Head and Neck Imaging

Galdino E. Valvassori, Richard A. Buckingham,
Barbara L. Carter, William N. Hanafee,
Mahmood F. Mafee

1118 Illustrations

1988
Georg Thieme Verlag   Thieme Medical Publishers, Inc.
Stuttgart · New York   New York

Galdino E. Valvassori, M.D.
Professor of Radiology and Otolarynology
Abraham Lincoln School of Medicine
University of Illinois
55 East Washington Street
Chicago, Illinois 60602, USA

Richard A. Buckingham, M.D.
Clinical Professor of Otolaryngology
Head and Neck Surgery
University of Illinois,
College of Medicine at Chicago
Chicago, Illinois 60612
Otologist, Resurrection Hospital
Chicago, Illinois 60631, USA

Barbara L. Carter, M.D.
Professor of Radiology and Otolaryngology
Chief of ENT Radiology and C.T. Body Scanning
New England Medical Center Hospital
171 Harrison Ave.
Boston, Massachusetts 02111, USA

William N. Hanafee, M.D.
Professor of Radiology
University of California
Department of Radiological Sciences
The Center for the Health Sciences
Los Angeles, California 90024, USA

Mahmood F. Mafee, M.D.
Professor of Radiology
Director of Magnetic Resonance
Imaging Center & Radiology Section-EEI
University of Illinois Hospital and Clinics
1853 West Polk Street
Chicago, Illinois 60680, USA

Cover design by Renate Stockinger

Library of Congress Cataloging-in-Publication Data

Head and neck imaging / Galdino E. Valvassori . . . [et al.].
p. cm.
Includes bibliographies and index.
ISBN 0-86577-302-5 (Thieme Medical)
1. Head--Imaging. 2. Neck--Imaging. 3. Head--Diseases--Diagnosis. 4. Neck--Diseases--Diagnosis. I. Valvassori, Galdino E.
[DNLM: 1. Head--radiography. 2. Neck--radiography. WE 705 H4303]
RC936.H426 1988
617'.5107572--dc19
DNLM/DLC
for Library of Congress   88-24815

Important Note: Medicine is an ever-changing science. Research and clinical experience are continually broadening our knowledge, in particular our knowledge of proper treatment and drug therapy. Insofar as this book mentions any dosage or application, readers may rest assured that the authors, editors and publishers have made every effort to ensure that such references are strictly in accordance with the state of knowledge at the time of production of the book. Nevertheless, every user is requested to carefully examine the manufacturers' leaflets accompanying each drug to check on his own responsibility whether the dosage schedules recommended therein or the contraindications stated by the manufacturers differ from the statements made in the present book. Such examination is particularly important with drugs which are either rarely used or have been newly released on the market.

© 1988 Georg Thieme Verlag, Rüdigerstrasse 14, D-7000 Stuttgart 30, Germany
Thieme Medical Publishers, Inc.
381 Park Avenue South, New York, N.Y. 10016

Typesetting: Druckhaus Dörr, Inh. Adam Götz, Ludwigsburg
(System: Linotype 5 [Linotron 202])
Printed in West-Germany by Grammlich, Pliezhausen

ISBN 3-13-696901-4 (Georg Thieme Verlag, Stuttgart)
ISBN 0-86577-302-5 (Thieme Medical Publishers, Inc., New York)

1 2 3 4 5 6

Preface

We are pleased to present this new volume of Imaging of the Head and Neck published by Georg Thieme Verlag. The previous volume titled Radiology of the Head and Neck published in 1982 has become obsolete due to the exponential changes that have occurred in computerization and the development of non ionizing magnetic resonance techniques. These techniques have changed the field of visualization of lesions of the head and neck to such an extent that even the term Radiology has been supplanted by the newer title Imaging.

Magnetic resonance imaging techniques have greatly improved methods of detection of acoustic neuromas, head and neck tumors and cervical metastases. When MR techniques are used in conjunction with CT imaging, very few lesions are now undetectable. The recent introduction of paramagnetic contrast agents and the promise of future development of clinical magnetic spectroscopy will further increase the accuracy of these imaging techniques in detecting any lesion which is now overlooked by today's methodology.

Should the reader compare this volume with the previous one, he will note that the Ear Section consists of CT and MR images to the exclusion of the many polytomograms which were the basis of this section in the previous edition. In the Larynx and Hypopharynx Section, MR has to a great extent replaced CT. In the Section on Paranasal Sinuses, CT and MR images are far more frequent than previously and have supplanted polytomography. Conventional radiography has not been neglected in this book, since conventional radiographs remain the starting point of many imaging studies.

To make this volume utilizable in the future, as newer techniques become available, the authors have presented basic concepts of image evaluations. Imaging data is correlated with clinical anatomical pathological features which the reader will be able to apply in the interpretation of newer techniques as they become available. Otoscopic and laryngeal endoscopic photographs will aid the reader in conceptualizing the relations between clinical and imaging findings.

We again wish to thank Doctor Günther Hauff, Herr Achim Menge, Herr Gert Krüger, Frau Margaret Hadler and Mrs. Jill Rudansky for their encouragement, cooperation and assistance without which we could not have presented this book.

The Authors

Contents

Part I
Radiology of the Temporal Bone
Galdino E. Valvassori and Richard A. Buckingham

Part II
Paranasal Sinuses, Nasal Cavity, Pterygoid Fossa, Nasopharynx, and Infratemporal Fossa
Barbara L. Carter

Part III
Oral Cavity, Oropharynx, Upper Neck and Salivary Glands
Mahmood F. Mafee

Part IV
Hypopharynx and Larynx
William N. Hanafee

Part I

Radiology of the Temporal Bone

Galdino E. Valvassori and Richard A. Buckingham

Chapter 1 **Conventional Radiography**

Introduction

Conventional radiography is of value in screening the entire temporal bone, and in determining the status of pneumatization of the mastoid and petrous pyramid. This method permits evaluation of the size and extent of relatively large lesions that arise in or extend from adjacent structures into the temporal bone. Smaller pathological processes are not visualized by this technique, and computed tomography (CT) is needed.

There are several conventional projections which we use for evaluation of the temporal bone. Five projections demonstrate the mastoid and middle ear. The Law, Schüller, and Owen are lateral or modified lateral views. The Chausse III and Towne projections are modified frontal views.

Three projections expose the petrous pyramids and inner ear. The transorbital is a frontal view, the Stenvers an oblique view, and the Towne a modified frontal view.

To obtain consistant satisfactory conventional radiographs of the temporal bone, we use a head unit. The table top and cassette holder are small so that the patient's shoulder can fit underneath. This allows a good approximation of the patient's head to the film. A transparent table top enables the technician to center the area of interest properly, since both entrance and exit points of the x-ray beam are visible. The unit should have a tube with a small 0.3 mm focal spot for increased definition. A slow to average speed screen film combination gives the best results.

A small port size reduces scatter radiation. When the port exceeds 7.5 cm in diameter, a fixed or moving grid will control scatter. To use the small port effectively, the technician must be properly trained in the basic anatomy of the skull and temporal bone so that he can position the patient's head accurately and correctly.

The lateral projections are used for the study of the mastoid and the mastoid pneumatization. To avoid superimposition of the two ears, the x-ray beam is directed obliquely. The degree of angulation is inversely proportional to the distance between the structures we wish to avoid superimposing.

The 15° angulation of the Law view frees one mastoid from superimposition by the contralateral mastoid. An increase of angulation to 30° in the Schüller projection eliminates superimposition and separates the external auditory canal and middle ear from the ipsilateral petrous pyramid.

To correctly interpret mastoid pneumatization, the radiologist and otologist must be aware of the great variation in the extent of pneumatization, the size of the air cells and the size of the mastoid.

It is important to remember that the air cells of the mastoid may appear on the conventional projections to be smaller than they actually are. This appearance is caused by the superimposition of several layers of cells on the single plane of the radiograph. Thus a large superficial mastoid air cell will appear to be septated due to septa of smaller underlying cells which are projected through the image of the larger cell.

There are four stages or degrees of pneumatization of the mastoid:

1. Pneumatization of the antrum only. In these temporal bones the antrum exists as a single, large, smooth-walled air cell without scalloping of its margin by any smaller air cells. The physician should not confuse a single large antral air cell with a cholesteatoma. In cholesteatoma, the antrum will be cloudy and there will be destruction in the middle ear, since most cholesteatomas have their origin in the middle ear.
2. The antrum and a few small periantral and perifacial cells are the only areas of mastoid pneumatization.
3. The antrum and the entire mastoid process are well pneumatized.
4. The pneumatization of the antrum and mastoid process may extend into the squamous and zygomatic portions of the temporal bone and even into the occipital bone.

Law Projection

The Law projection is used to study the mastoid, the extent of the pneumatization and the condition of the air cells (Fig. 1.1).

To obtain this projection, the midsagittal plane of the skull is parallel to the film plane, and there is a 15° cephalocaudad angulation of the x-ray beam. In a variation of this projection, the face is rotated 15° toward the film.

Interpretation

When the mastoid is well pneumatized, the Law view demonstrates the extent of the air cells into the mas-

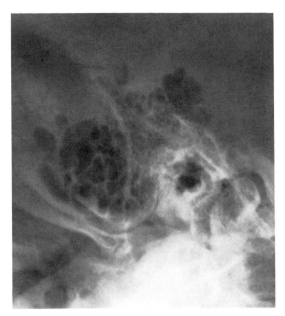

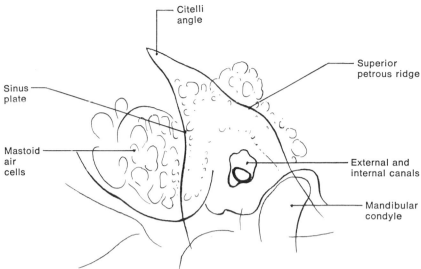

Figure 1.**1** **A** Law projection.   **B** Diagram of Law projection.

toid process, the temporal squama, the zygomatic arch and the occipital bone.

The internal and external auditory canals are superimposed and are surrounded by the dense bone of the petrous pyramid and otic capsule. The superior petrous ridge crosses the mandibular condyle anteriorly.

A sharp radiodense verticle line, the sinus plate, crosses the mastoid air cells posterior to the labyrinthine density. If the mastoid is well pneumatized, this sinus plate line separates the superficial air cells from the deeper air cells of the mastoid and of the petrous pyramid.

If the mastoid is poorly pneumatized, there are no cells posterior to the sinus plate.

The vertical line of the sinus plate merges posterosuperiorly with another similarly dense horizontal or oblique line. This dense line is the superior dural plate formed by the superior margin of the base of the pyramid in the region ot the tegmen of the antrum. The sharp angle at the junction of the sinus and dural plates is the sinodural angle of Citelli.

Indication

The Law view is useful for the study of pathologic processes involving the mastoid air cells and the sinus plate. However, since this projection does not give information about the external auditory canal or the middle ear cavity the Schüller projection is preferable.

Schüller Projection

The Schüller projection is another lateral view of the mastoid (Fig. 1.2).

In this projection, the sagittal plane of the head lies parallel to the table top, and the x-ray beam is rotated 30° cephalocaudad.

Interpretation

The extent of the pneumatization of the mastoid, the distribution and degree of aeration of the air cells, and the status of the trabecular pattern are revealed in the Schüller projection.

This view projects the internal auditory canal below the external auditory canal. The superior petrous ridge crosses the radiolucency of the external auditory canal and extends forward to reach the neck of the mandibular condyle.

As in the Law projection, the sinus and dural plate form sharply defined lines which merge posterosuperiorly at the angle of Citelli.

The Schüller projection exposes the upper portion of the external auditory canal, the epitympanum, and when the middle ear is aerated, portions of the incus and malleus.

Indication

This projection is used to determine the extent and degree of pneumatization of the mastoid and the condition of the air cells. The Schüller projection also supplies basic information about the size of the external auditory canal, and the relation of the external auditory canal to the sinus plate.

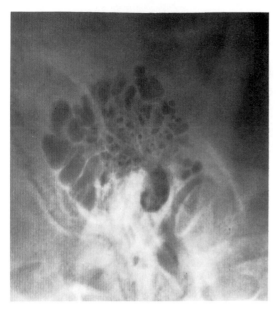

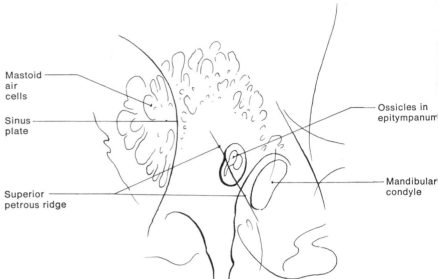

Figure 1.2   **A** Schüller projection.   **B** Diagram of Schüller projection.

Owen Projection

The Owen projection is a modification of the Mayer projection (Fig. 1.3). We prefer the Owen projection because there is less distortion of the anatomical structures.

In the Owen projection, the sagittal plane of the head first lies parallel to the x-ray film. Then the face is rotated 30° away from the film. The x-ray beam extends in a 30° to 40° cephalocaudad angle.

In the Schüller view, the petrous pyramid obscures the lower half of the lumen of the external auditory canal and middle ear. In the Owen projection the combination of 30° rotation of the face and the 30° to

40° cephalocaudad angulation move the projection of the pyramid downward and posteriorly.

The upper portion of the middle ear is now superimposed on the external auditory canal and appears as a well defined oval radiolucency. The angulation of the x-ray beam may vary from 30° to 40° depending on the anatomical relationship of the superior petrous ridge to the superimposed external auditory canal.

If the superior petrous ridge in the Schüller projection crosses the midportion of the external auditory canal, an angulation of the x-ray beam of 35° is sufficient. If the petrous ridge in the Schüller lies superior to the lumen of the external auditory canal, 40° angulation of the beam will be necessary. If, in the Schüller view,

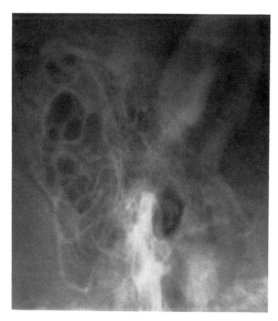

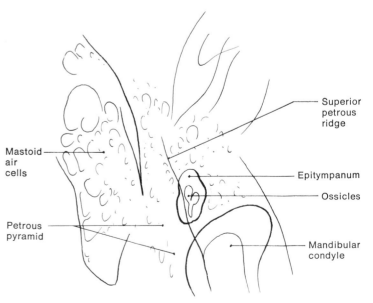

Figure 1.3   **A** Owen projection.   **B** Diagram of Owen projection.

the petrous ridge lies below the lumen of the external auditory canal, a 30° angulation of the beam will result in a good Owen projection.

Interpretation

The Owen view exposes the mastoid air cells adequately, but distorts them due to the angulation of head and x-ray beam. The Owen view exposes the sinus and dural plates but not as well as the Schüller.

The epitympanum and ossicles are discernible when the external auditory canal is sufficiently large and normally angulated. When the middle ear is aerated, the Owen view exposes the malleus head. The superimposition of the posterior wall of the external canal partially obstructs the view of the body of the incus.

The aditus and antrum extend posteriorly from the epitympanum from which they are separated by a bony contour formed by the posterior portion of the lateral epitympanic wall.

Indications and Limitations

The Owen projection visualizes the external auditory canal, the epitympanum, portions of the ossicles, and the mastoid air cells.

The effectiveness of the Owen view in visualizing the middle ear and epitympanum is limited if the external auditory canal is absent or stenosed, since absence of the external canal results in a bony mass obstructing the view of the middle ear and epitympanum.

Further, to recognize the ossicles, the middle ear must be aerated so that a clear air-bone interface exists between the ossicles and the middle ear space. In chronic infections of the middle ear and mastoid, the middle ear and epitympanum are filled with granulation tissue or cholesteatoma which obscure the ossicles.

Chausse III Projection

The Chausse III projection is a frontal view of the mastoid and middle ear cavity (Fig. 1.4). The projection allows satisfactory visualization of the epitympanum, the aditus, the mastoid antrum, and especially the anterior two-thirds of the lateral epitympanic wall.

As seen in horizontal sections, the lateral epitympanic wall forms an angle of 10° to 15° open anteriorly with the mid sagitall plane of the skull. At the aditus, the lateral epitympanic wall turns laterally to become the lateral wall of the mastoid antrum.

The Chausse III projection is complementary to the Owen view, since the Chausse III shows the anterior portion of the lateral epitympanic wall while the Owen view shows the posterior and aditus portions.

To obtain a Chausse III view, the head is positioned with the occiput on the table top, the chin flexed on the chest, and the head is rotated 10° to 15° to the opposite side of the ear examined. In a satisfactory Chausse III projection, the superior petrous ridge should form an continuous line with the superior orbital rim, and the lateral wall of the orbit should cross the lateral one-third of the internal auditory canal.

Interpretation

The vestibule and horizontal semicircular canal are the basic landmarks and are used to identify other structures. The horizontal semicircular canal bulges laterally into the radiolucency of the mastoid antrum. Inferolateral to the horizontal semicircular canal, there is a triangular bony mass made up medially by the malleus head and neck, and superolaterally by a portion of the incus body.

Lateral to the ossicles there is a sharply outlined and dense oblique line formed by the anterior portion of the lateral epitympanic wall. This line joins the superior wall of the external auditory canal to form a sharp spur, the scutum.

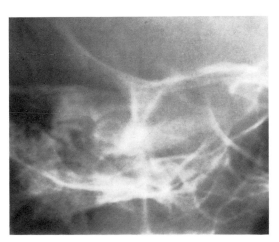

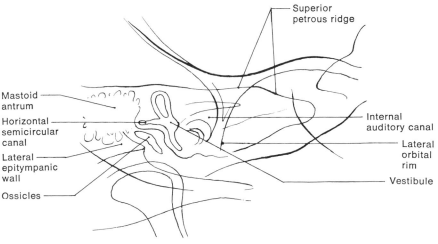

Figure 1.**4** **A** Chausse III projection.   **B** Diagram of Chausse III projection.

The mastoid antrum lies above the epitympanum. The antrum is separated from the epitympanum by a narrow radiolucent space, the aditus. The aditus is limited medially by the bulge of the horizontal semicircular canal and laterally by the epitympanic wall. The promontory forms the medial wall of the middle ear cavity. The internal auditory canal lies medial to the vestibule.

Indications

The Chausse III is the most reliable conventional projection for the study of the middle ear. With the Chausse III projection, middle ear structures are well seen in aerated middle ears but obscured in middle ears clouded by disease. In sclerotic mastoids, the superimposed dense mastoid bone obscures the middle ear and causes an apparent clouding.

The Chausse III is complementary to the lateral mastoid projections and is useful to study chronic otitis media and cholesteatomas, especially cholesteatomas with perforations of the pars flaccida of the tympanic membrane.

The Chausse III is the best of the conventional projections for visualization of fistulas of the horizontal semicircular canal.

Towne Projection

(Chamberlain-Towne, Worms and Bretton, Superorbital Projection of Lysholen)

In the Towne projection the mastoid air cells of both sides are well seen and can be easily compared because of the simultaneous exposure (Fig. 1.5). The epitympanum space and ossicles are poorly visualized. This projection exposes the internal auditory canal and labyrinth fairly well. A problem with the interpretation of the internal auditory canals arises in pneumatic and in sclerotic petrous pyramids. In pneumatic pyramids the air cells may confuse the contour of the internal auditory canals, while sclerotic bone may partially obliterate the view of the canals.

The Towne view is obtained with the patient's occiput on the x-ray film. The orbitomeatal line lies

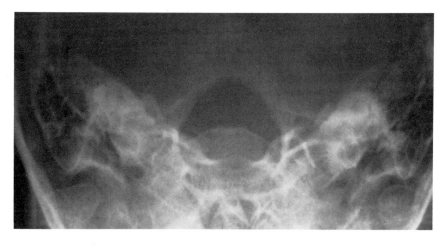

Figure 1.5   **A** Towne projection.

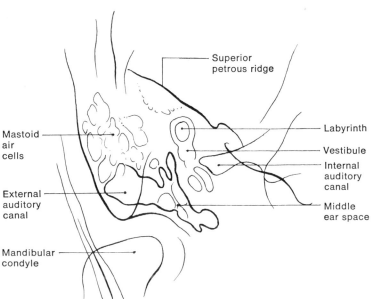

B Diagram of Towne projection.

perpendicular to the film. The x-ray beam is directed 30° caudad. Because of the angulation, the posterior aspect of the temporal bone and the occipital bone are well visualized.

Interpretation

In the Towne projection, the mastoid air cells lie at each lateral aspect of the radiograph. If the mastoids are not well pneumatized, the contours of the external auditory canals are visible above the temporomandibular joints. The superior petrous ridges and the posterior cells of the mastoid and petrous pyramid form the superior contour of the temporal bones, while the anterior cells are projected inferiorly.

The dense bone of the labyrinth lies medial to the mastoid air cells. The cochlea is projected inferior to the internal auditory canal which forms a radiolucent channel extending toward the petrous ridge.

The perilabyrinthine cells are usually well seen. The jugular fossa may be recognizable inferior to these cells.

Indication

The main indication for the Towne view is inflammation of the mastoid and petrous air cells.

This view is also useful for the study of the internal auditory canals in acoustic neuroma. With large glomus jugulare tumors, erosion of the jugular fossa and posteroinferior aspects of the petrous pyramid may be recognizable.

Transorbital Projection

The transorbital projection is one of the conventional radiographic views to expose the inner ear structures (Fig. 1.6).

This projection is satisfactory for the study of the internal auditory canal, which is exposed in its full length. This projection also visualizes the cochlea, the vestibule and the semicircular canals.

The main disadvantage of the transorbital projection is that large air cells in the petrous pyramid can obscure the contour of the internal auditory canal and may even create false contours. The transorbital view in therefore of greatest value in the study of the internal auditory canal in poorly pneumatized pyramids.

The occiput is placed on the x-ray film to magnify the orbital contour. The chin is flexed slightly so that the orbitomeatal line is perpendicular to the film plane. The x-ray beam is directed at a right angle to the film. For better details, each side should be radiographed separately, and the x-ray beam centered over each eye. In a proper transorbital view the superior petrous ridge should be projected 1 cm below the superior orbital rim.

Interpretation

The internal auditory canal forms a well defined radiolucency within the surrounding density of the pyramid. The vestibule lies at the lateral end of the internal canal. The semilunar lip of the posterior wall of the internal auditory canal forms the medial boundary of the canal. The radiolucent oval-shaped area medial to this lip represents the groove for the seventh and eighth cranial nerves on the longer anterior wall of the canal.

The cochlea appears below and is partially superimposed on the fundus of the internal canal. The petrous apex is obscured by superimposition of the medial orbital wall and paranasal sinuses.

Indication

The transorbital view is the best of the conventional projections for the study of possible acoustic neuromas, since it allows study of the shape and size of the internal auditory canal and of the length of the posterior wall.

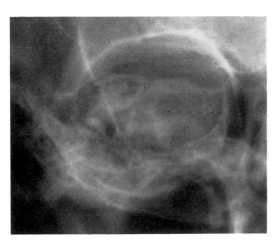

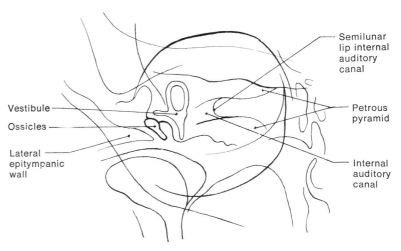

Figure 1.6 **A** Transorbital projection.   **B** Diagram of Transorbital projection.

Stenvers Projection

The Stenvers projection is the best view for the study of the petrous apex, the porus of the internal auditory canal, the vestibule, the semicircular canals, and the mastoid process air cells (Fig. 1.7).

In highly pneumatized temporal bones, petrous air cells obscure the contour of the internal auditory canal, and, as in the transorbital view, may cause false contours of the canal.

To obtain the Stenvers projection, the patient faces the x-ray film with the head slightly flexed. The head is rotated 45° toward the opposite side of the ear being examined. This position places the long axis of the petrous pyramid parallel to the film. The x-ray beam is angled 15° caudad.

Interpretation

The Stenvers view projects the mastoid process air cells laterally where they are free of superimposition.

The external auditory canal and middle ear cavity are poorly visualized. The vestibule and horizontal semicircular canals are well outlined lateral to the foreshortened internal auditory canal. The porus of the internal auditory canals forms an oval-shaped radiolucency medial to the semilunar lip of the posterior wall of the internal auditory canal. The petrous apex is seen in its entire contour. Under the pyramid, the hypoglossal canal is often seen on end above the condyle of the occipital bone.

Indication

The Stenvers view is useful in the study of pathological processes that involve the petrous pyramid and apex such as petrositis and tumors of various types.

The Stenvers projection cannot be used by itself for the study of the internal auditory canal, since the rotation of the pyramid foreshortens and distorts the contour of the canal.

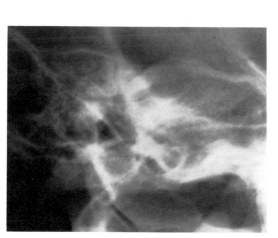

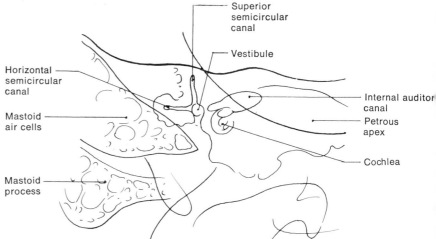

Figure 1.7   **A** Stenvers projection.   **B** Diagram of Stenvers projection.

Chapter 2 Serial CT Sections of Temporal Bone Anatomy

Introduction

High definition computed tomography has replaced multidirectional tomography as the radiographic study for the assessment of the temporal bone. Several factors are responsible:

1. CT sections offer high contrast images which allow excellent recognition of bony and soft tissue structures and pathology.
2. With CT it is possible to assess various parameters of the image, including adjacent intracranial and extracranial structures and pathology, by varying window width and level.
3. CT is the tomographic equipment used in most institutions in America at the present time.

High definition CT images are obtained with the use of special software reconstruction techniques, which reduce pixel size to 0.25 mm. Thin sections are achieved by narrowing the collimation of the x-ray beam and narrowing the aperture of each detector. Slice thickness is reduced to 1.5 mm and serial sections at 1.00 mm are achieved by overlapping sections by 0.5 mm.

Two or more projections are required for proper examination of the temporal bone. Use of the single axial projection can lead to misinterpretation of structures parallel to the plane of section, such as the floor of the external auditory canal and the tegmen of the mastoid and middle ear.

In routine CT examination of the temporal bone, enhancement of the images by infusion of contrast material is not necessary. Enhancement is indicated when the physician suspects vascular anomalies, tumors and intracranial complications such as brain abscesses. Enhanced CT will visualize involvement of the temporal bone and any intra- and extracranial extension of diesase.

CT enables the radiologist to measure tissue absorption with a cursor of variable size and obtain densitometric readings of selected areas of the temporal bone. This technique, however, is unreliable in differentiating fluids and soft tissues filling the mastoid air cells and middle ear because of partial volume averaging effects.

Dynamic CT uses fast, rotational scanning to diagnose and differentiate vascular masses of the temporal bone. A 30 to 45 cc bolus of contrast is rapidly injected intravenously, and 6 to 12 scans of a single pre-selected section showing the mass are obtained in 30 to 40 seconds. The first image exposes the mass before the contrast reaches it, and subsequent images show the progression and regression of the enhancement. A graph of the enhancement changes is obtained by plotting the density of the mass in CT numbers on the X-axis and the time on the Y-axis. Vascular masses are characterized by high peaks of 25 or more CT numbers with rapid wash-in and wash-out phases. The peak time and peak magnitude permit differentiation of arterial from venous structures and vascular tumors (Fig. 4.20 D and 4.23 E).

Projections

The normal temporal bone will be reviewed in four projections: axial or horizontal, coronal or frontal, sagittal or lateral, and 20° coronal oblique. Each CT image will be matched to a comparable tissue section and microradiograph of the tissue section of a temporal bone at the same level.

Axial or Horizontal Projection

Since the axial projection is the easiest to obtain, this is the standard view. The patient lies supine with the cantho-meatal line perpendicular to the tabletop. Sections at 1.5 mm increments are taken beginning at the arcuate eminence and continuing to the level of the floor of the hypotympanum and jugular fossa.

This projection delineates the anterior and posterior aspects and dimensions, but fails to demonstrate superior and inferior boundries of the temporal bone.

Coronal or Frontal Projection

The patient lies on the table prone or supine, with the head overextended and the gantry tilted so that the x-ray beam is perpendicular to a plane passing from the tragus to the inferior orbital rim. For this projection, the gantry must tilt 15°–20°.

Sections are taken from the bony eustachian tube to the loop of the posterior semicircular canal.

This projection is complementary to the axial, since it demonstrates the superior and inferior boundries and vertical dimensions of the bone.

20° Coronal Oblique

The patient lies prone with the head overextended and rotated 20° on a special head holder. Not all patients can tolerate this projection, especially if any degree of arthritis of the neck exists.

The projection is used primarily for study of the oval window, stapes and the tympanic segment of facial nerve. For oval window study, sections are taken at 1.0 mm increments.

Sagittal or Lateral Projection

Direct lateral sections are difficult to obtain and can only be performed in patients with supple necks. A true sagittal projection can never be fully accomplished. The patient lies prone on the table with the chest elevated by a support. The head is overextended, rotated and placed in a special head holder, so that the sagittal plane of the skull is more or less parallel to the x-ray beam.

Zonnenveldt in Holland has developed a swing table that facilitates positioning of the patient for the sagital projection.

Sagittal images, though not as satisfactory as direct CT, can be obtained by computer reformation of the raw data from serial axial sections. Whenever direct sagittal sections cannot be obtained, multidirectional tomography can be used when a unit is available.

The main reason for using this projection is to delineate the vertical portion of the facial nerve and the vestibular aqueduct.

CT of the Facial Canal

Involvement of the intratemporal portion of the facial nerve may result in facial nerve symptoms such as partial or complete paralysis, tics, hemifacial spasms, and alterations in hearing, taste and tearing.

The bony canal and the facial nerve pass through the temporal bone and can be visualized by CT. The facial nerve itself can best be visualized by MR.

CT sections are taken 1.5 mm apart, and contralateral views are obtained for comparison. The projection used in the study of the facial canal depends on the segment being examined. In the temporal bone, there are four segments of the facial canal which must be visualized.

1. First or internal auditory canal segment. Axial and coronal sections expose this segment. If an intracanalicular mass is suspected, an MR study or CT pneumocisternogram is required to determine the size and extent of the lesion.
2. Second or labyrinthine segment. This portion of the facial canal extends from the fundus of the internal auditory canal to the geniculate ganglion. This segment is the narrowest part of the facial canal. Axial and 20° coronal oblique sections expose the segment.
3. Third or tympanic segment. This segment extends from the geniculate ganglion along the medial wall of the tympanic cavity to the second or pyramidal turn of the facial nerve. The axial and 20° coronal oblique sections are best to expose this segment.
4. Fourth or mastoid segment. This segment stretches from the pyramidal turn to the stylomastoid foramen, and is best visualized by sagittal or coronal sections.

Axial Sections

Figure 2.1 exposes structures in a 2 mm thick axial section of a right, adult temporal bone, 2 mm inferior to the arcuate eminence.

The mastoid air cells occupy the lateral portion of the section; the anterior and posterior limbs of the superior semicircular canal are in the center. Subarcuate vessels pass between the limbs of the superior canal.

The superior petrosal sinus courses along the superior margin of the petrous apex.

Figure 2.2 shows the structures in a 2 mm thick axial section of a right adult temporal bone immediately inferior to Fig. 2.1.

The aditus of the mastoid antrum opens into the epitympanum. Mastoid air cells surround the epitympanum and antrum.

Superior portions of the malleus head and incus body appear in the epitympanum.

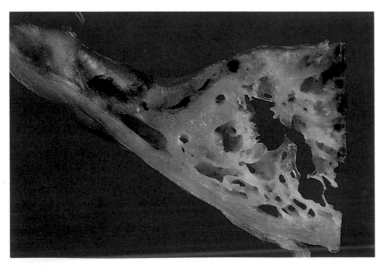

Figure 2.1   **A** Photograph of an axial macrosection 2 mm below the arcuate eminence.

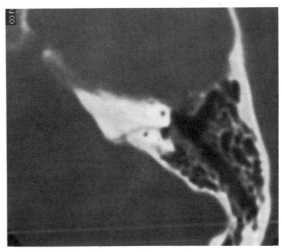

B CT corresponding to Fig. 2.1**A**.

anterior sur-
face petrous apex

subarcuate
blood vessels

anterior limb
superior semi-
circular canal

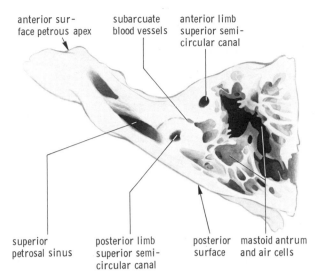

superior
petrosal sinus

posterior limb
superior semi-
circular canal

posterior
surface

mastoid antrum
and air cells

C Drawing of structures seen at this level.

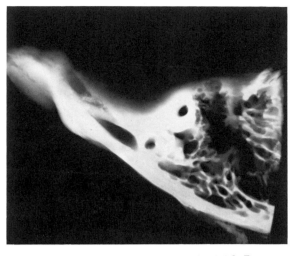

D Microradiograph corresponding to Fig. 2.**1A, B**.

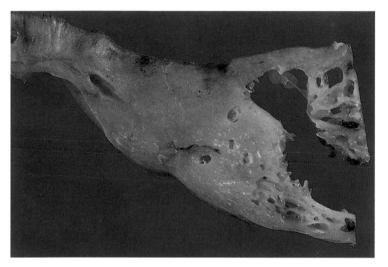

Figure 2.**2   A** Photograph of the axial macrosection immediately inferior to Fig. 2.**1A**.

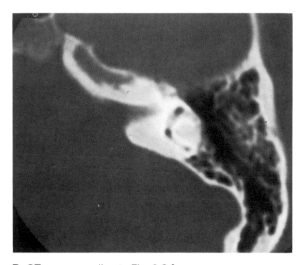

B CT corresponding to Fig. 2.**2A**.

facial nerve

ampulla super-
ior semicircu-
lar canal and
vestibule

horizontal
semicircular
canal

malleus and
incus

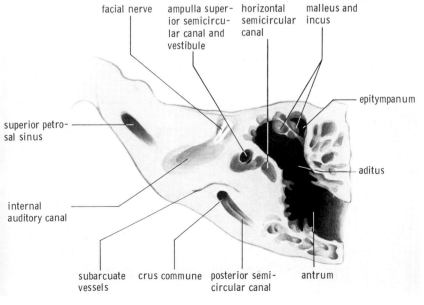

superior petro-
sal sinus

epitympanum

aditus

internal
auditory canal

subarcuate
vessels

crus commune

posterior semi-
circular canal

antrum

C Drawing of structures seen at this level.

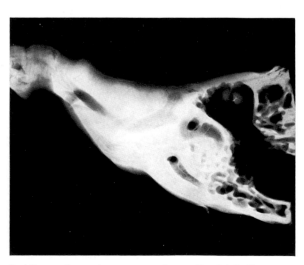

D Microradiograph corresponding to Fig. 2.**2A, B**.

The nonampullated limbs of the superior and posterior semicircular canals join at the crus commune.

The subarcuate vessels pass from the subarcuate fossa laterally between the limbs of the superior semicircular canal.

The horizontal semicircular canal forms the medial wall of the antrum, and the ampullated portions of the horizontal and superior semicircular canals open into the superior portion of the vestibule. This section also exposes the roof of the internal auditory canal.

Figures 2.3 to 2.5 reveal the structures in a 2 mm thick axial section of a right adult temporal bone immediately inferior to Fig. 2.2.

Mastoid air cells surround the antrum and extend lateral to the epitympanum. The malleus head and incus body occupy the epitympanum, and the incus short process rests in the fossa incudis.

The cavity of the epitympanum assumes a somewhat triangular shape at this level. The medial and lateral epitympanic walls converge posteriorly at the aditus, while the base of the triangle lies anterior. The medial wall forms a 20° to 25° angle with the sagittal plane crossing the fossa incudis. The lateral wall forms a 10° angle lateral to the sagittal plane at the fossa incudis.

The ampullated end of the horizontal semicircular canal enters the vestibule anteriorly (Fig. 2.4), and the nonampullated end opens into the posterior portion of the vestibule (Fig. 2.5).

The posterior semicircular canal extends posterolaterally from the crus commune.

The macula of the utricle stretches across the upper portion of the vestibule (Fig. 2.5 A).

The facial and superior vestibular nerves occupy the internal auditory canal.

The superior vestibular nerve arches towards, the utricular macula and the ampullae of the horizontal and superior semicircular canals (Fig. 2.4 A).

The petrous or labyrinthine portion of the facial nerve extends from the internal auditory canal to the geniculate ganglion. At the geniculate ganglion the nerve turns sharply into the horizontal position and extends posterior along the medial wall of the tympanum just below the horizontal semicircular canal (Fig. 2.4 A, 2.5 A, B). Superior portions of the basal and middle coils of the cochlea appear anterior to the fundus of the internal auditory canal.

The superior turn of the vestibular aqueduct passes adjacent to the posterior semicircular canal (Fig. 2.4 B, 2.5 B).

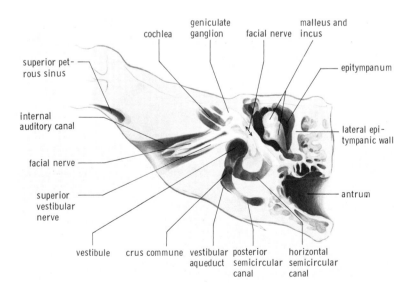

Figure 2.3 Drawing of structures seen in Fig. 2.4, 2.5.

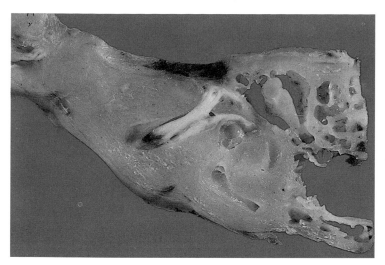

Figure 2.**4** **A** Photograph of the axial macrosection immediately inferior to Fig. 2.**2A**.

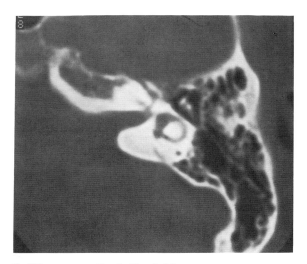

B CT corresponding to Fig. 2.**4A**.

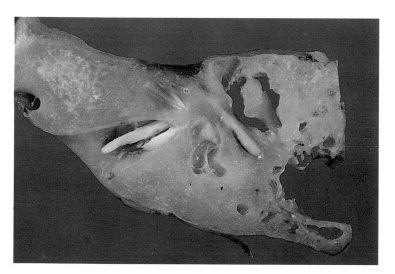

Figure 2.**5** **A** Photograph of axial macrosection 2 mm inferior to Fig. 2.**4A**.

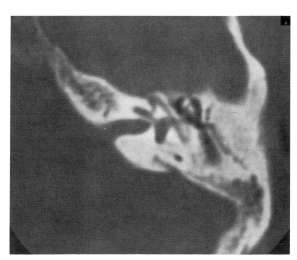

B CT corresponding to Fig. 2.**5A**.

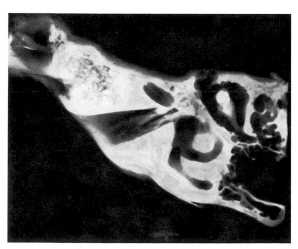

C Microradiograph of macrosection corresponding to Fig. 2.**4**, 2.**5**.

Figures 2.6–2.8 demonstrate the structures in 2 mm thick axial sections of a right adult temporal bone immediately inferior to Fig. 2.3–2.5.

The sections cross the mastoid antrum and the superior wall of the external auditory canal.

The tendon of the tensor tympani muscle stretches from the cochleariform process to the neck of the malleus. The tensor muscle appears on the surface of section (Fig. 2.8 A).

In the oval window, the stapes footplate is canted slightly downwards and the incudostapedial joint lies slightly below the level of the footplate (Fig. 2.8 A).

The facial nerve extends from the oval window to the second turn.

The stapedius tendon and the pyramidal eminence lie anteromedial to the facial nerve (Fig. 2.8 A).

The stapes footplate at this level forms the lateral wall of the vestibule. The membranous ampullated end of the posterior semicircular canal joints the utricle on the posteromedial margin of the vestibule (Fig. 2.8 A).

The nerve to the ampulla of the posterior semicircular canal leaves the internal auditory canal at the foramen singulare (Fig. 2.8 A, B).

The posterior semicircular canal lies anterior to the vestibular aqueduct. At this level the endolymphatic sac enters the vestibular aqueduct.

The section passes through the modiolus and three turns of the cochlea.

In the internal auditory canal, the cochlear nerve turns anteriorly into the modiolus 2 to 3 mm medial to the fundus of the canal.

The cochlear and inferior vestibular nerves lie in the inferior compartment of the internal auditory canal.

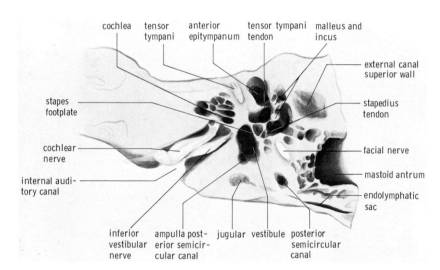

Figure 2.6 Drawing of structures seen in Fig. 2.7, 2.8.

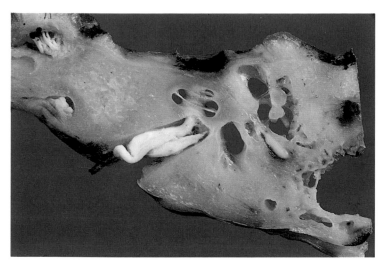

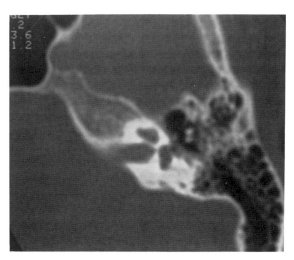

Figure 2.**7** **A** Photograph of the axial macrosection immediately inferior to Fig. 2.**5A**.

B CT corresponding to Fig. 2.**7A**.

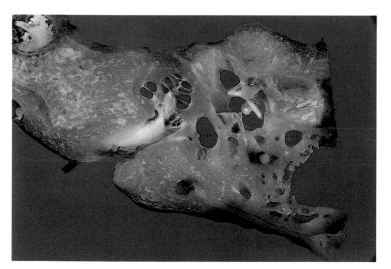

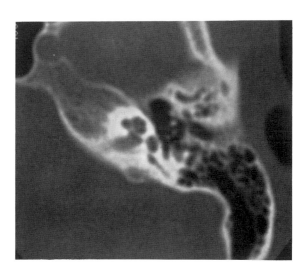

Figure 2.**8** **A** Photograph of axial macrosection 2 mm inferior to Fig. 2.**7A**.

B CT corresponding to Fig. 2.**8A**.

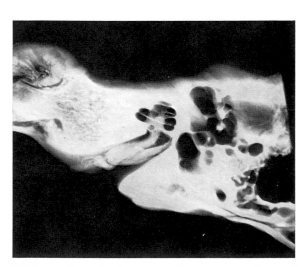

C Microradiograph of macrosection corresponding to Fig. 2.**7**, 2.**8**.

Figure 2.9 shows the structures in a 2 mm thick axial section of a right adult temporal bone immediately inferior to Fig. 2.6 to 2.8.

A section of the tympanic membrane with a portion of the malleus handle separates the external canal from the middle ear.

The lenticular process lies just posterior to the malleus handle. The tensor tympani canal lies on the anterior portion of the medial wall of the middle ear. The descending portion of the facial nerve lies in the posterior wall of the middle ear lateral to the pyramidal eminence and to the tympanic sinus.

The proximal portion of the basal coil of the cochlea forms the promontory of the medial wall of the middle ear. All three coils of the cochlea appear (Fig. 2.9). The spiral lamina separates the scala vestibuli from the scala tympani. In the niche of the round window, the round window membrane closes the scala tympani. At the fundus of the internal auditory canal, small twigs of the cochlear nerve supply part of the basal turn.

The ampulla of the posterior semicircular canal, as it enters the inferior and posterior portion of the vestibule lies close to the round window. The posterior semicircular canal arches posterior within the thickness of the tissue section between the facial canal anterior and the endolymphatic sac posterior (Fig. 2.9).

The dome of the jugular fossa lies medial to the middle ear.

The cochlear aqueduct passes from the posterior surface of the bone to the round window area.

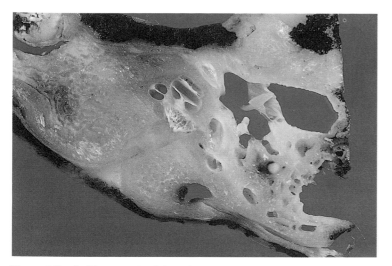

Figure 2.**9**   **A** Photograph of the axial macrosection immediately inferior to Fig. 2.**8A**.

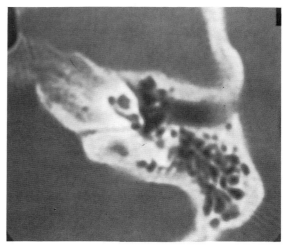

B CT corresponding to Fig. 2.**9A**.

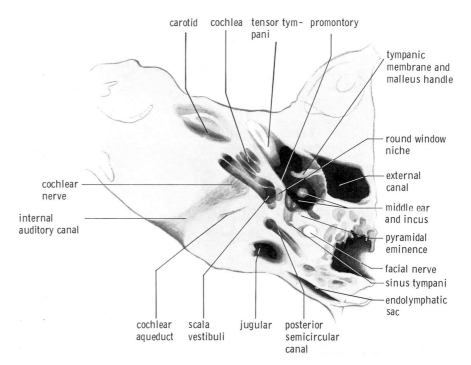

carotid   cochlea   tensor tym-   promontory
                    pani

tympanic membrane and malleus handle

round window niche

external canal

middle ear and incus

pyramidal eminence

facial nerve

sinus tympani

endolymphatic sac

cochlear nerve

internal auditory canal

cochlear aqueduct

scala vestibuli

jugular

posterior semicircular canal

C   Drawing of structures seen at this level.

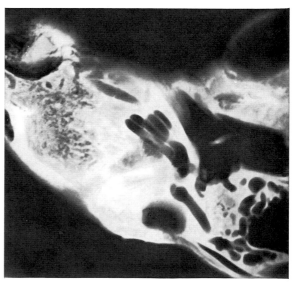

D Micrograph of macrosection corresponding to Fig. 2.**9A, B**.

Figure 2.10 reveals the structures in a 2 mm thick axial section of a right adult temporal bone immediately inferior to Fig. 2.9. The tip of the malleus handle lies in the umbo in a strip of the tympanic membrane. The tensor tympani muscle lies superior and lateral to the internal carotid artery. The carotid artery lies anterior to the basal turn of the cochlea on the medial wall of the bony eustachian tube. The descending facial nerve lies lateral to the jugular fossa. The inferior portion of the basal turn of the cochlea bounds the medial wall of the middle ear. The cochlear aqueduct lies medial to the jugular fossa and widens as it opens into the subarachnoid space.

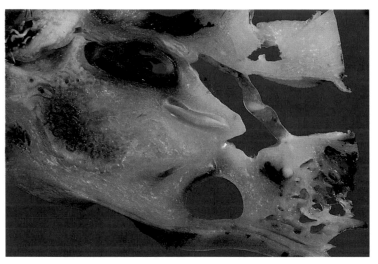

Figure 2.10   A Photograph of the axial section immediately inferior to Fig. 2.9 A.

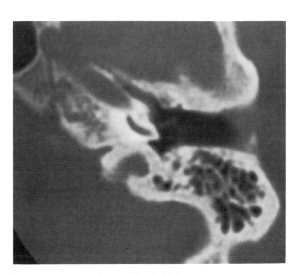

B CT corresponding to Fig. 2.10 A.

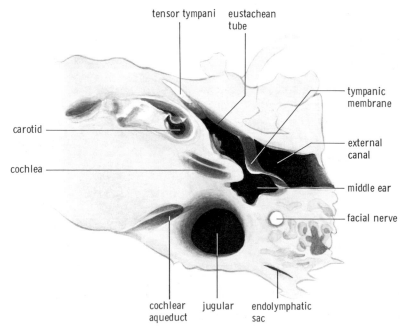

C Drawing of structures seen at this level.

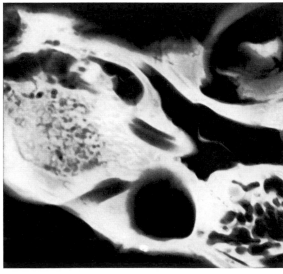

D Microradiograph of macrosection corresponding to Fig. 2.10 A, B.

Coronal Sections

Figure 2.11 exposes the structures in a 2 mm thick coronal section of a left adult temporal bone at the level of the anterior wall of the external auditory canal, the most anterior portion of the tympanic membrane, and the posterior aspect of the temporomandibular joint.

A small slice of the anterior portion of the malleus head appears in the epitympanum. A thin bony septum separates the hypotympanum from the carotid canal.

The geniculate ganglion of the facial nerve lies above the cochlea, while the tensor tympani canal lies on the medial wall of the middle ear.

The radiographic appearance of the cochlea is caused by the radiolucency of the modiolus and the bony spiral lamina. Thus the CT shows only the wall and lumen of the spiral cochlear canal and the septa that separate the basal, middle and apical coils.

Figure 2.11   **A** Photograph of coronal macrosection.

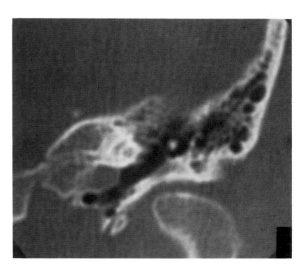

B CT corresponding to Fig. 2.11A.

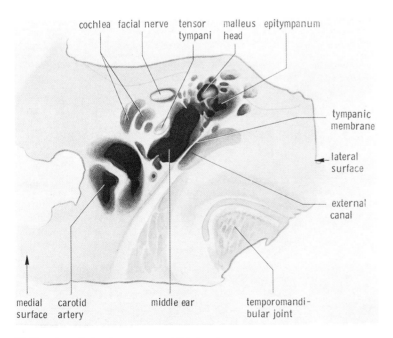

C Drawing of structures seen at this level.

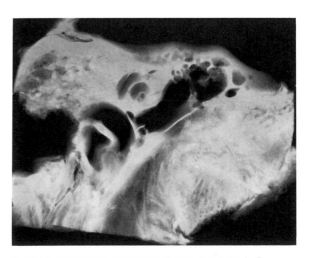

D Microradiograph corresponding to Fig. 2.11A, B.

Figure 2.12 demonstrates the structures present in a 2 mm thick coronal section of a left adult, temporal bone, immediately posterior to Fig. 2.11.

A thin section of tympanic membrane divides the external auditory canal from the middle ear. A small area of the pars flaccida is retracted above the mallear short process in the notch of Rivinus. The tendon of the tensor tympani stretches across the middle ear from the cochleariform process to the mallear neck.

The lateral wall of the epitympanum joins the superior wall of the external auditory canal in a sharp edge lateral to the malleus neck.

A portion of the body of the incus projects laterally from the articulation with the malleus head. This accounts for the characteristic bilobed appearance of the ossicular mass in the tomographs.

Within the thickness of the tissue section, the facial nerve bifurcates from the geniculate ganglion into the labyrinthine and tympanic segments. In **B** this bifurcation appears as paired, adjacent, circular foramina.

Portions of the basal, middle, and apical coils of the cochlea lie superior to the carotid canal.

Figure 2.13 demonstrates the structures in a 2 mm thick coronal section of a left adult temporal bone immediately posterior to Fig. 2.12.

The tympanic membrane with the malleus handle attached separates the external canal from the middle ear.

The inferior margin of the lateral attic wall and the superior wall of the external canal form a triangular projection with the apex directed medially.

Portions of the body and long process of the incus lie in the epitympanum between the prominence of the horizontal semicircular canal and the lateral epitympanic wall.

The tympanic portion of the facial nerve lies below the horizontal semicircular canal and above the anterior margin of the oval window. A small anterior portion of the stapes footplate and anterior crus are in the oval window. The proximal portion of the facial nerve lies in the upper compartment of the internal auditory canal.

The tissue section (Fig. 2.13 A) reveals the anterior wall of the vestibule, the horizontal and superior semicircular canals, and the internal auditory canal. Portions of the membranous labyrinth are present within the lumina of the vestibule and semicircular canals.

Below the facial nerve, the cochlear nerve enters the foraminous spiral tract of the modiolus.

The proximal part of the basal coil of the cochlea forms the promontory of the medial wall of the middle ear. The carotid artery lies inferiorly.

Figure 2.**12** **A** Photograph of coronal macrosection 2 mm posterior to Fig. 2.**11 A**.

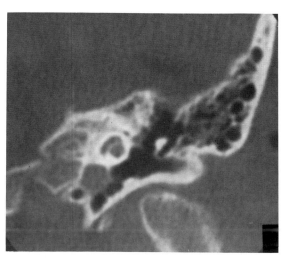

B CT corresponding to Fig. 2.**12 A**.

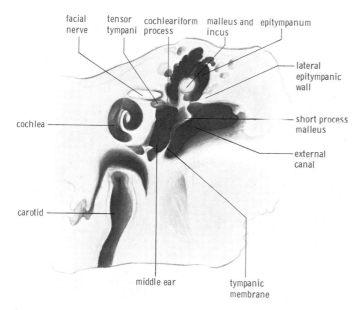

C Drawing of structures seen at this level.

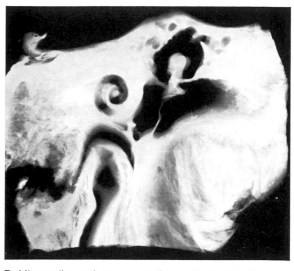

D Microradiograph corresponding to Fig. 2.**12A, B**.

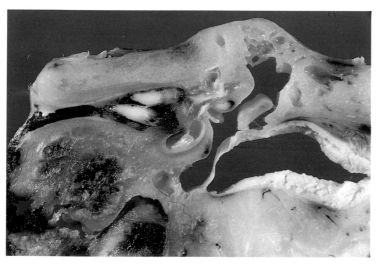

Figure 2.**13   A** Photograph of coronal macrosection 2 mm posterior to Fig. 2.**12A**.

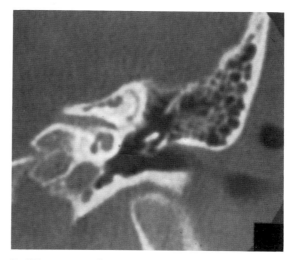

B CT corresponding to Fig. 2.**13A**.

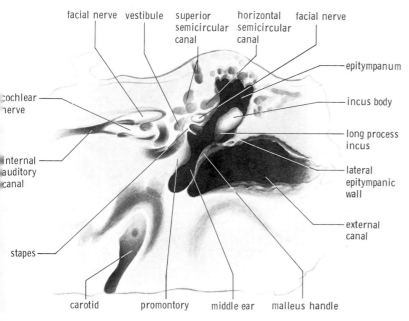

C Drawing of structures seen at this level.

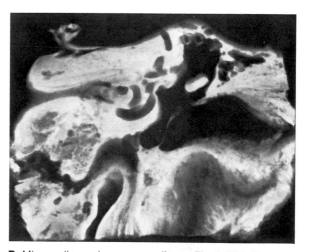

D Microradiograph corresponding to Fig. 2.**13A, B**.

Figures 2.14 to 2.16 show the structures in a 2 mm thick coronal section of a left adult temporal bone immediately posterior to Fig. 2.13.

The tympanic membrane separates the external and middle ears.

The long process of the incus extends to the stapes. A portion of the long process is missing in the tissue section (Fig. 2.15A). The tip of the short process of the incus lies in the aditus between the lateral epitympanic wall and the prominence of the horizontal semicircular canal (Fig. 2.15A). The mastoid antrum extends superior and posterior from the aditus.

The tissue sections expose the vestibule and the ampullated portions of the superior and horizontal semicircular canals. The utricle and the macula of the utricle occupy the upper portion of the bony vestibule. A portion of the saccule lies on the medial vestibular wall.

The facial nerve appears between the horizontal semicircular canal and the oval window. This section includes most of the stapes footplate and superstructure.

The scala vestibuli opens into the inferior portion of the vestibule, while the scala tympani extends to the round window.

There are segments of the facial and acoustic cranial nerves in the internal auditory canal.

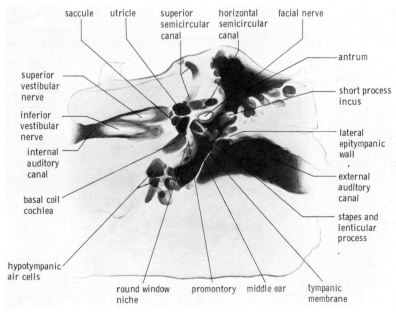

Figure 2.14 Drawing of structures seen in Fig. 2.15, 2.16.

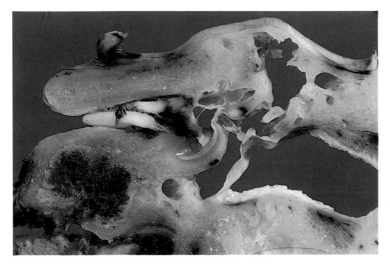

Figure 2.**15** **A** Photograph of coronal macrosection 2 mm posterior to Fig. 2.**13 A**.

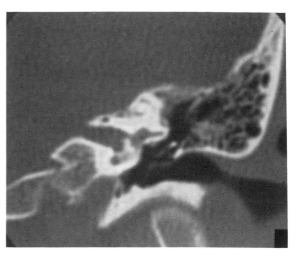

B CT corresponding to Fig. 2.**15 A**.

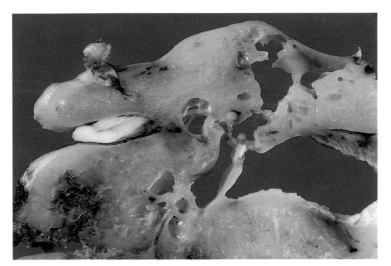

Figure 2.**16** **A** Photograph of coronal macrosection 2 mm posterior to Fig. 2.**15 A**.

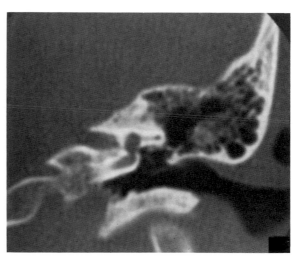

B CT corresponding to Fig. 2.**16 A**.

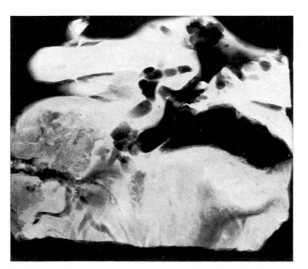

C Microradiograph corresponding to Fig. 2.**15**, 2.**16**.

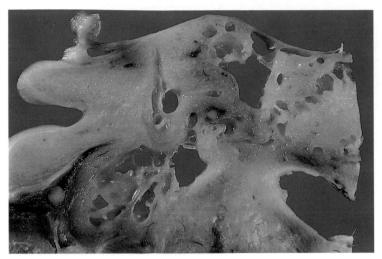

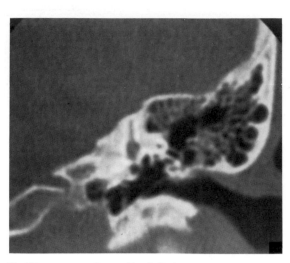

Figure 2.**17**   **A** Photograph of coronal macrosection 2 mm posterior to Fig. 2.**16 A**.

B CT corresponding to Fig. 2.**17A**.

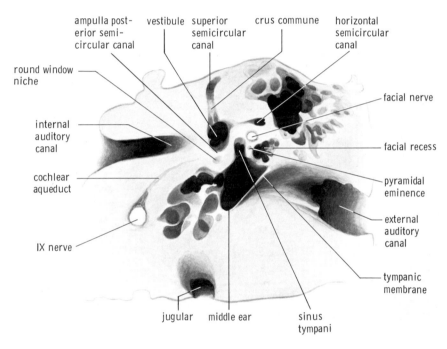

C Drawing of structures seen at this level.

ampulla posterior semicircular canal   vestibule   superior semicircular canal   crus commune   horizontal semicircular canal

round window niche

internal auditory canal

cochlear aqueduct

IX nerve

facial nerve

facial recess

pyramidal eminence

external auditory canal

tympanic membrane

jugular   middle ear   sinus tympani

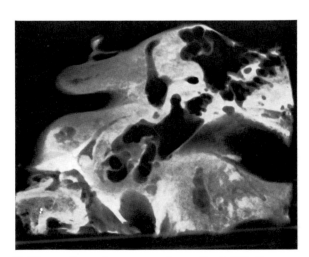

D Microradiograph corresponding to Fig. 2.**17A, B**.

Figure 2.**17** reveals the structures in a 2 mm thick coronal section of a left adult temporal bone immediately posterior to Fig. 2.**14** to 2.**16**.

The section exposes the external auditory canal and the posterior portion of the middle ear.

The horizontal semicircular canal protrudes into the mastoid antrum.

The superior semicircular canal joins the crus commune above the vestibule.

The facial nerve lies inferior to the horizontal semicircular canal. The pyramidal eminence with the tendon of the stapedius muscle is below the facial nerve. The extension of the middle ear medial to the pyramidal eminence represents the sinus tympani.

The facial recess lies between the facial nerve and the posterosuperior portion of the tympanic membrane. The ampullated end of the posterior semicircular canal opens into the inferior portion of the vestibule. A remnant of the round window niche appears at approximately the same level.

The posterior wall of the internal auditory canal is present.

The cochlear aqueduct stretches inferior from the round window area to the jugular foramen, (Fig. 2.**17 A, D**).

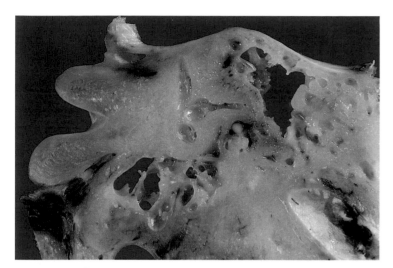

Figure 2.**18**   **A** Photograph of coronal macrosection 2 mm posterior to Fig. 2.**17 A**.

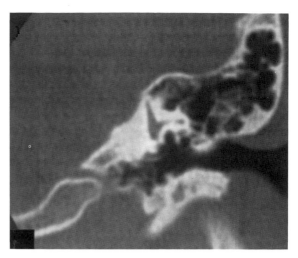

B CT corresponding to Fig. 2.**18 A**.

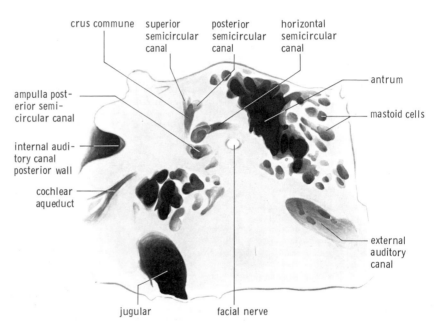

crus commune   superior   posterior   horizontal
                semicircular   semicircular   semicircular
                canal   canal   canal

ampulla post-   antrum
erior semi-
circular canal   mastoid cells

internal audi-
tory canal
posterior wall

cochlear
aqueduct

                                                                external
                                                                auditory
                                                                canal

jugular   facial nerve

C Drawing of structures seen at this level.

Figure 2.**18** shows the structures in a 2 mm thick coronal section of a left adult temporal bone immediately posterior to Fig. 2.**17**.

The section passes through the external auditory canal and mastoid air cells.

The posterior limb of the horizontal semicircular canal bulges into the mastoid antrum.

The crus commune, the posterior limb of the horizontal semicircular canal, and the ampulla of the posterior semicircular canal open into the posterior portion of the vestibule.

Portions of the membranous labyrinth are present within the bony canals (Fig. 2.**18 A**).

The pyramidal turn of the facial nerve lies under the horizontal semicircular canal.

Air cells lie inferior to the labyrinth.

The jugular opening of the cochlear aqueduct lies between the porus of the internal auditory canal and the jugular fossa (Fig. 2.**18 A, D**).

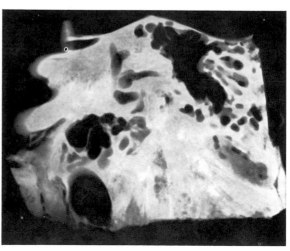

D Microradiograph corresponding to Fig. 2.**18 A, B**.

20° Coronal Oblique Sections

Figures 2.19 to 2.21 show the structures contained in a 2 mm thick, 20° coronal oblique section of a right adult temporal bone at the level of the cochlea.

The sections pass just anterior to the external auditory canal, through the anterior portion of the tympanic membrane, the cochlea, and the internal auditory canal. The section exposes the epi-, meso-, and hypotympanums. The tensor tympani muscle projects from the medial wall of the middle ear.

Above the cochlea, the facial nerve bifurcates from the geniculate ganglion into its petrous and tympanic segments.

Portions of three coils of the cochlea lie lateral to the internal auditory canal.

The CT shows only the contour of the lumen of the spiral canal of the cochlea and the bony septa between the coils, since the spongy modiolus and the spiral lamina are radiolucent.

The carotid artery appears inferior to the cochlea.

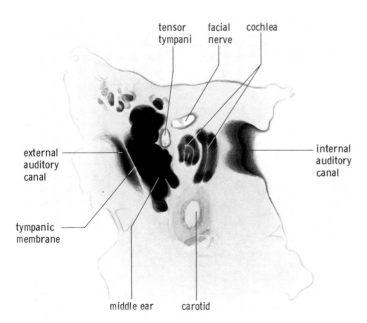

Figure 2.19 Drawing of structures seen in Fig. 2.20, 2.21.

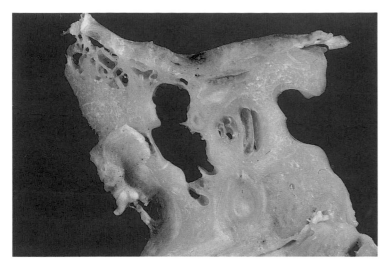

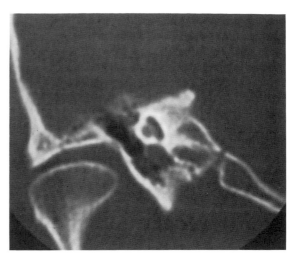

Figure 2.**20** **A** Photograph of 20° coronal oblique macrosection.

B CT corresponding to Fig. 2.**20A**.

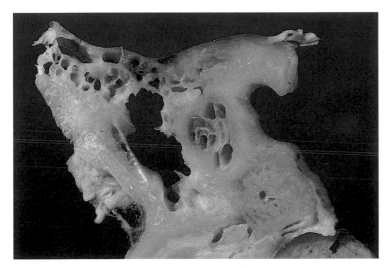

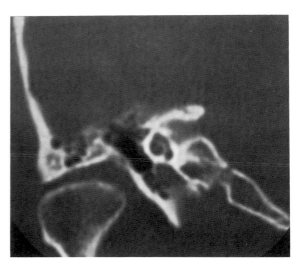

Figure 2.**21** **A** Photograph of 20° coronal oblique macrosection 2 mm posterior to Fig. 2.**20A**.

B CT corresponding to Fig. 2.**21A**.

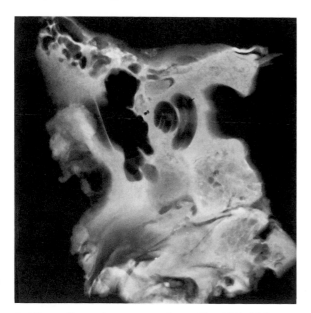

C Microradiograph corresponding to Fig. 2.**20**, 2.**21**.

Figure 2.22 shows the structures contained in a 2 mm thick 20° coronal oblique section of a right adult temporal bone immediately posterior to Fig. 2.19–2.21.

The section exposes a portion of the external auditory canal and an anterior strip of the tympanic membrane.

The head and part of the neck of the malleus lie in the epitympanum. The inferior and anterior margin of the lateral epitympanic wall is in close relation to the malleus neck.

The tensor tympani tendon lies on the medial wall of the middle ear below the horizontal portion of the facial nerve.

The proximal or petrous portion of the facial nerve stretches medially into the lumen of the internal auditory canal above the crista falciformis.

The cochlear nerve passes into the base of the modiolus below the crista falciformis. Portions of the middle and basal coils of the cochlea lie medial to the fundus of the internal auditory canal.

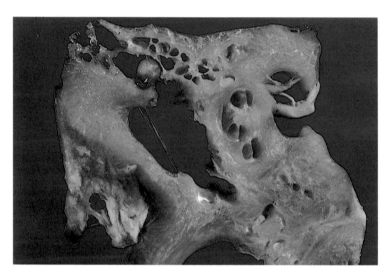

Figure 2.22   **A** Photograph of 20° oblique coronal macrosection 2 mm posterior to Fig. 2.21 A.

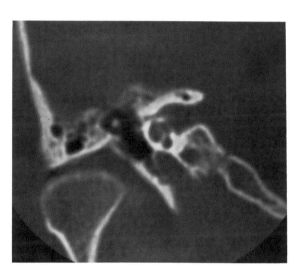

B CT corresponding to Fig. 2.22 A.

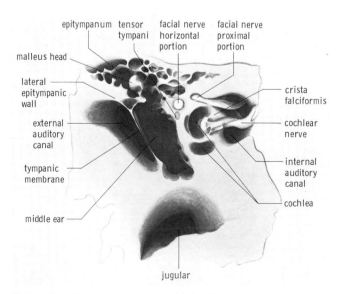

C Drawing of structures seen at this level.

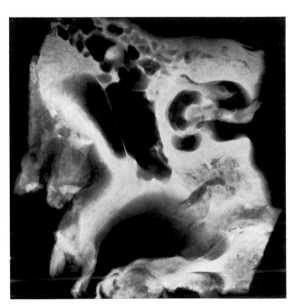

D Microradiograph corresponding to Fig. 2.22 A, B.

Figure 2.23 shows the structures contained in a 2 mm thick 20° coronal oblique section of a right adult temporal bone immediately posterior to Fig. 2.22.

The tympanic membrane and malleus handle separate the external canal from the middle ear.

The superior wall of the external auditory canal joins the inferior margin of the lateral attic wall in a sharp projection just above the short process of the malleus. In the epitympanum the body of the incus protrudes lateral from the head of the malleus (Fig. 2.23 A).

The tendon of the tensor tympani crosses the middle ear from the cochleariform process to the malleus. The horizontal portion of the facial nerve is closely related to the cochleariform process.

The promontory of the basal turn of the cochlea forms the medial wall of the tympanic cavity.

The superior and inferior vestibular nerves flare at the vestibular areas in the fundus of the internal auditory canal (Fig. 2.23 A). The crista falciformis divides the two branches of the vestibular nerve.

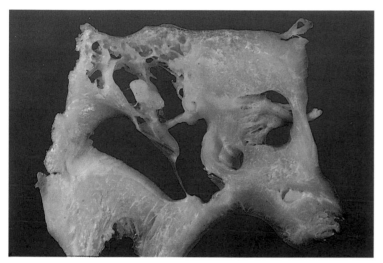

Figure 2.**23** **A** Photograph of 20° coronal oblique macrosection 2 mm posterior to Fig. 2.**22 A**.

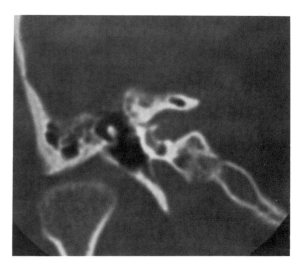

B CT corresponding to Fig. 2.**23 A**.

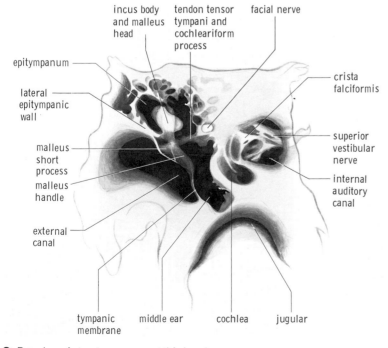

C Drawing of structures seen at this level.

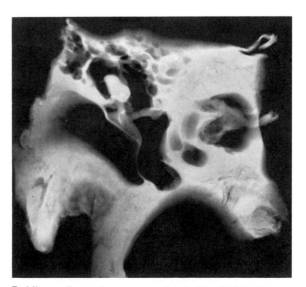

D Microradiograph corresponding to Fig. 2.**23 A, B**.

Figure 2.24 shows the structures contained in a 2 mm thick 20° coronal oblique section of a right adult temporal bone immediately adjacent to Fig. 2.23.

A strip of the tympanic membrane extends from the inferior margin of the lateral epitympanic wall to the anulus tympanicus inferior. The body of the incus lies in the epitympanum. The long process of the incus extends to articulate with the head of the stapes.

The facial nerve lies in the medial wall of the middle ear below the prominence of the horizontal semicircular canal.

The anterior portion of the stapes footplate closes the oval window. The anterior crus is attached to the footplate.

In the lumen of the promontory, the lamina spiralis separates the scala tympani from the scala vestibuli. The scala vestibuli opens into the vestibule above the scala tympani.

The ampullated ends of the superior and horizontal semicircular canals open into the vestibule. Segments of the membranous semicircular canals, the anterior portion of the utricle, the utricular macula, and the saccule occupy the lumen of the vestibule and bony canals (Fig. 2.24 A, D).

Only the fundus of the internal auditory canal remains (Fig. 2.24 D). A thin bony plate covers the jugular dome.

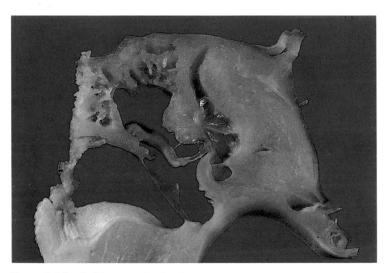

Figure 2.24   A Photograph of 20° coronal oblique macrosection 2 mm posterior to Fig. 2.23 A.

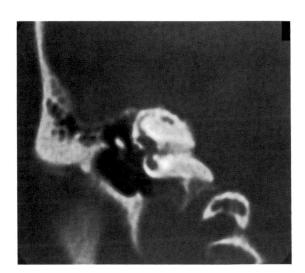

B CT corresponding to Fig. 2.24 A.

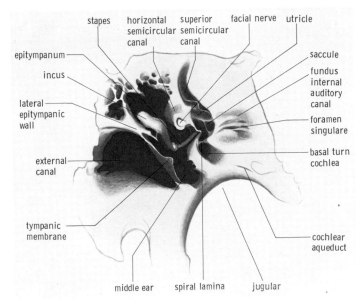

C Drawing of structures seen at this level.

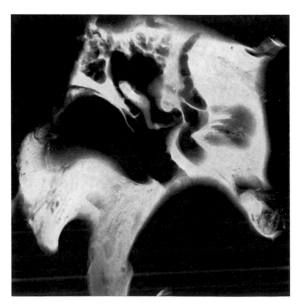

D Microradiograph corresponding to Fig. 2.24 A, B.

Figure 2.25 demonstrates the structures contained in a 2 mm thick 20° coronal oblique section of a right adult temporal bone immediately posterior to Fig. 2.24.

The section includes the external auditory canal, a thin section of tympanic membrane, the middle ear, and the aditus.

The body of the incus lies above the posterosuperior wall of the external auditory canal. The incus long process articulates with the stapes (Fig. 2.24 A, D).

The horizontal semicircular canal forms the medial boundary of the aditus of the mastoid antrum.

The facial nerve appears under the horizontal semicircular canal. The posterior half of the stapes footplate closes the oval window, and the posterior crus lies in the oval window niche. In the inferior aspect of the promontory, the round window membrane separates the round window niche from the scala tympani.

The superior semicircular canal arches upwards from the vestibule. The utricle occupies the upper portion of the bony vestibule.

The cochlear aqueduct arches within the thickness of the tissue section above the jugular fossa (Fig. 2.25 C, D).

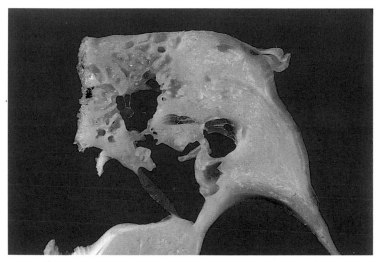

Figure 2.25 **A** Photograph of 20° coronal oblique macrosection 2 mm posterior to Fig. 2.24 A.

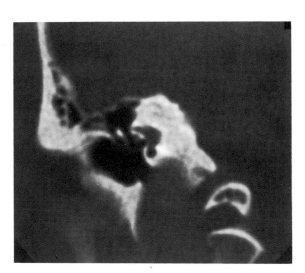

B CT corresponding to Fig. 2.25 A.

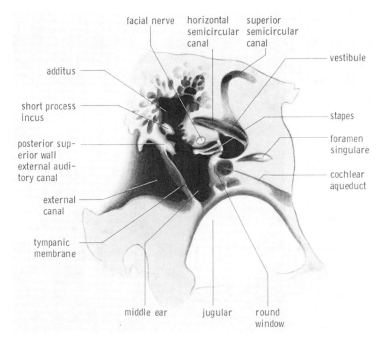

facial nerve   horizontal semicircular canal   superior semicircular canal

vestibule

additus

short process incus

posterior superior wall external auditory canal

external canal

tympanic membrane

stapes

foramen singulare

cochlear aqueduct

middle ear   jugular   round window

C Drawing of structures seen at this level.

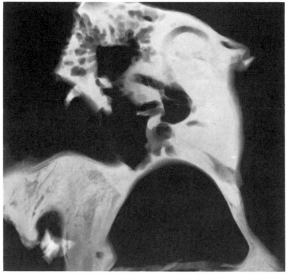

D Microradiograph corresponding to Fig. 2.25 A, B.

Figure 2.26 demonstrates the structures contained in a 2 mm thick 20° coronal oblique section of a right adult temporal bone immediately posterior to Fig. 2.25.

The section exposes the mastoid antrum with its surrounding air cells, the posterior wall of the external auditory canal, and the posterior part of the tympanic membrane.

The tip of the incus short process lies in the fossa incudis.

The facial nerve and the pyramidal eminence lie in the posterior wall of the middle ear below the horizontal semicircular canal.

The dome of the jugular fossa forms the floor of the hypotympanum.

The horizontal semicircular canal projects into the antrum.

The ampullated end of the posterior semicircular canal opens into the inferior portion of the vestibule (Fig. 2.26 A). The posterior margin of the round window lies opposite the posterior ampulla. Less than 2 mm, the thickness of this section, separates these two structures.

Portions of the membranous labyrinth occupy the lumen of the vestibule.

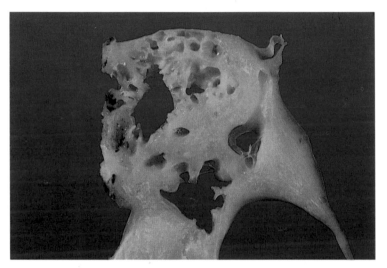

Figure 2.26   A Photograph of 20° coronal oblique macrosection 2 mm posterior to Fig. 2.25 A.

B CT corresponding to Fig. 2.26 A.

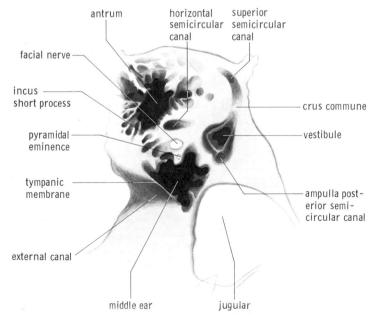

C Drawing of structures seen at this level.

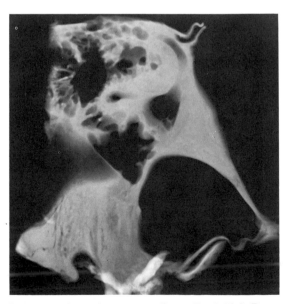

D Microradiograph corresponding to Fig. 2.26 A, B.

Sagittal Sections

The first sagittal section (Fig. 2.27), 2 mm thick, of this right adult temporal bone crosses the medial portion of the external auditory canal and the lateral portion of the epitympanum.

A small section of the tympanic membrane is attached to the posterosuperior wall of the external auditory canal.

The body of the incus is in the epitympanum and the short process in the fossa incudis.

The tegmen of the middle ear and mastoid forms the upper margin of the tissue section.

Mucosal strands stretch across the mastoid antrum. There are many small air cells in the mastoid.

The vertical portion of the facial nerve descends inferior.

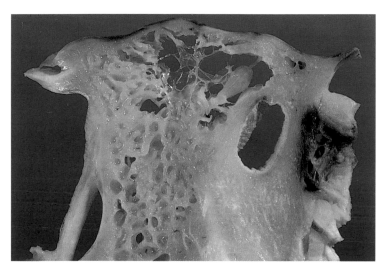

Figure 2.27 **A** Photograph of sagittal macrosection at the level of the lateral portion of the epitympanum.

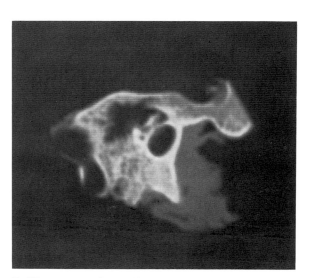

B CT corresponding to Fig. 2.27 **A**.

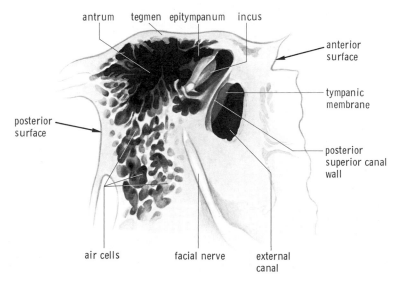

C Drawing of structures seen at this level.

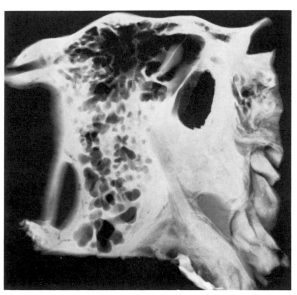

D Microradiograph corresponding to Fig. 2.27 **A, B**.

Figure 2.28 demonstrates the structures in the 2 mm thick sagittal section of a right adult temporal bone immediately medial to Fig. 2.27.

A thin strip of the tympanic membrane separates the external auditory canal anterior from the middle ear posterior.

The malleus head and neck occupy the anterior portion of the epitympanum.

The transected incus body articulates with the malleus head.

The short process of the malleus lies in contact with the tympanic membrane. The anterior tympanic spine is just anterior to the malleus short process. A segment of the chorda tympani crosses the middle ear.

The most lateral portion of the horizontal semicircular canal appears posteriorly.

The facial nerve descends from the pyramidal turn towards the stylomastoid foramen.

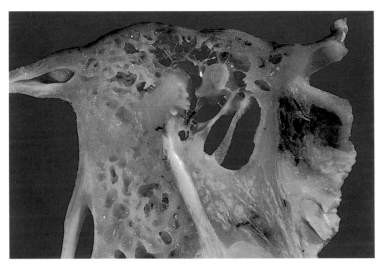

Figure 2.28   **A** Photograph of sagittal macrosection 2mm medial to Fig. 2.**27 A**.

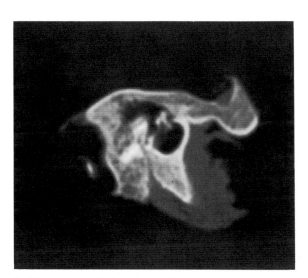

B CT corresponding to Fig. 2.**28 A**.

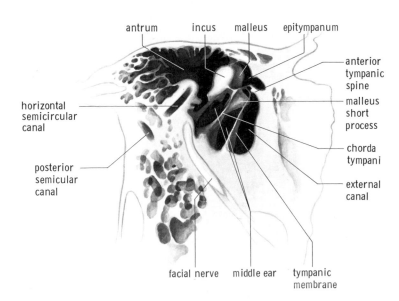

antrum   incus   malleus   epitympanum

horizontal semicircular canal

posterior semicular canal

anterior tympanic spine

malleus short process

chorda tympani

external canal

facial nerve   middle ear   tympanic membrane

C Drawing of structures seen at this level.

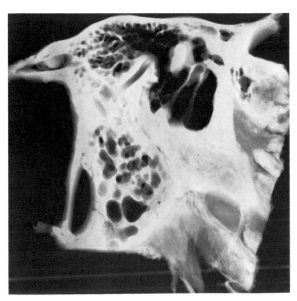

D Microradiograph corresponding to Fig. 2.**28 A, B**.

Figure 2.29 demonstrates the structures in a 2 mm thick sagittal section of a right adult temporal bone immediately medial to Fig. 2.28.

A thin strip of tympanic membrane attached to the malleus handle separates the external canal from the middle ear.

The anterior mallear ligament passes into the petrotympanic fissure above the anterior tympanic spine.

The remnant of the body of the incus articulates with the malleus head. The long process of the incus extends to the lenticular process. The horizontal and posterior semicircular canals are in the bone of the petrosa.

A segment of the facial nerve passes below the horizontal semicircular canal.

The pyramidal eminence and stapedius muscle are inferior to the facial nerve.

The endolymphatic sac lies beneath the dura of the posterior surface of the section.

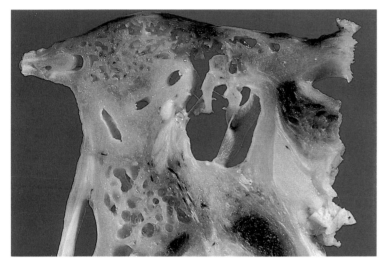

Figure 2.**29** **A** Photograph of sagittal macrosection 2 mm medial to Fig. 2.**28 A**.

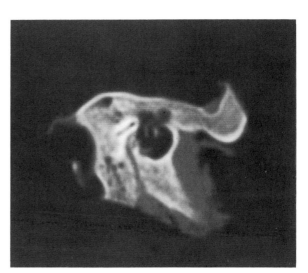

B CT corresponding to Fig. 2.**29 A**.

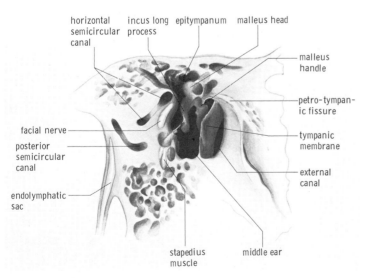

C Drawing of structures seen at this level.

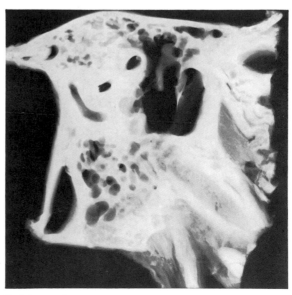

D Microradiograph corresponding to Fig. 2.**29 A, B**.

Figure 2.30 shows the structures in a 2 mm thick sagittal section of a right adult temporal bone immediately medial to Fig. 2.29.

The section includes the most anterior portion of the external auditory canal, the anterior portion of the tympanic membrane, and a thin section of the cochlear promontory.

The posterior half of the stapes footplate, head, and posterior crus occupy the oval window niche.

The tympanic sinus extends posteriorly between the oval and round windows (Fig. 2.30 A).

A section of the facial nerve is above the oval window. The cochleariform process and tensor tympani tendon are anterior to the facial nerve.

The three semicircular canals occupy the petrosa posteriorly. Segments of the membranous semicircular canals including their ampullated portions lie in the canal lumina.

The ampullated end of the horizontal semicircular canal opens into the vestibule just below the ampulla of the superior semicircular canal.

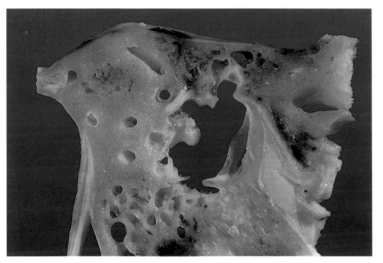

Figure 2.30   A Photograph of sagittal macrosection 2 mm medial to Fig. 2.29 A.

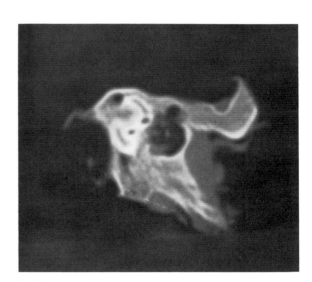

B CT corresponding to Fig. 2.30 A.

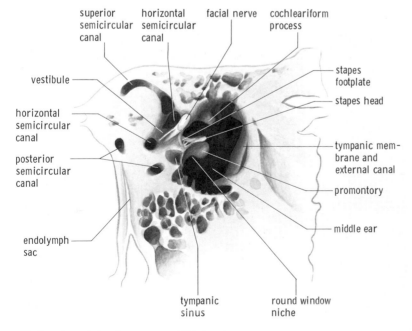

C Drawing of structures seen at this level.

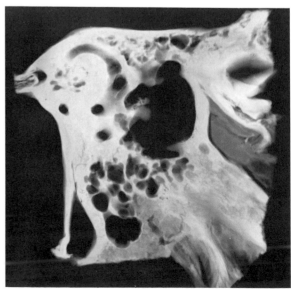

D Microradiograph corresponding to Fig. 2.30 A, B.

Figure 2.31 reveals the structures in a 2 mm thick sagittal section of a right adult temporal bone immediately medial to Fig. 2.30.

The section crosses the anterior portion of the middle ear and exposes the epi-, meso-, and hypotympanic portions of the middle ear.

The tensor tympani canal protrudes into the middle ear just below the facial nerve.

The anterior portion of the stapes footplate and the anterior crus lie in the anterior part of the oval window niche.

The promontory with the scala vestibuli and tympani lies anterior to the vestibule. The section exposes the round window niche and membrane.

The urticle stretches across the vestibule. Anterosuperiorly the utricular macula connects with the superior vestibular nerve.

The utricle joins the crus commune posterior and the ampullated end of the posterior semicircular canal inferior.

The bony vestibule narrows posteriorly toward the crus commune, which in turn branches to form the nonampullated limbs of the posterior and superior semicircular canals.

On the posterior aspect, the endolymphatic sac enters the vestibular aqueduct. The aqueduct extends to the vestibule medial to the crus commune.

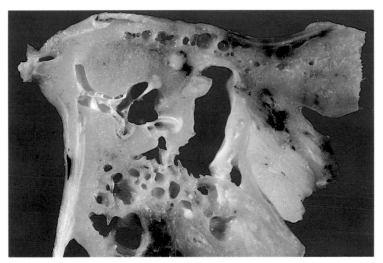

Figure 2.31   A Photograph of sagittal macrosection 2 mm medial to Fig. 2.30 A.

B CT corresponding to Fig. 2.31 A.

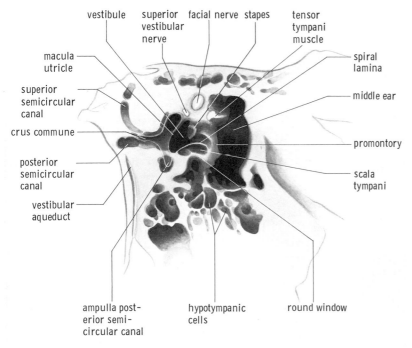

C Drawing of structures seen at this level.

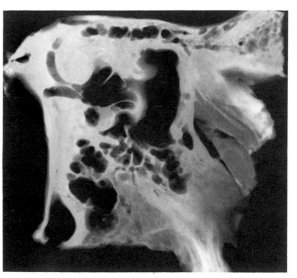

D Microradiograph corresponding to Fig. 2.31 A, B.

Figure 2.32 reveals the structures in a 2 mm thick sagittal section of a right adult temporal bone immediately medial to Fig. 2.31.

The middle ear narrows near the eustachian tube opening. The tensor tympani canal lies in the superior portion of the middle ear.

Within the thickness of the section, the facial nerve courses from the fundus of the internal auditory canal to the geniculate ganglion.

The scala tympani and the smaller scala vestibuli of the first portion of the basal turn of the cochlea lie inferior to the inferior vestibular nerve. The section exposes portions of the middle and apical coils of the cochlea.

A portion of the bony superior semicircular canal passes upwards from the crus commune.

The vestibular aqueduct curves around the medial portion of the crus commune within the thickness of the section.

The fundus of the internal auditory canal lies posterior to the cochlea on the medial surface of the section. The fundus contains portions of the superior and inferior vestibular and facial nerves.

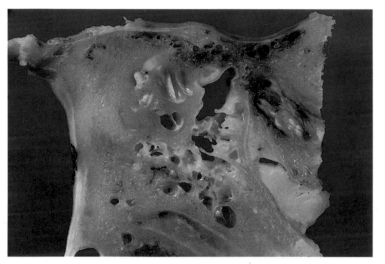

Figure 2.**32** **A** Photograph of sagittal macrosection 2 mm medial to Fig. 2.**31 A**.

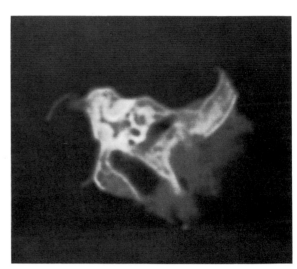

B CT corresponding to Fig. 2.**32 B**.

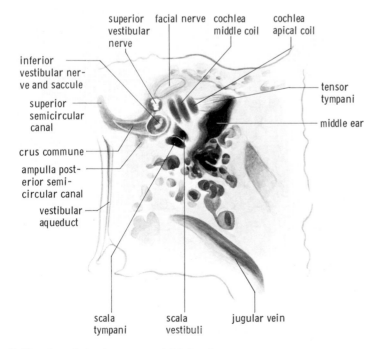

superior vestibular nerve

facial nerve

cochlea middle coil

cochlea apical coil

inferior vestibular nerve and saccule

superior semicircular canal

crus commune

ampulla posterior semicircular canal

vestibular aqueduct

tensor tympani

middle ear

scala tympani

scala vestibuli

jugular vein

C Drawing of structures seen at this level.

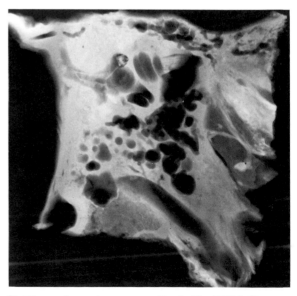

D Microradiograph corresponding to Fig. 2.**32 A, B**.

Figure 2.33 shows the structures in a 2 mm thick sagittal section of a right adult temporal bone immediately medial to Fig. 2.32.
The tensor tympanic canal protrudes into the eustachian portion of the middle ear.
The section exposes the modiolus and three turns of the cochlea. The modiolus is radiolucent and does not appear in the tomographs.

The lateral portion of the internal auditory meatus contains sections of the facial and acoustic nerves.
The carotid artery lies anterior and inferior to the cochlea, while the jugular fossa passes along the inferior surface of the section.

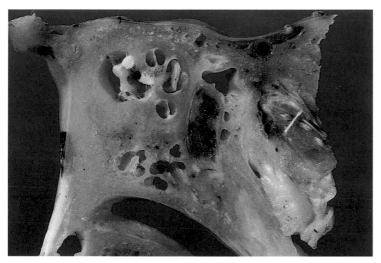

Figure 2.**33** **A** Photograph of sagittal macrosection 2 mm medial to Fig. 2.**32A**.

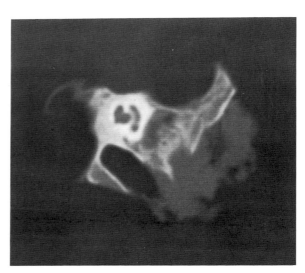

B CT corresponding to Fig. 2.**33A**.

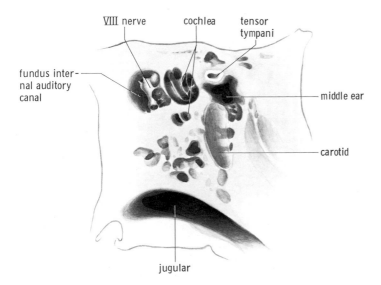

C Drawing of structures seen at this level.

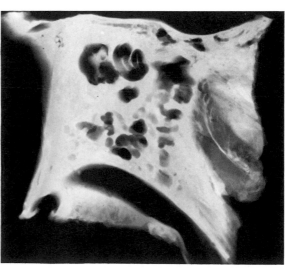

D Microradiograph corresponding to Fig. 2.**33A, B**.

Figure 2.34 shows the structures contained in a 2 mm thick sagittal section of a right adult temporal bone immediately medial to Fig. 2.33.

The tensor tympani is in the middle ear portion of the eustachian tube.

The carotid artery courses between the eustachian tube and the cochlea. Parts of the basal and middle coils of the cochlea lie anterior to the internal auditory meatus, while the jugular fossa forms the inferior margin of the section.

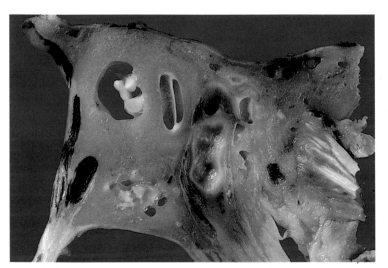

Figure 2.34   A Photograph of sagittal macrosection 2 mm medial to Fig. 2.33 A.

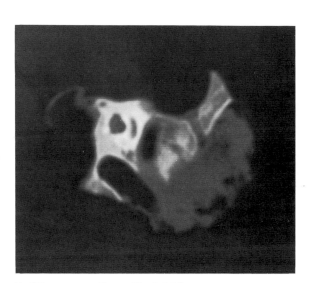

B CT corresponding to Fig. 2.34 A.

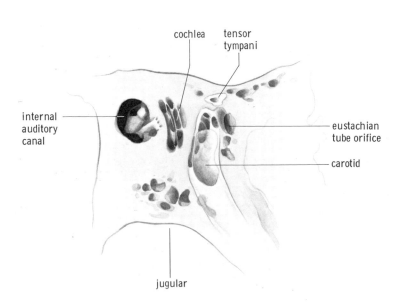

cochlea   tensor tympani

internal auditory canal

eustachian tube orifice

carotid

jugular

C Drawing of structures seen at this level.

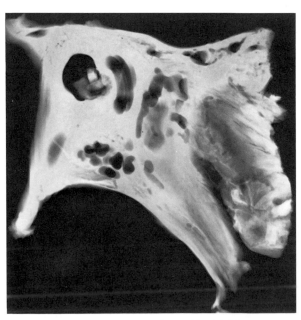

D Microradiograph corresponding to Fig. 2.34 A, B.

Chapter 3 Magnetic Resonance Imaging of the Temporal Bone

MR is an imaging technique that produces cross-sectional images in any plane without exposing the patient to ionizing radiation.

MR images are obtained by the interaction of hydrogen nuclei or protons, high magnetic fields, and radio frequency pulses.

The intensity of the MR signal to be converted to imaging data depends on the concentration or density of the hydrogen nuclei in the examined tissue and on two magnetic relaxation times, T1 and T2, which are tissue specific. One of the characteristics and advantages of MR is the feasibility of changing the appearance and information of the images by varying the relative contribution of the T1 and T2 relaxation times. Variation of relaxation times is obtained by changing the time between radio frequency pulses, TR or repetition time, and the time the emitted signal or echo is measured after the pulse, TE or echo time (Fig. 3.1).

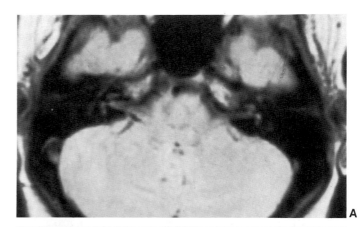

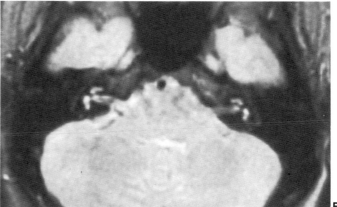

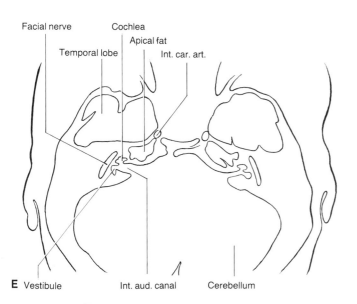

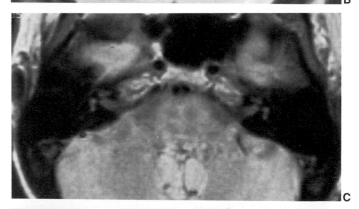

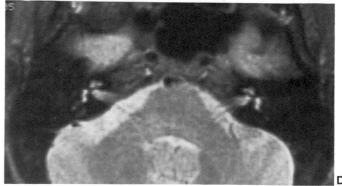

Figure 3.1 Normal temporal bone, axial MR images. **A, C** spin density weighted and **B, D** T2, **E** diagram.

These images are at the level of the internal auditory canal. The normal mastoid, external auditory canal, middle ear cavity, and ossicles appear black because of lack of signal from air and cortical bone. The internal auditory canals, cochleas, vestibules, and semicircular canals are recognizable because of the signal produced by fluids within the structures. The fat containing bone marrow within the petrous apices emits a strong signal. Notice that the fluid is brighter in the T2 images, while the signal intensity of the fat within the petrous apices is stronger in the spin density weighted images. The tympanic segment of both facial nerves are identified in images A and B as linear bands of medium signal intensity just lateral to the labyrinth.

The signal intensity of different tissues is directly proportional to the amount of free protons present within the tissue. Fat and body fluids contain large amounts of free proton, and therefore emit strong MR signals which are displayed as bright areas on the monitor and in the hard copy record. Air, cortical bone, and calcified tissue appear as dark areas, since they contain few free protons and emit a very weak MR signal (Fig. 3.2–3.4).

Blood vessels in which there is circulating blood appear in MR images as areas of void or no signal, because the magnetized protons of the circulating blood move out of the sections before their emitted signal can be detected (Fig. 3.2C). A high intensity signal will be detected from circulating blood vessels if a rapid scanning technique is used.

Pathological processes are recognizable when the proton density and relaxation times of the abnormal tissue are different from those of normal tissue.

Examination is performed with the patient supine and the plane extending from the tragus to the inferior orbital rim perpendicular to the table top.

Different projections are obtained by electronic adjustment of the magnetic field without moving the patient's head. Axial, coronal and sagittal projections are usually obtained.

T1 images obtained by a short TR and TE offer the best anatomical delineation (Fig. 3.2). T2 images obtained with long TR and TE better differentiate normal from pathologic tissues (Fig. 3.1 B, D).

Spin density weighted images generated by extending the TR, but with short TE, produce images that are related to proton density rather than magnetic relaxation characteristics. Proton density images, therefore, provide magnetic data that are not otherwise seen in T1 and T2 images.

Proton density sections resemble T1 images, but provide better differentiation of normal and abnormal tissues (Fig. 3.1 A, C).

The images in this chapter were obtained with a super conducting magnet and a magnetic field of 15 000 Gauss or 1.5 Tesla, two or four excitations and displayed on a 256 × 128 or a 256 × 256 matrix.

A strong magnetic field produces a high signal to noise ratio and sections as thin as 3.0 mm.

A further improvement in details is obtained from structures close to the surface of the body by the use of surface receiver coils.

Since cortical bone and air emit no signal, normal mastoid, external auditory canal, and middle ear cavity appear on MR images as black areas, and the contours of these structures are not visualized. The petrous pyramids are also dark, except for inner ear structures and the internal auditory canals, which appear bright from the signal emitted by the fluid within their lumens. Often a strong signal is emitted from fat in the diploe of the petrous apices.

Fluid and soft tissue changes caused by trauma, infection, or tumor of the temporal bone are seen in MR as areas of abnormally high signal intensity. MR is more sensitive than CT in detecting small soft tissue lesions in the temporal bone. However, the anatomical site of the lesions and presence and extent of bony destruction cannot be determined by MR, since all landmarks are absent in the MR images, except the lumen of the labyrinth. Because of these factors, CT remains at present the study of choice for identification of intratemporal bone pathology.

If the lesion extends beyond the limits of the temporal bone, or arises within the internal auditory canal or jugular fossa, MR details and defines involvement more precisely than CT. This is particularly true for glomus tumors, since involvement of the jugular vein and internal carotid artery is demonstrated in MR images without need for invasive vascular studies (Fig. 3.2C).

The present technique does not allow precise differentiation of soft tissue pathology, but this may become possible by future technical development in chemical shift imaging and spectroscopy.

The facial nerve is best demonstrated in T1 and spin density weighted images as a gray band (Fig. 3.1 A, B). The first three segments of the facial nerve are best seen in axial and coronal sections, the mastoid segment in the sagittal images.

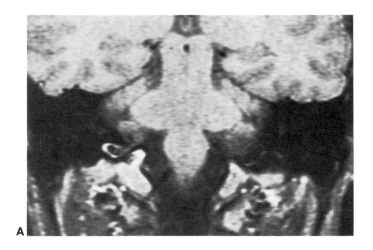

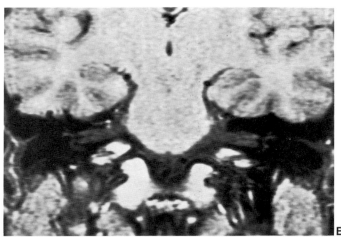

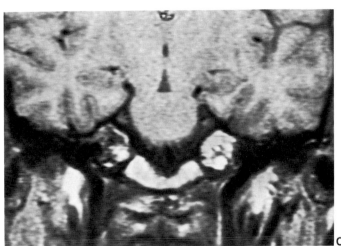

Figure 3.**2** Normal temporal bone coronal T1 images. **A** posterior section, the normal mastoids appear completely dark. **B** mid-section, the internal auditory canals, cerebellopontine cisterns, and segments of the cochleas, vestibules, and semicircular canals are visualized because of the signal produced by the fluid within these structures. Two linear bands brighter than fluid are observed in the lateral portion of the internal auditory canals produced by the myelinated portion of the 7th and 8th cranial nerves. At the fundus of the canal the two nerves appear separated by a dark line produced by the crista falciformis. **C** anterior section, the internal carotid arteries extend from the neck into the petrous pyramid. The areas of high signal intensity within the petrous apices and clivus are produced by fatty bone marrow. The 5th cranial nerves are visualized within the Meckel's caves above the petrous apices.

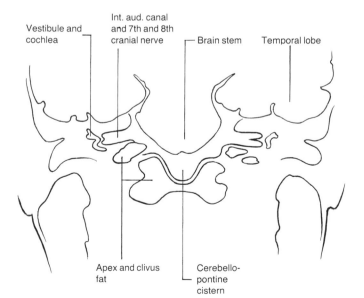

Figure 3.**3**   Diagram of structures seen in Fig. 3.**2B**.

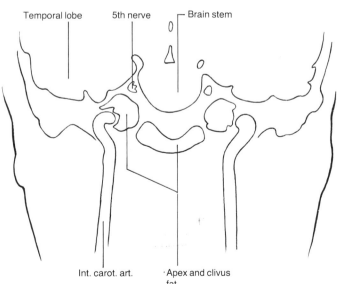

Figure 3.**4**   Diagram of structures seen in Fig. 3.**2C**.

Chapter 4 Congenital Abnormalities of the Temporal Bone

Tomography has permitted the accurate evaluation of large numbers of congenital deformities of the temporal bone, since the study can be made in the living patient. Prior to tomography, only a few post-mortem specimens of congenital defects were available for study, and surgery was performed without the benefit of knowing the precise type and degree of anomaly present. Congenital malformations are hereditary and transmitted by genetic defects or acquired during fetal life. The severity and degree depend on the causative factor or factors and the age at which the fetus was affected.

Congenital malformations of the temporal bone may be divided into three groups:

1. Defects of the sound-conducting apparatus, which include the anomalies of the external auditory canal, the middle ear, the ossicles, and the labyrinthine windows.
2. Malformations of the cochleovestibular perceptive apparatus. These include anomalies of one or more structures of the inner ear.
3. Abnormalities of blood vessels and nerves. Included in these lesions are anomalies of the course and position of the carotid artery, the jugular bulb, and the facial nerve.

Radiographic Evaluation

In congenital anomalies of the ear, a radiographic assessment is essential. Otoscopy is of little value in atresia and aplasia of the external auditory canal, and audiometry is unreliable in young children. A proper radiographic study should demonstrate the status of the anatomical structures of the ear. Such information is of value for the otologist in determining the proper treatment for conductive and sensorineural hearing losses.

Conventional radiography is of limited value except for the evaluation of the degree and development of the pneumatization of the mastoid. In agenesis and atresia of the external auditory canal, the dense atretic block obscures the middle ear in the Schüller and Owen projections, and a tomographic examination should be performed. The CT study should include axial and coronal sections. In selected cases, 20° coronal oblique and sagittal images are added to evaluate the labyrinthine windows and the mastoid segment of the facial canal. In young restless children, sedation is often necessary to immobilize them during the examination.

A good CT study will provide the surgeon with the following basic information about the feasibility of corrective surgery and in determining which type of surgery is indicated.

1. The degree and type of abnormality of the tympanic bone. These abnormalities may range from a relatively minor deformity to a complete agenesis of the external auditory canal.
2. The degree and position of the pneumatization of the mastoid air cells and mastoid antrum.
3. The position of the sigmoid sinus, the jugular bulb, and course of the carotid canal.
4. The development and aeration of the middle ear cavity.
5. The status of the ossicular chain, the size and shape of the ossicles, and the presence of fusion or fixation.
6. The patency of the labyrinthine windows.
7. The development and course of the facial nerve.
8. The relationship of the meninges to the mastoid and superior petrous ridge. The middle cranial fossa often forms a deep groove lateral to the labyrinth, which results in a low lying dura over the mastoid, epitympanum, and external auditory canal.
9. The degree of development and the morphology of the inner ear structures. Anomalies of the membranous labyrinth are not visible radiographically, but CT will detect abnormalities of the bony labyrinthine structures.

We studied more than 850 CT cases of congenital ear defects. About 60% of these cases had deformities of the external auditory canal, middle ear, or both structures. Inner ear abnormalities accounted for 30% of the congenital defects, and the remaining 10% had mixed defects of the external, middle, and inner ears.

Embryology

A short review of the embryology of the ear is helpful in understanding the radiographic changes seen in congenital malformations.

Embryology of the Outer and Middle Ear

In the four-week-old human embryo, three branchial arches separated by two branchial grooves appear. While the third arch and second groove disappear, the first branchial groove deepens to become the primitive external auditory meatus. Simultaneously

Figure 4.**1**   Three-month old fetus showing development of middle and external ears. There is a solid core of epithelial cells extending toward the first pharyngeal pouch from the primitive external acoustic meatus. (From Shambaugh GE: *Surgery of the Ear.* 2nd ed. Saunders, Philadelphia and London 1967)

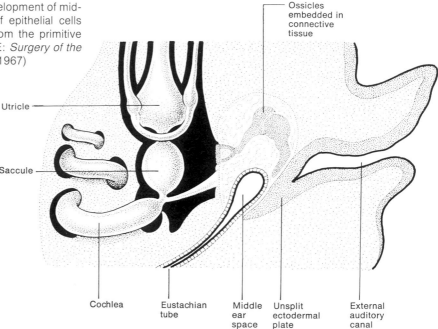

Utricle

Saccule

Cochlea

Eustachian tube

Middle ear space

Unsplit ectodermal plate

External auditory canal

Ossicles embedded in connective tissue

the first pharyngeal pouch evaginates, and for a short time comes in contact with the ectoderm of the first branchial groove. Mesenchyme soon grows between and separates these layers of ectoderm and endoderm.

At eight weeks of embryonic life, a solid core of epithelial cells grows inward from the primitive external meatus towards the epithelium of the pharyngeal pouch. The thin seam of intervening connective tissue will become the fibrous layer of the definitive tympanic membrane (Fig. 4.**1**).

This core of epithelial tissue from the ectoderm of the first groove remains solid until the seventh month of fetal life, when the core of epithelial cells splits, beginning in its deepest portion, where it forms the epithelium of the tympanic membrane. The dissolution of this core of epithelium then proceeds externally to join the lumen of the primitive external meatus. By this time, the other structures of the outer, middle, and inner ear are well formed.

This sequence of embryologic events explains how in some cases of stenosis or atresia of the outer portion of the external canal, the middle ear and tympanic membrane may be well formed.

The first pharyngeal pouch becomes the eustachian tube and middle ear, while the cartilage of the first and second brachial arches form the malleus, incus and part of the stapes. The ossicles grow only during the first half of fetal life, after which they ossify, having attained full adult size (Fig. 4.**1**).

The air cells of the temporal bone develop as outpouchings from the tympanum, epitympanum, antrum and eustachian tube. These outpouchings may appear in the 34-week-old fetus. When air enters the middle ear at birth, pneumatization occurs and cell development continues until early adult life, unless arrested by inflammatory processes.

Inner Ear

In the three-week-old human embryo, a plate-like ectodermal thickening occurs bilaterally near the hind brain. This is the otic placode, which forms in a few days an otic pit. The pit becomes an otocyst by the fourth week. By seven weeks, the otocyst has formed three semicircular canals and by the eleventh week the cochlea (Fig. 4.2). The primitive labyrinth enlarges until midterm when it reaches adult form and size. The endolymphatic duct and sac are the earliest appendages of the otic vessicle. They form at four and one half weeks of embryonic life when the otocyst divides into endolymphatic and utriculosaccular portions.

Throughout infancy and childhood, the endolymphatic duct and sac continue to change and enlarge to accommodate themselves with the growth of the surrounding temporal bone.

Differentiation of the sensory cells of the semicircular canals, utricle and saccule occur by the eighth week, but development of sensory cells of the cochlea does not begin until the twelfth week and is not complete until after midterm.

By the eighth embryonic week the precartilage surrounding the otic membranous labyrinth changes into an outer zone of true cartilage to form the otic capsule, while the inner zone of precartilage vacuolizes to form the perilymphatic spaces. These spaces appear around the vestibule, the scala tympani and vestibuli, and the semicircular canals, and coalesce until a continuous perilymphatic space surrounds the entire membranous labyrinth.

Ossification of the otic capsule does not occur until the cartilage has attained maximum growth and maturity at midterm.

The endochondral layer of the bone of the otic capsule is formed from cartilage which is not removed

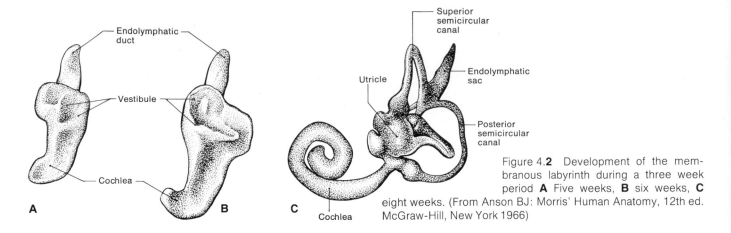

Figure 4.**2** Development of the membranous labyrinth during a three week period **A** Five weeks, **B** six weeks, **C** eight weeks. (From Anson BJ: Morris' Human Anatomy, 12th ed. McGraw-Hill, New York 1966)

and remodelled into periosteal haversian bone as in other bones of the body.

The first ossification center of the otic capsule appears around the cochlea in the 16th week of fetal life when the cochlea has reached adult size. Ossification of the 14 centers is almost complete by the 23rd week.

Anomalies of the Sound Conducting System

Anomalies of the sound conduction system can affect the external auditory canal, the mastoid, the middle ear cavity, the ossicles, and the labyrinthine windows.

Anomalies of the Tympanic Bone

The degree and type of anomaly of the tympanic bone range from mild stenosis to complete agenesis of the external auditory canal (Fig. 4.**3** to 4.**7**).

Embryologically, the definitive external auditory canals begin to form medially at the level of the tympanic membrane. An arrest in this developmental process may leave an atretic plate laterally, which causes a complete external canal atresia.

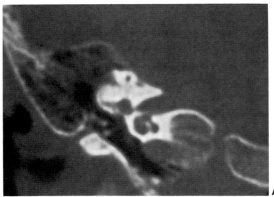

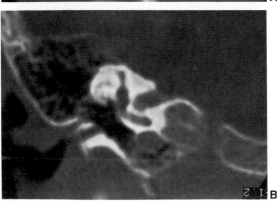

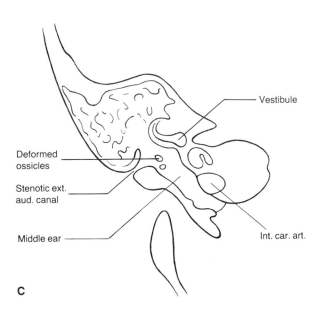

Figure 4.**3**   Dysplasia, tympanic bone. **A, B** coronal CT sections, left.

The external auditory canal is markedly stenotic. The middle ear is normal in size and aerated, but the ossicular chain is deformed. The oval window is closed by a thickened bony plate.

C Diagram of **A**.

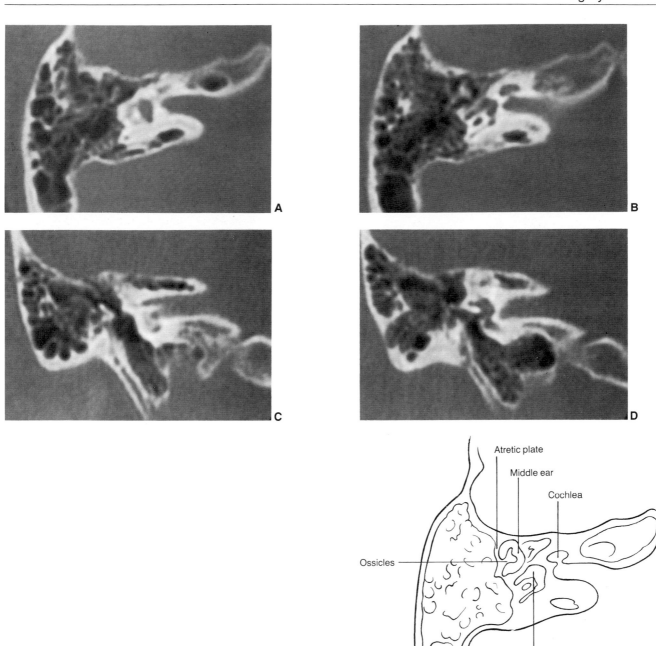

Figure 4.**4** Agenesis, external auditory canal. **A, B** axial, **C, D** coronal CT sections, right.
The mastoid and middle ear cavity are well developed and clear. The malleus head and the incus body are deformed, fused and fixed to the thick atretic plate. The horizontal semicircular canal is hypoplastic.
E Diagram of **B**.

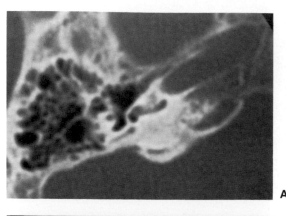

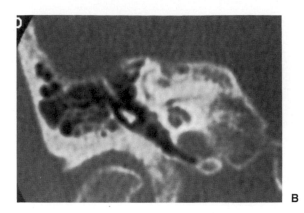

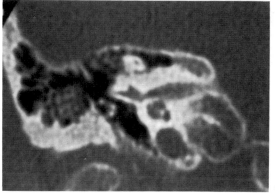

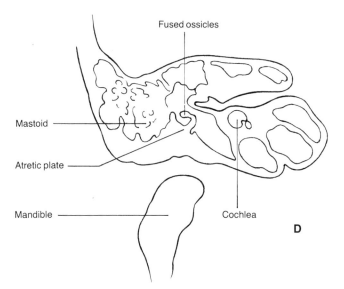

Figure 4.**5** Agenesis, external auditory canal. **A** axial, **B, C** coronal CT sections, right.
The mastoid is well pneumatized and clear. The middle ear is normal in size and aerated and closed by a thick atretic plate. The malleus is fixed to the atretic plate.
D Diagram of **C**.

Microtia

Microtia, or varying degrees of deformity of the auricle, is often associated with dysplasia of the external auditory canal. No direct relationship exists between the degree of severity of the auricular and external canal anomalies, though severe microtia is usually associated with severe agenesis of the canal.

In agenesis of the external auditory canal, often a small tissue tag and a small pit are present in place of the normal auricle and external canal.

These pits and tags usually have no topographic relationship to the mastoid and middle ear. To establish the position of the middle ear in relation to bone vestigial remnant of the external ear, we tape a radiopaque pellet over the pit. The CT will show the metallic marker and its relationship to the underlying structures. When the external auditory canal assumes a more verticale course than normal, CT will reveal this malposition.

The origin of the external auditory canal from the first branchial groove and adjoining branchial arch explains the frequent association of abnormalities of other structures with the same derivation. Mandibular facial dysostoses, the Treacher-Collins and the Franceschetti syndromes, frequently are associated with defects of the external canal and auricle.

In many cases of congenital agenesis of the external auditory canal, the temporomandibular joint is displaced posteriorly and lies lateral to the middle ear cavity (Fig. 4.6C). In some cases the mandibular condyle is hypoplastic and the temporomandibular fossa flat.

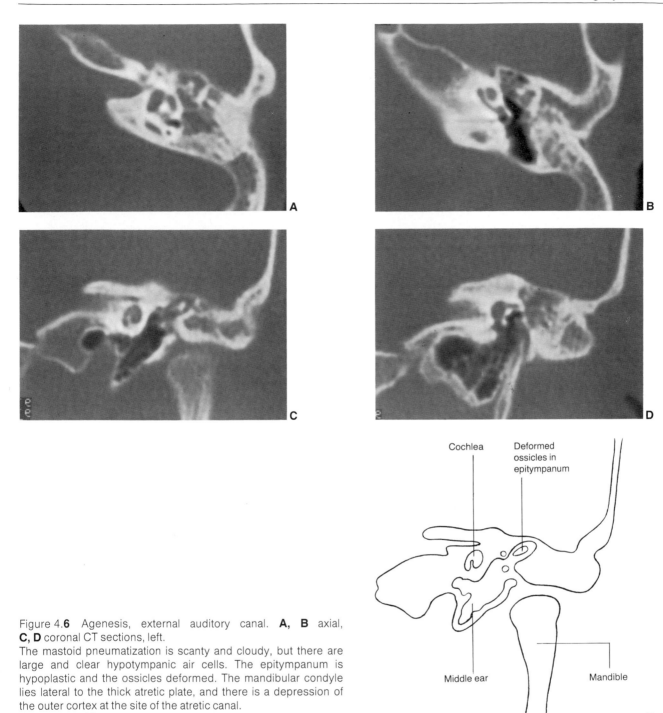

Figure 4.**6** Agenesis, external auditory canal. **A, B** axial, **C, D** coronal CT sections, left.
The mastoid pneumatization is scanty and cloudy, but there are large and clear hypotympanic air cells. The epitympanum is hypoplastic and the ossicles deformed. The mandibular condyle lies lateral to the thick atretic plate, and there is a depression of the outer cortex at the site of the atretic canal.
E Diagram of **C**.

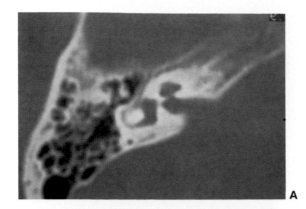

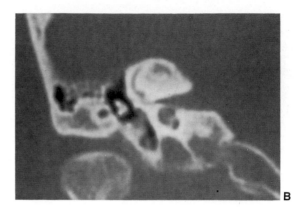

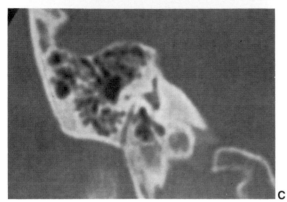

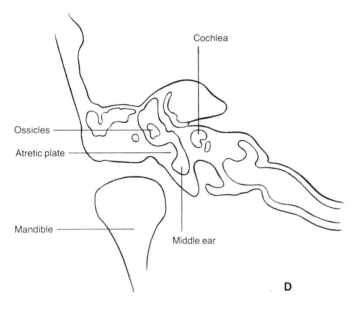

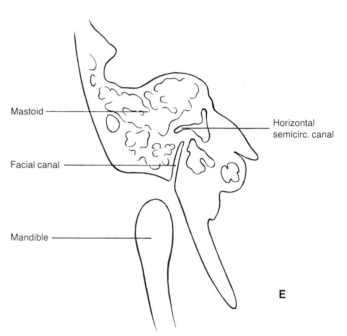

Figure 4.**7**   Agenesis, external auditory canal. **A** axial, **B, C** coronal CT sections, left.
The mastoid is well developed. The middle ear cavity is hypoplastic and there is a thick atretic plate projecting into the hypoplastic middle ear. The malleus and incus are fused and fixed to the anterior attic wall. The mastoid segment of the facial nerve is slightly rotated laterally.
D Diagram of **B**.
E Diagram of **C**.

Mastoid Pneumatization

Radiography reveals the degree of pneumatization of the mastoid. Pneumatization can be completely absent (Fig. 4.**8**) limited to a small mastoid antral cell, or completely normal (Fig. 4.**3**–4.**5**).
Conventional views and especially axial CT sections will determine the degree of pneumatization and the position of the sigmoid sinus in relation to the external canal, antrum, and middle ear.
Coronal sections are necessary to determine the relationship of the tegmental plate to the antrum and middle ear (Fig. 4.**8**). A low lying dura is common in congenital atresia, as the middle cranial fossa deepens to form a groove lateral to the labyrinth.

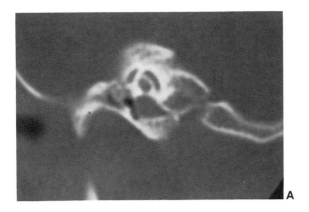
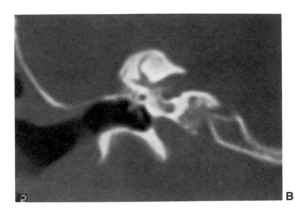

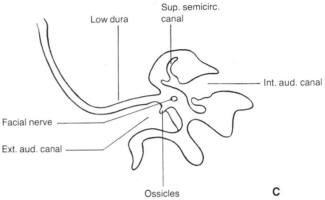
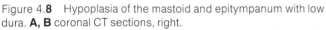

Figure 4.**8**   Hypoplasia of the mastoid and epitympanum with low dura. **A, B** coronal CT sections, right.
CT sections of the middle ear cavity show a small mastoid, hypoplasia of the epitympanum, a rudimentary ossicular mass and an extremely low dura lying at the level of the tympanic portion of the facial nerve.
C Diagram of **B**.

Anomalies of the Middle Ear

The degree of development and aeration of the middle ear is determined by axial and coronal CT sections.
The malformations of the middle ear vary from minor hypoplasia to almost complete agenesis. In the majority of cases associated with atresia, the middle ear cavity is slightly hypoplastic but is usually well aerated (Fig. 4.3–4.5).

Anomalies of the Ossicles

Anomalies of the incus and malleus occur in varying degrees. Axial and coronal sections expose the anomalies best. In cases of agenesis of the external auditory canal but relatively normal middle ear development, the malleus and incus are present but fused together and fixed to the atretic bone plate at the level of the neck of the malleus (Fig. 4.3–4.**10**).
In these cases, the long process of the incus is normal. If the atretic plate lies lateral to the level of the tympanic membrane, the ossicular chain may be entirely normal. When the middle ear cavity is hypoplastic, the malleus and incus exist as an amalgam of amorphous bone, and the long process of the incus is shortened or absent (Fig. 4.**8**).
In severe cases, the middle ear may be extremely hypoplastic, and only a rudimentary ossicular mass is present in an ectopic position (Fig. 4.7).
A congenital anomaly may be confined to the ossicular chain. The external auditory canal, the middle ear, and the ossicles are well formed, but the malleus or incus are fused to the epitympanic wall. The malleus is more commonly fixed than the incus (Fig. 4.**9**).
Tomography will demonstrate such an isolated fixation if there is ossified bone between the ossicle and the epitympanic wall or tegmen. In ears with a very low lying tegmental plate, it is difficult to determine the presence of fixation, since the space between the ossicle and the tegmen is very narrow.

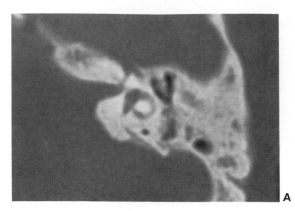

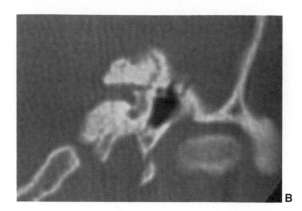

Figure 4.**9**   Congenital malleus fixation. **A** axial, **B** 20° oblique, CT sections, left.
The mastoid is hypoplastic, the dura is low, and the head of the malleus fused to the adjacent anterior epitympanic wall.
C Diagram of **A**.

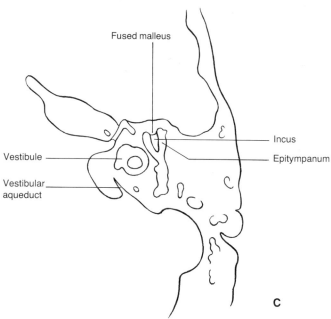

Fused malleus

Incus

Epitympanum

Vestibule

Vestibular aqueduct

C

Anomalies of the Labyrinthine Windows

Anomalies of the labyrinthine window and the stapes may be the only defect in the middle ear, or such lesions may be associated with other anomalies of the ossicles, the middle ear, and the external auditory canal. Stapes and oval window defects are more common than abnormalities of the round window.

In well developed and well aerated middle ear cavities, 20° coronal oblique and axial sections will detect defects of the stapes superstructure. The most common stapes anomaly is a single, thick monopolar stapes crus.

Congenital fixation of the stapes footplate is a common isolated defect, but CT can define a lesion only if the footplate is abnormally thickened and calcified. On CT, congenital fixation of the stapes resembles stapedial otosclerosis (Fig. 4.**10**).

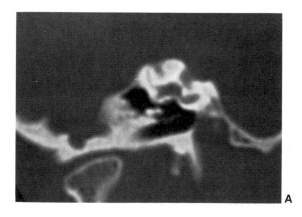

Figure 4.**10** **A** Congenital closure, oval window, 20° coronal oblique CT sections, right.
The patient has a craniofacial dysplasia. The temporal bones are distorted and the dura is low. The middle ear is aerated and the malleus and incus are normal, but the thick bony plate closes the

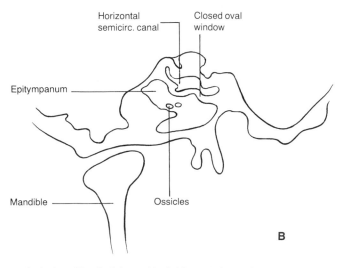

Horizontal semicirc. canal

Closed oval window

Epitympanum

Mandible

Ossicles

B

oval window. The facial canal is dehiscent above the oval window.
B Diagram of **A**.

Facial Nerve Anomalies

Congenital anomalies of the facial canal involve the size and the course of the canal.

There may be complete or partial agenesis of the facial nerve canal with total paralysis (Fig. 4.**11**). Occasionally the facial nerve canal may be unusually narrow and hypoplastic. In these cases, intermittent episodes of facial paresis may occur.

Minor variations of the course of the facial nerve are common and of no clinical or surgical significance (Fig. 4.**7**). More severe anomalies of the course of the facial nerve occur in the tympanic and vertical portions. Recognition of these anomalies is very important in planning surgical correction of ear disease. The horizontal segment at times is displaced inferiorly to cover the oval window or lies exposed over the promontory.

Anomalies of the mastoid segment are common in congenital atresia of the external auditory canal. The facial canal is usually rotated laterally (Fig. 4.**7**). The rotation varies from a minor obliquity to a true horizontal course.

Since facial nerve anomalies are common in congenital atresia, all such patients should have assessment preoperatively (Figs. 4.**7**, 4.**8**).

Anomalies of the Inner Ear

Most cases of congenital sensorineural deafness are caused by abnormal development of the membranous labyrinth. These lesions are not detectable by radiography.

Defects in the otic capsule are visible by CT. Anomalies of the otic capsule may involve a single structure or the entire capsule.

With recent advances in surgical procedures for profound sensorineural deafness, CT of the labyrinth is indicated for (1) diagnosis of the status of the otic capsule, (2) detection of cases possibly suitable for surgery of the endolymphatic sac or other inner ear structures, and (3) selection of possible candidates for cochlear implants.

The most severe anomaly of the otic capsule is the Michel type of deformity, which is characterized by a hypoplastic petrous pyramid and an almost complete lack of development of the inner ear structures. There is often a single labyrinthine cavity of varying size which occupies the space normally taken by the vestibule, cochlea and semicircular canals (Fig. 4.**12**). When facial nerve function is normal, the internal auditory canal is present but the lumen of the canal is narrowed to the size of the facial nerve. The external auditory canal and middle ear cavity are usually normal, but appear abnormally large in comparison with the small labyrinthine vestiges. The Michel deformity is usually bilateral. We have found this deformity associated with the Klippel-Feil anomaly in several cases.

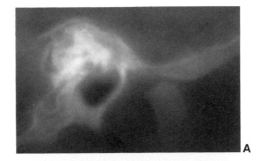
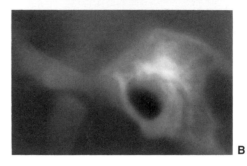
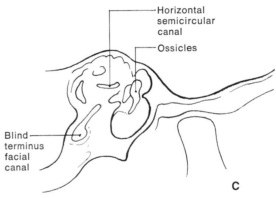

Figure 4.**11** Congenital atresia, facial nerve canal, sagittal tomogram. **A** right, **B** left, normal.
This three-year-old child has congenital right facial paralysis. The facial nerve ends in a blind cul-de-sac at the mid portion of the mastoid segment, **A**. The normal facial canal appears in the tomogram, **B**.
C Diagram of **A**.

A less severe deformity of the labyrinthine capsule is the Mondini type, which is characterized by an abnormal development of the cochlea and often is associated with an abnormality of the vestibular aqueduct, the vestibule, and the semicircular canals. The cochlea may be hypoplastic or of normal size, but the bony partition between the cochlear coils is hypoplastic or absent, which gives the appearance of an "empty cochlea" (Fig. 4.**13**). The vestibular aqueduct is often shortened and dilated (Fig. 4.**16**). The vestibule appears larger and the contour more globular than normal. There is often dilatation of the ampullated ends of the horizontal and superior semicircular canals (Fig. 4.**17**). The Modini deformity may be unilateral or bilateral.

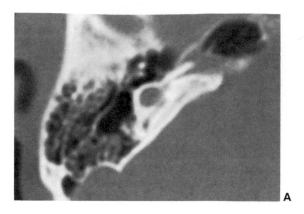

Figure 4.**12**   Michel anomaly. **A** axial, **B** coronal CT sections, right.

The mastoid and middle ear are normal, but the petrous pyramid is markedly hypoplastic. The inner ear structures are absent, except for a cavity in the region of the vestibule and horizontal semicircular canal. The internal auditory canal is very narrow and appears large enough to contain only the facial nerve.

C Diagram of **A**.

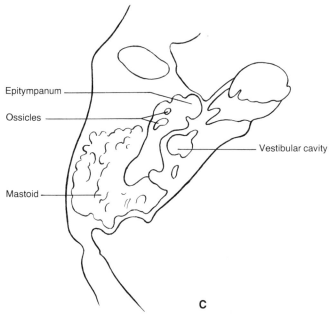

Figure 4.**13**   Mondini anomaly. **A** axial skull base, **B, C** coronal CT sections, left.

The cochlea is normal in size, but the absence of bony partitions causes the appearance of an empty cochlea, **B.** The vestibule is moderately dilated. The vestibular aqueduct is shortened and dilated, **A**.

D Diagram of **A**.
▼

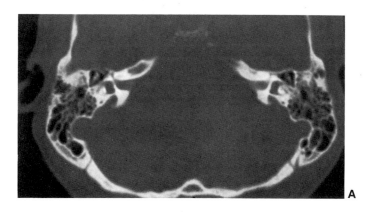

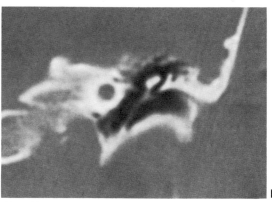

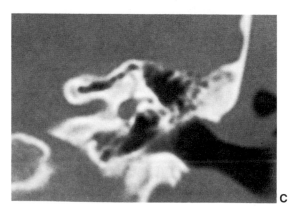

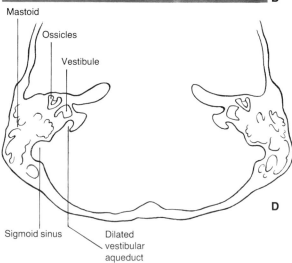

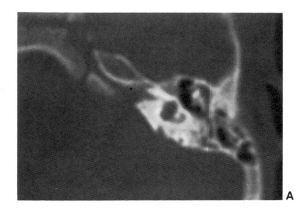

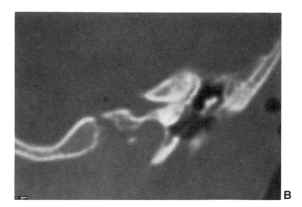

Figure 4.**14**   Agenesis, cochlea. **A** axial, **B** coronal CT sections, left.
There is severe hypoplasia of the cochlea. The horizontal semicircular canal is hypoplastic. The internal auditory canal is funnel shaped and narrows laterally.
C Diagram of **B**.

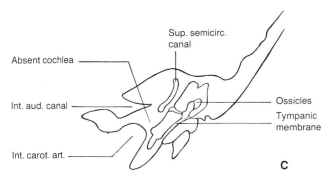

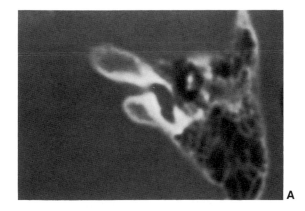

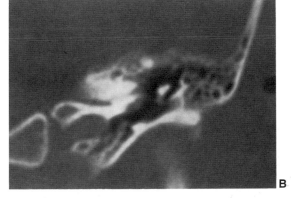

Figure 4.**15**   Agenesis, cochlea. **A** axial, **B** coronal, CT sections, left.
The cochlea is absent, the horizontal semicircular canal is hypoplastic, and the internal auditory canal is narrowed laterally. The oval window is closed by a thick bony plate.
C Diagram of **A**.

Cochlea

Various anomalies of the cochlea affecting the size, the lumen, and the bony partitions between the coils can be visualized by CT (Figs. 4.**14**, 4.**15**). The cochlear size varies from normal to complete absence. The lumen of the cochlea may be narrowed, obliterated, or grossly dilated. If the bony partitions between the cochlear coils are absent, the cochlea will appear as an empty shell.

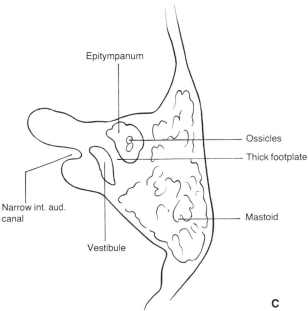

Vestibular Aqueduct Abnormalities

The vestibular aqueduct is a small bony canal which extends from the posteromedial wall of the vestibule to the posterior surface of the petrous pyramid. In the adult, the shape of the aqueduct forms an inverted J. The proximal segment, the isthmus, which arches medial to the common crus, is the narrowest segment of the aqueduct and measures 0.3 mm in diameter. As the aqueduct extends inferiorly, it widens and forms a triangular slit parallel to the posterior surface of the pyramid. The outer aperture of the aqueduct measures approximately 2.0–6.0 mm in the larger diameter and 1.0 mm in the shorter.

The aqueduct contains the endolymphatic duct which enlarges to end blindly in the endolymphatic sac lying on the posterior surface of the petrous bone.

Sagittal and axial sections are used to visualize the vestibular aqueduct. The postisthmic segment appears in more than 90% of normal ears, but the isthmic segment is seen in less than 50% because of the overlying radiolucency of the common crus.

Congenital widening of the aqueduct may occur without any other abnormalities (Fig. 4.16).

Radiographic evaluation is limited to the postisthmic segment. We measure the anteroposterior diameter in the sagittal sections midway between the outer aperture and the common crus. At this level, the normal aqueduct measures 0.5–1.0 mm in diameter. An aqueduct is considered abnormal when the lumen at the midpoint is wider than 1.5 mm or narrower than 0.5 mm. Occasionally an aqueduct is so narrow that it cannot be visualized the sections.

A dilated and shortened vestibular aqueduct similar in appearance to that of the Mondini deformity is occasionally present without other radiographically visualized abnormalities.

A narrow vestibular aqueduct is often associated with cochlear or vestibular disorders of the Ménière's type and is considered a predisposing factor to these disorders. Visualization of a normal size aqueduct does not rule out Ménière's type of otic pathology, since patients with this disorder often have a normal aqueduct.

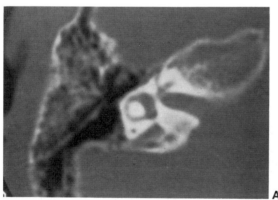

A

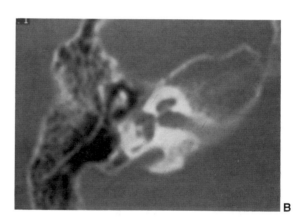

B

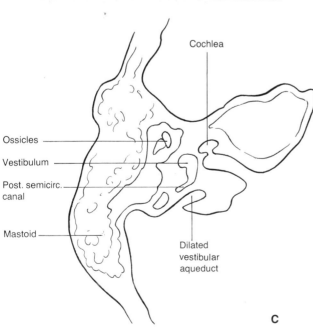

Cochlea

Ossicles

Vestibulum

Post. semicirc. canal

Mastoid

Dilated vestibular aqueduct

C

Figure 4.16   Congenital widening of the vestibular aqueduct. **A, B,** axial CT sections, right.

The vestibular aqueduct is abnormally wide and measures 4 mm in diameter. The remainder the of the inner ear structures are normal.

C Diagram of **B**.

Semicircular Canals and Vestibule

The semicircular canals are often congenitally deformed. This anomaly may be isolated or associated with other malformations of the bony labyrinth. The horizontal canal, which is the most commonly affected, may be shortened or dilated, or in the more severe defects exist merely as a lateral outpouching of the vestibule (Figs. 4.14, 4.15, 4.17). In these cases, there is absence of the bony core around which the canal normally loops. An isolated anomaly of the horizontal canal may occur with normal cochlear and vestibular function.

Hypoplasia or aplasia of the vestibule and semicircular canals can be present with or without other inner ear anomalies. This condition often occurs in association with the Waardenburg Syndrome.

Dilatation of the vestibule is often associated with an enlarged vestibular aqueduct (Fig. 4.13).

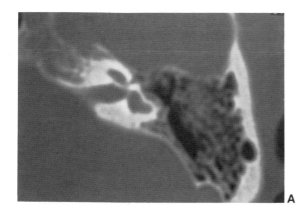

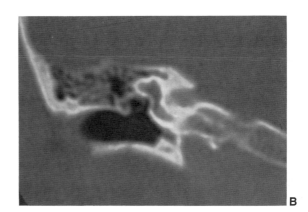

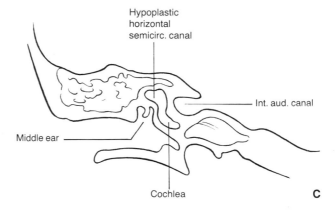

Figure 4.17 Congenital malformation of the vestibule and semicircular canals. **A** axial, **B** coronal CT sections, right.
The vestibule is hypoplastic and the oval window closed. The superior and posterior semicircular canals are absent. The horizontal canal is hypoplastic, forming a dilated pouch extending laterally from the vestibule.
C Diagram of **B**.

Anomalies of the Internal Auditory Canal

The most common anomaly of the internal auditory canal is an hypoplasia. The hypoplasia can be isolated or be associated with other anomalies (Fig. 4.**18**).

Rarely the canal is abnormally dilated and shortened. A dilated and shortened internal canal at times is associated with chronic hydrocephalus. In these cases, the dilatation is secondary to increased intracranial pressure and is not a congenital defect.

Anomalies of the Cochlear Aqueduct

In about 20% of the ears with congenital anomalies of the otic capsule, the cochlear aqueduct is abnormally dilated. A dilated cochlear aqueduct occurs occasionally as an isolated defect.

Isolated dilation of the aqueduct can cause a "labyrinth gusher" of cerebrospinal fluid, which sometimes occurs during stapedectomy for otosclerosis or congenital footplate fixation.

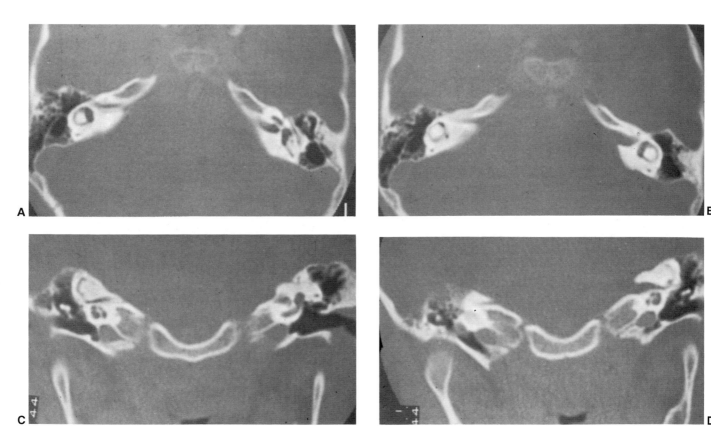

Figure 4.**18**   Hypoplasia, internal auditory canal. **A, B** axial sections, **C, D** coronal sections, right.

The right internal auditory canal is markedly hypoplastic when compared to the normal internal canal on the left side. The remaining inner ear structures are normal.

Congenital Obliterative Labyrinthitis

A lesion acquired late in fetal life may cause bony obliteration of the lumen of one or more of the inner ear structures which are already well formed. This type of obliteration cannot be differentiated radiographically from obliterative labyrinthitis secondary to postnatal infections (Fig. 4.19).

Cerebrospinal Fluid Otorrhea

Congenital defects causing cerebrospinal fluid otorrhea occur rarely and often result in repeated bouts of meningitis. The etiology is varied. In some instances, a defect in the tegmen and dura result in cerebrospinal fluid leaks. More rarely the otorrhea is the result of defects at the fundus of the internal auditory canal and in the stapes footplate with consequent communication between the subarachnoid space and the middle ear via the internal auditory canal and the vestibule. These patients are profoundly deaf.

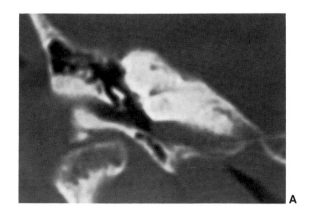

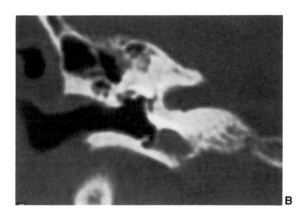

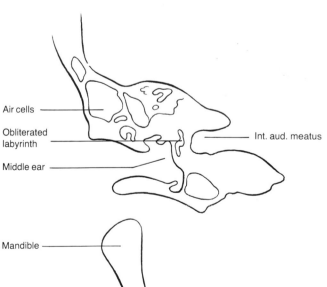

Figure 4.**19** Obliterative labyrinthitis. **A, B** coronal CT sections, right.
The middle ear cavity and mastoid are normal. The lumen of the inner ear structures is almost completely obliterated by bone.
C Diagram of **B**.

Imaging Assessment for Cochlear Implantation

Candidates for cochlear implants require a radiographic study to determine the feasibility of the procedure. CT can determine the size of the development of the mastoid, middle ear, round window, cochlea and cochlear lumen, the position of the dura and, of course, the facial nerve canal.

The otologic surgeon must know if the mastoid and middle ear are large enough to obtain access to the promontory and round window. If an intracochlear implant is contemplated, the surgeon should know if there is a patent round window and cochlear lumen. If the cochlear lumen is obliterated, the cochlea must be drilled or an extra cochlear device used.

Marked hypoplasia of the internal auditory canal indicates lack of development of the acoustic nerve, which will make an implant unfeasible.

MR is indicated to establish the presence and status of the eighth nerve and to rule out central pathology affecting the auditory pathways.

A postoperative CT study is required shortly after surgery to determine correct positioning of the electrodes. This is needed as a baseline for further studies should the electrode become displaced or non-functioning. Yearly follow-up examination will determine if the cochlear lumen remains patent and if the implant wires are intact.

Congenital Vascular Anomalies

Various techniques visualize anomalies of the jugular vein and the carotid artery as these structures course through the temporal bone.

Jugular Vein

There is a tremendous variation in the size of the jugular vein and bulb. These variations occur not only from patient to patient but from one side to the other in the same patient. The size of the jugular fossa is not a criterion of a pathologic process.

A normal jugular fossa may produce only a slight indentation on the undersurface of the petrous bone or extend upwards as high as the superior petrous ridge posterior to the labyrinth and the internal auditory canal (Fig. 4.20–4.22). In these instances, the jugular bulb projects so high that the vein blocks access to the internal auditory canal by the translabyrinthine route in acoustic neuroma surgery.

The jugular bulb at times projects into the hypo- or mesotympanum. There may be a bony cover over the jugular bulb (Fig. 4.20–4.22), or the vein may lie exposed in the middle ear in contact with the medial surface of the tympanic membrane. In these cases, such a high jugular bulb can be misdiagnosed as a glomus tumor.

There are three variations of high jugular bulbs projecting into the mesotympanum, which the radiologist should differentiate from pathological conditions.

1. The jugular fossa and bulb are high, and a soft tissue mass protrudes into the middle ear but is covered by a thin bony shell.
2. The jugular fossa and bulb are high, but there is an incomplete bony shell surrounding the soft tissue mass which protrudes into the middle ear.
3. The jugular fossa is not high but there is a large defect in the dome of the fossa. The jugular bulb herniates into the middle ear where it appears as a soft tissue mass. This variation may be confused with a glomus tumor but for the fact that the contour of the jugular fossa is normal except for the defect. In a few cases where the diagnosis is in doubt, a dynamic CT study at the level of the middle ear mass will produce a graph with a characteristic high venous peak at 20–25 seconds (Fig. 4.21 D). Jugular venography will show a normal jugular vein projecting into the middle ear to the level of the soft tissue mass appearing in the CT (Fig. 4.20). In an MR study, the middle ear mass will appear dark due to the signal void from the circulating venous blood.

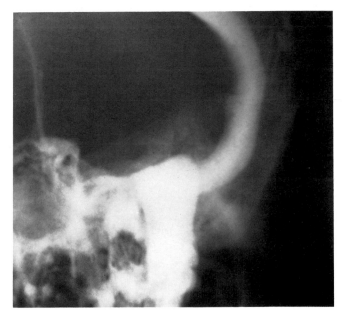

Figure 4.**20**　Retrograde jugular venogram, left. The jugular bulb protrudes into the middle ear to the level of the vestibule.

Figure 4.**22**　**A** High jugular bulb, otoscopic findings, left. ▶
The dome of the jugular bulb without a bony cover protrudes into the posterior mesotympanum and lies in contact with the tympanic membrane. The jugular bulb has the characteristic blue color of venous blood.
B Diagram of **A**.

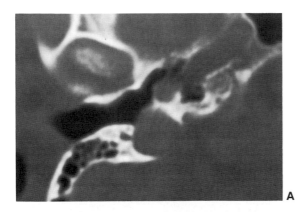

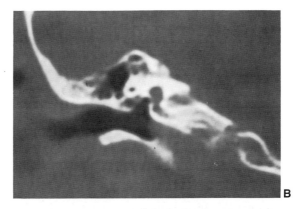

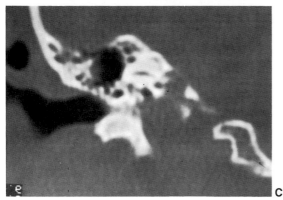

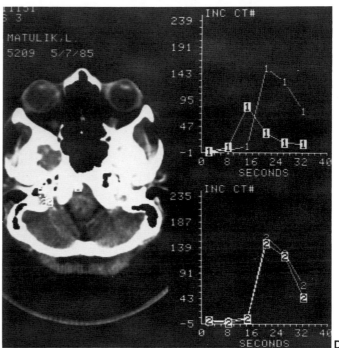

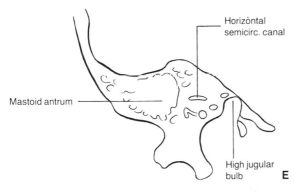

Horizontal
semicirc. canal

Mastoid antrum

High jugular
bulb

E

Figure 4.**21**   High jugular bulb. **A** axial, **B, C** coronal CT sections, **D** dynamic CT time-density study.
The large, deep jugular fossa extends to the level of the superior petrous ridge posterior to the labyrinth. The jugular bulb projects into the posterior inferior portion of the mesotympanum and appears as a middle ear mass with a partial bony shell, **A.** The dynamic CT study reveals that the time-density curve of the middle ear mass, curve 2, has an identical peak time as the curve obtained from the lateral sinus, non-boxed 1. Notice that the peak time of the curve obtained from the basilar artery, boxed 1, has a far shorter peak or transit time.
E Diagram of **C**.

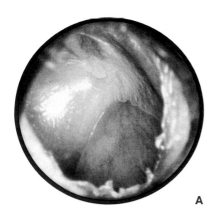

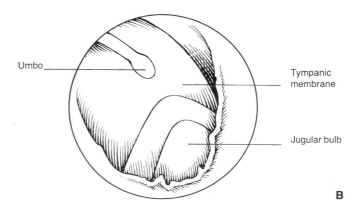

Umbo

Tympanic
membrane

Jugular bulb

Ectopic Carotid Artery

Minor variations in the intratemporal course of the internal carotid artery are not uncommon but are of no clinical significance.

The carotid artery may take an ectopic course through the middle ear (Figs. 4.23–4.28). This anomaly is rare but is of clinical importance. If surgery is contemplated, the otologic surgeon should be aware of the abnormal position of the artery in his surgical field. This lesion also may be misdiagnosed as a glomus or other type of middle ear tumor. We have recognized eight cases of this rare vascular anomaly. All were confirmed by angiographic studies.

Microscopic otoscopy shows a pinkish or white-blue mass lying in the inferior mesotympanum in contact with the medial surface of the tympanic membrane. The mass may or may not pulsate (Fig. 4.23).

The CT findings of an ectopic intratemporal carotid artery are:

1. There is a soft tissue mass extending throughout the entire length of the inferior portion of the middle ear cavity (Fig. 4.24 A).
2. There may be a thin bony wall partially surrounding the artery.
3. Contact of the mass with the tympanic membrane causes lateral bulging of the membrane. Medially the mass may cause indentation of the promontory (Fig. 4.24 C).
4. The arterial tissue mass may encroach on the incudostapedial joint and cause conductive deafness.
5. The normal proximal portion of the carotid canal is absent. The normal canal is always clearly visible below the cochlea in coronal and 20° coronal oblique sections (Fig. 4.24 C, D).

6. The anomalous carotid artery enters the temporal bone through a canal or dehiscent area in the floor of the posterior portion of the hypotympanum between the jugular fossa medially and the vertical portion of the facial canal laterally.

A dynamic CT study at the level showing the middle ear mass will produce a graph with a characteristic high arterial peak time at about 8–10 seconds (Fig. 4.24 E).

MR will show the presence of a vascular structure, but will not differentiate an ectopic carotid from a high jugular bulb.

Arteriography can confirm the CT findings. The arteriographic findings are (Figs. 4.25–4.28):

1. There is narrowing or tapering of the internal carotid artery at the site where the artery enters the base of the skull;
2. The proximal ectopic arterial segment lies at least 1 cm more laterally and posteriorly than normal. In the coronal plane, this arterial segment lies lateral rather than medial to the vertical plane which passes through the vestibule;
3. The proximal anomalous carotid artery segment follows a straight vertical course, while the proximal segment of a normal internal carotid artery curves gently medially and anteriorly;
4. The anomalous carotid artery makes a sharp 90° turn within the middle ear cavity. The artery then runs anteriorly throughout the middle ear and exits inferior to the cochlear apex, where it usually regains the normal course in the petrous pyramid.

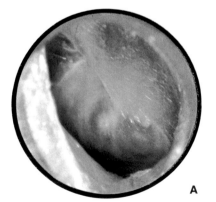

A

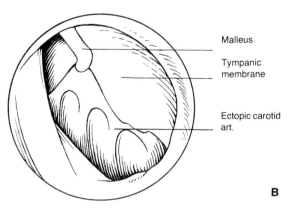

Malleus

Tympanic membrane

Ectopic carotid art.

B

Figure 4.23 **A** Ectopic internal carotid artery, otoscopic findings, left.

A deep, red-purple mass fills the inferior middle ear and herniates the tympanic membrane slightly. This lesion did not pulsate.
B Diagram of **A**.

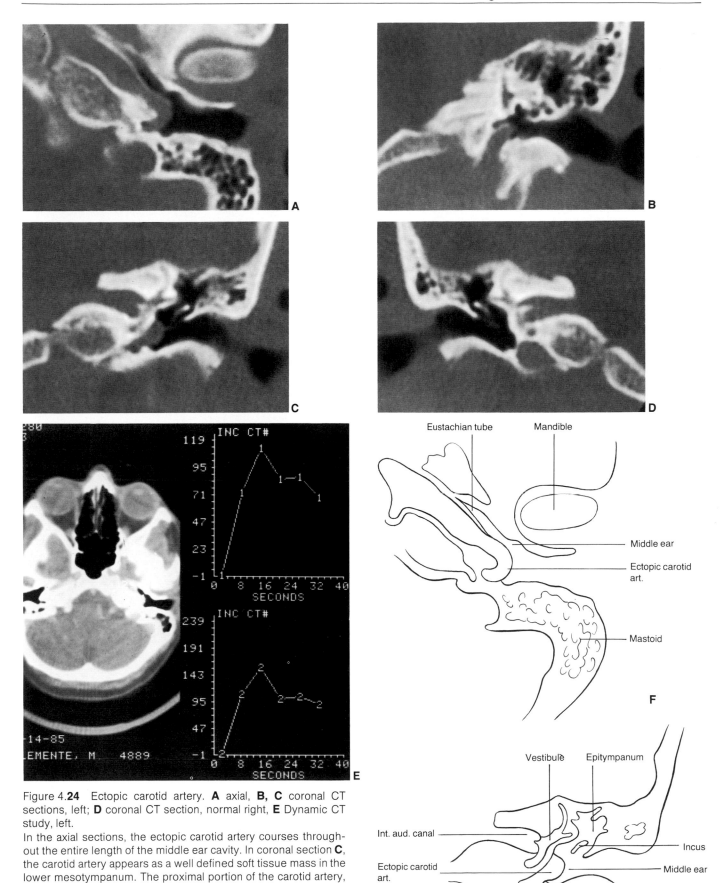

Figure 4.**24**   Ectopic carotid artery. **A** axial, **B, C** coronal CT sections, left; **D** coronal CT section, normal right, **E** Dynamic CT study, left.

In the axial sections, the ectopic carotid artery courses throughout the entire length of the middle ear cavity. In coronal section **C**, the carotid artery appears as a well defined soft tissue mass in the lower mesotympanum. The proximal portion of the carotid artery, normally seen under the cochlea, is absent. Compare corresponding sections of the normal right ear, **D**, where the carotid artery is normal. The ectopic carotid artery enters the middle ear through a posteriorly displaced canal and passes into the middle ear through a defect in the hypotympanic floor, **B**.

The dynamic CT study, **E** reveals that the time density curve of the middle ear mass, 1, has an identical peak time as the curve obtained from the internal carotid artery in its normal position in the anterior portion at the apex of the temporal bone, 2.

F Diagram of **A**.
G Diagram of **C**.

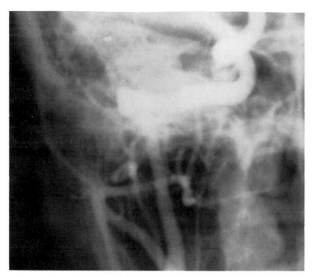

Figure 4.**25** Ectopic carotid artery, arteriogram, coronal projection, right. The narrow proximal internal carotid artery enters the middle ear and courses lateral to the vestibular plane

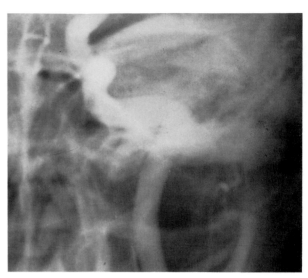

Figure 4.**26**   Corresponding arteriogram of normal left carotid for comparison

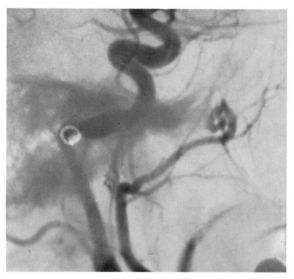

Figure 4.**27**   Ectopic carotid arteriogram, lateral projection, with subtraction. The ectopic carotid enters the posterior middle ear and makes a 90° turn anteriorly. The marker corresponds to the region of the vestibule.

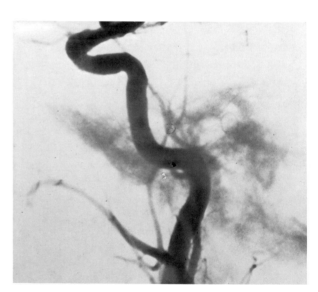

Figure 4.**28**   Corresponding arteriogram of the normal left carotid for comparison.

Chapter 5   Temporal Bone Trauma

Imaging studies of the temporal bone following head trauma are indicated when there is cerebrospinal fluid otorrhea or rhinorrhea, hearing loss, or facial nerve paralysis.

Demonstration of temporal bone fractures is important for therapeutic and medicolegal reasons.

In fractures of the base of the skull, the temporal bone is usually involved. The temporal bone can also be affected by fractures of the calvarium which extend into the skull base.

Temporal bone fractures are difficult to visualize radiographically. Conventional radiography is helpful in demonstrating fractures of the temporal squama and mastoid. When fractures involve the middle ear and petrous pyramid, CT is indispensible in demonstrating the extent of the lesion.

In acute head trauma with unconsciousness or neurological findings, a CT or MR should be performed first to rule out the possibility of intracranial hemorrhage.

Classification

Temporal bone fractures are divided into longitudinal and transverse lesions depending on the direction of the fracture line. Longitudinal fractures (Fig. 5.1) occur more frequently than transverse fractures in a ratio of 5:1. Classification of temporal bone fractures into longitudinal and transverse types is somewhat arbitrary, since most fractures follow a serpiginous course into the temporal bone.

Localized fractures of the mastoid and external canal are the result of direct trauma. An isolated fracture of the anterior wall of the external canal may result from indirect trauma from a blow to the mandible.

The typical longitudinal fracture involves the temporal squama and extends into the mastoid. The fracture usually reaches the external auditory canal and passes medially into the epitympanum. Medial extension into the petrosa from the epitympanum may occur, and the fracture line can pursue an intra- or extralabyrinthine course.

An intralabyrinthine course of the fracture is rare since the labyrinthine bone is relatively resistant to trauma. Extralabyrinthine extension of a longitudinal fracture occurs either anterior or posterior to the labyrinth, though anterior extension is more common.

A transverse fracture of the temporal bone typically crosses the petrous pyramid at right angles to the longitudinal axis of the pyramid. The fracture line usually follows the line of least resistance and runs from the dome of the jugular fossa through the labyrinth to the superior petrous ridge.

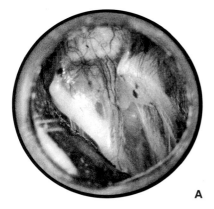

A

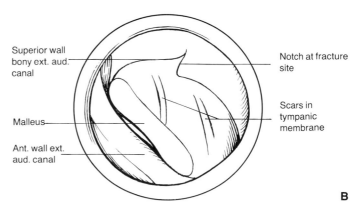

Superior wall bony ext. aud. canal

Notch at fracture site

Scars in tympanic membrane

Malleus

Ant. wall ext. aud. canal

B

Figure 5.**1** **A** Longitudinal fracture, otoscopic findings, left. This patient suffered a longitudinal fracture three years previously. The notch on the posterosuperior bony margin of the external auditory canal is a result of the slight displacement of the fracture which extended through the external auditory canal into the mastoid and ruptured the tympanic membrane.
B Diagram of **A**.

Clinical Findings

Clinical findings depend on the type of fracture. Hemotympanum and bleeding from the ear occur when the external auditory canal or tympanic membrane are involved.

When the tegmen is involved and the tegmental dura is torn, cerebrospinal fluid otorrhea occurs if the tympanic membrane is also ruptured. If the tympanic membrane is intact, the cerebrospinal fluid will flow into the eustachian tube and cerebrospinal rhinorrhea will result.

When the fracture line crosses the epitympanum, there is usually disruption of the ossicular chain with conductive deafness. Conductive deafness also occurs following displaced fractures of the anterior external canal wall and consequent canal stenosis. When the fracture line extends into the labyrinth, a total sensorineural deafness and vestibular paralysis occur. When the fracture runs into the petrous pyramid adjacent to but not involving the labyrinth, partial sensorineural deafness or vestibular paresis often result from labyrinthine concussion. In a longitudinal fracture with extralabyrinthine extension into the petrous pyramid, mixed hearing loss can result from simultaneous ossicular disruption and labyrinthine concussion.

Facial paralysis occurs immediately or after a few hours or days following trauma.

Immediate onset of facial paralysis is the result of severe direct trauma or bisection of the nerve by the fracture. Delayed facial paralysis is due to edema or hematoma of the nerve with or without fracture of the facial canal.

Radiographic Findings

Fractures with wide separation and displacement of the fragments are easily visualized radiographically. Microfractures and fractures with minimal separation and displacement can only be recognized if the radiographic plane passes at right angles to the plane of the fracture. For this reason, the radiographic projections vary for longitudinal and transverse fractures, and multiple conventional and CT projections are needed to demonstrate the contour of a serpiginous fracture.

The radiographic evaluation of a temporal bone fracture should begin with conventional views including the Schüller, Towne-Chamberlain, and Stenvers views. When a fracture line is detected in the temporal squama on the Schüller view and extends into the pyramid, the fracture will be of the longitudinal type (Fig. 5.2). If a fracture line is seen in the occipital bone in the Towne-Chamberlain or Stenvers projection, pyramidal extension of the fracture will be of the transverse type (Fig. 5.3).

CT permits precise evaluation of the course of fractures into the middle ear and petrous bone. This technique shows displacement and disruption of the ossicular chain, the site of facial nerve lesions, and tegmental injuries. In longitudinal fractures, the most revealing projections are the axial and sagittal, since in these projections the plane of the fracture will be at

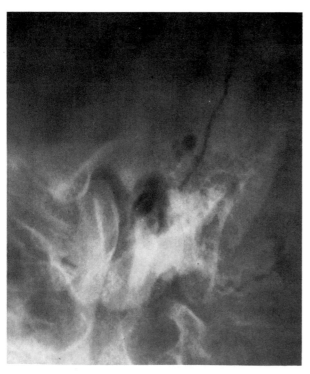

Figure 5.2 Longitudinal fracture, temporal bone, Schüller view, left. A longitudinal fracture line extends from the temporal squama, through the mastoid, into the external auditory canal.

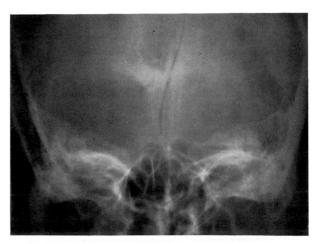

Figure 5.3 Transverse fractures, both temporal bones, Towne view. There are fractures of both petrous pyramids and a linear fracture of the occipital bone extending to the foramen magnum.

right angles to the section plane. Coronal and axial projections are required for demonstration of transverse fractures.

A fracture line may disappear at a certain level only to reappear a few mm distant. This apparent gap is not due to interruption of the fracture line, but rather to the fact that the plane of the fracture line changes course and becomes invisible in some of the sections.

CT and MR are useful in diagnosis of herniation of the brain, of the, meninges and fractures involving the tegmen. See Chapter 9, and Fig. 5.14.

Longitudinal Fractures

Longitudinal fractures of the temporal bone involve the mastoid and extend from the floor of the middle cranial fossa and tegmen downward and often forward to the posterosuperior wall of the external auditory canal (Fig. 5.4). There often is an extension of the fracture to the anterior wall of the external auditory canal and temporomandibular fossa (Fig. 5.5).

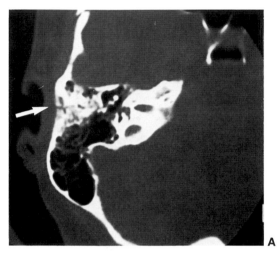
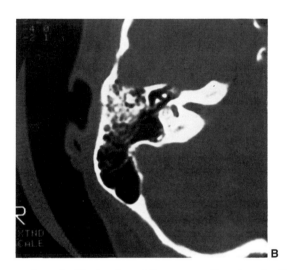

Figure 5.4 Longitudinal fracture. **A, B** axial sections, right. There is a fracture of the mastoid extending to the lateral epitym-

panic wall with clouding of the surrounding air cells. The incus is separated from the malleus head.

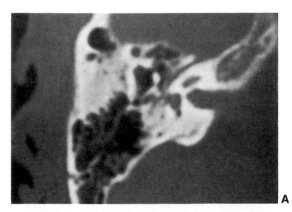
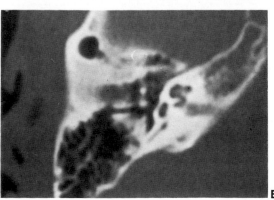

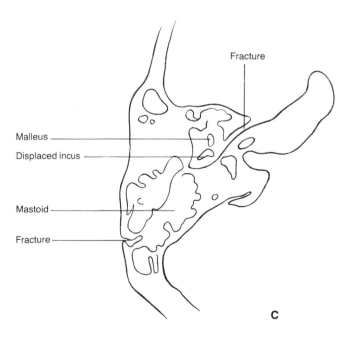

Figure 5.5 Longitudinal fracture temporal bone. **A, B** axial CT sections, right.
The longitudinal fracture reaches the posterior, superior canal wall and lateral epitympanic wall. The body of the incus is displaced and rotated posteriorly.
C Diagram of **A**.

A fracture of the posterior wall of the external auditory canal may extend medially to the facial nerve canal at or distal to the pyramidal turn of the nerve with a resultant facial paralysis.

Medial extension of a longitudinal fracture into the epitympanum results in a disruption of the ossicular chain, a tegmental fracture, and often a cerebrospinal otorrhea (Figs. 5.4, 5.5, 5.10).

We have observed luxation of the incus where the short process was propelled into the facial canal and paralyzed the facial nerve distal to the pyramidal turn.

A longitudinal fracture may extend into the petrous pyramid through the labyrinth, but more commonly anterior to the labyrinth. Anterior petrous extension occasionally causes a lesion of the facial nerve and canal at the superficial geniculate ganglion area. Our data show that in longitudinal fractures, the facial nerve is most commonly injured at the geniculate ganglion area.

Anterior extension of the longitudinal fracture may reach the carotid canal, injure the internal carotid, and lead to a post-traumatic aneurysm.

Transverse Fractures

Most transverse fractures of the temporal bone lie medial to the middle ear cavity and therefore usually involve the inner ear structures. The fracture may extend anteriorly into the floor of the middle cranial fossa and posteriorly into the occipital bone.

Most commonly, transverse fractures reach from the dome of the jugular fossa to the superior petrous ridge either medial or lateral to the arcuate eminence. Laterally placed fractures involve the promontory, the vestibule, the horizontal and posterior semicircular canals, and occasionally the tympanic segment of the facial nerve. Medially situated fractures involve the vestibule, the cochlea, the fundus of the internal auditory canal, and the crus commune (Fig. 5.3, 5.6).

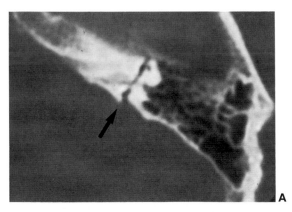

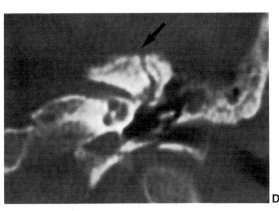

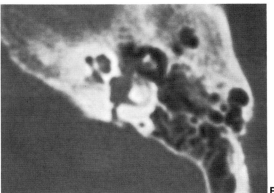

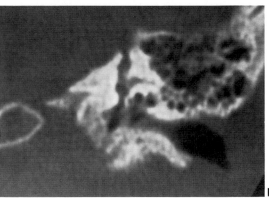

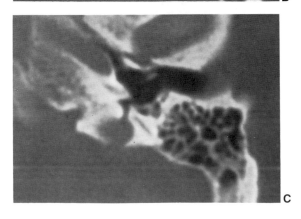

Figure 5.6 Transverse fracture, temporal bone. **A, B, C** axial, **D, E** coronal CT sections, left.
The fracture extends from the superior petrous ridge in the region of the arcuate eminence to the jugular fossa. The fracture involves three semicircular canals, and splits the vestibule, **B**. The facial canal is involved in the tympanic segment anterior to the oval window, **D**.

A more unusual type of transverse fracture occurs medial to the vestibule and bisects the internal auditory canal.

Direct Mastoid Fractures

Direct mastoid trauma produces a comminuted fracture of the mastoid cortex and trabeculae and diffuse clouding of the air cells from accompanying hemorrhage. Occasionally the fractures extend to the external canal and to the vertical segment of the facial canal and cause facial nerve paralysis (Figs. 5.7, 5.8).

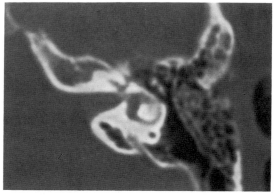

Figure 5.**7**   Direct fracture, mastoid, axial CT section, left. The mastoid cortex is fractured and depressed, the mastoid cells adjacent to the fracture are cloudy, and there is subluxation of the incudomallealar joint.

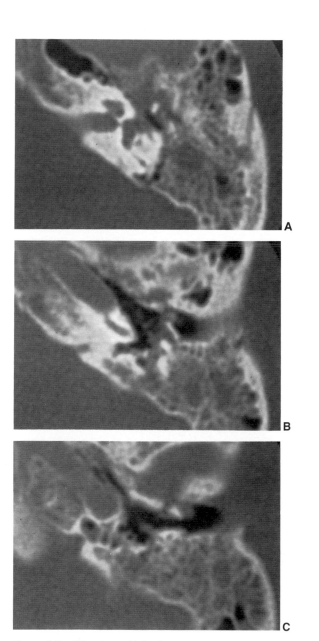

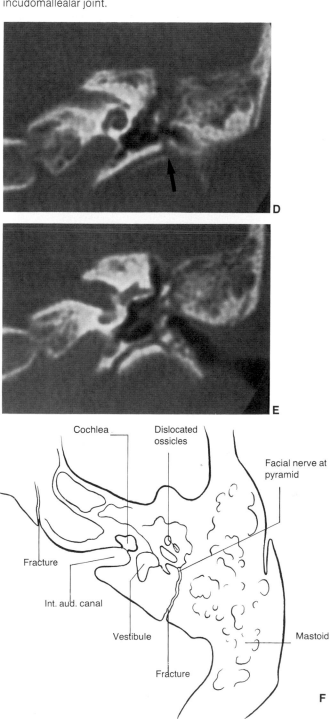

Figure 5.**8**   Direct, multiple fractures, temporal bone. **A, B, C** axial, **D, E** coronal CT sections, left.
Multiple fractures are present in the mastoid with extensive clouding of the air cells. The fractures involve the external auditory canal with depression and narrowing of the canal, **C** and **D**. The ossicular chain is disrupted, **A** and **E**. The facial canal is involved in the region of the second, pyramidal turn, **B**.
F Diagram of **A**.

Ossicular Dislocation

Following a temporal bone fracture, some patients develop a persistant conductive deafness which is usually secondary to disruption of the ossicular chain. The disruption is associated with a fracture usually of the longitudinal type. In some cases radiographic evidence of a fracture is absent, but disruption of the ossicles is evident on CT.

Ossicular disruption can also occur following direct trauma to the ear by foreign bodies perforating the tympanic membrane, from previous mastoid surgery, or by projectile missiles.

Dislocation of the malleus is rare because of the firm attachment of the malleus to the tympanic membrane and the strong anterior mallear ligament.

The incus is most commonly dislocated since its attachments to the malleus and stapes are easily torn (Figs. 5.4–10). When the incudomallear joint is disrupted, the body of the incus is usually rotated and displaced superiorly, posteriorly, and laterally. More rarely the incus body is displaced inferolaterally to

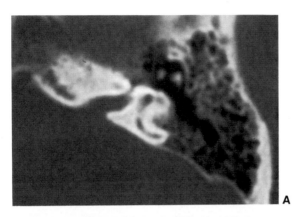

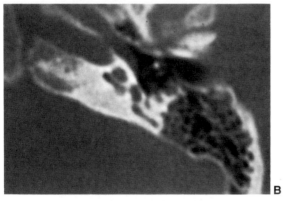

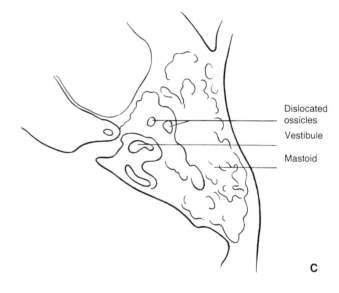

Figure 5.9   Ossicular dislocation. **A, B** axial CT sections, right. The incus body is dislocated anteriorly and laterally from the head of the malleus. The long process of the incus is rotated and separated from the stapes head.
C Diagram of **A**.

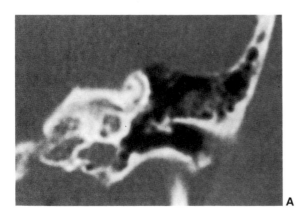

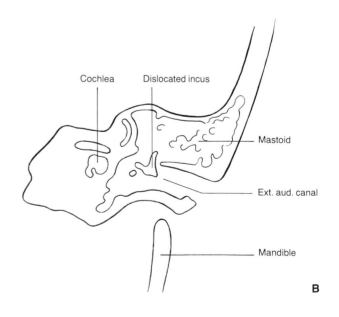

Figure 5.10   Incus dislocation, coronal CT section, right. Following a longitudinal fracture, the incus body is displaced and protrudes into the upper portion of the external auditory canal.
B Diagram of **A**.

abut against the superior portion of the tympanic membrane. Otoscopically the dislocated incus appears as a bony mass in the upper portion of the middle ear.

The most common site of ossicular chain disruption is the incudostapedial joint area. The disruption exists as a fracture of the lenticular process of the incus, a dislocation of the incudostapedial joint, or a fracture through the stapes superstructure.

Radiographic detection of disruption of the incudostapedial joint area is made by visualization of the separation of the incus long process from the stapes head and by recognition of displacement of the long process of the incus away from the stapes.

Isolated stapes footplate fractures cannot be visualized directly. In some cases of post-traumatic cerebrospinal rhinorrhea, air can be identified within the vestibular or cochlear lumens (Fig. 5.11).

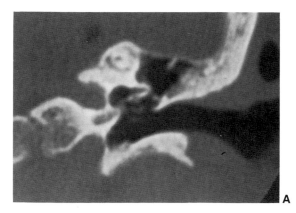

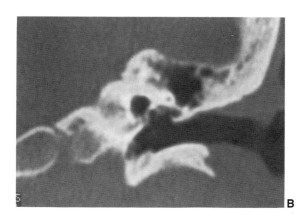

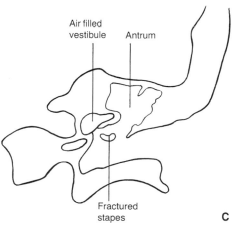

Figure 5.**11** Fracture of the stapes with pneumolabyrinth. **A, B** coronal sections, left. The stapes superstructure and footplate are fractured and air has entered the vestibule. The lumen of the vestibule is far darker than the adjacent lumen of the cochlea. **C** Diagram of **A**.

Projectile Missiles

Missiles such as bullets or metallic fragments from industrial accidents penetrate into the temporal bone and cause severe injury. The injury depends on the trajectory of the bullet and the site where the bullet fragments come to rest. Following industrial accidents, we usually find radio-opaque fragments lodged in the external auditory canal or middle ear (Fig. 5.12). Bullet wounds cause comminution of the temporal bone. There are multiple metallic bullet fragments, since bullets usually shatter on impact with the hard bone of the petrosa (Fig. 5.13).

Some bullet wounds cause mastoid and middle ear trauma with cerebrospinal fluid leaks, conductive deafness, and facial paralysis. When lesions involve the inner ear structures, there will be total sensorineural deafness and loss of vestibular function.

One serious problem with CT when large metallic fragments are present is the deterioration of the image by spark artifacts.

An MR study is contraindicated when there is the possibility of the presence of the ferromagnetic fragments within the temporal bone or brain.

Traumatic Facial Nerve Lesions

Traumatic lesions of the intratemporal portion of the facial nerve occur following head injuries of various types, especially with high speed vehicle accidents (Fig. 5.14).

A CT study should be performed in these cases to demonstrate the presence of (1) a temporal bone fracture, (2) the course of the fracture, and (3) the site of involvement of the facial canal.

This information is necessary if surgical decompression of the facial canal is planned.

The radiographic findings are variable:

1. There may be a complete disruption of the contour of a segment of the facial canal;
2. The canal may be transected by the fracture line;
3. There may be separation and depression of a fragment of the canal wall into the facial nerve;
4. The incus may be dislocated and the short process impelled into the facial canal immediately distal to the pyramidal turn.

Im some cases, the site of the involvement of the facial canal cannot be visualized by CT. However, by tracing the course of the fracture line, the site of the lesion can be determined.

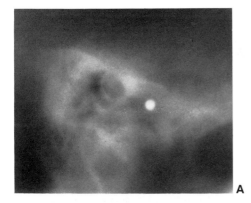

Figure 5.12 Metallic foreign body. **A** sagittal, **B** semiaxial tomogram, right.
A metallic foreign body, a large weld spark, lies in the eustachian tube portion of the middle ear.

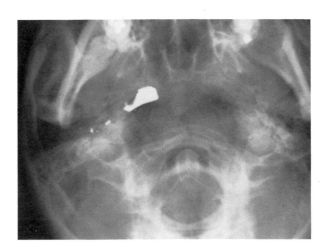

Figure 5.13 Bullet fragment, temporal bone, basal skull view, right.
The main portion of the bullet is lodged in the petrous apex. Metallic fragments outline the trajectory.

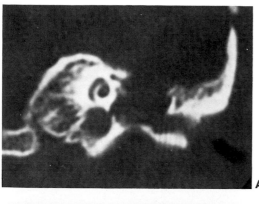

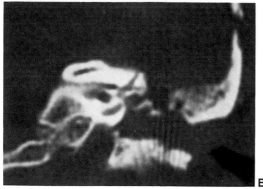

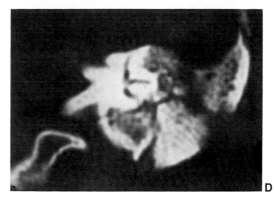

Figure 5.**14** Multiple fractures, with immediate facial paralysis and meningoencephalocele. **A, B, C, D** coronal CT sections, left. There are fractures of the temporal squama and tegmen. A large soft tissue mass with the same absorption coefficient as the brain extends into the middle ear through a large tegmental defect, **A**. In **B**, 3 mm posterior, there is a fracture with displacement of the lateral epitympanic wall. The incus is dislocated. The external canal and middle ear cavity are opacified by bleeding and edema. In **C**, 3 mm posteriorly, the fracture involves the tegmen of the antrum and crosses the posterior wall of the middle ear. In **D**, 3 mm posteriorly, the fracture transects the vertical segment of the facial nerve.

Classification of Imaging Findings

The facial nerve may be injured by transverse or longitudinal fractures. While the incidence of transverse fractures is less than that of longitudinal, more than 50% of transverse fractures have an associated lesion of the facial nerve. In these cases, the nerve involvement occurs within the internal auditory canal, labyrinthine, or tympanic segment.

Facial paralysis occurs in approximately 20% of longitudinal temporal bone fractures. About 50% of these lesions are located at or distal to the pyramidal turn, and 50% in the geniculate ganglion region.

When the geniculate ganglion area is involved, the longitudinal fracture crosses the mastoid, the external canal and attic and extends into the petrous pyramid anterior to the labyrinth. The fracture involves the facial canal in the region of the superficial and poorly protected anterior genu.

Iatrogenic Lesions

Facial nerve injury may occur following mastoid surgery. In these cases, the most common lesion occurs at the pyramidal turn. The facial canal in this area is disrupted and often there is an associated defect in the horizontal semicircular canal.

Chapter 6   Acute Otitis Media, Mastoiditis and Malignant Necrotizing External Otitis

Acute Otitis Media and Mastoiditis

Acute mastoiditis occurs as a complication or extension of an acute otitis media. Acute otitis media is an infection that begins in the upper respiratory tract and nasopharynx, ascends the eustachian tube, and affects the middle ear. Probably even in the early stages of acute otitis media, the inflammatory process extends to some degree into the epitympanum and mastoid antrum. Depending on the virulence of the infecting organism, the resistance of the host, and the type of treatment, the infection may or may not extend to involve the mastoid air cells and the air cells of the petrous pyramid.

Further progress of the infectious process, uncontrolled by proper therapy, leads to suppuration and destruction of air cell septa in the mastoid and petrous pyramid. This results in areas of coalescence and abscess formation.

Acute suppurative mastoiditis can extend beyond the borders of the temporal bone. (This was more common in the preantibiotic era than at present.) Erosion of the posterior wall of the mastoid over the sigmoid sinus results in extradural abscess formation and septic thrombosis of the sigmoid sinus. Temporal lobe and extradural abscesses may occur following erosion of the tegmen. Erosions of the cortex of the mastoid result in subperiosteal abscesses over the mastoid process and under the superior attachment of the sternocleidomastoid muscle (see Fig. 6.6). Extension of the infection from the mastoid medially into the petrous apex leads to a petrositis with serious neurological and intracranial complications.

Otoscopically, the tympanic membrane in acute otitis media is inflamed, reddened and most often bulges externally due to seropurulent fluid under increased pressure in the middle ear .(Fig. 6.1).

In some instances, antibiotic therapy will result in improvement of the otoscopic findings, while the deep mastoid infection persists and progresses to abscess formation and intracranial complications (see Fig. 6.4).

Facial paralysis may occur as a complication of acute or subacute otitis media. When paralysis occurs soon after the onset of an acute otitis media, the facial nerve paralysis is usually not due to erosion of the bony canal but to edema and inflammation of the nerve within the bony canal probably similar to Bell's palsy. Recovery of facial nerve function occurs in these cases with conservative treatment.

Facial paralysis occuring two weeks or more after the onset of a persistent acute otitis media usually indicates erosion of the bony facial canal and extension of the infection. CT is indicated, and surgery may be required in cases of this type.

Imaging Findings

The radiographic findings of acute mastoiditis depend on the stage of the inflammatory process and the extent of pneumatization of the temporal bone. Acute mastoiditis does not occur in acellular mastoids.

The earliest findings of an acute mastoiditis are a haziness of the middle ear cavity and the mastoid air cells. As the infective process worsens, diffuse clouding of the middle ear cavity and mastoid air cells occur. In the initial stage of the disease, the trabecular pattern of the mastoid air cells is intact (Fig. 6.2). However, mucosal edema and seropurulent fluid cause the trabecular pattern to be less well defined due to lack of the normal air bone interface between cells and trabeculae (Figs. 6.3, 6.4). A similar involvement usually occurs in the petrous air cells of well pneumatized petrous bones.

With progression of the disease, the trabecular pattern first becomes ill defined due to demineralization. This phase is followed by destruction of the trabeculae with formation of coalescent areas of suppuration (Fig. 6.5).

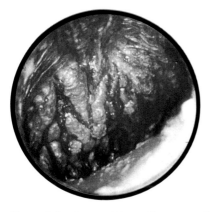

Figure 6.**1**   Acute otitis media, otoscopic findings, right. The tympanic membrane is grossly inflamed and bulges externally due to purulent discharge in the middle ear under increased pressure. The normal landmarks are missing and the superficial epithelium in the tympanic membrane is desquamating.

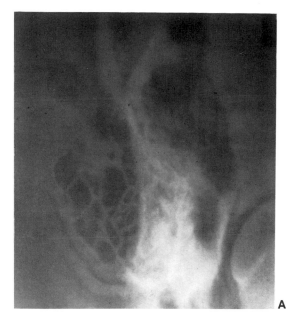
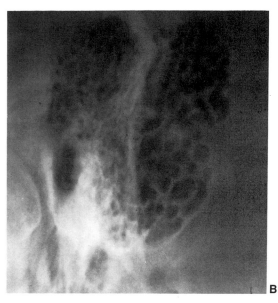

Figure 6.2 Acute mastoiditis. **A** Owen view, right ear. **B** Owen view of the opposite, normal ear. There is diffuse homogeneous clouding of the mastoid air cells with intact trabeculae, **A**. In **B,** the mastoid air cells are normal.

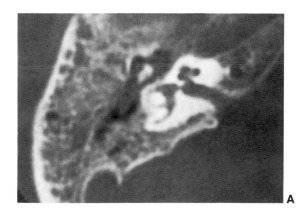
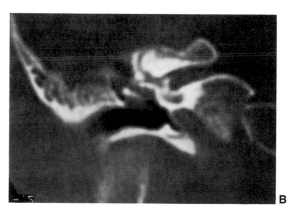

Figure 6.3 Acute mastoiditis and otitis media. **A** axial, **B** coronal CT sections, right.
There is a diffuse clouding of the well pneumatized mastoid. The trabecular pattern is intact. Fluid fills the upper portion of the middle ear, and the lateral wall of the attic and the ossicular chain are normal.

When a severe coalescent mastoiditis extends posteriorly, the sinus plate becomes poorly defined and partially eroded (Fig. 6.7). These findings indicate possible septic thrombosis of the lateral sinus, which can be demonstrated by MR. The thrombosis appears as an area of high signal intensity within the lumen of the sinus. Intracranial abscesses appear on CT as low absorption areas surrounded by an enhancing margin in the epidural, intradural, or parenchymal areas (Fig. 6.7).

Imaging Technique

Conventional x-rays, such as the Schüller, Owen, and Towne views, are usually sufficient to determine the degree of clouding of the air cells and demonstrate large areas of destruction. Axial and coronal CT sections reveal more discreet areas of mastoid or petrous coalescence and tegmental or sinus plate erosions (Figs. 6.6, 6.7). When an intracranial complication is suspected, the CT study of the brain with infusion of contrast material must be performed (Fig. 6.7). An MR study of the brain will also reveal otogenic intracranial pathology.

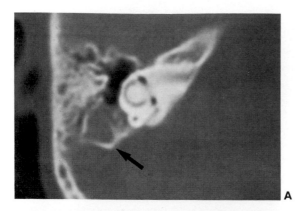

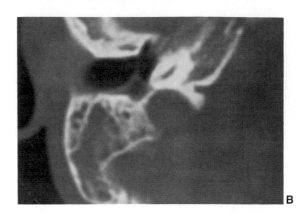

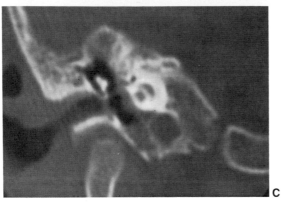

Figure 6.**4**   Acute mastoiditis with breakdown of trabeculae. **A, B** axial, **C** coronal CT sections right.

The middle ear cavity is aerated, but there is mucosal edema on the promontory. The mastoid air cells are cloudy, and the trabeculae are partially eroded with formation of a coalescent cavity extending from the antrum into the mastoid body.

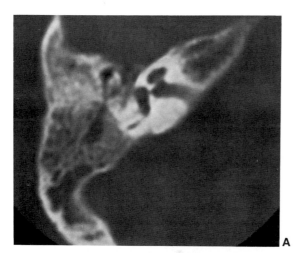

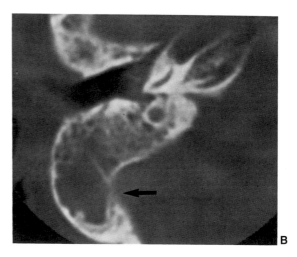

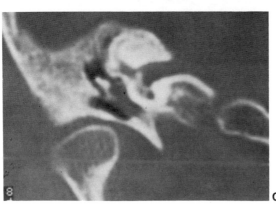

Figure 6.**5**   Acute otitis media with coalescent mastoiditis. **A, B** axial, **C** coronal CT sections, right.

The middle ear cavity is cloudy. The mastoid air cells are cloudy and the trabeculae and the mastoid process are destroyed with formation of the large abscess cavity.

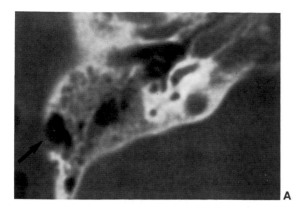

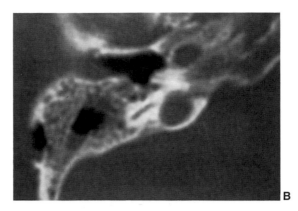

Figure 6.6 Acute mastoiditis with subperiosteal abscess. **A, B** axial CT, right.

The mastoid air cells are cloudy, and there are fluid levels within two large cells. The mastoid cortex overlying one of the large cells is eroded, forming a subperiosteal abscess.

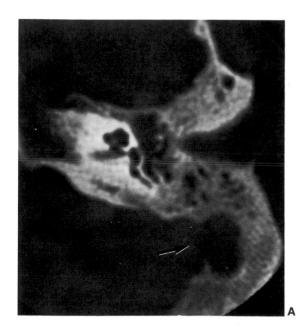

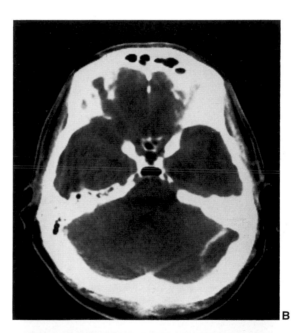

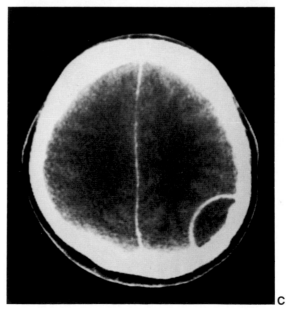

Figure 6.7 Acute mastoiditis with intracranial brain abscess. **A, B, C** axial CT, left.

In **A**, a large coalescent cavity has eroded the sinus plate and caused a septic thrombophlebitis of the lateral sinus. In **B** and **C**, a large epidural abscess extending supratentorily is visualized by contrast enhancement of the capsule.

Differential Diagnosis

On conventional radiography, the early findings of acute mastoiditis may be identical to the features of serous otitis media. In serous otitis media, sterile serous fluid fills the middle ear and at times the entire mastoid air cell system. Since the clinical features of serous otitis and acute otitis media are quite different, it is imperative that the radiologist have sufficient clinical information to avoid misdiagnosis.

Reticuloendotheliosis in the form of eosinophilic granuloma may cause a breakdown of the trabecular pattern similar to that of acute coalescent mastoiditis or petrositis. Clinical history and otoscopic findings will enable the radiologist to diagnose this lesion correctly (Pages 125, 129).

Malignant Necrotizing External Otitis

Malignant external otitis is an acute osteomyelitis of the temporal bone that occurs in older diabetic patients and is caused by the pseudomonas bacterium. The infection begins as an external otitis but spreads to involve the surrounding walls of the external canal. The process often extends into the middle ear and mastoid. The infection usually breaks through the floor of the external canal at the bony and cartilaginous junction, and spreads along the undersurface of the temporal bone to involve the facial nerve at the stylomastoid foramen. Further medial extension involves the jugular fossa and cranial nerves IX, X, XI, and XII. Anterior spread of the infection affects the temporomandibular joint.

Imaging Findings

CT is essential when studying malignant external otitis. Axial and coronal projections are indicated. The radiographic findings of malignant external otitis are similar to those of carcinoma of the external auditory canal. The bony canal appears eroded and partially destroyed, and the lumen is narrowed by soft tissue edema (Figs. 6.8, 6.9).

When facial nerve paralysis occurs, the facial canal in the early stage is normal, since the nerve is first affected at the stylomastoid foramen. CT a few days after the onset of the paralysis usually shows erosion of the contour of the stylomastoid foramen and of the adjacent mastoid segment of the facial canal. The lateral wall of the jugular fossa becomes eroded as the infection passes medially.

If the anterior wall of the external canal is destroyed and the infection involves the mandibular fossa, the mandibular condyle is displaced anteriorly. The muscles of mastication are often swollen, and the adjacent perifascial planes obliterated.

The mastoid air cells may become involved by direct posterior extension or via the middle ear (Fig. 6.8). The lateral attic wall and floor of the middle ear often are destroyed (Fig. 6.9). In severe, advanced cases the entire petrous pyramid may be involved in a severe demineralizing, osteomyelitic process which may spread to the adjacent occipital bone and cervical spine, and even to the contralateral temporal bone.

Healing Stages

If surgical and antibiotic therapy are successful in arresting the spread of and eliminating the infection, follow up CT studies show remineralization of the petrous pyramid, mastoid, occipital bone and other involved structures.

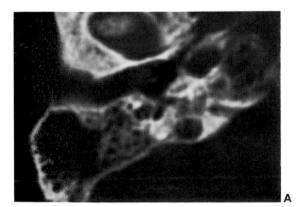

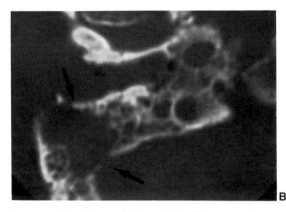

Figure 6.8 Malignant necrotizing external otitis. **A, B** axial, CT sections, right.
There is marked soft tissue swelling of the external auditory canal which obstructs the canal in this diabetic patient. The posterior bony canal wall is partially eroded adjacent to a large coalescent cavity in the mastoid. The sinus plate is thinned and partially dehiscent.

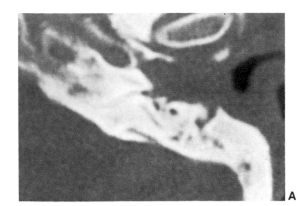

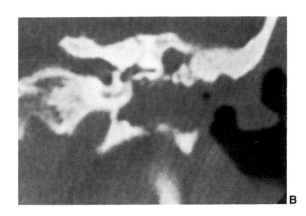

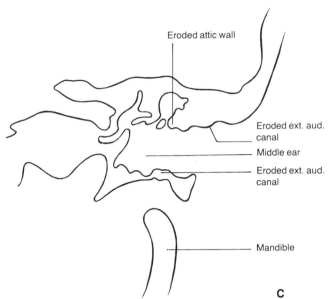

Eroded attic wall

Eroded ext. aud. canal

Middle ear

Eroded ext. aud. canal

Mandible

C

Figure 6.**9** Malignant necrotizing otitis externa. **A** axial, **B** coronal, CT sections, left.

The lumen of the external canal is obliterated by inflamed soft tissues and the bony canals walls are irregularly eroded. The erosion extends superiorly and blunts the lateral attic wall. The infection has spread to involve the middle ear and mastoid.

C Diagram of **B**.

Chapter 7 Chronic Otitis Media and Mastoiditis

Chronic otitis media and mastoiditis are the result of an infection by an organism of low virulence or of an acute infection with incomplete resolution. In the United States today due to improved general health, antibiotics and vaccines, acute otitis rarely progresses to chronic otitis media. In the preantibiotic era a single, severe infection by a virulent organism associated with decreased host resistance often resulted in severe destruction of the middle ear and scarring, which led to chronic suppuration.

Another type of chronic otitis media is the result of faulty middle ear aeration and eustachian malfunction. This is chronic adhesive otitis media and is relatively more common today in the United States.

Clinical Findings

The clinical findings in chronic otitis media and mastoiditis are perforation of the tympanic membrane, chronic suppurative discharge and poor hearing in the affected ear. The mucosa of the middle ear is involved in a chronic inflammatory process, which also affects the epitympanum, mastoid antrum, and mastoid air cells.

Chronic suppurative otitis media and mastoiditis must be differentiated from chronic adhesive otitis media in which there are varying degrees of middle ear atelectasis.

Otoscopic Findings

In the active stage of chronic otitis and mastoiditis, there is a central type of tympanic membrane perforation and a suppurative discharge from the middle ear. The tympanic membrane is thickened and reddened, and the mucosa of the middle ear is edematous and hyperemic. There is often a granulomatous polyp of varying size that arises from the margin of the tympanic membrane perforation or from the mucosa of the medial wall of the middle ear. With subsiding of active infection, a perforation will persist without discharge and the middle ear mucosal edema resolves (Fig. 7.1).

In chronic adhesive otitis media, there usually is a deep atelectatic, retracted pocket in a portion of the tympanic membrane which appears as a perforation. Careful microscopic otoscopy, however, will show that the atelectatic pocket is an area of retracted, ectatic atrophic tympanic membrane and not a perforation (see Fig. 7.4). Chronic adhesive otitis media may evolve into a cholesteatoma, another form of chronic mastoiditis which will be discussed separately in Chapter 8.

Imaging Techniques

Conventional radiography is usually sufficient to evaluate the degree of development of the mastoid, the trabecular pattern and the degree of involvement of the air cells (Figs.7.2–7.3). For more precise evaluation of the middle ear, axial and coronal CT sections are obtained. For unilateral disease, images are taken in two projections of the involved side, but only axial sections of the uninvolved side for comparison.

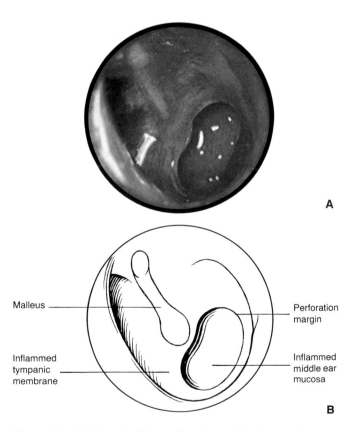

A

Malleus

Inflammed tympanic membrane

Perforation margin

Inflammed middle ear mucosa

B

Figure 7.1 **A** Chronic otitis media, otoscopic findings, left. There is a posterior perforation in this chronically inflamed tympanic membrane. The middle ear mucosa is thickened and reddened. Purulent secretion was aspirated prior to photography. **B** Diagram of **A**.

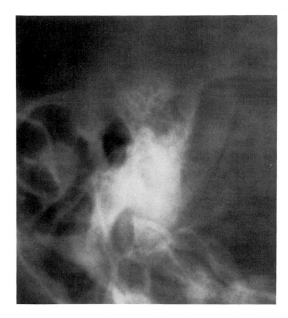

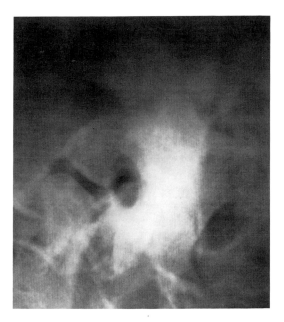

Figure 7.**2** Chronic mastoiditis, Schüller view, left. There is a non-homogeneous clouding of the mastoid air cells with thickening of the trabeculae. Some air cells appear constricted by reactive new bone formation.

Figure 7.**3** Chronic mastoiditis, acquired sclerotic type, Schüller view, left. The air cells are completely obliterated by reactive new bone formation.

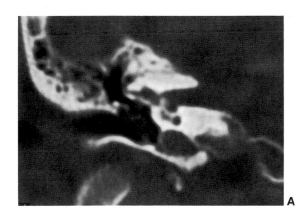

A

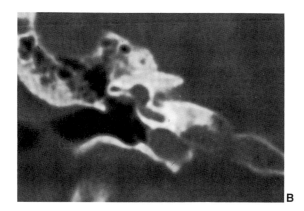

B

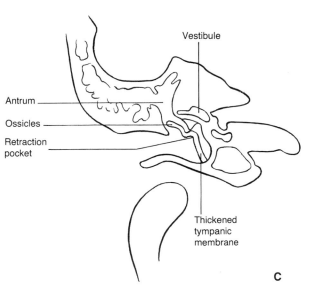

Vestibule

Antrum

Ossicles

Retraction pocket

Thickened tympanic membrane

C

Figure 7.**4** Chronic otitis media with posteriorsuperior retraction pocket, pars tensa. **A, B** coronal sections, right.

There is a deep retraction pocket of the posterosuperior quadrant of the pars tensa. The pocket extends into the oval window area and erodes the long process of the incus and stapes superstructure.

C Diagram of **A**.

Mastoid Pneumatization

The pneumatization of the mastoid and the petrous pyramid varies from person to person and to a lesser degree from side to side in the same individual.

Im some mastoids, pneumatization is limited to a single antral air cell. The small mastoid process contains either a spongy diploe far less dense than the surrounding cortex, or the entire mastoid may be as dense as cortical bone. These same features exist in the petrous pyramids of poorly pneumatized bones.

In larger mastoids, the pneumatization extends into the mastoid tip and petrous pyramid and apexes. At times the pneumatization invades the squamous portion of the temporal bone, the zygoma and the occipital bone.

In poorly pneumatized but non-infected bones, the mastoid antrum is obscured in the lateral conventional views by the overlying dense bone and appears as single smooth cavity in the Towne view. This single smooth cavity is often misdiagnosed as cholesteatoma. CT will demonstrate that the antrum is free of disease and that the middle ear and ossicular chain are normal.

Imaging Findings

Chronic Mastoiditis

Radiographic findings in chronic mastoiditis are a non-homogenous clouding of the mastoid antrum and air cells with varying degrees of change in the mastoid trabeculae. Mastoid inflammation produces thickening of some trabeculae secondary to reactive new bone formation and at the same time demineralization of other trabeculae. At this stage of the process, the air cells appear cloudy and fewer than normal, and the residual trabeculae are thickened (Fig. 7.2).

As the chronic inflammatory process continues, the air cells become constricted as reactive new bone thickens the remaining trabeculae (Fig. 7.6). In the final stage of the process, the air cells are obliterated and the mastoid appears completely sclerotic (Fig. 7.3). The lumen of the mastoid antrum and residual air cells are usually filled with granulation tissue and appear cloudy.

The Middle Ear

For proper evaluation of the middle ear in chronic otitis media, we utilize CT. The radiographic appearance of the middle ear depends on the degree of inflammatory changes in the mucosa and the aeration of the middle ear.

In chronic suppurative otitis media and mastoiditis, the residual portion of the tympanic membrane is usually thickened and visible. The middle ear is partially or completely cloudy during active suppuration. If there is no active infection the middle ear is aerated. In chronic adhesive otitis media, CT sections demonstrate thickened portions of the tympanic membrane retracted to the promontory and a contracted middle ear space (Figs. 7.4, 7.7).

Erosion of the long process of the incus commonly occurs in chronic otitis media, and the malleus handle is often foreshortened. Erosion of the malleus head and incus body in the epitympanum is rare unless cholesteatoma is present. In some ears when the long process of the incus is eroded, the tympanic membrane retracts and attaches itself to the stapes head forming a natural myringostapediopexy (Fig. 7.7).

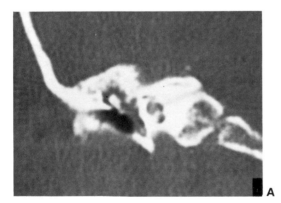
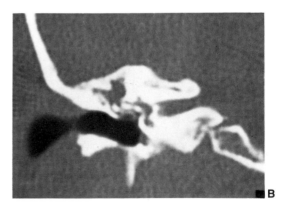

Figure 7.5 Chronic otitis media. **A, B** coronal CT sections, right.
The middle ear space is cloudy and contracted. Small tympanosclerotic deposits lie within the tympanic membrane and in the middle ear, **A**. There is marked retraction of the posterior portion of the tympanic membrane at the level of the promontory. The long process of the incus is eroded, and the mastoid antrum is cloudy, **B**.

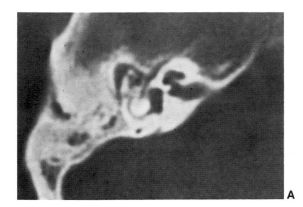

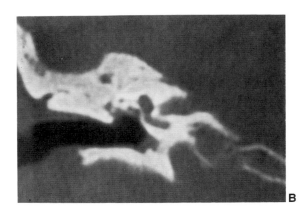

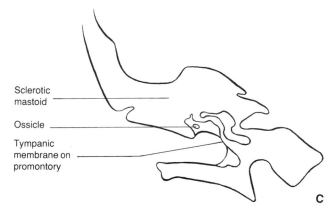

Figure 7.**6**   Chronic mastoiditis and otitis media. **A** axial, **B** coronal, CT sections, right.

The mastoid trabeculae are markedly thickened and almost completely obliterate the air cells including the antrum. The epitympanum appears constricted by reactive new bone formation. The head of the malleus and incus body are deformed and fixed. The middle ear space is absent, the tympanic membrane appears to be plastered onto the medial wall of the middle ear, and the malleus handle and long process of the incus are eroded.

C Diagram of **B**.

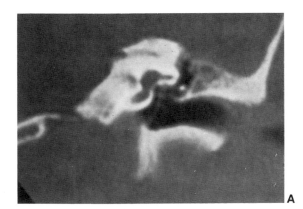

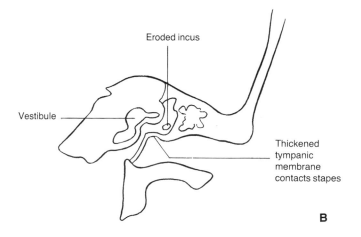

Figure 7.**7**   **A** Chronic otitis media, coronal CT section, left. The long process of the incus is eroded, and the tympanic membrane retracted to the level of the stapes head forming a myringostapediopexy.

B Diagram of **A**.

Cholesterol Granuloma

Cholesterol granuloma is a nonspecific chronic inflammation of the middle ear and mastoid. Histologically a cholesterol granuloma consists of a mass of chronic inflammatory tissue containing clefts of cholesterol crystals surrounded by giant cells.

When a cholesterol granuloma occurs in the middle ear behind an intact tympanic membrane, otoscopically it resembles a glomus tumor. In CT the granuloma appears as a well defined soft tissue mass when the middle ear is aerated. Unfortunately the middle ear mucosa is usually inflamed and the granuloma cannot be discerned. The bony contour of the middle ear is intact, but the ossicles are often eroded by the granulomatous process (Fig. 7.8).

Petrous Pyramid Cholesterol Granuloma

Cholesterol granulomas of the petrous apex occur in extensively pneumatized temporal bones as expansile lesions which thin and erode the surrounding bone. Large lesions erode the bony labyrinth. This lesion is indistinguishable on CT from a congenital cholesteatoma of the petrous apex. Both cholesteatoma and granuloma appear in preinfusion studies as low density lesions which do not enhance except for the faint ring in the capsule (Figs. 7.9–7.11).

By MR it is now possible to differentiate these two lesions. On MR the cholesterol granuloma usually appears as a bright lesion characterized by a short T1 and long T2 relaxation time. Areas of signal void in cholesterol granuloma are produced by deposition of hemosiderin. Congenital cholesteatomas appear less bright in the T1 images than cholesterol granulomas (Figs. 7.9E, F, G, 7.11).

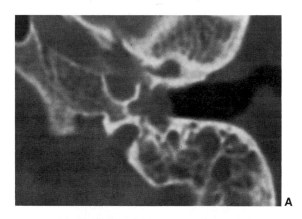

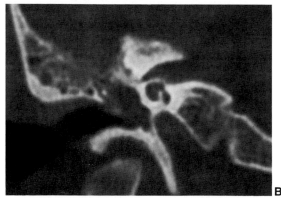

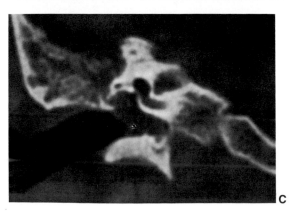

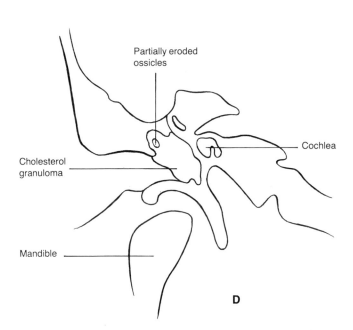

Figure 7.8   Cholesterol granuloma, middle ear and mastoid. **A** axial, **B, C** coronal CT sections, left.
A large soft tissue mass fills the mesotympanum, partially eroding the ossicles. The tympanic membrane bulges externally and the mastoid air cells and antrum are cloudy.
D Diagram of **B**.

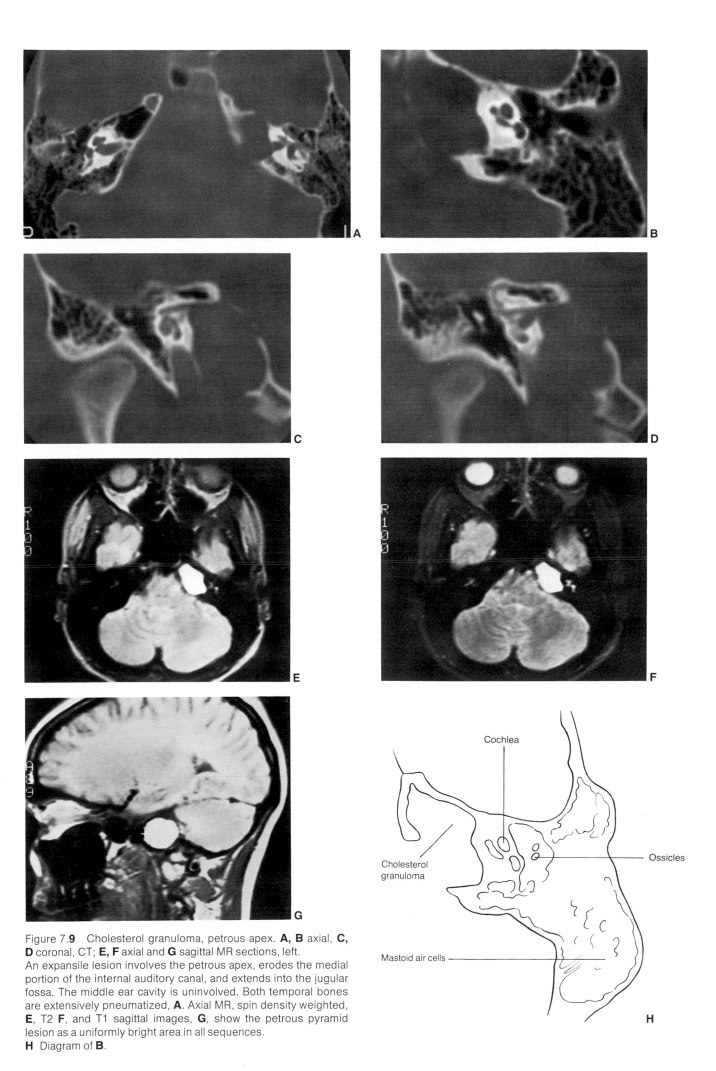

Figure 7.9   Cholesterol granuloma, petrous apex. **A, B** axial, **C, D** coronal, CT; **E, F** axial and **G** sagittal MR sections, left.
An expansile lesion involves the petrous apex, erodes the medial portion of the internal auditory canal, and extends into the jugular fossa. The middle ear cavity is uninvolved. Both temporal bones are extensively pneumatized, **A**. Axial MR, spin density weighted, **E**, T2 **F**, and T1 sagittal images, **G**, show the petrous pyramid lesion as a uniformly bright area in all sequences.
H Diagram of **B**.

Cochlea

Cholesterol granuloma

Ossicles

Mastoid air cells

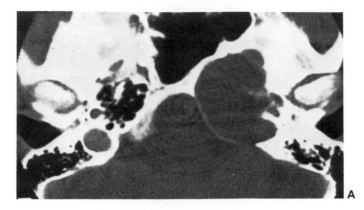
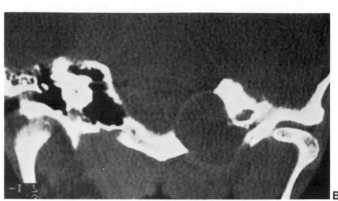

Figure 7.**10** Cholesterol granuloma, petrous pyramid. **A** axial, **B** coronal, enhanced CT sections, left.
A large expansile lesion involves the left petrous apex and the adjacent aspect of the occipital bone. The mass has a low density and does not enhance except for its capsule.

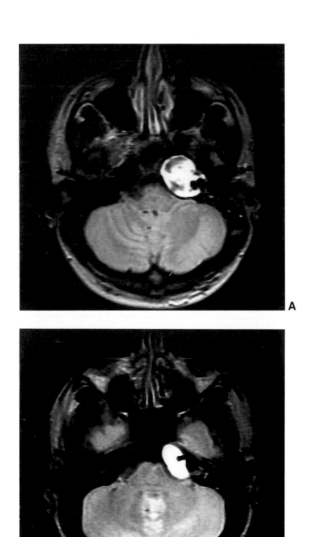

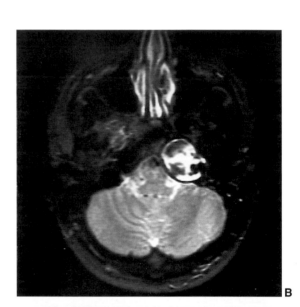

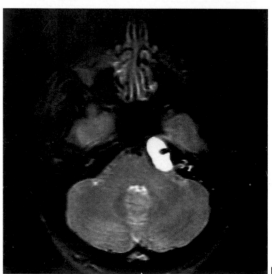

Figure 7.**11** Cholesterol granuloma. **A, C** spin density weighted, **B, D** T2, axial MR sections, same ear as Fig. 7.**10**. A large lesion is demonstrated in the region of the left petrous apex. The mass has a high signal intensity in both sequences, except for several areas of void in its inferior portion, presumably due to deposits of hemosiderin.

Tympanosclerosis

Tympanosclerosis consists of deposits of hyalinized and often calcified fibrotic granulation tissue in the middle ear, epitympanum, and tympanic membrane (Fig. 7.12). Tympanosclerosis occurs most commonly as deposits of thickened hyalinized tissue within the layers of the tympanic membrane, on the promontory, and in the epitympanum surrounding and fixing the ossicles.

Tympanosclerotic deposits, if large enough and calcified, are recognizable by CT. The deposits appear as punctate or linear densities within the tympanic membrane or applied to the contour of the promontory (Fig. 7.13).

Large deposits of tympanosclerosis in the epitympanum appear as ill defined calcified masses that surround the ossicles. The normal ossicular contour is lost (Fig. 7.14).

An isolated plaque of tympanosclerosis in the anterior or superior epitympanum may ankylose the malleus head to the tegmen (Fig. 7.15).

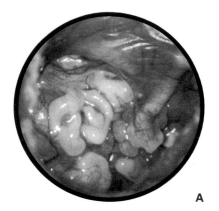
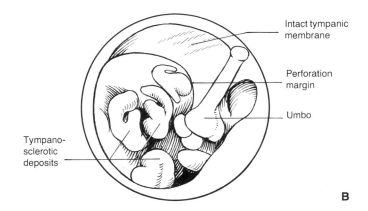

Figure 7.**12**   **A** Tympanosclerosis of the middle ear, otoscopic findings, right.
There is a large tympanic membrane perforation, and white globular deposits of tympanosclerosis line the exposed medial wall of the middle ear.
B Diagram of **A**.

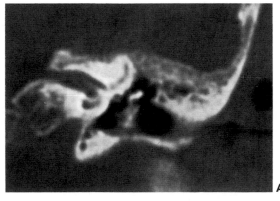
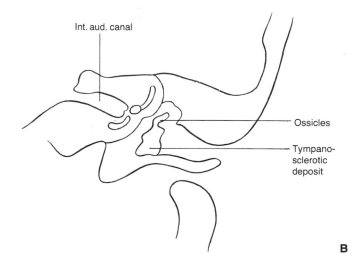

Figure 7.**13**   **A** Chronic otitis media, coronal CT section, left.
The tympanic membrane is thickened by a large tympanosclerotic focus. The middle ear is aerated but the mastoid air cells are cloudy.
B Diagram of **A**.

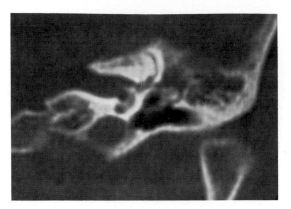

Figure 7.**14**   Chronic otitis media, coronal CT section, left. Large tympanosclerotic deposits surround and fix the ossicles in the epitympanum. The epitympanum and mastoid air cells are cloudy and the tympanic membrane is thickened and retracted.

Chronic Granulomatous Disorders

Tuberculosis

Tuberculosis of the ear is rarely seen in the United States today. In the few cases we have studied radiographically, the findings were similar to chronic otitis media and mastoiditis. The diagnosis of tuberculosis is made by acid fast smear, biopsy, and bacteriologic studies (Fig. 7.**16**).

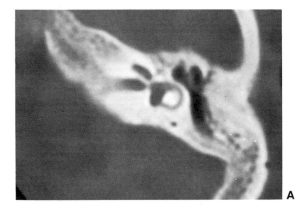

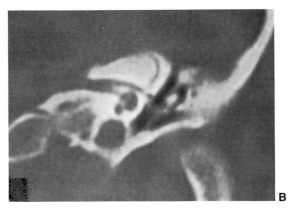

Figure 7.**15**   Chronic otitis media. **A** axial, **B** coronal CT sections, left.
Tympanosclerotic deposits fix the malleus head to the anterior wall and tegmen of the epitympanum. The middle ear cavity is partially cloudy and the tympanic membrane thickened.
C Diagram of **B**.

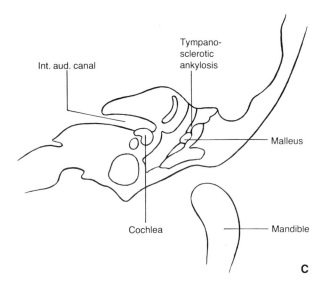

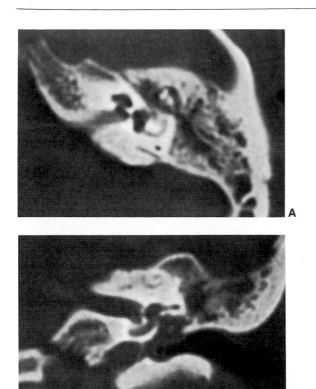

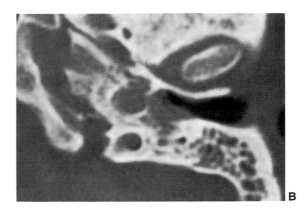

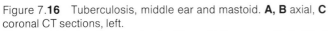

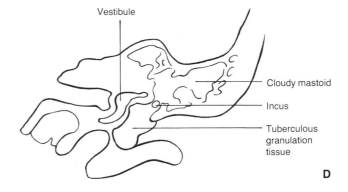

Figure 7.**16**   Tuberculosis, middle ear and mastoid. **A, B** axial, **C** coronal CT sections, left.
The mastoid air cells are cloudy. The middle ear cavity is filled with a soft tissue mass surrounding, but not eroding, the ossicles. The tympanic membrane bulges externally.
D Diagram of **C**.

Chapter 8 Cholesteatoma of the Middle Ear and Mastoid

A cholesteatoma is an epidermoid cyst which histologically consists of an inner layer of desquamating stratified squamous epithelium apposed on an outer layer of subepithelial connective tissue. The lumen of the cyst is filled with desquamated epithelial debris. The subepithelial connective tissue layer is usually involved by a chronic inflammatory process characterized by deposition of cholesterol crystals, and infiltration of giant cell and round cells.

The epithelial cyst enlarges progressively because of accumulation of epithelial debris within its lumen. As the cyst enlarges and comes in contact with contiguous bony structures of the middle ear, mastoid and petrous pyramid, erosion of these structures occurs due to pressure necrosis and enzymatic lysis of bone.

Cholesteatomas may be congenital or acquired. Congenital cholesteatomas originate from epithelial rests within or adjacent to the temporal bone. Acquired cholesteatomas arise in the middle ear and extend into the mastoid and occasionally into the petrous pyramid. There is another distinct form of cholesteatoma which arises in the external auditory canal and often follows previous irradiation of the head.

Acquired Cholesteatoma of the Middle Ear and Mastoid

The etiology of acquired cholesteatoma is not known, and there are four main theories that attempt to explain the pathogenesis. Regardless of their etiology, acquired cholesteatomas slowly expand to erode middle ear and mastoid structures.

The pathogenesis of acquired cholesteatoma may occur in one of the four following manners:

1. **Negative pressure theory.** Poor aeration of the middle ear, probably related to malfunction of the eustachian tube, results in a relative negative pressure in the middle ear. This negative pressure causes medialward retraction of the pars flaccida or of atrophic areas of the pars tensa of the tympanic membrane. The retracted areas deepen to form pits, and epithelial debris collects within the lumen of the retracted pockets. When egress of the debris is impaired, encystment and cholesteatoma formation ensues. Many authors call this type of lesion occuring in the pars flaccida a primary acquired cholesteatoma.

2. **Migration theory.** This theory postulates that a previous necrotic otitis media destroys the marginal portion of the pars tensa of the tympanic membrane.

Epithelium from the external auditory canal grows into the middle ear at the margin of the perforation, encysts and forms a cholesteatoma. Most authors refer to this type of cholesteatoma as a secondary acquired cholesteatoma.

Epithelium from the surface of the tympanic membrane may also migrate into the middle ear from the rim of a central perforation of the pars tensa to form a cholesteatoma.

3. **Metaplasia theory.** Following middle ear infection, the middle ear mucosa undergoes a metaplasia to desquamating stratified squamous epithelium. Encystment follows, and a cholesteatoma is formed.

4. **Papillary ingrowth theory.** This theory has been advanced by Rüedi. An inflammatory stimulus causes invasive hyperplasia of the basal layer of the stratified squamous epithelium of the tympanic membrane. The hyperplastic basal cells infiltrate into the subepithelial connective tissues, extend into the middle ear, desquamate, encyst, and form a cholesteatoma.

Clinical and Otoscopic Findings

Most cholesteatomas originate from the stratified squamous epithelium of the tympanic membrane or external auditory canal and develop in the middle ear or epitympanum. As they enlarge, they destroy the ossicles and adjacent bony structures and extend into the mastoid.

Acquired cholesteatomas are characterized by a tympanic membrane perforation of the pars flaccida, the pars tensa or combined perforation of both pars flaccida and pars tensa. There is usually an associated chronic infection, a history of chronic aural discharge, and a conductive or mixed deafness (Figs. 8.1, 8.7).

Most perforations are of the marginal type since part of their circumference lies in contact with the bony margin of the tympanic sulcus or notch of Rivinus. Some cholesteatomas occur with central perforations of the pars tensa.

The characteristic of cholesteatoma is that the lumen of the tympanic membrane perforation contains varying amounts of epithelial debris. In chronically infected cholesteatomas, granulomatous tissue and polyps accompany the epithelial debris.

Otoscopically, the otologist can diagnose most cholesteatomas but cannot determine the size and extent of the lesion in the epitympanum and mastoid.

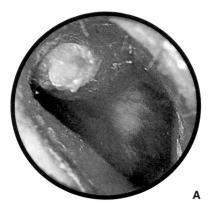

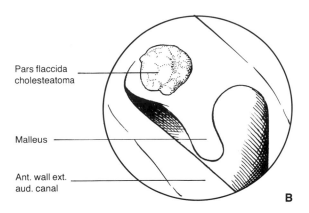

Pars flaccida
cholesteatoma

Malleus

Ant. wall ext.
aud. canal

Figure 8.**1**   **A** Cholesteatoma, pars flaccida, otoscopic findings, left.
There is a perforation of the pars flaccida filled with necrotic epithelial debris. The notch of Rivinus is slightly enlarged.
B Diagram of **A**.

A small epitympanic perforation filled with epithelial debris may be the only otoscopic evidence of a large cholesteatoma (Fig. 8.**1**). On the other hand a large tympanic membrane perforation filled with debris may be found to be associated with a relatively small lesion. Without a proper CT evaluation, the otologist has no insight into the size of the lesion, or the status of the ossicles, the labyrinth, the tegmen or the facial nerve.

Imaging Techniques

Radiographic evaluation of the middle ear and mastoid for cholesteatoma is done by tomographic techniques. CT is the method of choice, since it reveals the presence of soft tissue masses and erosion of the bony structures such as ossicles and labyrinth far better than conventional tomography. In addition CT demonstrates extension of cholesteatoma into the petrous apex and erosion of the tegmen and sinus plates. In cases of acute exacerbation with intracranial complications, CT with infusion or MRI will demonstrate intracranial pathology such as extradural, cerebral, and cerebellar abscesses.

Conventional Radiography

The study of cholesteatoma with conventional radiographs is limited due to the superimposition of many complex and minute structures on a single plane. Conventional radiography should only be used when tomography is not available, since this technique will only delineate large, extensive lesions. The most useful projections for the study of cholesteatoma are the Schüller, Owen and Chausse III. Large cholesteatomas cause smooth walled cavities in the mastoid, often eroding the posterosuperior wall of the bony external auditory canal.

CT

Coronal and axial projections are required for a CT study of cholesteatoma.
For the study of the tympanic segment of the facial nerve, oval window niche and horizontal semicircular canal erosion, 20° coronal oblique sections are occasionally added.
When sagittal sections are required for the study of the mastoid segment of the facial canal, we use either reconstructed sagittal images or multidirectional tomographs.

Magnetic Resonance Imaging

MR images obtained with surface coils demonstrate the presence of cholesteatoma, which appears as a mass of medium signal intensity in T1 and high intensity in T2 images (see Figs. 8.**25**, 8.**27**). However, it is difficult to differentiate the actual cholesteatoma mass from the surrounding fluid or imflammatory tissues. The most important limitations are that MR images have no bony landmarks and do not allow localization of the process, and give no information concerning the status of the ossicles or other bony structures.

Diagnosis of Cholesteatoma

The diagnosis of acquired cholesteatoma is based on the detection of a soft tissue mass and erosion of the lateral epitympanic wall, posterosuperior canal wall, and ossicles. Erosions of one or more of these structures is found in a great majority of cholesteatomas. Erosion of the long process of the incus occurs commonly in chronic otitis media as well as cholesteatoma, and is not a specific finding for cholesteatoma. The superstructure of the stapes may be eroded in cholesteatomas. The detection of stapes erosion is difficult because of the small size of the structure and because cholesteatoma and inflammatory tissue in the middle ear obscure the stapes.

The evaluation of the extent of the lesion depends on the recognition of changes in the aditus, antrum, mastoid, and petrous pyramid. With cholesteatomas, there is a soft tissue mass in the meso- or epitympanum. If the middle ear cavity is aerated, the soft tissue mass is well outlined. When fluid or inflammatory tissue in the middle ear cavity surround the cholesteatoma, the mass is obscured, since the radiographic densities of the cholesteatoma and inflammatory tissue and fluid are very similar.

Use of the cursor to measure absorption coefficients and to differentiate cholesteatoma from surrounding fluid and granulation tissue is unsatisfactory because of partial volume averaging and limited differential absorption between these tissues.

Patterns of Imaging Findings

Different patterns of radiographic findings can be observed in the study of cholesteatomas. When we analysed these patterns, a correlation was found between the site of the tympanic membrane perforation and the radiographic findings. Cholesteatomas of the pars flaccida, known as primary acquired cholesteatomas, have a characteristic radiographic pattern (Figs. 8.1–8.5).

Cholesteatomas arising from the pars tensa, usually the posterosuperior portion, known as secondary acquired cholesteatomas, have a radiographic pattern distinct from pars flaccida lesions (Figs. 8.8–8.14).

At times, a cholesteatoma may involve both the pars flaccida and pars tensa. These lesions produce a radiographic pattern that is a combination of the two types (Fig. 8.15). In extensive, far advanced choles-

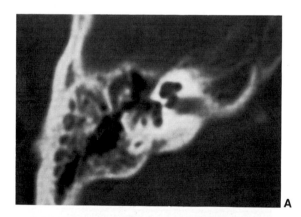

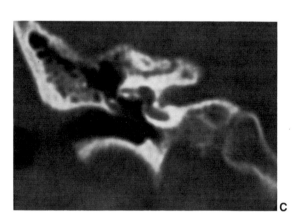

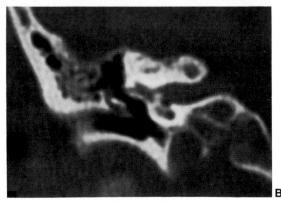

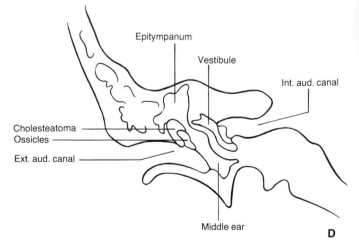

Figure 8.2   Cholesteatoma, pars flaccida. **A** axial, **B, C** coronal, CT sections, right.
The inferior margin of the anterior lateral attic wall is eroded by a soft tissue mass which lies lateral to the ossicles. The ossicular chain is intact.
D Diagram of **B**.

teatomas of either the pars flaccida or pars tensa, there is destruction of most of the structures in the meso- and epitympanum and no distinct pattern remains (Fig. 8.17–8.19).

Pars Flaccida Cholesteatomas

Cholesteatomas arising from the pars flaccida are the easiest lesions to diagnose radiographically, because the lateral epitympanic wall is eroded (Figs. 8.2–8.5). In pars flaccida cholesteatomas, the tympanic cavity is usually contracted and narrowed by retraction of the pars tensa of the tympanic membrane, since the pars tensa is usually thickened and the retracted membrane becomes visible.

The typical CT pattern of a pars flaccida choles-teatoma consists of one or more of the following findings:

1. There is erosion of the anterior portion of the lateral epitympanic wall.
2. There is erosion of the anterior tympanic spine.
3. A soft tissue mass lies in the epitympanum lateral to the ossicles.
4. There is an increased distance between the lateral epitympanic wall and the ossicles. This increase is due to medial displacement of the ossicles and to erosion of the lateral epitympanic wall.
5. When cholesteatoma fills the epitympanum and extends to the tegmen, the epitympanum acquires a smooth shell-like outline.

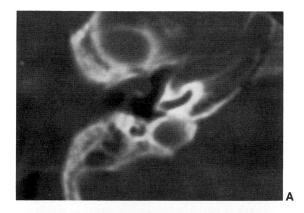

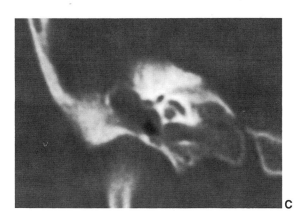

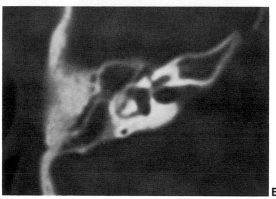

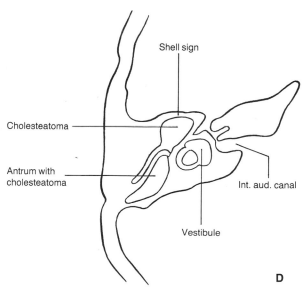

Figure 8.3 Cholesteatoma, pars flaccida. **A, B** axial, **C** coronal CT sections, right.

A soft tissue mass fills the epitympanum and erodes the anterior portion of the lateral epitympanic wall. The ossicles are eroded and the contour of the epitympanum appears to have a smooth shell-like contour. The lesion extends inferiorly to the level of the umbo, leaving the inferior middle ear free of cholesteatoma.
D Diagram of **B**.

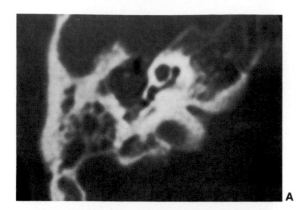

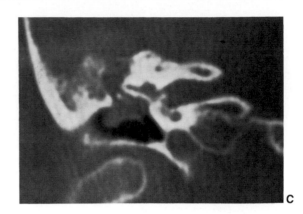

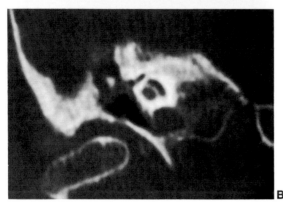

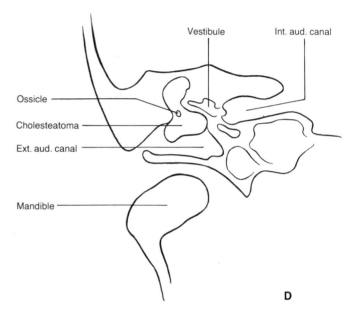

Figure 8.**4**   Cholesteatoma, pars flaccida, **A** axial, **B, C** coronal CT sections, right.
The cholesteatoma fills the epitympanum and erodes the lateral attic wall. The mass extends inferiorly into the posterosuperior portion of the mesotympanum and bulges laterally into the external auditory canal, **C**.
D Diagram of **C**.

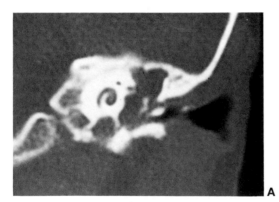

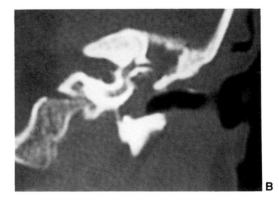

Figure 8.**5**   Cholesteatoma, pars flaccida, **A, B** coronal, CT sections, left.
The bony lateral epitympanic wall is eroded and a large cholesteatoma fills the entire middle ear cavity. The aditus is enlarged, and the bony capsule of the horizontal canal is eroded, resulting in a fistula of the semicircular canal.

Ossicles

When the cholesteatoma is limited to the anterior portion of the epitympanum, the adjacent aspect of the malleus head is eroded and has a concave, rather than a convex, outline. If the cholesteatoma extends into the posterior epitympanum, the body of the incus will be eroded. The long process of the incus is usually spared in pars flaccida cholesteatomas, unless the cholesteatoma sac is large and extends into the posterior middle ear. In more advanced lesions, both the malleus head and incus body are eroded (Fig. 8.3).

Epitympanic Retraction Pockets

An epitympanic retraction pocket is an invagination of the pars flaccida of the tympanic membrane without accumulation of epithelial debris. Since these lesions can be a precursor of a cholesteatoma, they must be followed carefully by the otologist.

Blunting of the lateral epitympanic wall is observed in simple retraction pockets of the pars flaccida. If the pars flaccida is thickened, the membrane is clearly visible. There is no soft tissue mass, since there is no encystment of accumulated debris within the lumen of the pocket (Fig. 8.6).

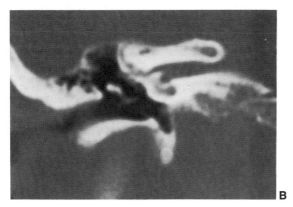

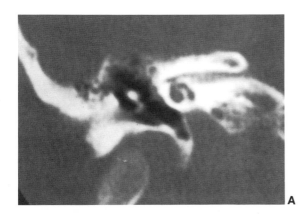

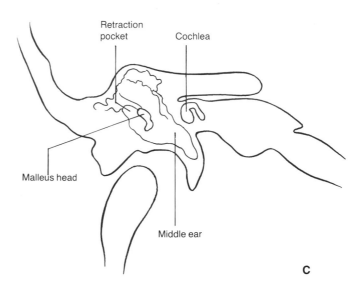

Figure 8.**6**   Epitympanic retraction pocket, **A, B** coronal CT sections, right.
The inferior margin of the lateral epitympanic wall is eroded, but there is no soft tissue mass in the epitympanum lateral to the malleus head. In **A**, the retracted tympanic membrane stretches from the superior aspect of the malleus head to the lateral epitympanic wall.
C Diagram of **A**.

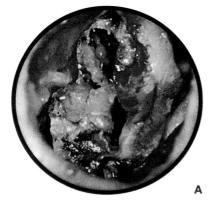

Figure 8.**7**   **A** Cholesteatoma, pars tensa, otoscopic findings, right.

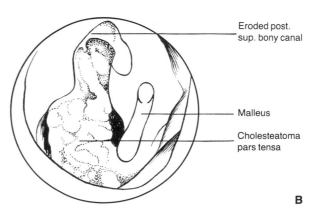

There is a posterosuperior perforation filled with epithelial debris and granulation tissue. The cholesteatoma has partially eroded the posterosuperior bony external canal.
B Diagram of **A**.

Pars Tensa Cholesteatomas

Cholesteatomas of the pars tensa are more difficult to diagnose than pars flaccida lesions because the lateral epitympanic wall may be intact. In early cases, bony erosion is limited to the long process of the incus and this is not a specific finding for cholesteatomas.

The radiographic pattern for cholesteatoma of the pars tensa consists in findings common to all pars tensa cholesteatomas and of findings that depend on the site of origin of the lesion in the pars tensa.

The findings common to all pars tensa cholesteatomas are one or more of the following: (Figs. 8.8–8.16)

1. There is a soft tissue mass in the middle ear.
2. The long process of the incus is eroded.
3. The soft tissue mass of the middle ear extends into the epitympanum medial to the ossicles.
4. The malleus head and incus body are displaced laterally by the soft tissue mass of the cholesteatoma sac. The malleus head is usually displaced but intact while the displaced incus body is often eroded.

The most frequently occuring type of pars tensa cholesteatoma arises from the posterosuperior margin of the membrane. In these cases there is often blunting of the posterior portion of the lateral epitympanic wall and erosion of the posterosuperior bony canal wall.

Cholesteatomas may arise from central or anterosuperior perforations of the pars tensa. In these cases, the posterosuperior bony wall of the external auditory canal is intact, but the other findings of pars tensa cholesteatoma are present in large lesions. Early lesions may be confined to the medial surface of the tympanic membrane (Fig. 8.12). Cholesteatomas of the posterior pars tensa can extend into the sinus tympani (Figs. 8.10, 8.13). When they do, they are best visualized in axial sections. Occasionally projections of the cholesteatoma extend into the eustachian tube (Fig. 8.14).

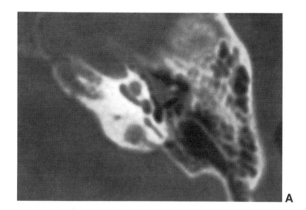

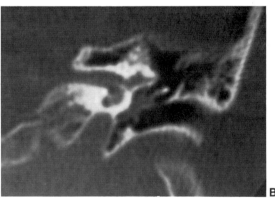

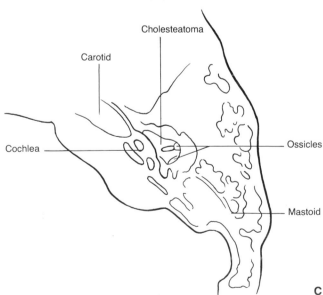

Figure 8.8   Cholesteatoma, pars tensa. **A** axial, **B** coronal, CT sections, left.
A small soft tissue mass lies in the mesotympanum. The long process of the incus is intact and uninvolved.
C Diagram of **A**.

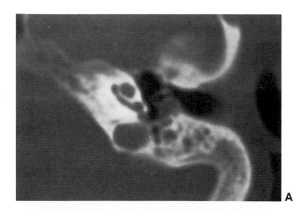

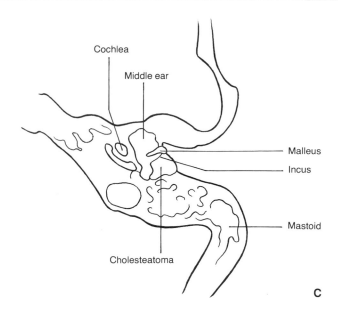

Figure 8.**9**   Cholesteatoma, pars tensa. **A** axial, **B** coronal, CT sections, left.
A soft tissue mass occupies the posterosuperior portion of the middle ear. The mass abuts and partially erodes the long process of the incus.
C Diagram of **A**.

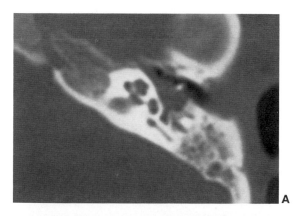

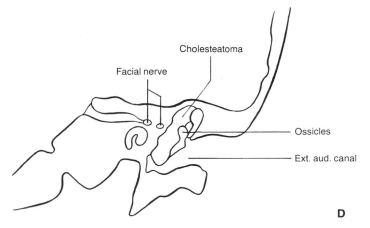

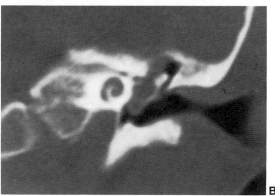

Figure 8.**10**   Cholesteatoma, pars tensa. **A** axial, **B, C** coronal, CT sections, left.
A soft tissue mass fills the posterior portion of the middle ear and extends into the attic medial to the ossicles. The posterosuperior

bony canal wall anulus is blunted and the long process of the incus eroded. The lesion extends into the sinus tympani, **A**.
D Diagram of **B**.

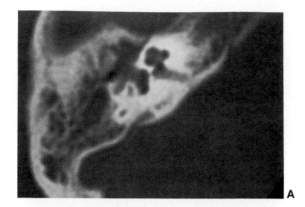

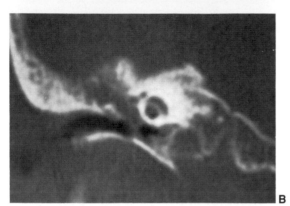

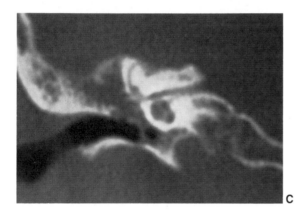

Figure 8.11   Cholesteatoma, pars tensa. **A** axial, **B, C** coronal, CT sections, right.

The cholesteatoma fills the posterosuperior quadrant of the mesotympanum, extends into the attic medial to the ossicles, and displaces the ossicles laterally. The long process of the incus is eroded as is the Koerner's septum.

D Diagram of **B**.
E Diagram of **C**.

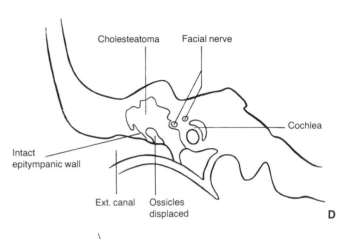

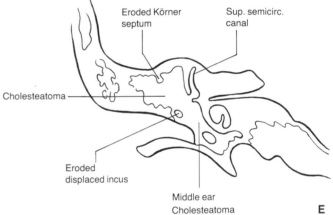

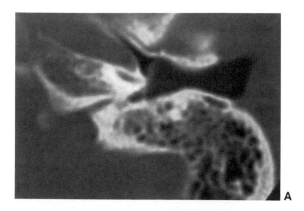

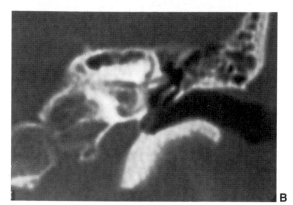

Figure 8.**12** Cholesteatoma, pars tensa. **A** axial, **B** coronal CT section, left.
A small soft tissue mass in the lower mesotympanum lies on the medial surface of the tympanic membrane, which appears thickened. The middle ear is aerated, and the ossicles are intact.
C Diagram of **B**.

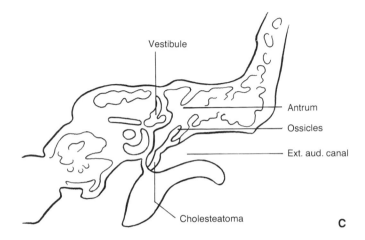

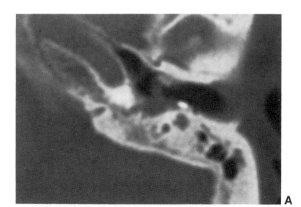

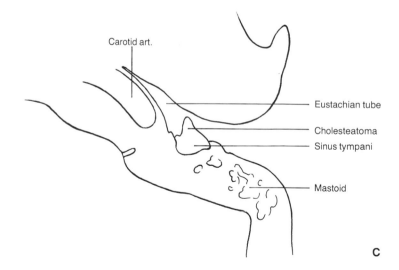

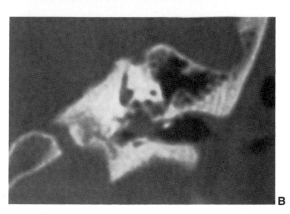

Figure 8.**13** Cholesteatoma, pars tensa, involving the sinus tympani. **A** axial, **B** coronal CT sections, left.
A soft tissue mass fills the posterior portion of the mesotympanum and sinus tympani.
C Diagram of **A**.

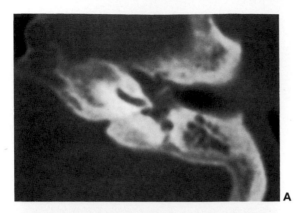

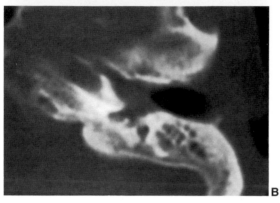

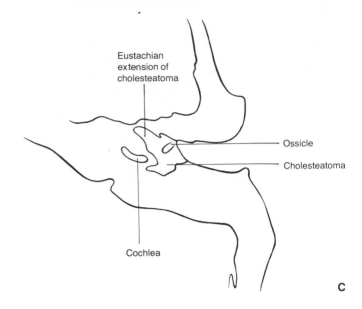

Figure 8.**14**   Cholesteatoma, pars tensa, with eustachian tube extension. **A, B** axial, CT sections, left.
A cholesteatoma fills the middle ear. A lobulated projection of the cholesteatoma extends deeply into the eustachian tube lumen.
C Diagram of **A**.

Combined Pars Flaccida and Pars Tensa Cholesteatomas

In cholesteatomas that arise from combined perforations of the pars tensa and pars flaccida, the radiographic findings are a combination of the two patterns (Fig. 8.**15**).

At times, the entire pars flaccida and pars tensa are absent. The predominance of the findings depends on which portion of the tympanic membrane is more extensively involved. In lesions with total absence of the tympanic membrane, the mesotympanum appears aerated and matrix lines the middle ear.

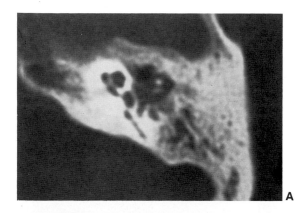

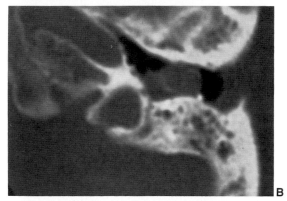

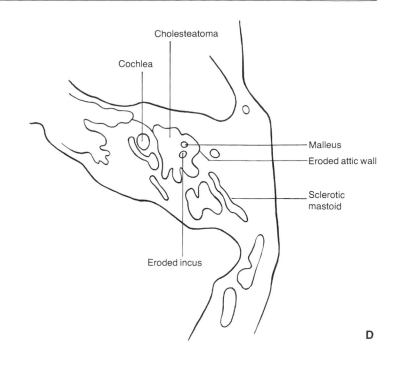

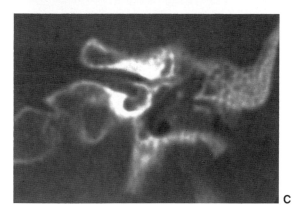

Figure 8.**15** Cholesteatoma, pars flaccida, and pars tensa, combined. **A, B** axial, **C** coronal, CT sections, left.

The cholesteatoma extends into the mesotympanum medial to the ossicles and erodes the long process of the incus, **A**. A large polyp completely obstructs the lumen of the external auditory canal, **B**. The inferior margin of the lateral epitympanic wall is eroded, as is the lateral surface of the malleus head by cholesteatoma, **C**. The mastoid is sclerotic.

D Diagram of **A**.

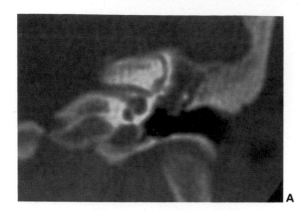

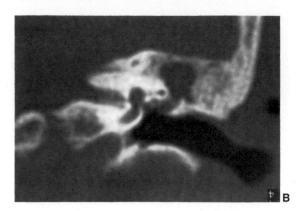

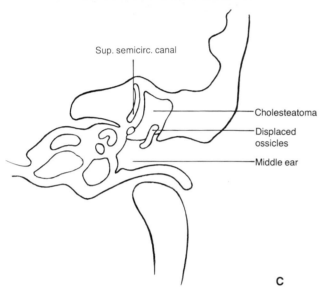

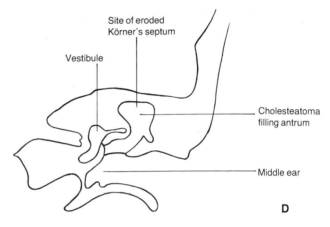

Figure 8.**16**   Cholesteatoma, pars tensa. **A, B** coronal, CT sections, left.

A soft tissue mass extends from the posterosuperior quadrant into the epitympanum medial to the ossicles, which are displaced laterally. The lesion fills the mastoid antrum, which is enlarged and has a smooth outline. The Koerner's septum is eroded completely.

C Diagram of **A**.
D Diagram of **B**.

Evaluation of the Extent of Cholesteatoma

The radiographic detection of the extent of a cholesteatoma beyond the limits of the meso- and epitympanum depends on the recognition of soft tissue and
bony changes in the aditus, the antrum, the mastoid,
and the petrous pyramid.

Aditus

Enlargement of the aditus is best seen in axial CT, and
indicates extension of the cholesteatoma posterosuperiorly. The short process of the incus which
lies in the adjacent fossa incudis is usually eroded
(Fig. 8.**17**).

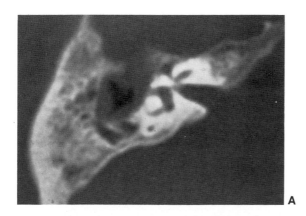

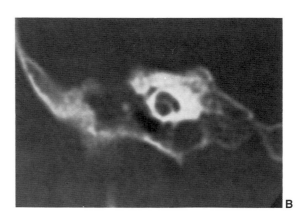

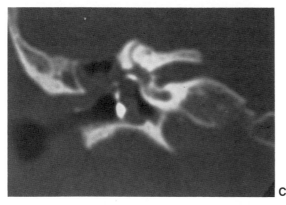

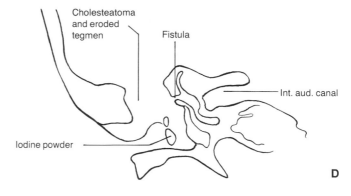

Figure 8.**17** Cholesteatoma, **A** axial, **B**, **C** coronal, CT sections, right.
A large cholesteatoma fills the epitympanum and erodes the
lateral epitympanic wall. The mass extends into the mastoid
antrum, enlarges the aditus and erodes and fistulizes the capsule
of the horizontal semicircular canals. The tegmen of the mastoid
is eroded. The outer surface of the thickened tympanic membrane is coated by an iodine containing theraputic powder.
D Diagram of **C**.

Antrum

When the cholesteatoma extends into the mastoid antrum, a mass is visible which partially or completely fills the lumen. As the cholesteatoma erodes the air cells that line the walls of the antrum, the contour becomes smooth. Further extension of the cholesteatoma results in enlargement of the antral cavity (Fig. 8.16–8.18). Superior extension of the cholesteatoma causes progressive erosion of the Koerner's septum (Figs. 8.11, 8.16). The Koerner's septum is a rather constant landmark in pneumatized mastoids and appears as a thick bony septum extending from the tegmen medially and inferiorly into the antrum and aditus (Fig. 8.22). Complete amputation of the septum indicates extension of the cholesteatoma to the tegmen of the antrum (Fig. 8.16).

Mastoid

Further extension of the cholesteatoma into the mastoid causes progressive destruction of the trabecular pattern and formation of a large, smooth-walled cloudy cavity (Figs. 8.16–8.19). Occasionally, the cholesteatoma may insinuate itself into the mastoid air cells without eroding the bony trabeculae. This type of involvement, usually seen in children, causes a cloudiness of the mastoid air cells which cannot be distinguished radiographically from simple mastoiditis.

Natural Radical

Occasionally, an extensive mastoid cholesteatoma will erode the posterior portion of the lateral epitympanic wall and the posterosuperior wall of the bony external auditory canal. The cholesteatoma exteriorizes itself, discharges into the external auditory canal, and forms a "natural radical" mastoid cavity. In these cases there is a defect of varying size in the mastoid and adjacent posterosuperior external canal wall.

Complications

Complications of cholesteatomas occur when the lesion erodes the anatomical boundaries of the middle ear, antrum, and mastoid or involves the facial nerve.

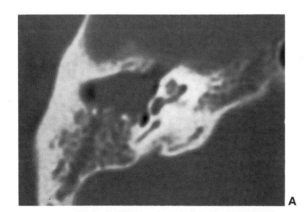

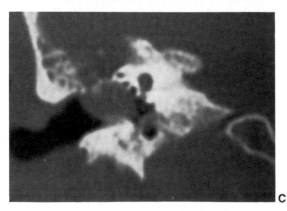
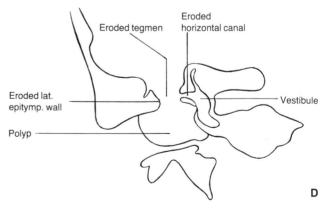
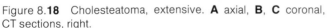

Figure 8.18   Cholesteatoma, extensive. **A** axial, **B**, **C** coronal, CT sections, right.
There is a large polyp filling the external auditory canal. The lateral epitympanic wall is eroded and cholesteatoma fills the epitympanum and mastoid. The tegmen is eroded and the capsule of the horizontal semicircular canal is markedly thinned. The vertical portion of the facial canal is eroded from the pyramidal turn to the stylomastoid foramen.
D Diagram of **B**.

The most common complications are:

1. Erosion of the tegmen or sinus plate
2. Erosion of the labyrinthine wall with fistula formation
3. Extension of the cholesteatoma into the petrous pyramid
4. Erosion of the facial nerve canal.

Tegmen, Sinus Plate Erosion, and Intracranial Complications

Erosion of the tegmen usually occurs in large cholesteatomas (Figs. 8.17–8.19). In coronal sections, the tegmen slopes downward anteriorly and is not well visualized in this projection. When tegmen erosion is suspected, direct or reconstructed sagittal CT or multidirectional tomography is indicated.

Meningeal and intracranial complications may occur in association with tegmental erosions, and a CT study with infusion of the brain will show such lesions as otogenic abscesses (Fig. 6.7). Erosion of the posterior wall of the mastoid and the sinus plate occur in extensive cholesteatomas and may lead to septic thrombophlebitis of the lateral sinus and to cerebellar abscess formation.

Labyrinthine Fistulae

Labyrinthine fistulae occur most commonly in the lateral portion of the horizontal semicircular canal, which bulges into the antrum. Radiographically a fistula of the horizontal semicircular canal is characterized by flattening of the normal convex contour of the canal and by erosion of the labyrinthine capsule over the lumen of the canal.

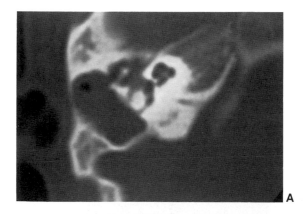

A

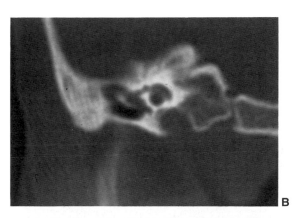

B

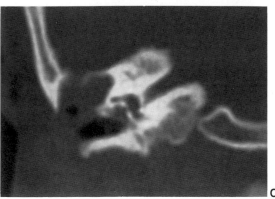

C

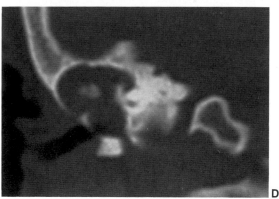

D

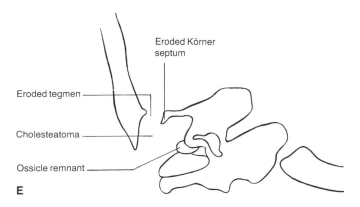

E

Eroded Körner septum

Eroded tegmen

Cholesteatoma

Ossicle remnant

Figure 8.**19** Cholesteatoma, extensive. **A** axial, **B**, **C**, **D** coronal, CT sections, right.
An extensive cholesteatoma fills and erodes the epitympanum and the entire mastoid. The lesion has destroyed the posterosuperior bony external canal wall, eroded the tegmen, C, and eroded and fistulized the posterior semicircular canal. The mastoid segment of the facial canal is eroded and the facial nerve exposed.
E Diagram of **C**.

Fistulae at the lateral prominence of the horizontal semicircular canal are seen in axial and coronal sections (Fig. 8.17–8.19). Fistulae of either the anterior or posterior aspect of the horizontal canal are exposed best in axial sections. Fistulae of other areas of the labyrinth are rare and usually occur in large cholesteatomas, which erode into the pyramid. Horizontal semicircular canal fistulae are rare in small or moderately sized pars flaccida cholesteatomas because the ossicles are interposed between the sac and the bony horizontal canal.

In far advanced cases, a fistula may occur in association with dissolution of the ossicles.

Fistulae of the horizontal semicircular canal are not uncommon in pars tensa cholesteatoma, because extension of the cholesteatoma from the middle ear is medial to the ossicles and in contact with the bony horizontal semicircular canal.

Should infection spread via the fistula to the labyrinth to produce labyrinthitis, severe vertigo and deafness occur. The end result of a septic labyrinthitis is a partial or total bony obliteration of the vestibule, semicircular canal, and cochlea (Figs. 4.19, 9.3).

Petrous Extension of Cholesteatoma

Extension of acquired cholesteatomas into the petrous pyramid occurs in large cholesteatomas that arise in well pneumatized petrous bones. In the medialward extension, the cholesteatoma follows the course of least resistance and erodes the thin walls of the petrous air cells (Fig. 8.19).

The paths most commonly followed by petrous extensions are:

1. Anterosuperiorly, above the cochlea, involving the geniculate ganglion and extending to the suprameatal area of the petrous bone.
2. Posterosuperiorly, between the limbs of the superior semicircular canal to reach the fundus of the internal auditory canal. These lesions may broach the wall of the internal auditory canal.
3. Infralabyrinthine, inferior to the cochlea and internal auditory canal. Such lesions may break into the jugular fossa.

The cholesteatoma may extend to reach the petrous apex by any of these routes.

Facial Nerve

Facial nerve paralysis can occur if the cholesteatoma erodes the facial nerve canal and exposes the nerve. The exposed nerve must be compressed by the cholesteatoma or affected by an inflammatory process to cause paralysis. The demonstration of the facial nerve canal erosion is important to the otologic surgeon, since he should be aware of the erosion preoperatively to avoid damage to the exposed nerve (Figs. 8.18, 8.19, 8.24). The most common site of facial nerve canal erosion is the area extending from the oval window to the proximal portion of the vertical segment. Erosion of the anterior portion of the tym-

panic segment and geniculate ganglion may occur in large epitympanic lesions. Erosion of the mastoid segment of the nerve occurs in lesions that involve the entire mastoid.

Involvement of the tympanic segment of the nerve is best seen in coronal and 20° coronal oblique sections. Mastoid segment erosions are best seen in sagittal and coronal sections. In 50% of cases, the bony canal of the horizontal portion of the facial nerve will be congenitally dehiscent. Therefore, evidence of defects of the bony canal of this segment of the nerve does not indicate erosion by cholesteatoma. But erosions of the bony canal in the vertical portion or the geniculate ganglion area are significant, since they indicate erosion by cholesteatoma.

Congenital Cholesteatoma of the Middle Ear

Congenital cholesteatomas histologically are epidermoid tumors originating from embryonic epidermoid rests located anywhere in the temporal bone or in the adjacent extradural or epidural spaces. The clinical symptomatology of congenital cholesteatoma depends of the size and the site of the lesion (Fig. 8.20).

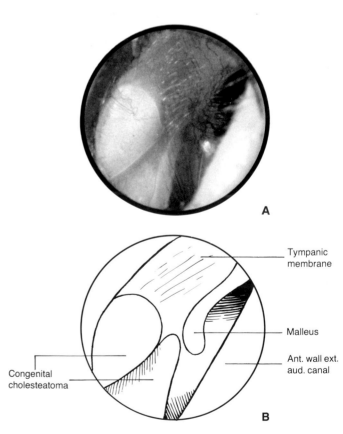

Figure 8.**20** **A** Cholesteatoma, congenital, otoscopic findings right ear.
A whitish mass of necrotic epithelial debris fills the posteroinferior portion of the middle ear medial to and in contact with an intact tympanic membrane.
B Diagram of **A**.

Clinical Findings

Otoscopically congenital middle ear cholesteatomas appear as whitish globular masses lying medial to an intact tympanic membrane. There is usually no history of antecedent inflammatory ear disease. Occasionally there is an associated serous otitis media.

CT sections show a well defined soft tissue mass within the middle ear (Fig. 8.21–8.23). If the cholesteatoma involves the entire middle ear space or if there is an accompanying serous otitis media, the entire tympanic cavity appears cloudy.

The cholesteatoma mass may erode portions of the ossicular chain. In congenital cholesteatoma the tympanic membrane often bulges laterally (Figs. 8.21–8.23). This lateral bulging seen on coronal and axial sections enables the radiologist to differentiate the mass of the congenital cholesteatoma from serous otitis media. In both instances, the middle ear will appear cloudy, but in serous otitis media the tympanic membrane is retracted medially.

The inferior margin of the lateral epitympanic wall, which is typically eroded in acquired cholesteatoma, is intact in congenital lesions. The medial aspect of the lateral epitympanic wall is often eroded from within when the congenital lesion extends into the epitympanum.

Congenital cholesteatomas arising in the mastoid are very rare and appear as areas of destruction of the trabecular pattern produced by the cystic mass in the mastoid. In such cases, the middle ear cavity is normal in contradistinction to acquired cholesteatoma where the middle ear is always involved.

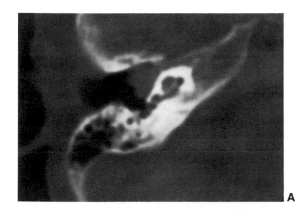

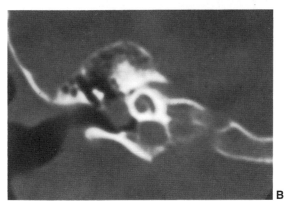

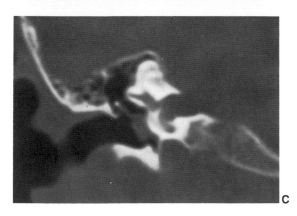

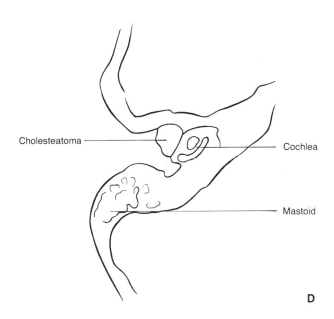

Figure 8.**21** Cholesteatoma, congenital. **A** axial, **B**, **C** coronal, CT sections, right.

A soft tissue mass fills the anterior portion of the mesotympanum and produces and outward bulge of the intact tympanic membrane. The lesion encroaches upon the incudostapedial joint. The remaining middle ear and mastoid are normal.

D Diagram of **A**.

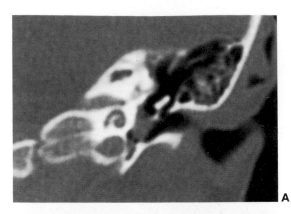

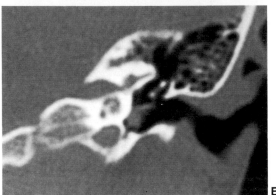

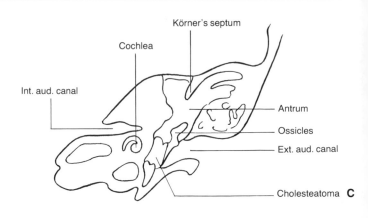

Figure 8.**22**   Cholesteatoma, congenital. **A**, **B** coronal CT sections, left.
A well defined soft tissue mass lies in the mesotympanum. The mass extends from the intact tympanic membrane to the promontory. The middle ear and mastoid are well aerated.
C Diagram of **A**.

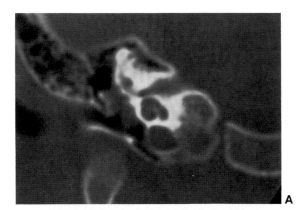

Figure 8.**23**   Cholesteatoma, congenital. **A**, **B** coronal CT sections, right.
A large soft tissue mass fills most of the mesotympanum and displaces the intact tympanic membrane laterally. The mass extends into the epitympanum medial to the ossicles and erodes the long process of the incus.
C Diagram of **B**.

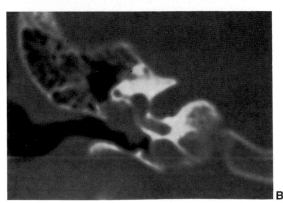

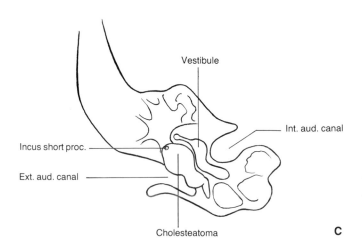

Petrous Pyramid and Epidural Cholesteatomas

The majority of these lesions arise in the petrous apex or adjacent epidural spaces. The first sign of a congenital cholesteatoma of the pyramid is often a facial paralysis of slow onset followed by sensorineural hearing loss caused by erosion of the labyrinth. In the early stages, the middle ear may be normal. Radiographic findings depend on whether the choles-teatoma arises from within the petrous apex or from the adjacent epidural or extradural spaces.

When the cholesteatoma arises from within the petrous apex, computerized tomography will show an expansile, cystic lesion in the apex (Fig. 8.24, 8.26). The involved area of the pyramid is expanded, and the superior petrous ridge is usually elevated and thinned out. As the lesion expands, the internal auditory canal and labyrinth become eroded. Choles-

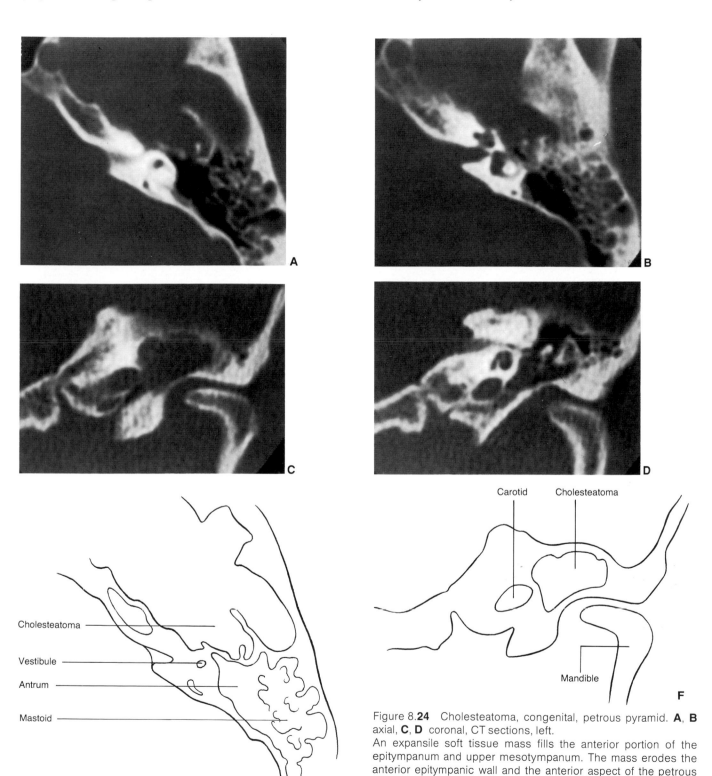

Figure 8.24 Cholesteatoma, congenital, petrous pyramid. **A**, **B** axial, **C**, **D** coronal, CT sections, left.
An expansile soft tissue mass fills the anterior portion of the epitympanum and upper mesotympanum. The mass erodes the anterior epitympanic wall and the anterior aspect of the petrous pyramid. The facial canal in the region of the geniculate ganglion is eroded, **B**, **C**.   **E** Diagram of **A**.   **F** Diagram of **C**.

teatomas arising from the epidural or extradural spaces of the superior aspect of the pyramid cause a scooped out defect on the superior aspect of the pyramid (Fig. 8.27). The defect is caused by erosion of the pyramid from without, and there is no bony rim as in lesions arising from within the pyramid.

Infusion CT shows no mass enhancement, except for a thin and often incompletely visualized capsule. The CT findings are identical to those of a cholesterol granuloma (see Figs. 7.9–7.11). Cholesteatoma and cholesterol granuloma can be differentiated from each other by MRI, since in the T1 sequence, the cholesterol granuloma is bright, but the cholesteatoma less bright (Figs. 8.24–8.27).

Cholesteatomas originating in the jugular fossa area can cause bony changes similar to glomus jugulare tumors. Both lesions expand the jugular fossa and erode the posteroinferior aspect of the petrous pyramid and adjacent occipital bone. Bolus infusion CT allows differentiation of the two lesions, since glomus tumors enhance but cholesteatomas do not.

Congenital cholesteatomas of the cerebellopontine angle produce signs and symptoms similar to an acoustic neuroma.

In cholesteatoma of the angle, the lumen of the internal auditory canal is usually not expanded, but there is erosion and shortening of the posterior wall of the internal canal. Again differentiation is easily made by CT with infusion.

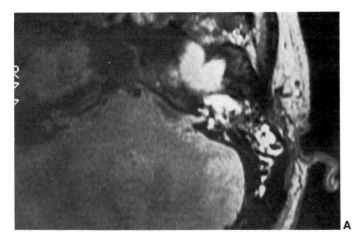

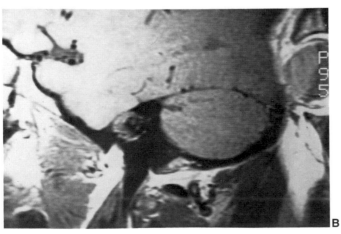

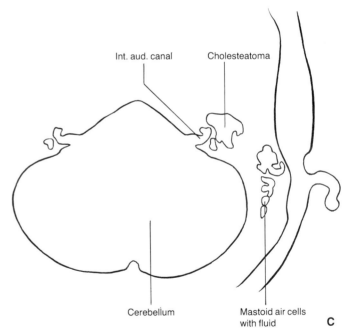

Figure 8.25 Cholesteatoma, congenital, petrous pyramid. **A** axial T2, **B** sagittal spin density weighted MR sections, same ear as Fig. 8.24.

The cholesteatoma appears in the T2 images as a high signal intensity mass involving the anterior aspect of the petrous pyramid and middle ear cavity, **A**. In the sagittal spin density weighted sections, the signal intensity is less than in T2, **B**. In the axial T2 images, fluid in the mastoid air cells appears bright.

C Diagram of **A**.

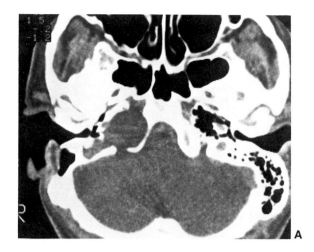

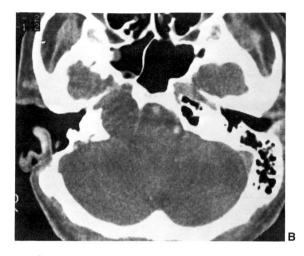

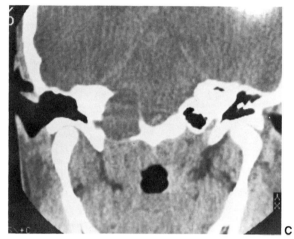

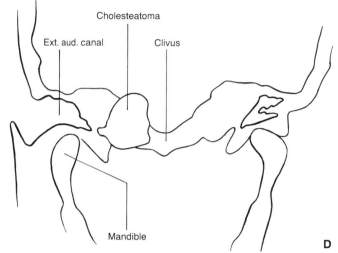

Figure 8.**26**   Cholesteatoma, petrous apex. **A**, **B** axial, **C** coronal, CT sections, right.
The right petrous apex is destroyed by an expansile low density lesion. Infusion shows enhancement of the capsule. The lesion involves the clivus and occipital condyle. There is an old mastoidectomy defect.
D Diagram of **C**.

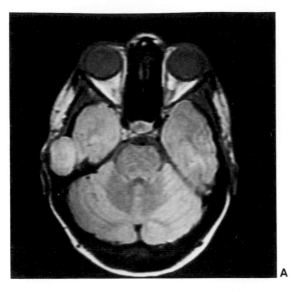

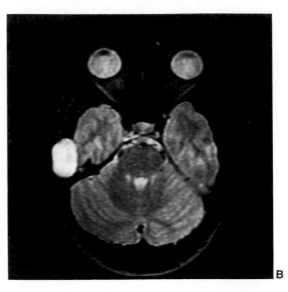

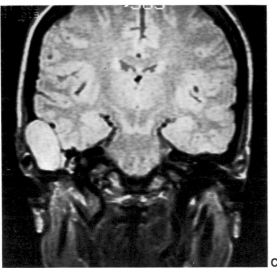

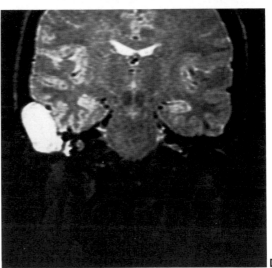

Figure 8.**27**   Congenital cholesteatoma. **A, B** axial, **C, D** coronal MR sections, right.
There is a large extradural mass in the lateral portion of the right middle cranial fossa. The mass erodes the adjacent upper aspect of the temporal bone and bulges into the external auditory canal. The lesion is characterized by a signal of medium intensity in spin density weighted images, **A, C**, and by a signal of higher intensity in the T2 images, **B, D**.

Cholesteatoma of the External Auditory Canal

There are two types of cholesteatoma of the external auditory canal. The first type, keratosis obliterans, is caused by osteomas, stenosis of the canal or hard masses of cerumen. Blockage of the external canal for a long period permits epithelial debris to accumulate in the canal and enlarge the bony contour of the external canal. CT shows concentric enlargement of the bony external auditory canal by a soft tissue mass medial to the site of the canal stenosis or obstruction (Fig. 8.**28**, 8.**29**).
The other type of cholesteatoma of the external canal is called invasive keratitis and is characterized by localized accumulations of desquamated debris in the bony canal (Fig. 8.**30**).

Removal of the debris reveals deep localized erosions of the bony canal wall and areas of exposed, necrotic bone. Occasionally the lesions extend and involve almost the entire circumference of the external canal. There often is a history of antecedent radiotherapy to the area of the ear. In invasive keratitis, tomography shows erosion of the cortex of the involved portion of the canal. In larger lesions there are scooped out defects of the bony canal wall. When the lesion is diffuse, there is expansion of the involved canal segment without obstruction of the canal lumen. When the external canal cholesteatoma is large, it erodes the anulus and extends into the middle ear, attic and mastoid.

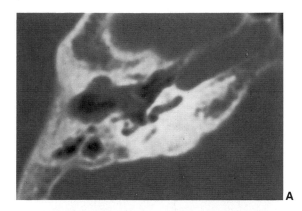

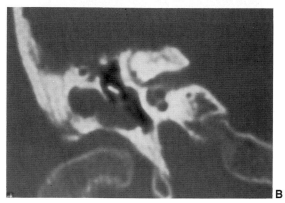

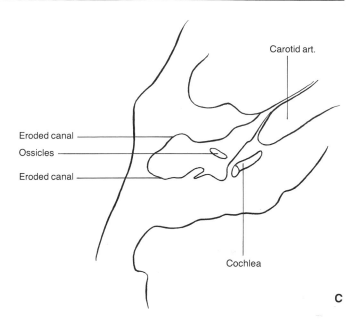

Figure 8.**28** Cholesteatoma, external auditory canal. **A** axial, **B** coronal, CT sections, right.

A soft tissue mass obstructs the external auditory canal and erodes the bony canal walls. The mass extends into the posterosuperior quadrant of the tympanic cavity, **A**.

C Diagram of **A**.

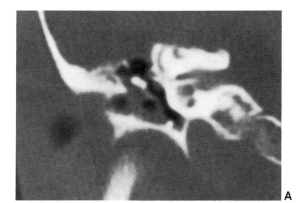

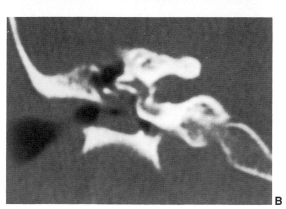

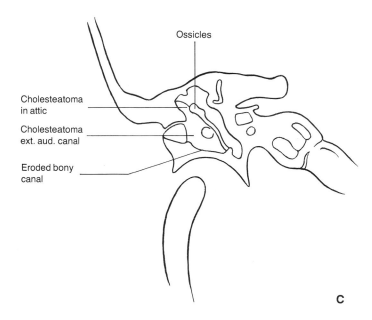

Figure 8.**29** Cholesteatoma, external auditory canal. **A**, **B** coronal, CT sections, right.

The cholesteatoma fills the medial portion of the external canal, erodes the inferior margin of the epitympanic wall, and extends into the attic lateral to the ossicles.

C Diagram of **A**.

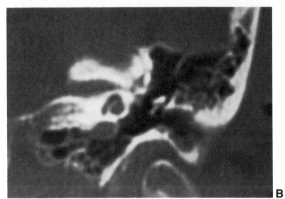

Figure 8.**30** Cholesteatoma, external auditory canal, post-irradiation therapy. **A**, **B** coronal CT sections, left.
There is localized erosion of the lateral portion of the floor of the external auditory canal. Necrotic debris overlies the erosion. This patient had x-ray therapy to the head twenty years previously.
C Diagram of **B**.

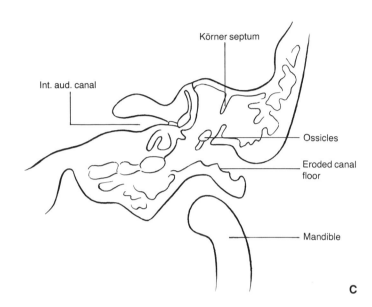

Chapter 9 **Postoperative and Postirradiation Imaging of the Temporal Bone**

Postoperative radiographs of the ear are difficult to interpret. The bony landmarks are usually missing, and there is often clouding of the mastoid cavity because of recurrent pathologic changes or because tissue grafts or flaps were used to fill the mastoidectomy cavity. In addition, with passage of time new bone formation may partially fill in the surgical defects.

To understand and interpret the postoperative radiographic findings of the ear, the radiologist should be acquainted with the basic techniques of middle ear and mastoid surgery.

Simple and Radical Mastoidectomies

Mastoid surgery may be divided into simple and radical procedures.

Simple Mastoidectomy

A simple mastoidectomy consists of drilling away the external mastoid cortex and exenterating the mastoid air cells.

Air cell exenteration extends to the mastoid antrum. When indicated by the pathology, the dissection will extend to the epitympanum. The surgeon drills between the dural plate and the superior wall of the external auditory canal and leaves the inferior margin of the lateral epitympanic wall intact.

At times the surgeon may only explore the antrum and epitympanum. In these cases he removes only enough mastoid cortex and mastoid air cells to expose these areas.

Radical and Modified Radical Mastoidectomies

The essential feature which differentiates a simple mastoidectomy from one of the various types of radical mastoidectomies is that in the radical procedure the mastoid bridge is removed. During the surgical dissection of the mastoid, the lateral portion of the posterosuperior bony canal wall and upper portion of the lateral epitympanic wall are first drilled away. This leaves a bony arch called the mastoid bridge which is made up of the medial portion of the posterosuperior bony canal wall and the inferior margin of the epitympanic wall.

This bridge is removed during one of the last stages of the operation and converts a simple mastoidectomy into a radical mastoidectomy. Removal of the bridge transforms the mastoid cavity and the external canal into a common cavity.

The modified radical mastoidectomy is the most commonly performed type of radical mastoidectomy. In the modified radical mastoidectomy, remnants of the tympanic membrane and ossicles are retained to preserve hearing.

In the true radical mastoidectomy, which is rarely performed, all middle ear structures and tympanic membrane remnants are removed.

Tympanoplasty

Tympanoplasties are surgical procedures of the middle ear and mastoid designed to improve hearing. There are five classical types of tympanoplasties. In Type I and II a graft is used to cover defects of the tympanic membrane. In Type III and IV usually some form of mastoidectomy and ossicular reconstruction are performed. Type V is rarely performed and consists of a fenestration of the horizontal semicircular canal and preservation of a reduced middle ear space.

Imaging Findings

Postoperative radiography of the ear is difficult and CT is essential to evaluate pathology correctly. The postoperative radiographic evaluation of the ear requires a knowledge of (1) the pathology for which the surgery was performed, (2) the type of surgery performed, and (3) the clinical and otoscopic findings that make further x-ray studies necessary.

In postoperative radiography of the ear, an almost infinite spectrum of findings may occur depending on variables of the preoperative pathology, the surgical procedure, and recurrent or residual disease.

Ideally, whenever the surgeon feels that at the end of the surgery there is residual disease, he should secure a postoperative study which can serve as a base line for subsequent evaluations.

Mastoid Cavity

A disease-free surgical cavity appears as well defined and sharply outlined defect in the mastoid, epitympanum, and external canal depending on the type of surgery performed. Small defects in the tegmen produced during surgery are of no significance.

The mastoid cavity is usually clear unless some form of fibromuscular flap was used to fill the mastoid. The radiologist must be informed about the use of such flaps.

Following radical mastoidectomy, the mastoid and external ear common cavity must be cleaned periodically to prevent accumulation of necrotic epithelial debris and cerumen. Usually the cavity is not completely filled with debris, so that the images show only partial cloudiness. If debris has been allowed to accumulate over a period of years, the cavity will appear completely cloudy. Infection and recurrent cholesteatoma will also fill and opacify the mastoid cavity, which becomes poorly defined and irregular due to osteitis of the walls, and leads to abscess formation (Fig. 9.1).

The trabeculae of the residual air cells become demineralized and in long-standing infections, sclerotic (Fig. 9.2). If recurrent cholesteatoma is filling the mastoidectomy cavity, there is expansion of the

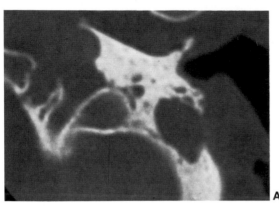

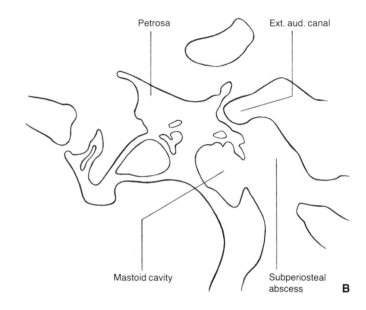

Figure 9.1 **A** Cholesteatoma, recurrent, with subperiosteal abscess, mastoid tip, axial CT, left.
There is a smooth walled and cloudy cavity in the mastoid tip, which contains necrotic epithelial debris. The cortex is eroded, and there is a subperiosteal abscess in continuity with the cavity. The abscess produces a marked soft tissue swelling overlying the mastoid.
B Diagram of **A**.

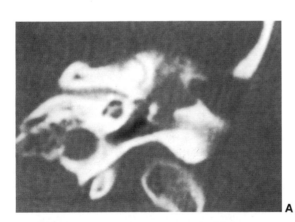

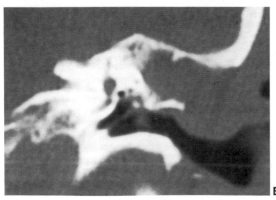

Figure 9.2 Cholesteatoma, recurrent, post simple mastoidectomy, **A**, **B** coronal, CT sections, left.
Recurrent cholesteatoma fills the epitympanum and mastoid cavity. The superior bony canal is preserved. There are residual mastoid air cells in the medial portion of the cavity.
C Diagram of **B**.

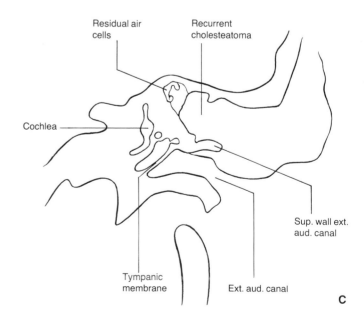

cavity and thinning of the walls, which lead to erosions in the tegmen and sinus plates (Fig. 9.2). Fistulae of the labyrinth may be present. If a fistulized labyrinth becomes infected, partial or complete bony obliteration may occur (Fig. 9.3). Recurrent cholesteatoma may erode the facial canal and extend into the labyrinth (Fig. 9.4). Recurrent cholesteatoma should be differentiated from cholesterol granuloma cysts, which have a somewhat smooth margin (Fig. 9.5). In doubt, MR will differentiate these lesions.

Stenosis of the External Auditory Canal

At times following myringoplasty and tympanoplasty where the external canal is preserved, the canal becomes filled with a fibrous scar. The tympanic membrane graft may also heal in a position far lateral to the bony sulcus. CT will show the amount and extent of the soft tissue stenosis of the external canal, as well as the position of the lateralized tympanic membrane graft (Figs. 9.3, 9.5).

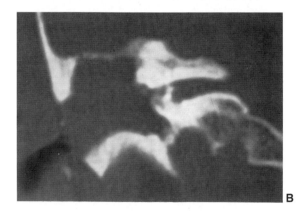

A

B

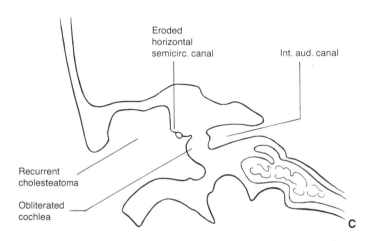

Figure 9.**3**   Cholesteatoma, recurrent, with obliterative labyrinthitis. **A, B** coronal CT sections, right.
There is soft tissue stenosis of the external auditory canal, and a recurrent cholesteatoma fills the mastoidectomy cavity and middle ear. There is a horizontal semicircular canal fistula which lead to suppurative labyrinthitis and consequent partial bony obliteration of the lumen of the cochlea, vestibule, and semicircular canals.
C Diagram of **B**.

C

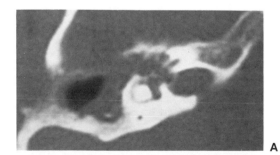

A

B

Figure 9.**4**   Cholesteatoma, recurrent, post modified radical mastoidectomy. **A** axial, **B** coronal, CT sections, right.
The recurrent cholesteatoma fills the medial portion of the mastoidectomy cavity and erodes into the cochlea and vestibule. The tegmen is eroded. The entire tympanic segment of the facial canal from the geniculate ganglion to the pyramidal turn is eroded.
C Diagram of **B**.

C

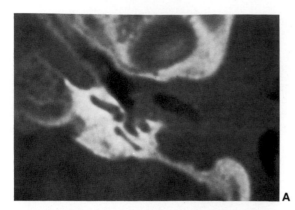

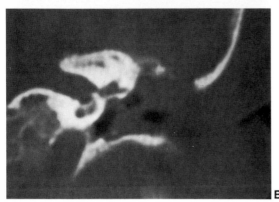

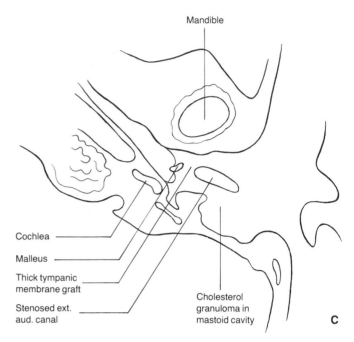

Figure 9.5 Postoperative stenosis, external canal. **A** axial, **B** coronal, CT sections, left.
Following modified radical mastoidectomy, the external canal is markedly stenotic and the tympanic membrane graft markedly thickened. There is a homogeneous clouding of the mastoid cavity due to a cholesterol granuloma cyst.
C Diagram of **A**.

When scar tissue fills the canal, the air column of the external canal ends in a blind sac lateral to the bony sulcus.

After radical mastoidectomy, the external auditory canal may become stenosed or obliterated by fibrosis due to recurrent or persistent infection.

Middle Ear

The middle ear cavity may be normal in size or contracted but still aerated following successful mastoid surgery. Clouding of the middle ear cavity is evidence of recurrent infection or cholesteatoma.

At times following tympanoplasty, the graft used to reconstruct the tympanic membrane becomes displaced laterally (Fig. 9.5). Thickened, scarred, lateralized grafts are seen in axial and coronal sections.

Ossicles

The appearance of the ossicular chain will depend on whether the ossicles have been removed at surgery, left in place, or transposed.

The body of the incus is the ossicle most often transposed. When properly transposed, the body of the incus can be easily seen lying in the posterosuperior quadrant of the middle ear between the tympanic membrane or malleus handle and the oval window region.

With recurrent infection, the incus may be resorbed.

Placement of the incus between the tympanic membrane or malleus handle and the stapes may fail, and the incus may migrate inferiorly where it is visualized tomographically. Recurrent cholesteatoma can displace a transposed incus inferiorly.

Facial Canal

The appearance of the facial canal in the postoperative CT study varies with the extent of the pathology and the surgery. The facial canal may be normal and uninvolved, eroded by the original lesion, dissected at surgery, or traumatized at surgery (Fig. 9.4).

Meningocele and Meningoencephalocele

A soft tissue mass contiguous to a defect in the tegmen of the mastoid suggests the possibility of a meningocele or meningoencephalocele. If the brain and meninges herniate into the relatively small space of the antrum or epitympanum, the constant pulsation of the cerebrospinal fluid is transmitted through the walls of the meningocele to cause a gradual resorption of the surrounding bony walls (Fig. 9.6, 9.7).

CT demonstrates the bony defect in the tegmen and a soft tissue mass filling the mastoid cavity. This soft tissue lesion cannot be reliably differentiated from a recurrent cholesteatoma, since the absorption coefficients of both lesions are similar. The differentiation between a meningocele and an cholesteatoma can be made by MR. On MR, cholesteatoma appears as a

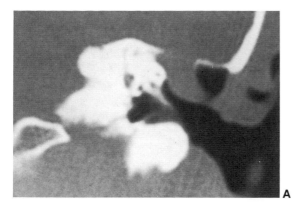

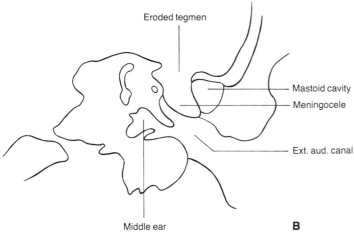

Figure 9.**6 A** Meningocele, post modified radical mastoidectomy, coronal CT, left.
A large defect in the tegmen permits herniation of a meningoencephalocele into the mastoid cavity.
B Diagram of **A**.

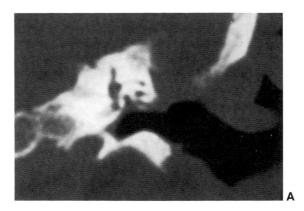

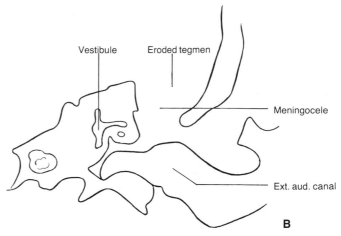

Figure 9.**7 A** Meningocele, post modified radical mastoidectomy, coronal CT section, left.
The tegmen of the mastoid cavity is defective, and a meningocele herniates into the mastoid antrum.
B Diagram of **A**.

lesion of high medium signal in the T1 and high signal intensity in T2 images. A meningocele will have the same characteristics as cerebrospinal fluid: low medium signal intensity in T1 and high intensity in the T2 images. On MR, meningoencephaloceles have the same characteristics of the adjacent brain, which are quite different from a cholesteatoma.

Postirradiation Changes

Following high dosage radiotherapy to the temporal bone for intra- and extracranial malignancies, radionecrosis may ensue. These changes occur several years post-therapy and range from minimal ulceration of the external auditory canal to extensive necrosis of the temporal squama, mastoid and petrous pyramids (Fig. 9.8).

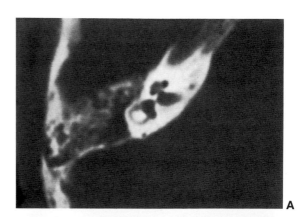

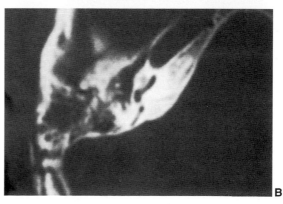

Figure 9.**8** Osteoradionecrosis. **A**, **B** axial, CT sections, right. ▶
This patient was treated for carcinoma of the parotid 11 years previously. There is extensive dissolution and decalcification of the temporal squama of the mastoid and the tympanic bone. There is a soft tissue stenosis of the external auditory canal. The middle ear is clouded.

Chapter 10 Tumors

Benign Tumors

Benign tumors of the temporal bone originate in the squama, the mastoid, and the petrous pyramid or from adjacent structures, such as meninges, the jugular vein, and cranial nerves. At times, benign tumors arising from structures adjacent to the temporal bone and external auditory canal can impinge on the temporal bone and external canal. Lipomas and occasionally pleomorphic adenomas of the parotid gland can become large enough to narrow or obstruct the external canal (Fig. 10.1). Acoustic neuromas, because of their distinctive characteristics and diagnostic problems, will be discussed separately in Chapter II.

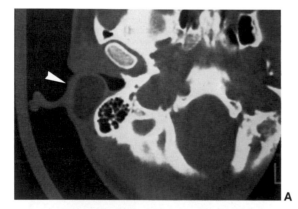

Figure 10.**1** Lipoma retroauricular region. **A** axial, **B** coronal CT sections, right. A well defined low density soft tissue mass lies lateral to the right mastoid. The mass encroaches upon and narrows the lumen of the cartilaginous portion of the external auditory canal, arrow **A**.

Exostoses

Exostoses are the most common tumor of the external auditory canal. Exostoses represent local or diffuse areas of hyperostosis often caused by frequent swimming. They are usually multiple, large or small, and often are bilateral. Small lesions cause no symptoms, while large lesions obstruct the canal.

Exostoses have a variable CT appearance. Small lesions appear as dense nodules, protruding into the lumen of the external auditory canal. More diffuse lesions appear as dense bony ridges which stretch along the canal walls. Occasionally the entire circumference of the canal ist thickened and the lumen is constricted.

Osteoma

Osteomas are benign bony tumors which are usually single and may occur anywhere in the temporal bone. There are two types, cancellous and compact. Radiographically, the compact lesion appears as well defined, occasionally lobulated dense bony mass. Cancellous osteomas appear as partially ossified masses.

A common site is the external auditory canal, where the osteoma appears as a single bony mass occluding the lumen (Fig. 10.**2**). This lesion may cause retention of epithelial debris and cerumen, which results in cholesteatoma of the external auditory canal.

Osteomas may also occur as a solitary lesion in the squama, mastoid, middle ear and petrous pyramid. In the squama, an osteoma produces a hard bony mass on the surface of the bone usually above and posterior to the auricle. When they occur in the mastoid, osteomas are usually asymptomatic unless they encroach upon the facial nerve.

Osteomas may lie in the middle ear and cause conductive hearing loss by impinging upon the ossicular chain (Fig. 10.**3**).

In the petrous pyramid, osteomas usually are situated in the region of the porus of the internal auditory canal. Rarely they may encroach on the neurovascular structures of the internal auditory canal and cause hearing and vestibular disturbances.

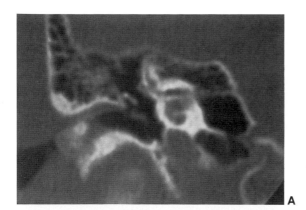

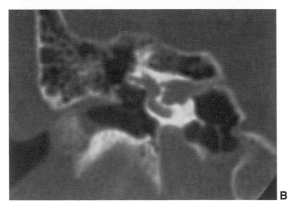

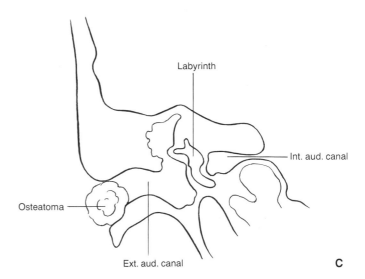

Figure 10.**2**   Osteoma external auditory canal **A**, **B** coronal CT sections, right. A large cancellous osteoma obstructs the lumen of the outer portion of the right external auditory canal. The middle ear cavity is normal.
C   Diagram of **B**.

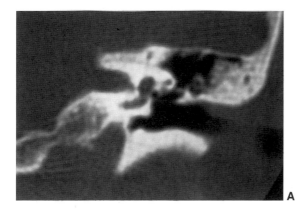

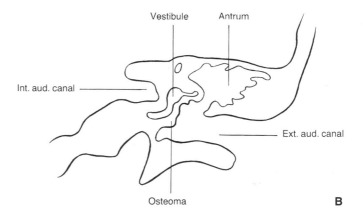

Figure 10.**3**   Osteoma of the middle ear cavity, coronal CT section left, **A**. A small bony mass protrudes into the middle ear space from the promontory. The middle ear cavity appears otherwise normal.
B   Diagram of **A**.

Adenoma

Adenomas usually occur in the fibrocartilaginous portion of the external auditory canal. As with other benign tumors of the external canal, radiography is not indicated unless the lesion obstructs the canal and obscures the view of the tympanic membrane or middle ear.

Middle ear adenomas are rare. The lesion has a tendency to recur after surgery and may degenerate into adenocarcinoma. A middle ear adenoma appears in CT sections as a diffuse or localized non-specific soft tissue mass (Fig. 10.4). There is no bony erosion unless malignant degeneration of the adenoma into adenocarcinoma has occurred.

Hemangioma

Hemangiomas are rare tumors of the temporal bone. The clinical and radiographic features depend on the anatomical location (Fig. 10.5).

They may occur in the temporal squama where they produce an area of radiolucency with typical spoke-like trabeculation.

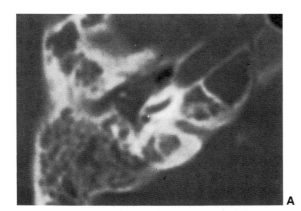

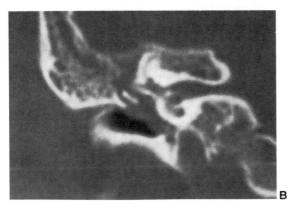

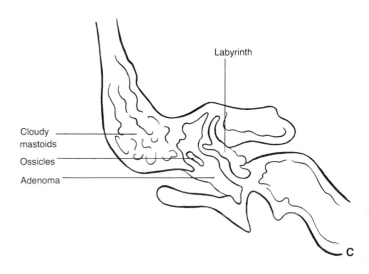

Figure 10.**4**   Adenoma middle ear cavity. **A** axial, **B** coronal CT sections, right. A lobulated soft tissue mass fills most of the mesotympanum and attic surrounding but not eroding the ossicles. The tumor extends into the sinus tympani and mastoid antrum. The lateral wall of the attic is intact. The mastoid air cells are cloudy due to fluid.
C Diagram of **B**.

Labyrinth

Cloudy mastoids
Ossicles
Adenoma

A hemangioma of the external canal can fill and enlarge the bony canal. Often there are phleboliths within the lesion. Figure 10.5 shows a hemangioma arising from the tympanic membrane. A hemangioma of the middle ear results in a poorly defined soft tissue mass which may be associated with ossicular erosion. Hemangiomas can be differentiated from glomus jugulare tumors because hemangiomas do not erode the hypotympanic floor.

A dynamic CT study with bolus injection of contrast demonstrates a highly vascular mass. Peak time will depend on the type of hemangioma. Some hemangiomas of the middle ear cavity, however, cannot be differentiated from glomus tympanicums.

Hemangiomas of the petrous pyramid produce a diffuse, mottled demineralization with multiple honeycombed radiolucencies.

A hemangioma may lie in the internal auditory canal and cerebellopontine angle and mimic an acoustic neuroma. Differentiation can be made by MR or subtraction arteriography.

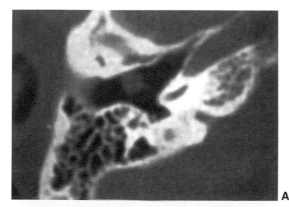

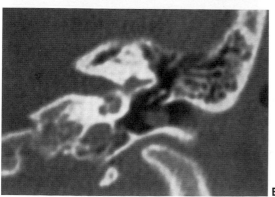

Figure 10.5 Capillary hemangioma, right tympanic membrane. **A** axial, **B** coronal CT sections. A well defined soft tissue mass lies within the medial portion of the right external auditory canal. The mass appears attached to the outer surface of the tympanic membrane.
C Diagram of **B**.

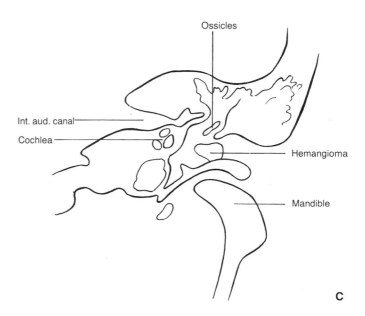

Meningioma

Meningiomas arise from the meningeal covering of the temporal bone and from meningeal extension within the internal auditory canal.

The most common type of meningioma arises from the dura covering the petrous ridge. Radiographically the findings vary from hyperostosis to moth-eaten erosion, which can progress to frank destruction of the petrous bone. Often there is a combination of these findings (Figs. 10.6–10.9).

One form of hyperostotic meningioma is the en plaque lesion. A characteristic manifestation of this lesion is the presence of a calcified layer separated from the surface of the temporal bone by a radiolucent band (Fig. 10.6). Some meningiomas erode the tegmen and break into the middle ear cavity (Fig. 10.9). The occasional ectopic meningioma can involve the middle ear cavity without erosion of the tegmen. Facial nerve involvement can occur in the region of the geniculate ganglion. Erosion of the labyrinth is rare.

Computerized tomography with bolus infusion is indicated in cases where a meningioma is suspected, since this technique will demonstrate the involvement of the base of the skull and the presence of any intracranial component of the tumor (Figs. 10.7–10.9). En plaque lesions are frequently not recognized because of lack of enhancement of the sheet-like tumor. Meningiomas arising within the internal auditory canal and cerebellopontine angle cistern mimic acoustic neuromas clinically and radiographically (Fig. 10.7). Differential diagnosis can be made if there is hyperostosis of the walls of the internal auditory canal and of the crista falciformis, or if there are calcifications scattered within the mass.

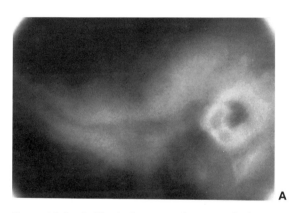

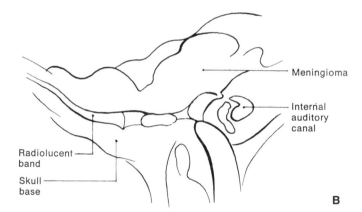

Figure 10.6 **A** Meningioma, en plaque, sagittal tomogram, left. There is marked hyperostosis on the superior surface of the temporal bone, which extends anteriorly along the floor of the middle cranial fossa. A radiolucent band separates the lesion from the underlying skull base.
B Diagram of structures seen at this level.

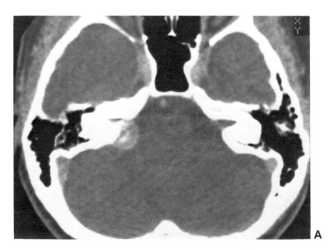

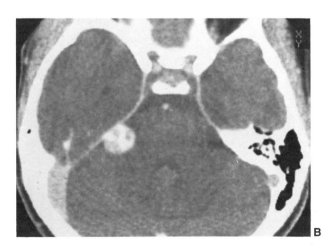

Figure 10.7 Meningioma, cerebellopontine angle, **A, B** axial, CT sections, right.
After infusion, a partially calcified soft tissue mass protrudes from the internal auditory canal into the cerebellopontine cistern. The lesion extends superiorly to the tentorium, **B**. There is hyperostotic narrowing of the right internal auditory canal, **A**.

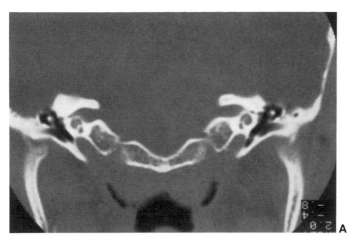

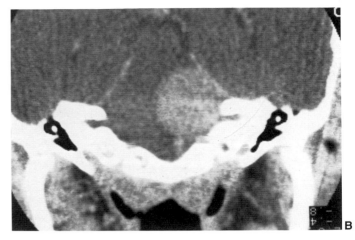

Figure 10.**8** Meningioma cerebellopontine angle. **A**, **B** coronal CT sections, left. A large enhanced mass fills the right cerebellopontine cistern, **B**. The mass reaches the tentorium and com- presses the brainstem. The right internal auditory canal is not enlarged, **A**.

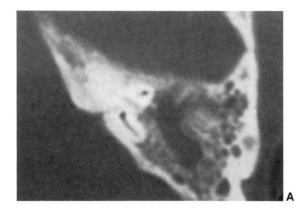

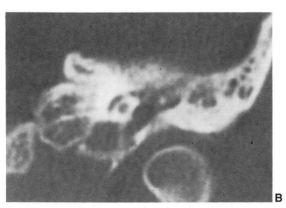

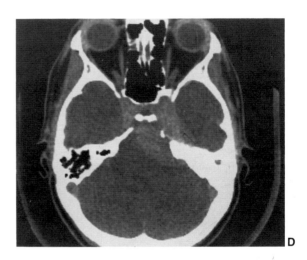

Figure 10.**9** Meningioma with involvement of the left middle ear and posterior cranial fossa. **A** axial, **B**, **C** coronal, **D** post-infusion axial CT sections.

A soft tissue mass fills the middle ear cavity and mastoid. There is erosion of the anterior aspect of the petrous pyramid and irregular thickening of the tegmen tympani, **A**, **C**. The post-infusion section, **D**, reveals the presence of a large enhanced mass involving the dura and extradural spaces in the cranial fossa adjacent to the left petrous pyramid. The mass extends into the middle cranial fossa in the region of the cavernous sinus.

E Diagram of **C**.

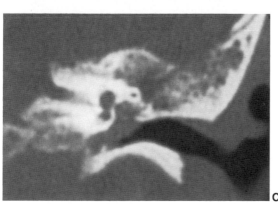

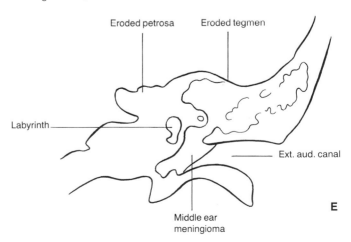

Computerized tomography usually will not differentiate meningioma and acoustic neuroma and other cerebellopontine angle masses.

On MR, meningiomas have a heterogenous appearance. The majority are isodense with the surrounding brain tissue in T1 weighted images, but often appear as areas of decreased signal intensity in the delayed T2 images. However, other meningiomas appear as bright masses with high signal intensity in T2 images.

Neuromas of the Facial Nerve

Intratemporal neuromas or neurilemomas of the facial nerve occur rarely.

The clinical findings depend on the site of origin and size of the lesion. Lesions arising within the internal auditory canal may present symptoms mimicking an acoustic neuroma. Neuromas that arise within the facial canal usually cause a peripheral facial paralysis or tic. When a neuroma arises within the tympanic portion of the facial nerve canal, the first symptom may be conductive deafness due to encroachment of the tumor on the ossicular chain.

In our series of facial neuromas, the most common site of involvement is the geniculate ganglion region, with enlargement of the bony canal seen by CT and thickening of the nerve seen on MR (Fig. 10.12).

Imaging Findings

Initially facial nerve neuromas cause thickening of the nerve and expansion of the lumen of the bony nerve canal. To detect early changes, it is necessary to compare the affected and normal sides. Enlargement of the lesion results in erosion of the bony canal and involvement of the adjacent structures of the petrous pyramid, middle ear and mastoid (Figs. 10.10–10.12). When the tumor extends into the middle ear, a well defined soft tissue mass appears (Figs. 10.10, 10.11). Lesions arising in the internal auditory canal cause enlargement of the canal. CT pneumocisternography or MR are indicated in these cases to diagnose the presence of a mass and to determine the size of the lesion.

A facial nerve neuroma limited to the internal auditory canal cannot be differentiated from an acoustic neuroma.

If the neuroma extends into the labyrinthine segment of the fallopian canal, CT will show enlargement of the bony canal and MR, enlargement of the nerve in this area.

Vth Nerve Neuromas

Neuromas of the Vth nerve arising from the gasserian ganglion tend to enlarge superiorly into the middle cranial fossa. Occasionally these tumors cause indentation and erosion of the superior petrous ridge medial to the internal auditory canal.

Axial and coronal CT sections will demonstrate the site and degree of bony involvement.

The tumor mass is better demonstrated in coronal and axial MR images. The lesion varies from thickening of the nerve to masses of variable size, characterized by high signal intensity in the T2 images.

IX, X, XI, XIIth Nerve Neuromas

Neuromas of the IXth, Xth, XIth and XIIth nerves arise in the jugular fossa or in the hypoglossal canal. They produce paralytic lesions of various types. As the tumor enlarges, it produces a progressive expansion of the jugular fossa and hypoglossal canal similar to the lesions of a glomus jugulare tumor. Neuromas can also extend intracranially into the posterior cranial fossa and the foramen magnum.

Contrary to glomus jugulare tumors, neuromas of the IX, X, XI and XII nerves do not extend into the middle ear, and they produce a more sharply defined expansion of the jugular fossa than do glomus tumors.

The diagnosis and evaluation of the size and extent of the lesion is made with CT and bolus infusion or MR imaging.

Contrast CT will show an enhanced soft tissue mass. The computer generated time density curve is quite different from the high peak curves of the glomus tumors.

MR images demonstrate a mass with a high signal intensity in the T2 images.

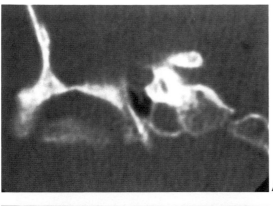

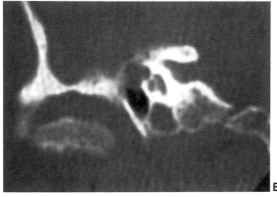

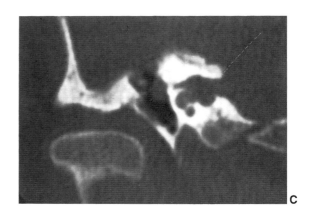

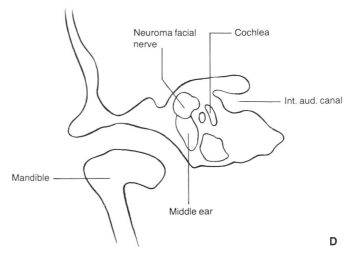

Figure 10.**10**   Facial neuroma. **A**, **B**, **C** 20 degree coronal oblique CT sections right. A soft tissue mass expands the facial canal in the region of the anterior genu and adjacent proximal portion of its tympanic segment. The mass bulges into the attic anterior and medial to the ossicles, **C**.
D Diagram of **B**.

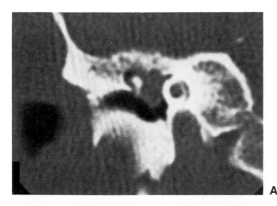

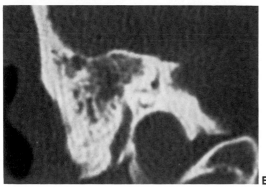

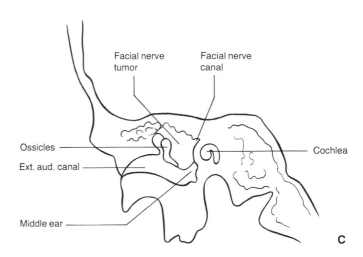

Figure 10.**11**   Facial nerve neuroma. **A**, **B** coronal CT sections, right, same ear as Fig. 10.**12**.
A soft tissue mass fills the middle ear medial to the malleus, **A**. In **B**, a section 6 mm posterior, the extension of the neuroma into the vertical portion of the facial nerve has produced an expansion of the bony canal.
C Drawing of **A**.

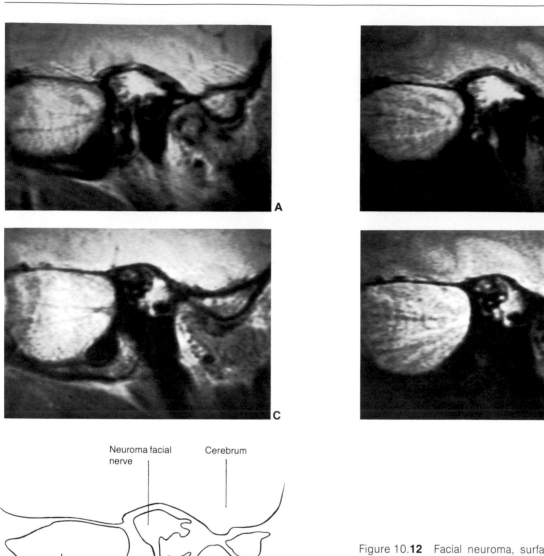

Figure 10.**12** Facial neuroma, surface coil images. **A**, **C** spin density weighted, **B**, **D** T2 sagittal MR sections, right, same ear as Fig. 10.**11**.
A soft tissue mass characterized by a high signal in both spin density weighted and T2 images fills the middle ear cavity and extends into the mastoid segment of the facial canal, which appears dilated in its mid portion.
E Drawing of **A**.

Eosinophilic Granuloma

Eosinophilic granuloma is a benign chronic granuloma related to other diseases of the reticuloendothelial system such as Letterer-Siwe, Hand-Schüller-Christian, and histiocystosis X. The etiology is unknown, but eosinophilic granuloma is commonly classified as a benign tumor. Eosinophilic granuloma of the temporal bone usually involves the mastoid. Radiographically the findings are similar to an acute mastoiditis with areas of coalescence. The involved mastoid air cells appear cloudy, and the trabecular pattern is destroyed with formation of a cavity. The mastoid cortex may be thinned, destroyed, or expanded (Figs. 10.**13**, 10.**14**).

The differential diagnosis from acute mastoiditis is made by clinical history. In acute mastoiditis, there are fever, tenderness, and draining from the ear. In eosinophilic granuloma, there are no systemic symptoms and the swollen mastoid is not tender. There may be discharge from the ear and granulation in the middle ear and external canal.

When the disorder affects the squama, eosinophilic granuloma causes lytic areas of variable size. There is no reactive new bone at the margins of the lesion.

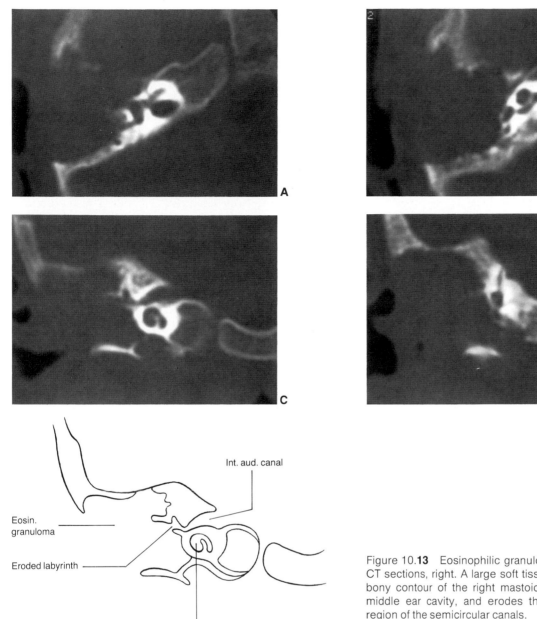

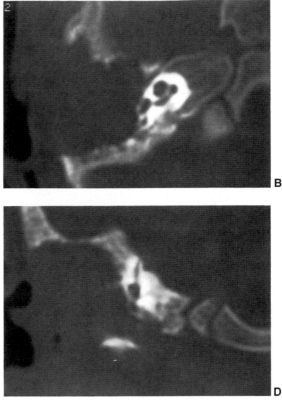

Int. aud. canal

Eosin.
granuloma

Eroded labyrinth

Cochlea   E

Figure 10.13   Eosinophilic granuloma. **A**, **B** axial, **C**, **D** coronal
CT sections, right. A large soft tissue mass fills and destroys the
bony contour of the right mastoid, external auditory canal, and
middle ear cavity, and erodes the labyrinthine capsule in the
region of the semicircular canals.
E Drawing of **C**.

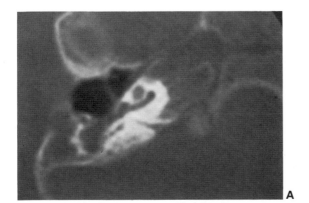

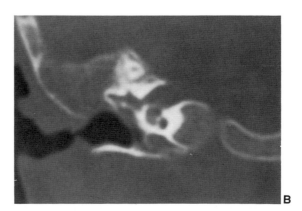

Figure 10.14   Eosinophilic granuloma. **A** axial, **B** coronal CT
sections, right, same ear as Fig. 10.13. Follow-up study 4 months
later following radiation therapy treatment. There has been a
dramatic improvement due to marked shrinkage of the soft tissue
mass and partial remineralization of the involved portion of the
temporal bone.

Glomus Tumors

Glomus tumors, also called chemodectomas and non-chromaffin paragangliomas, are benign tumors arising in the middle ear or jugular fossa from minute glomus bodies which are found chiefly in the jugular fossa and on the promontory of the middle ear.

The symptomatology depends on the site and size of the lesion. Lesions arising in the jugular fossa, called glomus jugulare tumors, encroach upon the adjacent cranial nerves and may cause paralysis of these nerves. The tumor usually involves the middle ear, where it may cause conductive deafness by encroaching upon the ossicular chain. As the lesion enlarges, it extends into the mastoid and external auditory canal. Involvement of the labyrinth causes tinnitus, sensorineural deafness, and vertigo. Glomus tympanicum is a lesion that arises from glomus bodies along the Jacobson's nerve on the promontory. Early, these lesions are small and confined to the middle ear, where they may encroach upon the ossicles. If the lesion enlarges inferiorly and destroys the hypotympanic floor, it becomes indistinguishable from a glomus jugulare tumor.

Otoscopic Findings

The characteristic finding of a glomus tumor is the presence of a reddish purple mass in the middle ear. In the early stages, the mass lies medial to the intact tympanic membrane. Contact of the tumor with the tympanic membrane often causes a curvilinear air-tumor interface. Since both glomus jugular and glomus tympanicum tumors arise in the inferior portion of the middle ear, otoscopic differentiation between the two types is impossible.

As the lesions enlarge, the tympanic membrane is sloughed, and reddish purple polypoid masses appear in the external auditory canal. These polypoid lesions bleed easily and profusely when manipulated, while inflammatory polyps of chronic otitis media bleed only slightly. The diagnosis should be confirmed by biopsy. This procedure should be performed after radiographic evaluation to avoid obscuring the mass by hemorrhage.

When confined to the middle ear and lying behind an intact tympanic membrane, the otoscopic appearance of a glomus tumor may be confused with a high jugular bulb, an ectopic internal carotid artery or with a cholesterol granuloma of the middle ear (Figs. 10.15, 10.16). See also pages 60–64.

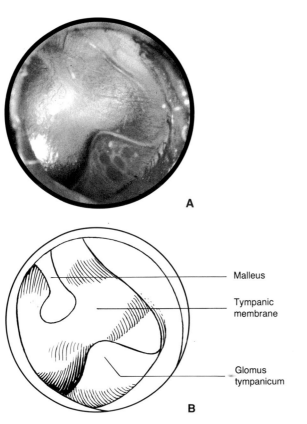

Figure 10.**15** **A** Glomus tympanicum, otoscopic findings, left. A purple-red mass lies in the inferior portion of the middle ear in contact with the tympanic membrane.
B Diagram of **A**.

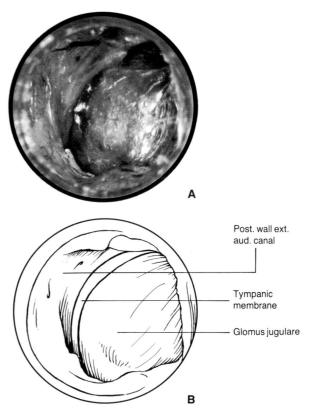

Figure 10.**16** **A** Glomus jugulare tumor, otoscopic findings, right.
A large glomus jugulare fills the middle ear and herniates the tympanic membrane into the external auditory canal. The lesion has a characteristic red-purple color of glomus tumors.
B Diagram of **A**.

Imaging Techniques

CT is the most useful technique for the diagnosis and evaluation of the extent of glomus tumors. MR is indicated in large tumors. Arteriography and retrograde venography have been largely supplanted by CT and MR.

CT

Axial and coronal CT sections before and after bolus injection of contrast are indicated. Images are studied for soft tissue and bone. A dynamic CT study of a preselected section showing the tumor mass will differentiate a glomus tumor from other vascular lesions such as high jugular bulb. The computer generated density time curve reveals a high, early, quasiarterial peak, rather than a delayed venous peak of a high jugular bulb, Figs. 10.19, 10.23.

MR

An MR ist best performed with surface coils to obtain better tumor definition. The tumor mass appears as a mass of medium signal intensity different from surrounding structures. With this technique, involvement of the jugular vein or carotid artery can be seen, since these vessels are visible in MR without the need for contrast injection (Figs. 10.22, 10.24).

Arteriography

Arteriography is indicated to identify the feeding vessels of the glomus tumor prior to embolization or surgical ligation and tumor removal. Common carotid artery injection is used to visualize feeding vessels, which can come from both the external and internal carotids. The ascending pharyngeal artery is the most common feeder. A vertebral arteriogram will visualize feeders from the vertebro-basal circulation.

Subtraction should be used to delineate the vascular mass and feeding vessels otherwise obscured by the density of the surrounding temporal bone (Fig. 10.25).

Retrograde Venography

Retrograde jugular venography is seldom indicated since MR images can visualize tumor extension into the vein (Figs. 10.26).

The study is done by percutaneous puncture of the jugular vein with a Seldinger needle. The stylet is withdrawn and a guide wire is advanced through the needle lumen into the internal jugular vein to the bony roof of the jugular fossa. The needle is removed, and a radiopaque polyethylene catheter is threaded into the jugular vein over the guide wire, which is in turn removed.

Imaging Findings

Glomus Tympanicum (Fig. 10.15)

CT and MR are important in establishing the diagnosis and essential in determining the size and extent of the lesion (Figs. 10.17–10.19).

In glomus tympanicum, CT examination shows a soft tissue mass of variable size usually in the lower portion of the tympanic cavity. When inflammation or serous fluid fills the middle ear and surrounds the tumor, the contour of the mass is obscured. A large glomus tympanicum filling the entire middle ear causes a bulge of the tympanic membrane laterally and a concave erosion of the bone of the promontory. The lesion may also extend posteriorly into the mastoid and inferiorly into the hypotympanic cells. The floor of the hypotympanum is usually intact. Should the lesion erode into the jugular fossa, the tumor becomes indistinguishable from a glomus jugulare.

Subtraction arteriography demonstrates the vascular mass in the middle ear and the supplying vessels. Jugular venography will be negative.

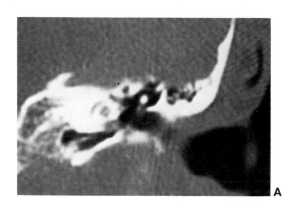
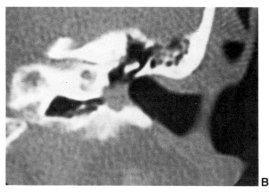

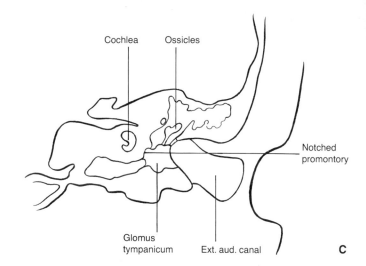

Figure 10.**17**   Glomus tympanicum. **A**, **B** coronal, CT sections, left.

An enhanced soft tissue mass fills the lower portion of the mesotympanum. The mass bulges the tympanic membrane laterally, notches the promontory medially, and impinges on the incudostapedial joint. The jugular fossa is uninvolved.

C Diagram of **B**.

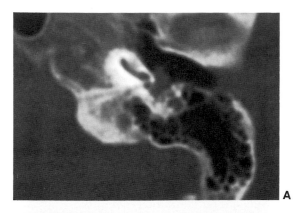

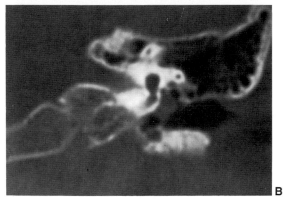

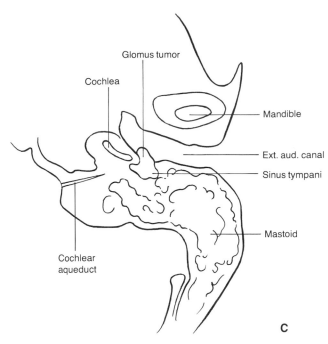

Figure 10.**18**   Glomus tympanicum. **A** axial, **B** coronal, CT sections, left.
A well defined and enhancing soft tissue mass lies in the posterior portion of the mesotympanum. The lesion extends into the sinus tympani. The jugular fossa and carotid canal are normal.
C Diagram of **A**.

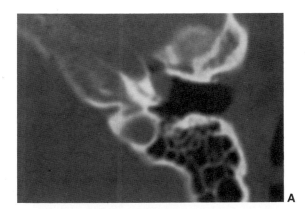

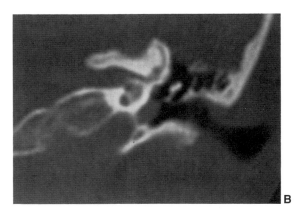

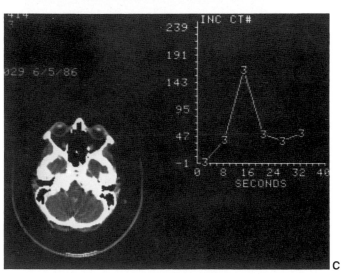

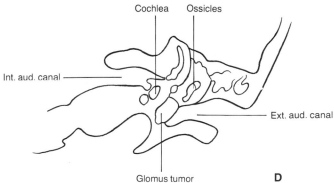

Figure 10.**19**   Glomus tympanicum tumor. **A** axial, **B** coronal CT sections, and **C** dynamic circulation study, left. A well defined soft tissue mass lies in the inferior portion of the mesotympanum. The remainder of the middle ear is aerated and no bony erosion is identified. The carotid canal is in normal position. The dynamic circulation study reveals the tumor to be highly vascular with an arterial peak time.
D Diagram of **B**.

Glomus Jugulare (Fig. 10.**16**)

Typical CT findings of a glomus jugulare tumor are (Figs. 10.**20**–10.**24**):

1. Erosion of the cortical outline and enlargement of the jugular fossa. The size of the jugular fossa is extremely variable, and asymmetry of the two jugular fossae is a common finding. A large jugular fossa is not indicative of a glomus tumor unless there is associated cortical erosion.
2. Erosion of the triangular bony septum which divides the jugular fossa from the outer opening of the carotid canal. This finding appears on sagittal images.
3. Erosion of the floor of the middle ear cavity.
4. An enhancing soft tissue mass of variable size projecting into the middle ear cavity from the jugular fossa. The mass may extend superiorly to encroach upon the ossicular chain. Further extension may occur into the mastoid. Lateral extension of the mass erodes the tympanic membrane and fills the external canal.
5. Erosion of the posteroinferior aspect of the petrous pyramid. This is typical of medial extension of the glomus. The glomus first undermines the posteroinferior aspect of the petrosa and erodes the external aperture of the cochlear aqueduct (Figs. 10.**21**–10.**23**). Further enlargement of the lesion leads to partial or complete destruction of the petrous apex. The labyrinth becomes skeletonized, but is seldom invaded.
6. The adjacent aspect of the occipital bone is also involved and gradually eroded in large lesions. Further medial extension involves the hypoglossal canal and reaches the foramen magnum.
7. Large tumors erode the posterior aspect of the petrous pyramid and protrude extradurally into the posterior fossa (Figs. 10.**21**–10.**23**).
8. Inferior extension within and along the jugular vein occurs at times. Such extension is better visualized in MR, since with CT, not only the tumor enhances, but also the adjacent musculature which impairs tumor delineation.

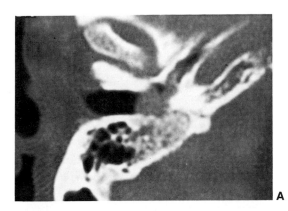

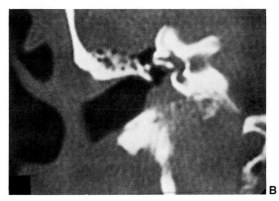

Figure 10.20   Glomus jugulare. **A** axial, **B** coronal, CT sections, right.
The jugular fossa is enlarged, the hypotympanic floor eroded and the hypotympanic cells cloudy. An enhancing soft tissue mass protrudes into the inferior mesotympanum and displaces the tympanic membrane laterally.
C Diagram of **B**.

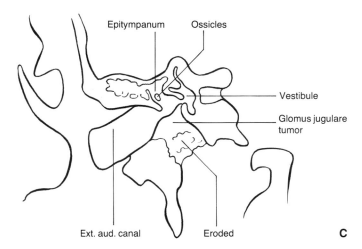

MR Imaging

MR is indicated for large glomus jugulare tumors with extratemporal extension. The tumor appears in both T1 and T2 images as a non-homogeneous mass of medium signal intensity. Several small areas of void or no signal are scattered throughout the tumor mass, produced by intralesional blood vessels. The signal intensity is easily differentiated from surrounding intracranial and extracranial soft tissues (Figs. 10.22, 10.24).

The main advantage of MR is that the jugular vein and the internal carotid artery are visualized without need for invasive vascular procedures. MR will demonstrate displacement, narrowing, encroachment or obstruction and thrombosis of these vessels. Extension of the tumor within the lumen of the vessels can be clearly identified. When extensive skull-base surgery is contemplated, it is essential to know precisely if the great vessels are compromised by tumor.

Jugular Venography

When the jugular vein is involved, retrograde jugular venography will show any partial or complete obstruction in a vessel. When MR is not available, venography is the best method to demonstrate a downward extension of a glomus tumor into the neck within the lumen or along the wall of the jugular vein. This information is necessary to outline the inferior margin of the radiotherapy ports.

Arteriography

Subtraction arteriography is not required to diagnose the glomus tumor, but as indicated it identifies feeding vessels of the lesion prior to embolization or surgical ligations.

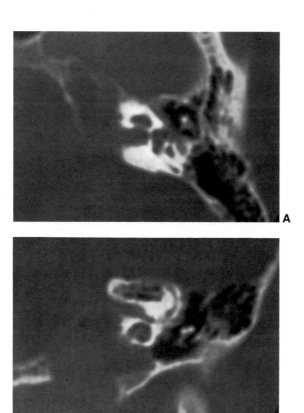
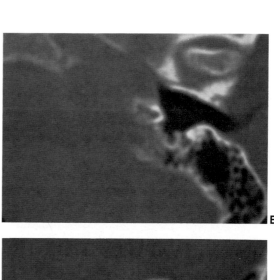
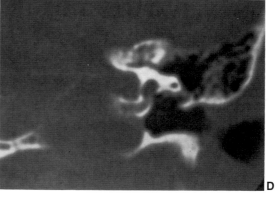
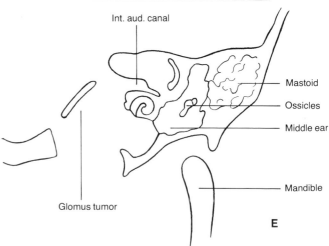
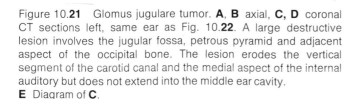

Figure 10.21   Glomus jugulare tumor. **A, B** axial, **C, D** coronal CT sections left, same ear as Fig. 10.**22**. A large destructive lesion involves the jugular fossa, petrous pyramid and adjacent aspect of the occipital bone. The lesion erodes the vertical segment of the carotid canal and the medial aspect of the internal auditory but does not extend into the middle ear cavity. **E** Diagram of **C**.

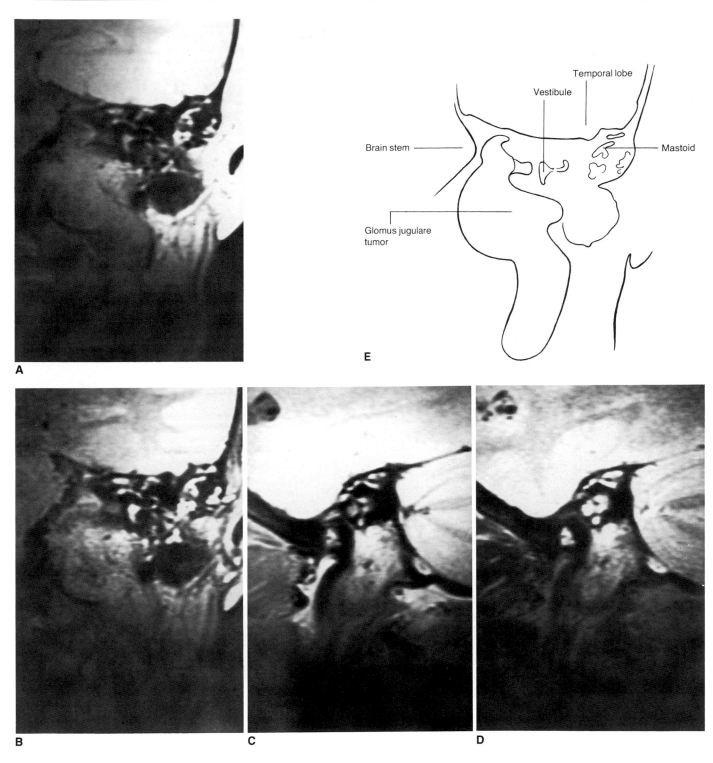

Figure 10.**22**   Glomus jugulare tumor. **A**, **B** coronal, **C, D** sagittal MR sections, left, same ear as Fig. 10.**21**. **A** and **C** spin density weighted and **B** and **D** T2 surface coil images.

A large soft tissue mass extends from the jugular fossa into the petrous pyramid. The mass is characterized by mixed intensity signals in both sequences and contains several void areas, presumably blood vessels. The tumor obstructs the jugular bulb and reaches but does not involve the carotid artery.
E Diagram of **A**.

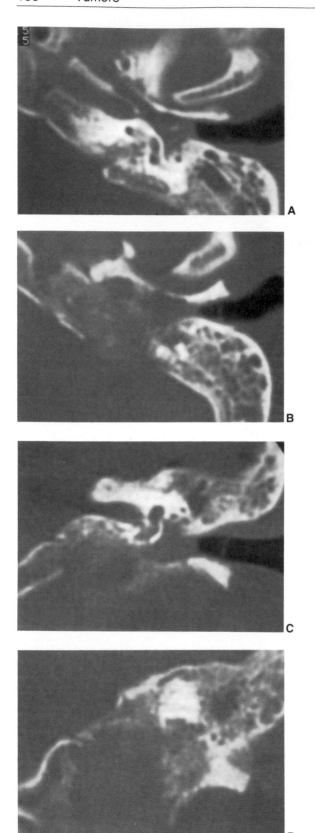

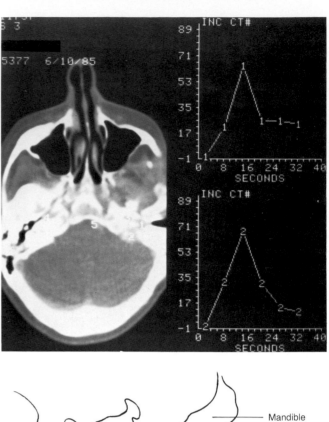

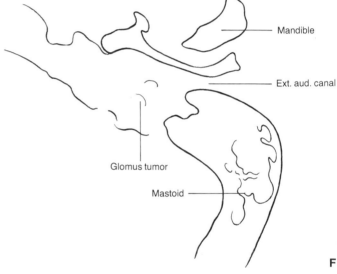

Figure 10.**23** Glomus jugulare tumor. **A**, **B** axial, **B, C** coronal CT sections, left and, **E,** dynamic circulation study, same ear as Fig. 10.**24**. The jugular fossa is enlarged and its bony contour eroded. The tumor infiltrates into the sublabyrinthine and perifacial air cells and involves the mastoid segment of the facial canal. The hypotympanic floor is eroded and a large soft tissue mass fills the mesotympanum and bulges laterally into the external auditory canal. The dynamic circulation study, **E**, shows the tumor mass to be highly vascular and having an arterial peak time.
F Diagram of **B**.

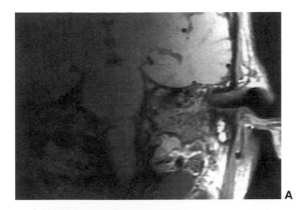

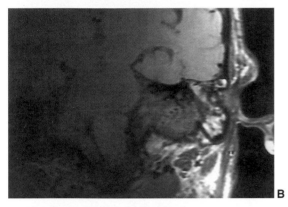

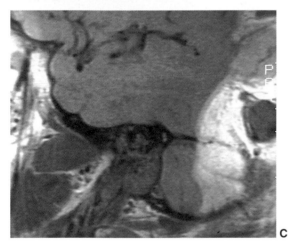

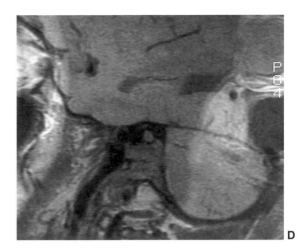

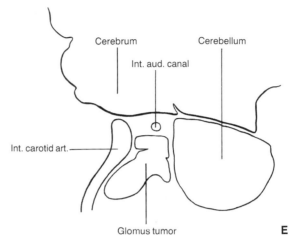

Cerebrum   Cerebellum

Int. aud. canal

Int. carotid art.

Glomus tumor   E

Figure 10.**24**   Glomus jugulare tumor. **A**, **B** coronal, **C**, **D** sagittal T1 surface coil MR sections, left, same ear as Fig. 10.**23**. A large soft tissue mass involves the undersurface of the entire left temporal bone and extends into the middle ear cavity. The mass is characterized by a signal of medium intensity and contains several dark areas, presumably blood vessels. Notice that the jugular bulb and adjacent portion of the jugular vein are obliterated by the tumor, while the carotid artery, **D**, is not involved. The brighter signal within the mastoid air cells is due to fluid.
E Diagram of **D**.

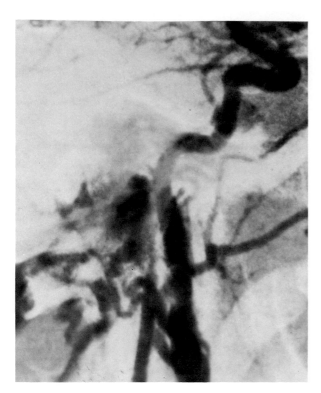

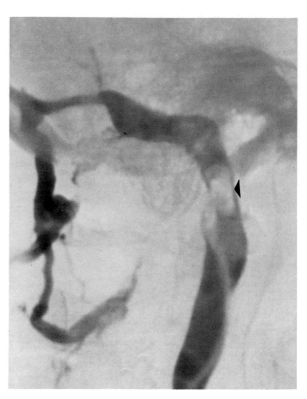

Figure 10.**25**   Glomus jugulare, carotid angiogram with subtraction, right.
A vascular mass lies in relation to the inferior aspect of the petrous pyramid. The ascending pharyngeal artery, which feeds the glomus tumor, is dilated.

Figure 10.**26**   Glomus jugulare, retrograde venogram, right.
A filling defect, arrow, is present in the jugular vein 1 cm below the dome of the jugular bulb.

Malignant Tumors

Primary Malignancies

Carcinoma

Carcinomas of the temporal bone arise chiefly from the external auditory canal. Primary carcinomas of the middle ear cavity are extremely rare since most middle ear carcinomas actually begin in the external canal at the anulus and infiltrate from there. Carcinomas of the canal tend to infiltrate and spread deep into the surrounding portions of the temporal bone. The predominant symptoms are pain and bleeding. Since there is no subcutaneous tissue between the skin and the periosteum of the external canal, carcinomas infiltrate the periosteum early, causing severe pain (Fig. 10.28).

Extension

Carcinomas of the external canal can extend anteriorly into the temporomandibular joint, posteriorly into the mastoid and facial nerve, inferiorly into the neck and medially into the middle ear. Further medial extension involves the jugular fossa and the petrous pyramid.

Otoscopic Findings

Otoscopically in carcinoma of the external canal, there is a granular ulcerating lesion that bleeds easily on contact with an instrument. All such granular lesions of the external and middle ear should be biopsied (Fig. 10.27).

Figure 10.27 Carcinoma of the external auditory canal, otoscopic findings, right. A large granular squamous carinoma fills the external auditory canal.

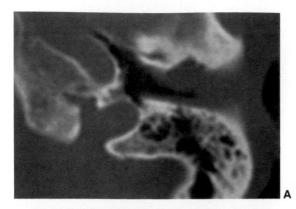

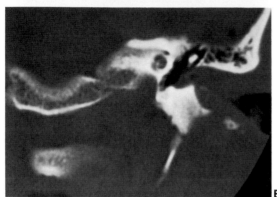

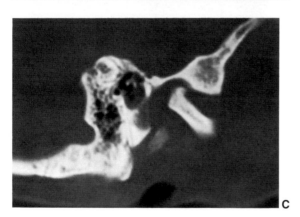

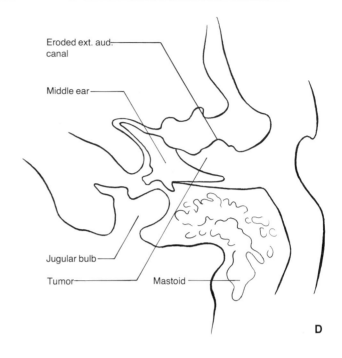

Figure 10.**28** Carcinoma, external auditory canal. **A** axial, **B** coronal, **C** direct sagittal CT sections, left. The left external auditory canal appears enlarged due to erosion of the lateral portion of its floor and inferior portion of its anterior wall by the malignant tumor. A soft tissue mass fills the lumen of the canal but does not extend into the middle ear cavity, which appears intact.

D Diagram of **A**.

Imaging Assessment

The role of CT in temporal bone carcinomas is twofold: to demonstrate bony erosions characteristic of carcinomas and to delineate the extent of the lesion. This information will enable the surgeon to determine the resectability of the lesion. When radiotherapy is indicated, the radiographic evaluation will help in establishing the size of the treatment ports.

CT examination consists of axial and coronal sections. Contrast enhancement will demonstrate extratemporal extension of the lesion. Direct or reformated sagittal sections should be obtained for study of the vertical portion of the facial nerve canal.

Findings

In an early lesion, CT will show an irregular soft tissue mass within the external canal and erosion and destruction of portions of the bony wall.

Spread of tumor through the anterior canal wall will result in erosion of the temporomandibular fossa and anterior displacement of the condyle.

Extension into the mastoid causes a typical moth-eaten appearance of the bone.

The vertical segment of the facial canal is involved most commonly in posterior extensions.

As the lesion extends medially there will be a soft tissue mass in the middle ear. From the middle ear, the lesion often extends inferiorly into the jugular fossa or medially into the petrous pyramid. Petrous extension usually results in skeletonization of the labyrinth, since the otic capsule is relatively resistant to infiltration.

Far advanced carcinomas cause massive destruction of the temporal bone and adjacent bony structures. In these cases CT and MR will demonstrate intracranial and neck extension of the tumor.

Sarcoma

Sarcomas of the temporal bone are extremely rare. They usually occur in children and arise from the middle ear or petrous pyramid. Histologically they are rhabdomyosarcoma, fibrosarcoma, lymphosarcoma, osteogenic sarcoma, chondrosarcoma and undifferentiated sarcoma.

Imaging Technique

CT studies consist of axial and coronal sections. Infusion studies and MR will demonstrate intra- and extracranial extensions of the lesion.

Findings

If the lesion originates in the middle ear, there will be a soft tissue mass which often causes lateral bulging of the tympanic membrane. The mastoid air cells appear cloudy in early lesions, but with growth of the tumor they are destroyed.

The external auditory canal is usually intact. Sarcomas tend to spread into the eustachian tube. Sar-

comas that arise in the nasopharynx and eustachian tube extend retrogradely to involve the middle ear and temporal bone.

The pyramid is often completely destroyed either by lesions arising in the petrosa or by extension of the highly malignant tumor from the middle ear.

Secondary Malignancies

Secondary involvement of the temporal bone by malignant tumors occurs by direct extension from lesions in adjacent structures and by metastases.

Direct Extension

The most common lesion that involves the temporal bone by direct extension is carcinoma of the parotid. As the lesion extends upwards from the parotid, it involves the base of the skull and the temporal bone. The floor of the external canal and the inferior surface of the mastoid are usually eroded by tumor. The lesion may obstruct the external auditory canal. Involvement of the stylomastoid foramen will cause facial nerve paralysis. These tumors have a tendency to spread from the foramen along the facial nerve and erode and expand the facial nerve canal (Fig. 10.29).

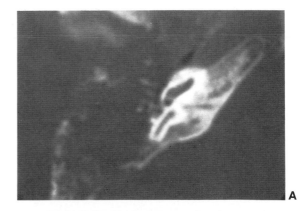

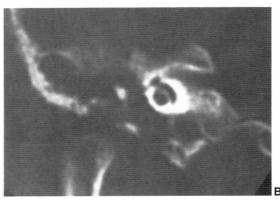

Figure 10.**29**   Recurrent carcinoma of the parotid, post radiation therapy. **A** axial, **B** coronal CT sections, right. A large soft tissue mass fills the external auditory canal, mastoid, and middle ear cavity, destroying the bony boundaries of these structures. The lesion involves the labyrinthine capsule in the region of the horizontal semicircular canal. The moth-eaten destruction of the temporal squama is presumably due to radionecrosis.

CT will demonstrate erosions of the temporal bone. Enhanced CT combined with sialography or MR will demonstrate the site and extent of the parotid tumor.

Metastatic Extension

The most common metastatic lesion of the temporal bone is carcinoma of the breast. Lung, prostate, and kidney and other lesions also metastasize to the temporal bone (Figs. 10.30, 10.31). Any area of the temporal bone may be involved, and symptomatology varies depending on the location of the lesion. The lesion may be destructive, as with lung metastasis, osteoblastic as with carcinoma of the prostate, or mixed, destructive and sclerotic, as with breast carcinoma.

CT or MR should be performed to rule out intracranial extension of the temporal bone lesion and to establish the extent of the temporal bone involvement. CT also helps to rule out the presence of other intracranial metastases.

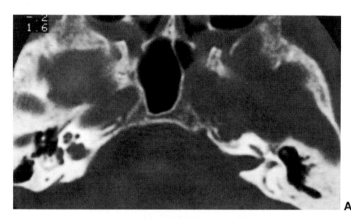

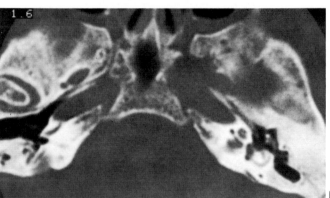

Figure 10.**30**   Metastatic carcinoma of the lung, **A**, **B** axial CT sections. A large destructive lesion involves the left petrous apex, clivus, and floor of the middle cranial fossa including the foramen ovale. The lesion extends into the left sphenoid sinus.
C Diagram of **B**.

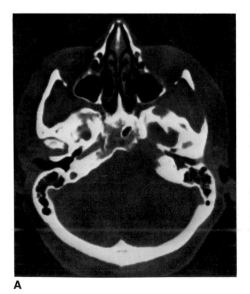

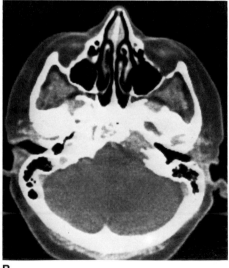

Figure 10.**31**   Metastatic carcinoma of the breast. **A**, **B** axial, CT sections. A large destructive lesion involves the left petrous pyramid, clivus, and adjacent floor of the middle cranial fossa. An enhanced soft tissue mass fills the bony apical defect, **B**.

Chapter 11 Internal Auditory Canal and Acoustic Neuroma

Acoustic neuromas are the cause of unilateral sensorineural hearing loss and vestibular function loss in approximately 10% of the patients with these presenting symptoms.

Acoustic neuromas usually arise within the lumen of the internal auditory meatus and, as they slowly enlarge, erode the bony margins of the meatus. Erosion of the meatus is visible radiographically. Acoustic neuromas account for approximately 10% of all intracranial tumors and 90% of all cerebellopontine angle tumors.

An acoustic neuroma is a benign, encapsulated, slowly growing tumor of one of the branches of the eight cranial nerve. The lesion arises from proliferation of the neurilemmal or Schwann cells. Histologically, the tumors are made up of streams of elongated spindle cells with fairly large nuclei, which often are arranged in a palisading pattern. The larger tumors may undergo cystic degenerative changes within the tumor mass. Approximately two thirds of acoustic neuromas arise from the vestibular division of the eighth nerve and one third from the cochlear division. Most acoustic nerve tumors arise within the lumen of the internal auditory canal at the junction between the neurilemmal sheaths deriving from the peripheral ganglia and the neuroglial fibers which extend peripherally from the brainstem. Early growth of an acoustic neuroma occurs within the lumen of the internal auditory canal without producing significant symptoms until the perineural subarachnoid space is filled with tumor mass. Once the lesion has expanded to come in contact with the walls of the internal auditory canal, pressure of the growing tumor results in erosion of the walls of the internal auditory canal and consequent enlargement of the canal. A few acoustic neuromas arise within the cerebellopontine cistern and do not extend into the internal auditory canal. Other lesions that occur in the cistern and mimic acoustic neuromas clinically are meningioma, epidermoids, and arachnoid cysts.

Bilateral acoustic neuromas are extremely rare except in patients with neurofibromatosis.

The most common initial symptom of an acoustic neuroma is unilateral sensorineural hearing loss. Vestibular disturbances such as mild dizziness and a sensation of imbalance occasionally occur as the first symptoms. The otolaryngologist is usually the first physician to see these patients.

The otolaryngologist uses a series of hearing tests that help in differentiating cochlear from retrocochlear lesions and in selecting patients for referral for imaging studies. The commonly used tests are pure tone air and bone conduction audiometry, speech discrimination tests, adaptation tests such as the tone decay test, tympanometric stapedial reflex measurements, and brainstem evoked responses.

Caloric tests and electronystagmography determine the function of the vestibular portion of the eighth nerve. Vestibular function is abnormal in over 80% of acoustic neuromas. The facial nerve is rarely involved in neuromas because of the resistance of the motor fibers of the seventh nerve to pressure.

As the neuromas grow, they extend medially into the cerebellopontine angle. Upward extension of the lesion causes pressure on the fifth cranial nerve. Loss of the cranial corneal reflex on the ipsilateral side may be the first sign of pressure on the fifth nerve.

Further enlargement of the tumor mass will produce encroachment on other cranial nerves with paralytic lesions of fifth through twelfth nerves. Encroachment on the cerebellum and brainstem likewise occurs in larger lesions. Far advanced lesions of this severity fortunately are rarely seen today because of improved methods for early diagnosis.

With early diagnosis, increased cerebrospinal fluid pressure and papilledema occur extremely rarely. Cerebrospinal fluid proteins are elevated only in the larger tumors.

Normal Internal Auditory Canal

The petrous pyramids lie in the base of the skull at approximately 45° to the sagittal plane of the skull. The internal auditory canal enters the petrous pyramid from the posteromedial surface, at the junction of the anterior two fifths with the posterior three fifths of the long axis of the pyramid. The long axis of the canal forms a right angle with the sagittal plane of the skull and an angle of about 45° with the long axis of the petrous pyramid (Fig. 11.1–11.3).

The opening or porus of the canal is shaped much like the bevel of a needle, with the maximum diameter in the same axis as the petrous pyramid. The posterior, superior, and inferior lips of the porus are prominent and are made up of dense bone. The anterior lip is usually poorly demarcated because the anterior wall of the canal blends smoothly with the posteromedial surface of the petrous bone.

The internal auditory canal contains the facial nerve, the nervus intermedius, the acoustic nerve, consist-ing of cochlear and vestibular portions, and the internal auditory artery. The nerves are enclosed within a common arachnoid sheath.

In approximately 20% of normal ears, the anterior inferior cerebellar artery loops into the canal.

Imaging Techniques

Imaging studies are essential in the diagnosis of acoustic neuromas and other lesions of the cerebellopontine angle. The techniques used for the study of the internal auditory canal and cerebellopontine angle cistern are conventional radiography, CT and MR.

Conventional Radiography

Conventional x-ray projections are unsatisfactory except for visualizing gross enlargements of the internal auditory canal. Superimposition of petrous air cells and other structures obscure the details of the internal canals. The transorbital and Towne views

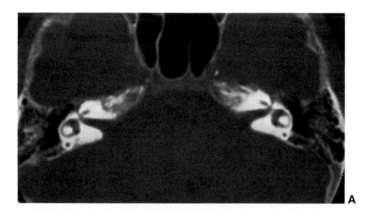
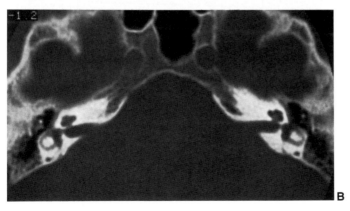

Figure 11.**1** Normal internal auditory canal. **A**, **B** axial CT sections.
A Section through the upper compartment of the internal auditory canal. The facial nerve canal extends from the fundus of the canal to the geniculate ganglion area.
B Section crossing the inferior compartment of the canal shows the opening at the base of the modiolus for the cochlear nerve. The opening of the internal auditory canal has a bevel shape with the posterior wall forming a sharp margin, while the anterior margin blends smoothly with the posteromedial surface of the petrous bone.

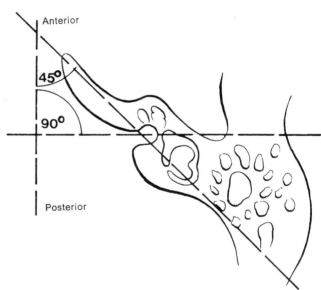

Figure 11.**2** Diagram of internal auditory canal relationship. The long axis of the petrous pyramid forms an approximately 45° angle with the sagittal plane. The internal auditory canal enters the pyramid at an angle of 90° to the sagittal plane.

demonstrate the full length of the canal. The Stenvers projection shows the porus of the internal canal, but the canal appears foreshortened.

CT

CT has replaced multidirectional tomography in the study of the internal auditory canals. In order to evaluate the entire contour of the internal auditory canal, both axial and coronal sections 1.5 mm apart are taken through the canal. Anterior and posterior canal walls are seen in axial sections, and the superior and inferior walls appear in the coronal sections.

CT studies should be performed on all patients with unilateral sensorineural hearing and vestibular losses of unknown origin. Audiometric and vestibular tests have a high degree of sensitivity but cannot provide a definitive diagnosis of acoustic neuroma.

Both sides should always be examined for comparison. The two internal auditory canals of the same patient normally are symmetrical. But variations of the sizes and shapes of the internal auditory canals of different patients are very common and often quite pronounced. There are several factors to consider in evaluating the internal auditory canal: shape, diameter, length, cortical outline, and position of the crista falciformis. Both internal auditory canals of the same patient must be compared to determine significant differences.

The shape of the normal internal auditory canals viewed on CT varies considerably from one patient to the next, but must be the same for the two canals of the individual patient. In 50% of the cases, the canals are cylindrical, and the vertical diameter is the same throughout the length of the canal. In 25%, the canals have an oval shape and the middle portion is larger than the medial and lateral ends. In the remaining 25%, the canals taper either medially or laterally.

The vertical diameter of the normal internal auditory canal may vary from 2–12 mm and the mean diameter is about 5 mm. In 95% of normal patients, the difference between the paired internal auditory canals does

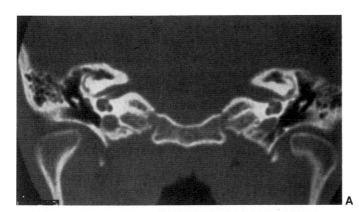
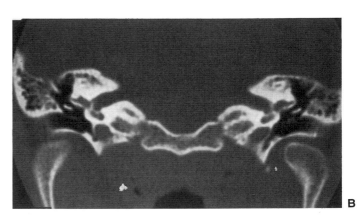
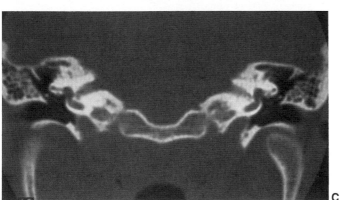
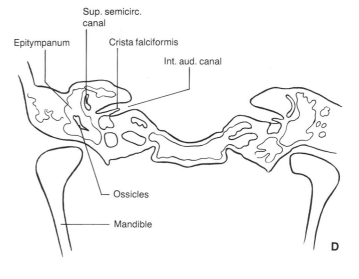

Figure 11.**3** Normal internal auditory canal. **A, B, C** coronal CT sections.
A The most anterior section shows the crista falciformis dividing the lateral portion of the canals.
B Midcanal section, **C** posterior section showing the posterior wall of the internal auditory canal.
D Diagram of **A**.

not exceed 1 mm. Measurement should be obtained in comparable sections at points equidistant from each vestibule.

The length of the canal is the shortest distance between the vestibule and the medial lip of the posterior wall. The length ranges from 4–15 mm with a mean of 8 mm. Again both sides must be compared. In 95% of normal patients, there is a 2 mm or less difference in the length of the posterior wall of the two canals.

The normal internal auditory canal is surrounded by a layer of well defined cortical bone, which is particularly evident when the canal is surrounded by diploic or pneumatized bone.

The crista falciformis is a horizontal bony septum dividing the lateral portion of the internal auditory canal into a smaller upper and larger lower compartment. The position of the crista should be above the midpoint of the vertical diameter and should be symmetrical in the two canals.

Abnormal Internal Auditory Canal

The internal auditory canal is enlarged in 75 to 80% of acoustic neuromas (Figs. 11.4, 11.7). In the remaining 20 to 25% of tumors, the two canals are symmetrical,

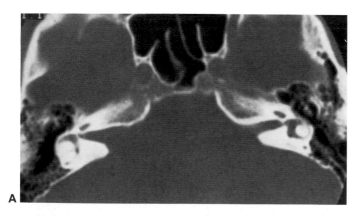
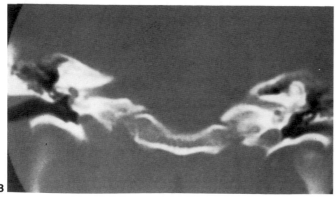

Figure 11.4　Acoustic neuroma right. **A** axial, **B** coronal CT sections. The right internal auditory canal is enlarged and wider than the left. The posterior wall of the right canal is blunted and slightly shorter than the left **A**.

or the difference in size is within the limits of normal variation. Changes in the bony contour of the internal auditory canal depend on the size and site of the lesion. Tumors limited within the internal canal often cause bowing of the canal walls, which gives the canal an oval contour. Lesions extending into the cerebellopontine cistern erode the medial portion of the canal, and the canal becomes funnel shaped. Canal measurements must be corrected for the magnification factor of the images.

Widening of 2 mm or more of any portion of one internal auditory canal when compared with the corresponding segment of the opposite canal should cause suspicion of a tumor.

Widening of 1–2 mm of any portion of the canal on the affected side in comparison with the corresponding segment of the opposite side is suggestive, but not conclusive, for a lesion.

Shortening of the posterior wall by at least 3 mm in comparison with the opposite side is usually indicative of a tumor, while shortening of 2–3 mm of the posterior wall is a less positive sign of a lesion. A change in the relationship of the crista falciformis to the superior and inferior canal walls on the affected side of more than 1 mm when compared with a normal side, may indicate the site of origin of the tumor.

Visualization of Acoustic Neuromas

CT combined with infusion of contrast or cisternography, and MR are the most conclusive studies for the diagnosis of cerebellopontine angle masses. These procedures permit precise determination of the size and extent of the lesion and indicate to the surgeon the best surgical approach for tumor removal.

Computerized Tomography

CT examination consists of scans obtained first before and then after drip infusion or bolus injection of contrast material. The first examination shows indirect signs of the tumor mass such as displacement of the fourth ventricle, narrowing of the opposite cerebellopontine cistern by the displaced brainstem, and, in a large lesion, presence of obstructive hydrocephalus. The tumor is usually not recognizable since it is isodense to the surrounding brain structures and is usually not surrounded by edema. The post-infusion study demonstrates the actual tumor mass following enhancement by the contrast material (Figs. 11.5–11.8, 11.17).

Maximal tumor enhancement occurs approximately one-half hour after the infusion, and at this time 1.5 mm axial sections are taken through the cerebellopontine cistern and internal auditory canals. If a tumor is visualized, coronal sections are obtained to show the vertical extent of the tumor. In large lesions, there is a central area of decreased absorption presumed to be produced by cystic degeneration of the tumor.

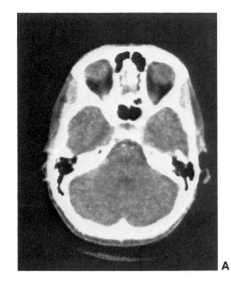 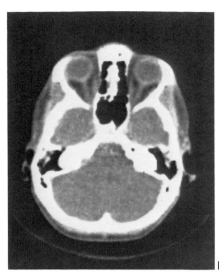

Figure 11.**5** Acoustic neuroma. **A**, **B** axial, post infusion CT, right.
A small enhanced lesion lies at the widened porus of the right internal auditory canal. The small tumor mass protrudes slightly into the cerebellopontine cistern.

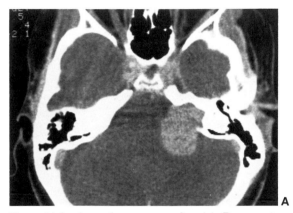 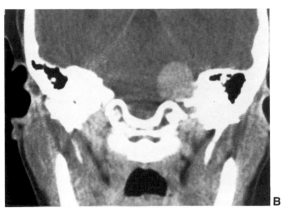

Figure 11.**6** Acoustic neuroma. **A** axial, **B** coronal, post infusion CT, left.

A large tumor mass expands the internal auditory canal and extends deep into the cerebellopontine cistern. The fourth ventricle is compressed.

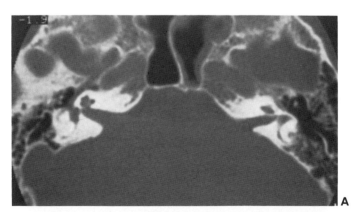 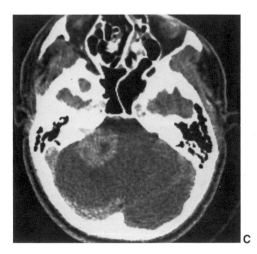

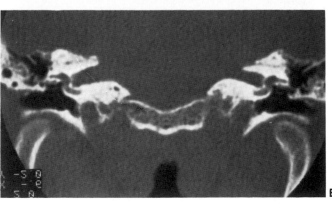

Figure 11.**7** Acoustic neuroma. **A** axial, **B** coronal CT sections of the temporal bones and **C**, post infusion axial section of the posterior cranial fossa. The right internal auditory canal is enlarged and wider than the left, particularly at the medial end and porus. Following infusion of contrast material, a large enhanced mass is noticed in the region of the right cerebellopontine cistern.

Acoustic neuromas smaller than 0.8 cm in the cistern or limited to the internal auditory canal cannot be visualized by this infusion technique. Therefore, a opaque or pneumocisternography is indicated to rule out lesions 0.8 cm or smaller in diameter.

Another important application of CT is for the evaluation of the postoperative patient. In the immediate postoperative period when intracranial complications occur, CT can demonstrate intracranial hemorrhage or brain edema and hydrocephalus. In the late postoperative period when there is a suspicion of recurrent tumor or when a subtotal resection was done, CT with infusion is more valuable than cisternography in delineating the size of the recurrent or residual lesion and in evaluating the progression of the tumor (Fig. 11.8).

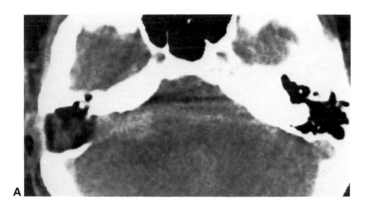

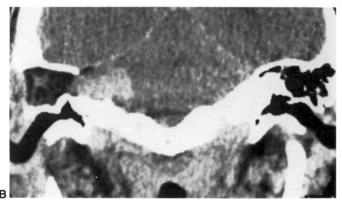

Figure 11.8 Recurrent acoustic neuroma. **A** axial, **B** coronal post infusion CT sections. The surgical defect of a translabyrinthine approach to the internal auditory canal is noticed on the right. The recurrent tumor appears as an enhanced soft tissue mass extending from the medial aspect of the defect into the cerebellopontine cistern.

CT-Pneumocisternography

CT pneumocisternography is best done with a high definition scanner and 1.5 mm sections. Two to three cc of gas are injected by lumbar puncture into the subarachnoid space with the patient in the lateral decubitus position lying on the normal side. Air, CO_2 or O_2 can be used. The patient is instructed to elevate his torso so that he rests on his elbow. At the same time, the chin is tilted upward so that the air will rise into the cerebellopontine angle.

After the air has filled the cerebellopontine angle, the patient again assumes a lateral decubitus position and scans are obtained. The head is then rotated 180 degress, the air shifts to the opposite side, and the normal canal is scanned.

When no tumor is present, the air will outline the contours of the internal canal and cistern. The 7th and 8th cranial nerves are clearly demonstrated as they stretch from the brainstem into the internal auditory canal (Figs. 11.9, 11.10).

When the tumor is very small, air outlines the localized swelling of the nerve within the internal auditory canal. In larger tumors which fill the internal canal completely, CT shows failure of air to enter at the porus (Figs. 11.11–11.16). When the tumor protrudes into the cerebellar pontine cistern, CT shows the contour of the extracanalicular mass and the obstruction of the internal canal. Vascular loops of the anterior inferior cerebellar artery can be visualized when the artery is fixed by adhesions or cross compressed by the 7th and 8th nerves (Fig. 11.18).

Occasionally, air will not enter the internal auditory canal because of the formation of a surface tension membrane at the interface between the gas and the cerebrospinal fluid at the porus. This surface tension membrane bulges laterally and this feature helps to differentiate it from an actual intracanalicular tumor mass.

CT Opaque Cisternography

Amipaque®, a brand of metrizamide, is used for opaque cisternography. This contrast material, while being absorbed rapidly, is a brain irritant at full strength, and, to avoid convulsions, should be used at low concentrations of 170 mgI per ml. We prefer to use gas as a contrast to avoid central nervous system complications.

Another reason for preferring gas is that when the internal auditory canal is narrow, it is easier to recognize a small amount of intracanalicular air than metrizamide. The absorption differential between air and bone is greater than that between metrizamide and bone.

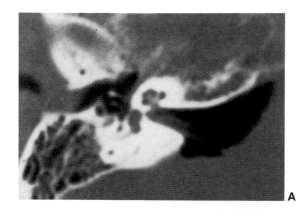

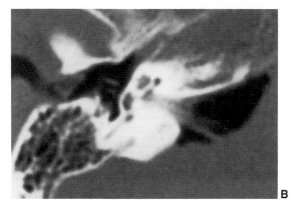

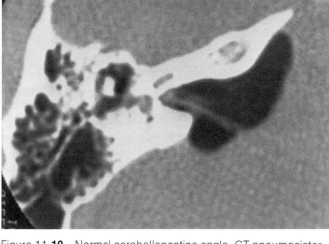

Figure 11.**10**   Normal cerebellopontine angle. CT pneumocister-nography, right.
Pneumocisternography shows that air fills the cistern and the internal auditory canal. The normal 7th and 8th nerves extend from the brainstem to the fundus of the canal.

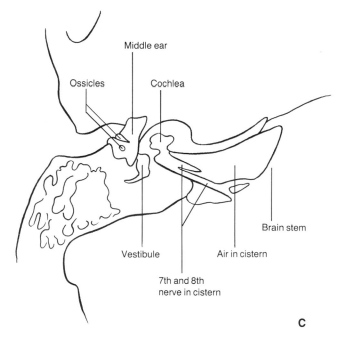

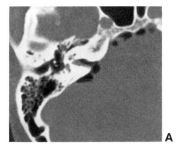

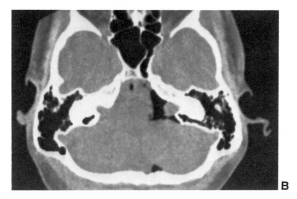

Figure 11.**9**   Normal cerebellopontine pneumocisternogram. **A**, **B** axial CT sections, right. The gas fills the cerebellopontine cistern and the internal auditory canal. The normal 7th and 8th cranial nerves are well visualized as they stretch from the brainstem into the interal auditory canal.
C Diagram of **A**.

Figure 11.**11**   Acoustic neuroma, CT pneumocisternography. **A** right, and **B** left axial CT sections.
The tumor, **B**, enlarges the left internal auditory canal. The air in the cistern outlines the medial aspect of the mass. **A** is the normal right side for comparison.

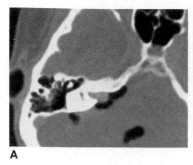
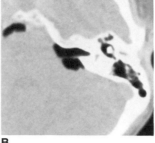

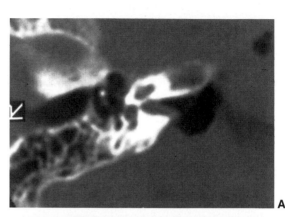

Figure 11.**12** Acoustic neuroma, CT pneumocisternography. **A** right, **B** left axial CT sections.
A small tumor mass, **A**, fills and expands the right internal auditory canal and protrudes into the cerebellopontine cistern. The proximal portion of the 8th nerve is normal and enters the medial aspect of the tumor.
B is the normal left side for comparison.

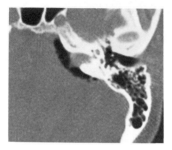

Figure 11.**13** Acoustic neuroma, CT pneumocisternography, left axial CT section.
The air in the cistern outlines the tumor mass, which bulges medially into the cistern from the enlarged internal auditory canal.

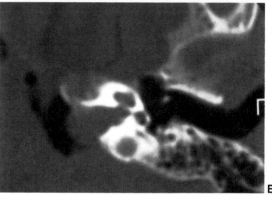

Figure 11.**15** Left acoustic neuroma, bilateral cerebellopontine pneumocisternogram. **A** right, **B** left axial CT sections. A tumor mass fills and expands the left internal auditory canal, **B**. The lesion bulges into the adjacent cerebellopontine cistern but does not reach the brainstem. The right side, **A**, is normal.

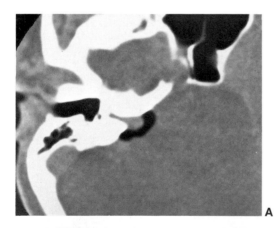

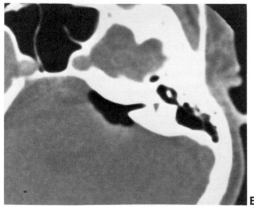

Figure 11.**14** Acoustic neuroma, CT pneumocisternography. **A** right and **B** left axial CT sections.
A small tumor, **A**, fills the internal auditory canal, which is not enlarged. The tumor extends 6 mm into the cistern. **B** is the normal side for comparison.

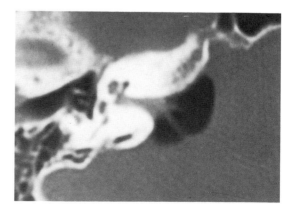

Figure 11.**16** Acoustic neuroma, cerebellopontine pneumocisternogram, axial CT section, right. The tumor mass fills the right internal auditory canal and protrudes slightly into the adjacent cerebellopontine cistern. Notice the uninvolved cisternal portion of the acoustic nerve.

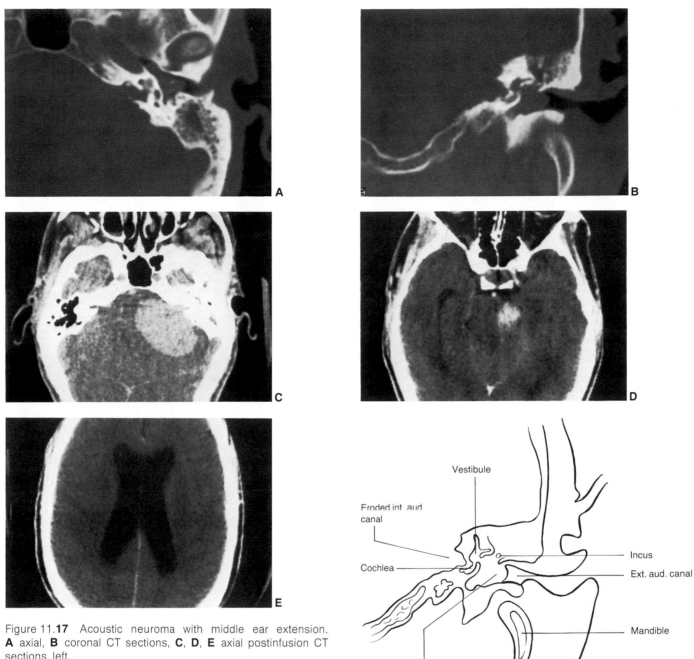

Figure 11.**17** Acoustic neuroma with middle ear extension. **A** axial, **B** coronal CT sections, **C, D, E** axial postinfusion CT sections, left.

A large soft tissue mass fills the left middle ear cavity and bulges into the external auditory canal. The internal auditory canal is expanded and largely eroded, **A, B**. A large enhanced soft tissue mass fills the left cerebellopontine cistern and compresses the brainstem, **C, D**. The mass herniates superiorly through the tentorial notch and causes an obstructive hydrocephalus, **E**.
F Diagram of **B**.

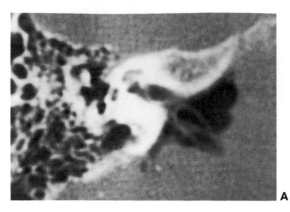

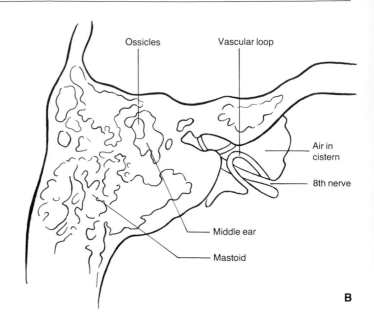

Figure 11.**18** **A** Vascular loop, axial CT cerebellopontine pneumocisternogram, right. The gas fills the right internal auditory canal and cerebellopontine cistern. A large vessel, presumably the anterior cerebellar artery, forms a large loop within the cistern. The vessel crosses and seemly compresses the nerve close to its exit from the brainstem and at the porus of the internal auditory canal.
B Diagram of **A**.

MR

MR is by far the preferred method of detecting and visualizing acoustic tumors without exposing the patient to ionizing radiation and without the necessity of a spinal puncture (Figs. 11.19–11.23). Both large and small tumors can be seen in one diagnostic procedure. Intravenous injection of paramagnetic agents, such as Gadolinium DTPA, have further improved tumor visualization. Both axial and coronal continuous 3 mm sections are taken using two to four excitations and a 256 × 128 matrix. The coronal sections are T1 images (600 TR/25 TE) and axial sections are spin density weighted (2000 TR/20 TE) and T2 (2000 TR/80 TE).

Large neuromas extending in the cerebellopontine cistern are easily recognizable as masses of higher signal intensity than the surrounding brain in the T2 images. In the T1 and spin density weighted images, the tumor mass is isodense to the gray matter. The tumor often impinges and indents the adjacent brainstem or cerebellum and is surrounded by a dark line produced by the infolded meninges (Fig. 11.22).

Smaller tumors with extracanalicular projections are best seen in the T1 and spin density weighted images as masses of higher signal intensity than the surrounding cerebrospinal fluid (Fig. 11.21).

Small intracanalicular lesions are seen in T1 images (Figs. 11.19, 11.20). These small images appear as localized areas of thickening of the 8th nerve or as masses of higher signal intensity than cerebro-spinal fluid, partially or completely filling the internal auditory canal. Small tumors are often completely obscured by the surrounding cerebrospinal fluid in the spin density weighted and T2 images.

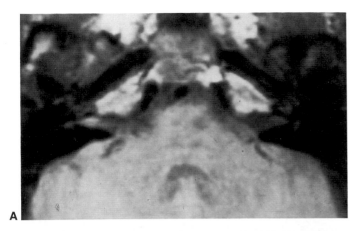

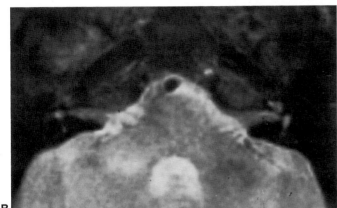

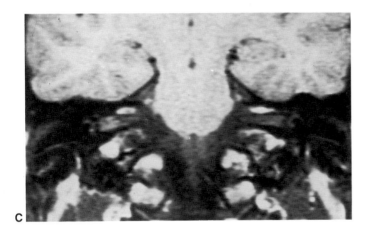

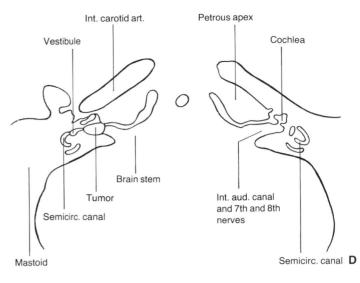

Vestibule

Int. carotid art.

Petrous apex

Cochlea

Brain stem

Tumor

Semicirc. canal

Mastoid

Int. aud. canal
and 7th and 8th
nerves

Semicirc. canal **D**

Figure 11.**19** Acoustic neuroma, intracanalicular. **A** spin density weighted, axial, **B** T2 axial and, **C** T1 coronal MR images, right.

A high signal intensity mass is recognizable in the T1 and spin density weighted images, **A** and **C**, in the lateral portion of the right internal auditory canal, which is slightly expanded. The lesion is obscured by the identical signal intensity of the cerebrospinal fluid in the T2 image, **B**.

D Diagram of **A**.
E Diagram of **C**.

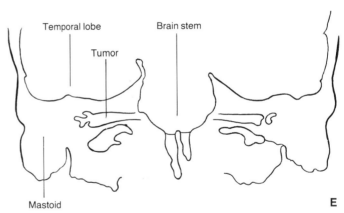

Temporal lobe

Tumor

Brain stem

Mastoid

E

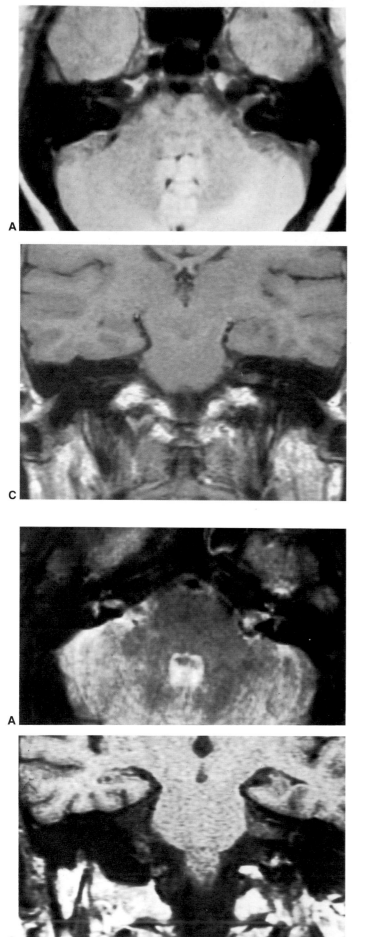

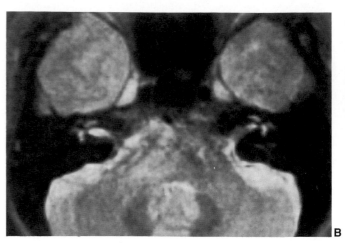

Figure 11.**20** Acoustic neuroma, **A** spinal density weighted, **B** T2 axial, and **C** coronal T1 MR images, left. In the T1 image, a small soft tissue mass is demonstrated within the left internal auditory canal. The lesion is not recognizable in the spin density and T2 weighted images.

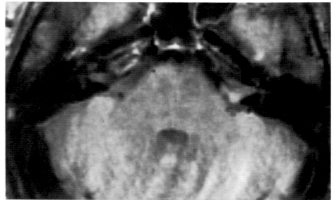

Figure 11.**21** Acoustic neuroma. **A** spin density weighted, **B** T2 axial, **C** T1 coronal, MR images, left.
The left internal auditory canal appears filled and expanded by a soft tissue mass of signal intensity higher than cerebrospinal fluid in the T1 and spin density weighted images, **A** and **C**. The mass bulges into the adjacent cerebellopontine cistern. In the T2 images, **B**, the lesion has the same signal intensity as cerebrospinal fluid, but the extracanalicular component of the mass produces a slight indentation of the brainstem.

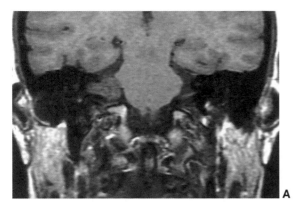

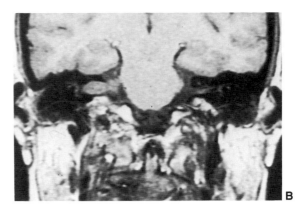

Figure 11.**22** Acoustic neuroma. **A**, **B** coronal MR T1 images. Soft tissue mass of higher signal density than cerebrospinal fluid fills and expands the right internal auditory canal. The mass extends into the cerebellopontine cistern, reaching and indenting the brainstem.

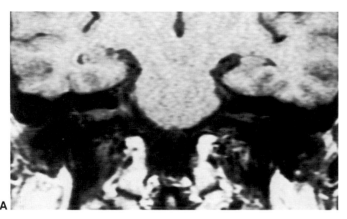

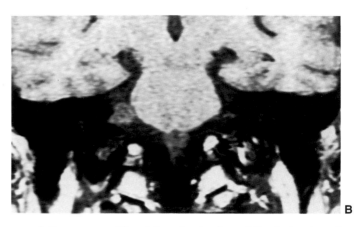

Figure 11.**23** Acoustic neuroma. **A**, **B** coronal T1 MR images, right.
The right internal auditory canal is filled and slightly expanded by a soft tissue mass. The cisternal extension of the lesion is well seen in **B** as a mass of higher signal intensity than the surrounding cerebrospinal fluid.

Chapter 12   Otosclerosis and Bone Dystrophies

Otosclerosis

Otosclerosis is a primary focal disease of the labyrinthine capsule. The otosclerotic foci may be single or multiple and undergo periods of resorption and redeposition of bone at variable intervals. There appears to be an hereditary factor in the etiology. The most common site of a focus is in the labyrinthine capsule just anterior to the oval window. This focus tends to extend posteriorly to fix the stapes footplate and at times invade and thicken the footplate. Similar foci occur in other areas of the labyrinthine capsule, particularly in the cochlea.

Involvement of the oval window with fixation of the stapes causes conductive deafness. Cochlear foci produce sensorineural deafness by an unknown mechanism.

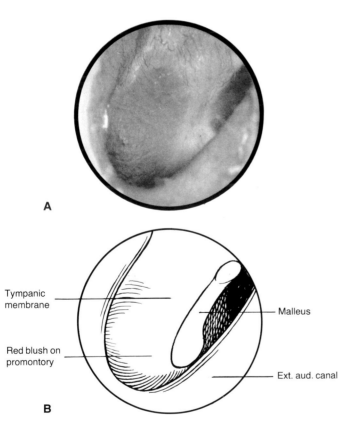

A

B

Tympanic membrane

Red blush on promontory

Malleus

Ext. aud. canal

Figure 12.**1**   Otosclerosis, Schwartze's Sign, otoscopic findings, right.
A A red blush of the promontory seen through the intact tympanic membrane is a sign of cochlear otosclerosis and demineralization.
B Diagram of **A**.

Histologically the foci that arise in the endochondral layer vary in appearance. In an active focus, there is a loose and irregular network of bony trabeculae with numerous blood vessels, osteoblasts and osteoclasts. In a mature focus there is a dense type of bone which is relatively avascular and acellular. These foci may progressively enlarge and extend to the endosteal and periosteal layers of the labyrinthine capsule. Periosteal involvement produces exostotic-like lesions protruding into the lumen of the tympanic cavity.

The progression of otosclerosis is characterized by remission and exacerbation. The disease may be quiescent for relatively long periods of time, or there may be rapid progression with deterioration of the hearing.

Clinical Course

Otosclerosis usually begins in young adults as a gradually progressive conductive or mixed type of deafness. The hearing loss which at the onset is usually conductive may stabilze for relatively long periods of time. Progression usually occurs in bouts of exacerbations until there is maximum conductive deafness. Further deafness may then occur due to superimposed sensorineural hearing loss caused by involvement of the cochlea by the otosclerotic process.

In the usual case of otosclerosis, the tympanic membrane and the middle ear appear normal on otoscopy. When there is severe involvement of the cochlea and promontory by large, active and vascular otosclerotic foci, the mucosa of the promontory becomes hyperemic. This hyperemia is visible through the normal tympanic membrane and causes a blush of the promontory, called the Schwartze sign (Fig. 12.**1**).

CT of the Labyrinthine Windows

CT is used to study and diagnose otosclerosis of the labyrinthine windows, the cochlea and other inner ear structures.

The projections used for the study of the labyrinth windows and cochlear capsules are the axial and 20° coronal oblique. The first projection demonstrates the cochlear coils and the round window. For exposure of the oval window, the 20° coronal oblique is far superior to the coronal projections.

The oval window lies in the medial labyrinthine wall of the middle ear cavity. The long axis of the window measures 3–4 mm and forms an angle of about 20° open posteriorly with the sagittal plane of the skull. The vertical axis of the window measures 1.5–2 mm.

The 20° coronal oblique projection demonstrates the oval window. Beginning at the level of the anterior aspect of the cochlea, sections 1 mm apart are taken that will pass through the oval window area.

The oval window appears as a well defined bony dehiscence in the lateral wall of the vestibule below the ampullated limb of the horizontal semicircular canal.

The footplate of the stapes is sectioned at right angles to the long axis. A normal footplate appears as a fine line extending across the oval window. The round window membrane closes the scala tympani and is located deep in the round window niche. On axial sections, the round window niche is well seen on the inferior aspect of the promontory below the oval window.

Radiographic Findings of Fenestral Otosclerosis

The radiographic appearance of otosclerosis of the oval window depends on the degree of maturation and the extent of the pathological process.

In mature otosclerosis, the oval window becomes narrowed or closed by calcified foci (Fig. 12.2).

In active otosclerosis or otospongiosis, the poorly calcified foci may not be recognizable. The margin of the oval window becomes decalcified so that the oval window seems larger than normal (Figs. 12.7, 12.11). The extent of the involvement varies. When otosclerosis involves the margin only, there is narrowing of the aperture of the oval window. Occasionally the footplate of the stapes becomes greatly thickened with minimal involvement of the surrounding oval window margin. In diffuse otosclerosis, the entire footplate is involved as well as the oval window margin. In these cases the oval window appears completely obliterated by a thick bony plate.

The otosclerotic process may involve the vestibular aspect of the footplate and oval window margin to encroach upon the vestibule.

The round window may be involved by an isolated focus or by extension of a large focus from the oval window area. There are areas of demineralization or sclerotic foci which surround and encroach the round window. It is difficult to predict the functional loss of hearing from round window otosclerosis, since it is known that a minute opening in the round window is sufficient for hydrodynamic function.

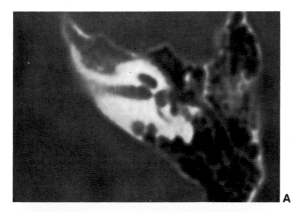

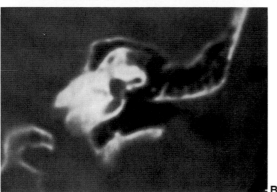

Figure 12.**2**   Left stapedial otosclerosis. **A** axial, **B** 20 degree coronal oblique sections, left. The oval window appears closed by a thickened footplate in both projections. The cochlear capsule is normal.
C Diagram of **B**.

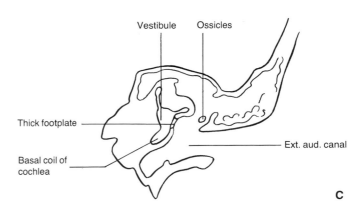

Pre- and Postoperative Evaluation of the Labyrinthine Windows

Otosclerosis is diagnosed clinically by the otologist on the basis of otoscopy, audiometry and tuning fork tests. The clinical evaluation cannot determine the extent or the degree of the pathological involvement of the footplate.

CT can visualize the extent of the pathology of the oval window and footplate and can be used in those cases where the clinical diagnosis of otosclerosis is in doubt and in some bilateral cases for selection of the ear to be operated. CT is also indicated in patients with pronounced mixed deafness to determine the presence of capsular involvement (Figs. 12.2–12.**14**).

Post-stapedectomy CT

CT is helpful in determining the cause of immediate and delayed vertigo and post-stapedectomy hearing loss. The position of the prosthesis is usually evident in CT section, Figs. 12.**3**–**6**. But because of partial volume averaging effects, thin metalic prostheses may not often be seen. Thicker metallic prostheses are distorted in CT images by volume averaging and spark artifacts.

Multidirectional tomography allows a more precise evaluation of the position of the metallic strut. CT can visualize some thick plastic prosthetic struts.

In cases where severe sensorineural deafness or vertigo follow immediately after surgery, CT or multidirectional tomography can demonstrate protrusion of the prosthesis into the vestibule (Figs. 12.**4**, 12.**5**).

When conductive deafness develops after an initial hearing improvement, the cause may be reobliteration of the oval window with fixation or dislocation of the prosthesis (Fig. 12.**6**). If the oval window remains patent, conductive deafness can occur from separation of the lateral end of the prosthesis from the incus or from necrosis of the long process of the incus. At times the lateral end of the strut is attached to the long process but the medial end is dislocated from the oval window. When a radiolucent prosthesis has been used, the position of the strut is difficult to determine.

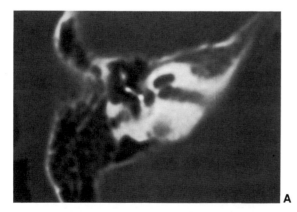

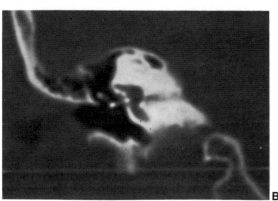

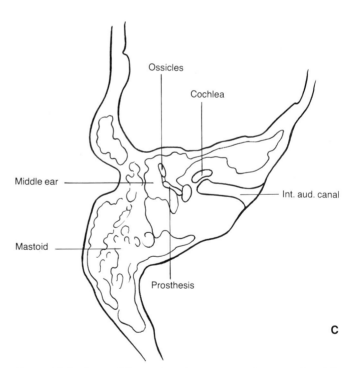

Figure 12.**3**   Stapedial otosclerosis, post stapedectomy. **A** axial, **B** 20 degree coronal oblique sections, right. A metallic prosthesis extends from the long process of the incus to the oval window which appears patent. Notice that the prosthesis is in good relationship to the long process of the incus and to the oval window opening. The cochlear capsule is intact.
C Diagram of **A**.

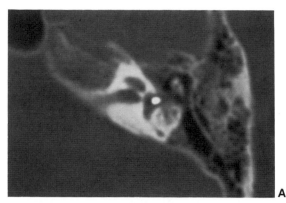

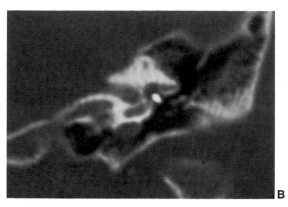

Figure 12.**4** Left stapedial otosclerosis, post stapedectomy. **A** axial, **B** 20 degree coronal oblique sections, left. The oval

window is patent but the medial end of the strut protrudes into the vestibule.

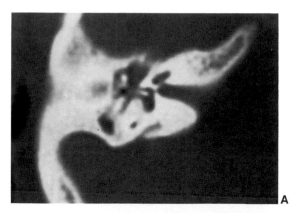

Figure 12.**5** Right fenestral otosclerosis post stapedectomy. **A** axial, **B** coronal CT sections, right. A metallic prosthesis extends from the long process of the incus to the oval window, which appears patent. The medial end of the strut protrudes for at least 2 mm into the vestibule. The changes in the middle ear cavity are due to a chronic otitis media.
C Diagram of **B**.

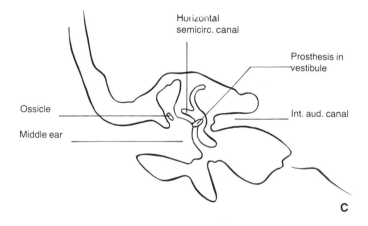

Figure 12.**6** Otosclerosis post stapedectomy, coronal oblique section, left. The lateral end of the prosthesis is displaced downward and separated from the long process of the incus.

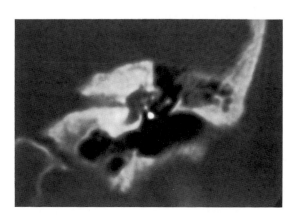

CT in Cochlear Otosclerosis

CT visualizes otosclerotic foci within the cochlear capsule.

The normal cochlear capsule appears as a sharply defined dense bony shell outlining the lumen of the cochlear coils.

When the otosclerotic foci affect the cochlear capsule, there is a variable disruption of the density and outline of the capsule (Figs. 12.7–12.14).

In the interpretation of the radiographic findings of cochlear otosclerosis, three factors must be considered:

1. The otosclerotic foci must be 1 mm or larger in diameter to be visible in the sections.
2. The density of the otosclerotic focus must be different from the density of the normal otic capsule.
3. Since the normal labyrinthine capsule is very dense, sclerotic foci can only be recognized when they are apposed to the periosteal or endosteal surfaces of the capsule.

The radiographic changes of cochlear otosclerosis are classified according to the extension of the process and maturation of the focus.

The otosclerotic process may be limited to a small portion of the basal turn of the cochlea immediately adjacent to the anterior margin of the oval window, spread into the basal turn, or involve other areas of the cochlea. Occasionally the fundus of the internal auditory canal, the semicircular canals, and the vestibule are affected.

The radiographic appearance of the otosclerotic lesion varies with the stage of maturation of the disease. In the demineralizing or spongiotic stage, the normally sharp outline of the capsule becomes interrupted and may disappear completely. The demineralization of the capsule causes loss of the normal different density between the lumen of the cochlear coils and the capsule. A typical sign of cochlear otosclerosis is the formation of a double ring effect due to the confluence of spongiotic foci within the thickness of the capsule (Figs. 12.8, 12.14). This band of intracapsular

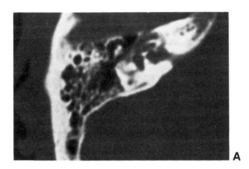

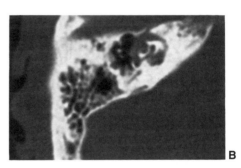

Figure 12.7   Otosclerosis, **A**, **B** axial CT sections.
The contour of the cochlear capsule is destroyed by severe demineralization. The residual dense areas are calcified fragments of the cochlea.

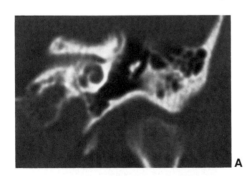

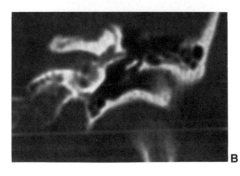

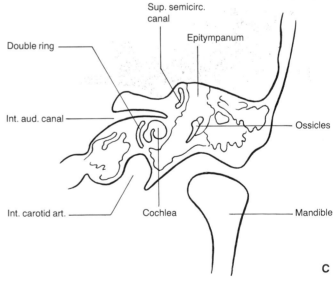

Figure 12.8   Otosclerosis. **A**, **B** coronal CT sections, left.
The anterior portion of the footplate is thickened, **B**. Confluent spongiotic foci lie in the medial aspect of the cochlear capsule, imparting a double ring appearance.
C Diagram of **A**.

demineralization may be limited to a segment of the capsule or follow almost the entire cochlear contour. This double ring effect sign is seen in cochlear otosclerosis and, in addition, in osteogenesis imperfecta and tertiary syphilis.

In the mature or sclerotic stage, there are localized or diffuse areas of thickening of the capsule due to apposition of new otosclerotic bone. Such foci when seen on end appear as areas of roughening or scalloping of the outer or inner outline of the capsule.

When spongiotic and sclerotic changes occur simultaneously, there is a mosaic pattern characterized by a mixture of areas of decreased density intermingled with areas of increased density. A similar mosaic pattern occurs as the result of several small spongiotic foci scattered throughout an otherwise normal capsule.

CT Densitometry

Quantitative assessment of the involvement of the cochlear capsule by otosclerosis is made by CT densitometric studies. Using the smallest cursor, 0.25 × 0.25 mm, the contour of the cochlear capsule is scanned and 31 densitometric readings are obtained. Readings are taken from two axial sections, the lower section passing through the basal turn and round window niche, the upper crossing the modiolus and three cochlear coils. Fifteen readings are taken from the lower section and sixteen from the upper. A densitometric profile of the capsule is obtained by plotting the densitometric values against the 31 points where the readings were obtained (Fig. 12.9). The topographic distribution of the 31 measured points, which begin at the promontory and pass through the 3 cochlear coils to reach the anterior aspect of the vestibule, is shown in Fig. 12.10. The horizontal axis of the graph indicates the areas where the measurements were taken and the vertical axis shows the density of the capsule expressed in CT numbers.

Curves from the patients are compared to previously obtained curves from normal ears. Variations of density exceeding standard deviations of 10 to 15% for each point indicate cochlear involvement.

CT densitometry is an objective approach to the identification of otosclerotic foci in the cochlear capsule and determination of the degree of maturation of the disease. Densitometry is also useful in the evaluation of the progress of the disease after medical therapy and for following the natural course of the disease (Figs. 12.12–12.14).

Densitometric curves similar to otosclerotic occur in Paget's Disease, osteogenesis imperfecta and tertiary syphilis. Differentiation is made by other clinical, radiographic and laboratory studies.

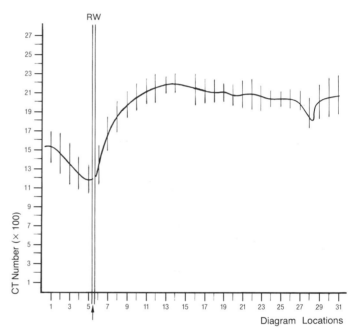

Figure 12.9 Densitometric curve with standard deviations of the normal cochlear capsule.
CT numbers are listed on the vertical axis, and the sites of the cursor readings on the horizontal axis starting shortly before the round window. RW is the location of the round window niche.

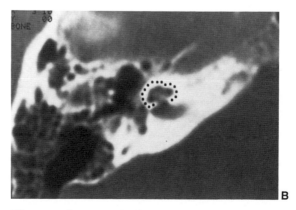

Figure 12.10 Topographic localization of 31 densitometric readings of the cochlear capsule. **A** lower section crossing round window niche, **B** mid modiolar section.

Fifteen readings are obtained from the lower section, five along the promontory and ten along the medial aspect of the basil turn. Sixteen readings are obtained in the upper section following the contour of the cochlea, and the results are plotted on the graph.

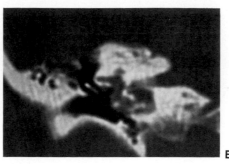

Figure 12.**11** Otosclerosis. **A**, **B** coronal CT sections, right.
Large otospongiotic foci have demineralized the cochlea. The contours of the cochlear capsule and the oval window are almost completely obliterated.

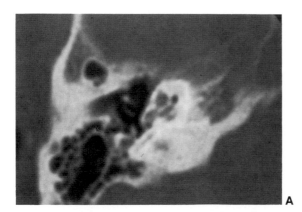

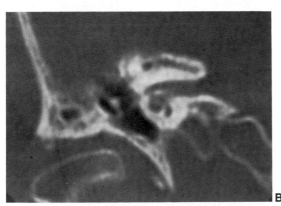

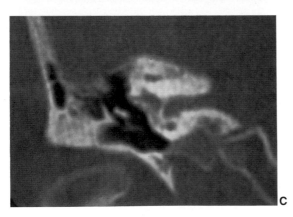

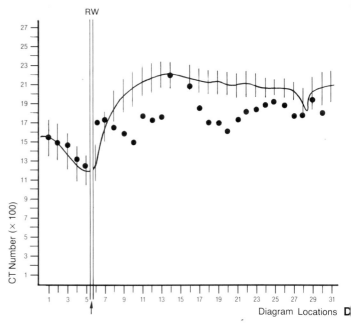

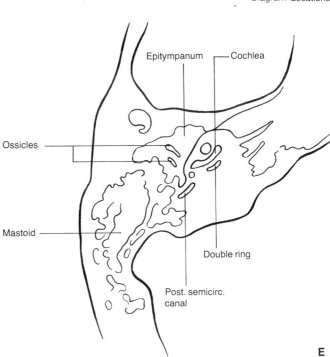

Figure 12.**12** Stapedial and cochlear otosclerosis. **A** axial, **B, C** 20 degree coronal oblique sections and **D**, densitometric profile, right. The footplate of the stapes is thickened, **C**. Multiple spongiotic foci are noticed in the capsule of the apical, middle coils and medial aspect of the basal turn of the cochlea with formation of a faint double ring.

Black dots are readings for this ear. Normal curve and standard deviations are above, **D**.
E Diagram of **A**.

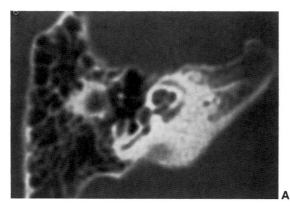

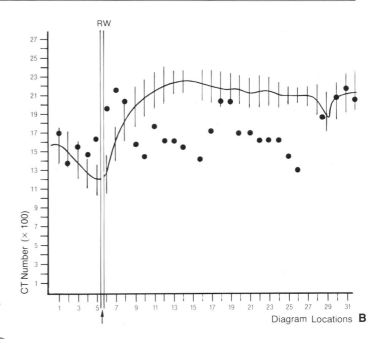

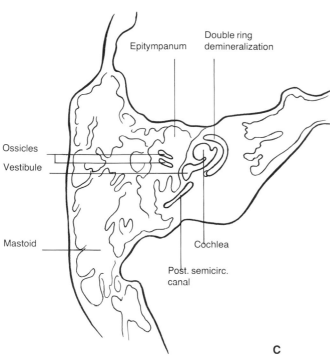

Figure 12.**13** Cochlear otosclerosis. **A** axial CT section, and **B** densitometric profile. A large band of intracapsular demineralization surrounds the cochlea. The densitometric profile, black dots, demonstrates that the involvement spares the promontory. Normal curve above.
C Diagram of **A**.

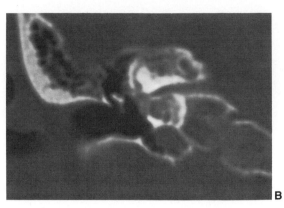

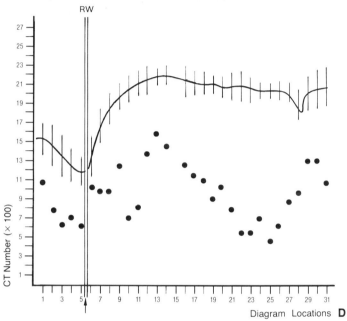

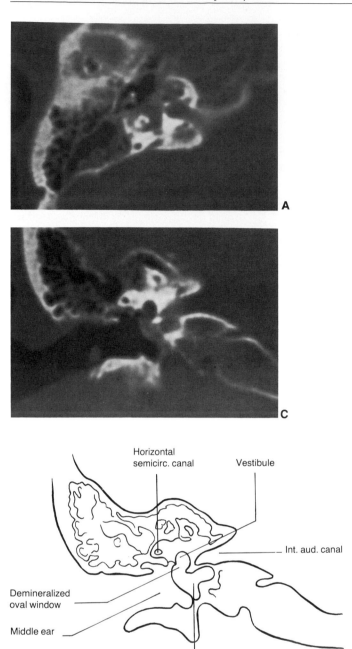

Figure 12.**14**   Cochlear otosclerosis. **A** axial, **B**, **C** coronal CT sections, **D** densitometric profile, right.

There are severe spongiotic changes throughout the cochlear capsule with formation of a double ring effect. The involvement is particularly severe in the basal turn and apical coil. The densitometric profile, **D**, black dots, demonstrates the severity of the process. The lowest regions of the densitometric curves correspond to the areas of most severe demineralization at 3–5 and 20–27 on the horizontal axis of the graft. Normal curve above. **E** Diagram of **C**.

Paget's Disease

Paget's disease can affect the calvarium and the base of the skull including the petrous pyramids. When the disease process extends into the otic capsule, there will be a mixed or sensorineural hearing loss which is progressive.

Radiographic Findings

Even in the absence of typical changes elsewhere in the skeleton, the diagnosis of Paget's disease can be made by recognition of pathognomonic features in the petrous pyramid.

In Paget's disease there is an active stage with progressive bone resorption followed by a stage of irregular reconstruction leading to a hypertrophied, irregularly mineralized bone.

The haversian bone of the petrosa is affected first, with spread of the disease from the apex laterally. At first, due to severe demineralization of the petrosa, the labyrinthine capsule becomes more prominent than normal. Involvement of the otic capsule begins at the periosteal surface. Slow demineralization occurs which produces first thinning and finally complete dissolution of the capsule. This results in a washed out appearance of the entire petrous bone characteristic of Paget's disease. The internal auditory canal is usually the first structure involved followed by the cochlea and the vestibular system (Figs. 12.15–12.17). In the late stage of the disease, deposition of irregular mineralized new bone occurs which results in thickening and enlargement of the petrous bone. The stapes footplate is often affected by the disease process, more rarely the malleus and incus are involved.

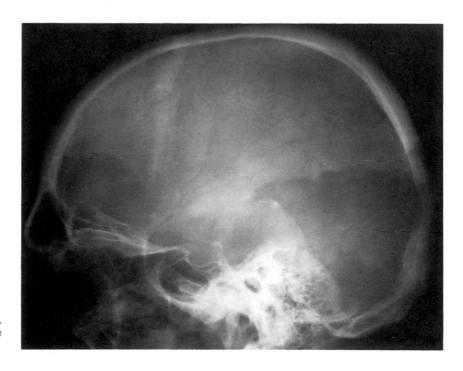

Figure 12.**15** Paget's Disease, lateral skull. Two sharply defined areas of demineralization, osteoporosis circumscripta, are present in the occipital and frontal bones.

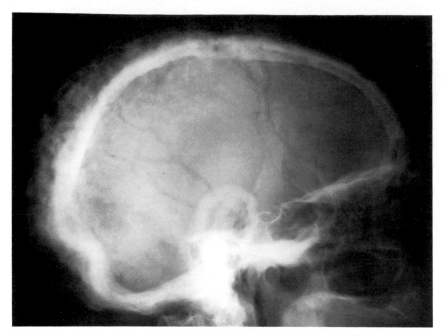

Figure 12.**16**   Paget's Disease, lateral skull.
The calvarium is markedly thickened and the pathologic remodeling of bone causes an irregular recalcification of the thickened
calvarium.

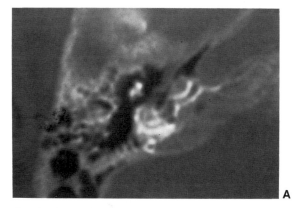

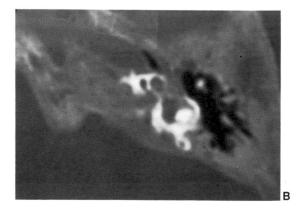

Figure 12.**17**   Paget's disease. **A**, **B** axial CT sections right and
left. There is a classic washed out appearance of both temporal
bones due to severe demineralization. Both labyrinthine capsules
are thinned out and partially erased.

Osteogenesis Imperfecta

Osteogenesis imperfecta or fragilitas osseum is characterized by abnormally thin and fragile long bones with a history of multiple fractures, by a blue color of the sclerae and by severe mixed deafness. In some forms of the disease, one or more of the features may be absent. The head is large, the calvarium abnormally thin, and the otic capsules are involved. The CT findings resemble those of active, cochlear otosclerosis, but are much more diffuse and involve the entire otic capsule (Fig. 12.18).

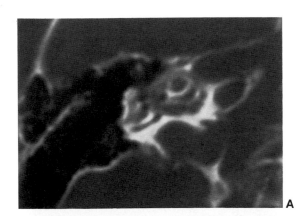

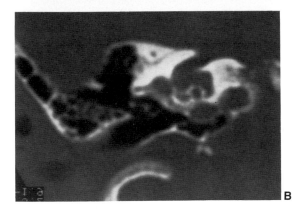

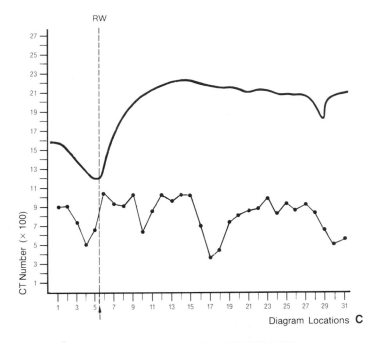

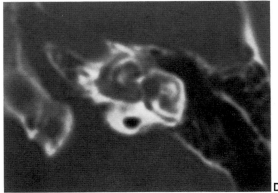

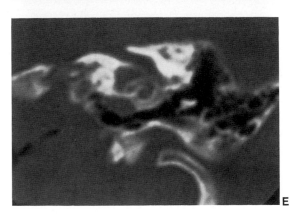

Figure 12.18 Osteogenesis imperfecta. A axial, B 20 degree coronal oblique section, C densitometric profile of the right ear and D, axial and E 20 degree coronal oblique sections, left. The cochlear capsules are almost complete erased. The involvement extends to the fundus of the internal auditory canals and to the vestibules. The densitometric profile of the right capsule provides a quantitative assessment of the involvement, C, black dots. Normal curve above.

Osteopetrosis

Osteopetrosis, Albers-Schönberg disease, marble bone disease is a rare bone disease characterized by formation of new bone while resorption of bone is diminished. This results in sclerosis of bone with obliteration of the medullary cavities and diploic spaces and narrowing of the foramina of the skull.

The petrous bone shows a complete lack of pneumatization and an homogenous diffuse sclerotic appearance.

Progression of the disease results in narrowing of the internal auditory canals and encroachment on the neurovascular bundles. Facial paralysis may occur on the same basis.

Fibrous Dysplasia

Fibrous dysplasia is an osseous dystrophy of unknown etiology which may involve the skull. There are two different types of changes that occur in the skull. In the calvarium and mandible there is expansion of the affected portion by multiple cystic lesions. In the base of the skull including the temporal bone, proliferation of bone occurs which leads to marked thickening and sclerosis of the affected areas. Involvement by fibrous dysplasia is usually unilateral which leads to asymmetry (Fig. 12.19). In the temporal bone, the squama becomes thickened and the pneumatic system obliterated. The external

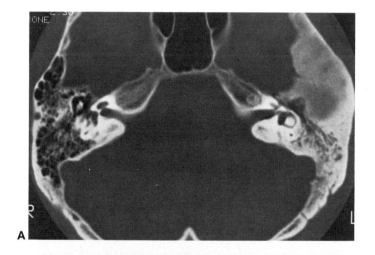

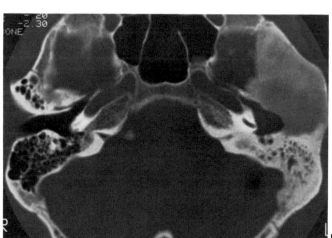

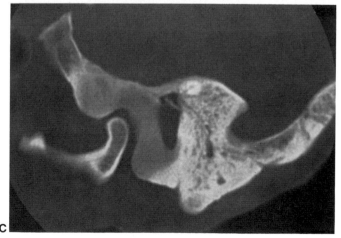

Figure 12.**19**   Fibrous dysplasia. **A**, **B** axial, **C** direct sagittal CT sections, left.

The temporal squama is markedly thickened. The disease extends to the temporomandibular fossa, which is shallow. The proliferative hyperostotic process obliterates some of the mastoid air cells and obstructs the external auditory canal. Because the external canal is obstructed, cholesteatoma fills the middle ear.

auditory canal is often stenosed by new bone formation. As the petrous pyramid becomes thickened and dense, the outline of the labyrinthine capsule becomes poorly distinguishable from the surrounding bone. Further progression may lead to narrowing of the internal auditory canal and obliteration of the lumen of the labyrinth.

Craniometaphyseal Dysplasia

Craniometaphyseal dysplasia is a genetic disorder characterized by alterations in the metaphyses of the long bones and by bony overgrowth of the skull, particularly the face and jaw.

The skull shows marked thickening and increased density of the calvarium with obliteration of the diploic space. The base of the skull, the maxilla and mandible become enlarged, thickened and sclerotic. The paranasal sinuses are obliterated (Fig. 12.20 A). In the temporal bone, the external auditory canal and middle ear are gradually filled in by new dense bone formation.

The petrous pyramids are thickened and the lumen of the labyrinth becomes obliterated (Fig. 12.20 B). The temporal bone and labyrinthine capsule are also involved in other rare congenital disorders and bony dysplasias such as cleidocranial dysostosis and Hurler's syndrome.

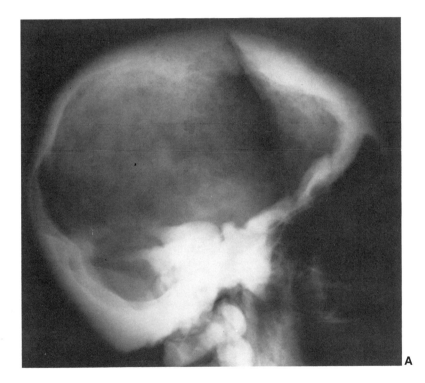

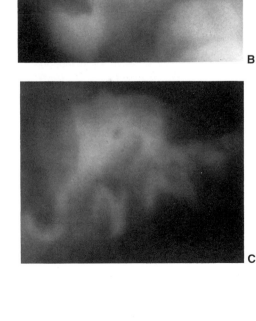

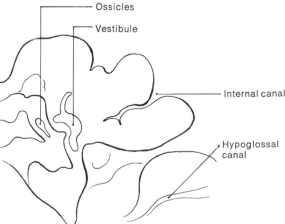

Figure 12.20 Craniometaphyseal dysplasia. **A** lateral skull, **B** coronal tomogram, right, **C** sagittal tomogram, right.
The calvarium and petrous pyramid are thickened by dense sclerotic bone. The process partially obliterates the lumens of the labyrinth and internal auditory canal. The hypoglossal canal is narrowed.
D Diagram of structures seen in **B**.

Bibliography

Anson BJ, Donaldson JA: The surgical anatomy of the temporal bone and ear. Saunders, Philadelphia 1967

Bast TH, Anson BJ: The temporal bone and the ear. Thomas, Springfield 1949

Buckingham RA, Valvassori GE: Tomographic and surgical pathology of cholesteatoma. Arch Otolaryngol 91: 464–469, 1970

Buckingham RA, Valvassori GE: Tomographic evaluation of cholesteatomas of the middle ear and mastoid. Otolaryngol Clin North Am 6: 363–377, 1973

Curati WL, Graif M, Kingsley DPE, et al: Acoustic neuromas: Gd-DTPA enhancement in MR imaging. Radiology 158: 447–451, 1986

Curtin HD: Radiologic approach to paragangliomas of the temporal bone. Radiology 150: 837–838, 1984

Curtin HD, Vignaud J, Bar D: Anomaly of the facial canal in a Mondini malformation with recurrent meningitis. Radiology 144: 335–341, 1982

Dulac GL, Vignaud J, Bar D: Anomaly of the facial canal in a Mondini malformation with recurrent meningitis. Radiology 144: 335–341, 1982

Dulac, GL, Claus E, Barrois J: Otoradiology. X-Ray Bull Special Issue. Agfa-Gevaert, Lille 1973

Hasso AN, Jones JL: Temporal bone: Normal and abnormal. In Haaga JR, Alfidi RJ (eds): Computed Tomography of the Whole Body, 2nd ed. St. Louis, CV Mosby Co, 1988

Johnson D, Voorhees R, Lufkin R, et al: Cholesteatoma of the temporal bone: Role of computed tomography. Radiology 148: 733–737, 1983

Kricheff II, Pinto RS, Bergeron RT, Cohen N: Air-CT cisternography and canalography for small acoustic neuromas. Am J Neurorad 1: 57–63, 1980

Lo WMM, Solti-Bohman LG, McElveen JT: Aberrant carotid artery: Radiologic diagnosis with emphasis on high-resolution computed tomography. Radiographics 5: 985–993, 1985

Mafee MF, Singleton EL, Valvassori GE, et al: Acute otomastoiditis and its complications: Role of CT. Radiology 54: 391–397, 1985

Mafee MF, Valvassori GE, Shugar MA, et al: High resolution and dynamic sequential computed tomography: Use in the evaluation of glomus complex tumors. Arch Otolaryngol 109: 691–696, 1983

Phelps PD, Lloyd GAS: Traumatic lesions of the temporal bone. In Radiology of the Ear. Oxford, Blackwell Scientific Publications, 1983

Rosenwasser H: Glomus jugulare tumors. Arch. Otolaryngol 1968 (monograph)

Sackett JF, Strother CM, Quaglieri CE, et al: Metrizamide – CSF contrast medium. Radiology 123: 779–782, 1977

Shaffer KA, Haughton VM, Wilson ChR: High resolution computed tomography of the temporal bone. Radiology 134: 409–414, 1980

Shambaugh GE Jr: Surgery of the ear, second edition. Saunders, Philadelphia 1967

Schuknecht HF: Pathology of the ear. Harvard University Press, Cambridge 1974

Spalteholz W, (trans. by) Barker LF: Hand atlas of human anatomy, Vol. III. Lippincott, Philadelphia 1943

Swartz JD, Faerber EN: Congenital malformations of the external and middle ear: High resolution CT findings of surgical import. AJR 144: 501–506, 1985

Valvassori GE, Pierce RH: The normal internal auditory canal. Am J Roentgenol 92: 1232–2141, 1964

Valvassori GE: The interpretation of the radiographic findings in cochlear otosclerosis. Ann Otol (St. Louis) 75: 572–578, 1966

Valvassori GE, Clemens JD: The large vestibular aqueduct syndrome. Laryngoscope 88: 723–728, 1978

Valvassori GE, Clemis JD: Abnormal vestibular aqueduct in cochleovestibular disorders. Adv Otorhinolaryngol 24: 100–105, 1978

Valvassori GE, Dobben GD: Vestibular basilar insufficiency. Ann Otol (St. Louis) 88: 689–692, 1979

Valvassori GE, Buckingham RA: Tomography and Cross Sections of the Ear. W. B. Saunders, Philadelphia. Thieme, Stuttgart 1975

Valvassori GE, Dobben GD: CT densitometry of the cochlear capsule in otosclerosis. AJNR 6: 661–667, 1985

Valvassori GE, Mafee MF: The temporal bone. In: Carter BL (ed): Computed Tomography of the Head and Neck. New York, Churchill Livingstone, 1985, pp. 171–205

Valvassori GE: Applications of magnetic resonance imaging in otology. AM J Otol 7: 262–266, 1986

Valvassori GE: Diagnosis of retrocochlear and central vestibular disease by magnetic resonance imaging. Ann otol rhin laryng 97: 19–22, 1988

Valvassori: GE, Morales Garcia F, Palacios E, Dobben GD: MR of the normal and abnormal auditory canal. AJNR 9: 115–119, 1988

Valvassori GE, Mafee MF: Diagnostic imaging in otolaryngology. Otolaryng Clinic North Am 21, number 2, 1988

Zooneveld FW: Computed tomography of the temporal bone and orbit. Urban and Schwartzenberg, Munich, 1987

Part II

Paranasal Sinuses, Nasal Cavity, Pterygoid Fossa, Nasopharynx, and Infratemporal Fossa

Barbara L. Carter

Paranasal Sinuses and Nasal Cavity

Chapter 1 **Anatomy**

Paranasal Sinuses

The paranasal sinuses and nasal cavity are present at birth but the sphenoid sinuses are too small to be seen and the frontal sinuses actually develop later from the ethmoids. The maxillary and ethmoid sinuses are visible at birth. All sinuses continue to grow, attaining their full sizes after the late teens. The **frontal** sinuses develop as outgrowths from the ethmoids, vary considerably in size and depth from one patient to another and though often somewhat symmetrical, may vary considerably from one side to the other. They may be completely absent, hypoplastic or very large (Fig. 1.**1**). Each frontal sinus opens into the middle meatus of the nasal cavity (Fig. 1.**2**) above and anterior to the hiatus semilunaris via the nasofrontal duct, entering directly or traversing the anterior part of the ethmoid labyrinth. The **ethmoid** sinuses vary considerably in size and number from 3 to 23 on each side.[16, 88] They are arranged in three groups, with the anterior and middle groups opening to the middle meatus on or above the bulla ethmoidalis (Fig. 1.**2**).[138] The posterior group opens to the superior meatus. The middle turbinate, which is part of the ethmoid bone, may be pneumatized with ethmoid air cells

(Fig. 1.**3**). Supraorbital cells are often present as an outgrowth of the ethmoid or frontal sinuses (Fig. 1.**4**). The lateral wall of the middle and posterior ethmoid sinuses (medial wall of the orbit) is a very thin or delicate bone called the lamina papyracea. The roof of the ethmoid cells or labyrinth is superior and lateral to the cribriform plate (see Fig. 2.**8**).

The **maxillary** sinuses are usually symmetric but they too can vary in development, with one appearing small or hypoplastic (Fig. 1.**5**). An underdeveloped, thick-walled sinus should not be mistaken for a diseased sinus. Bilateral hypoplasia may result in a relatively large nasal cavity (Fig. 1.**6**). Large maxillary sinuses extend into the zygoma laterally and down to the alveolar process of the maxilla inferiorly. Septae occur within the sinus cavity occasionally (Fig. 1.**7**) and rarely create a separate compartment within the main chamber (Figs. 1.**8**, 1.**9**)[65, 128] The ostium of the maxillary sinus opens to the hiatus semilunaris below the bulla ethmoidalis (Fig. 1.**2**), and is relatively high on the lateral wall of the nasal cavity under the middle turbinate. A second orifice is often seen behind the hiatus. A plate of bone called the ethmomaxillary plate (see Fig. 2.**3**) separates the maxillary sinus from the ethmoid sinuses. Along the roof

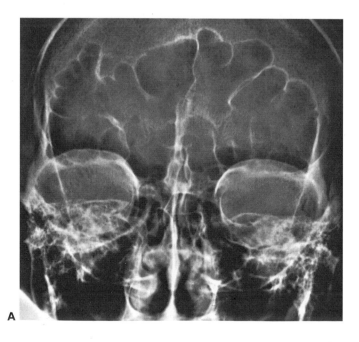
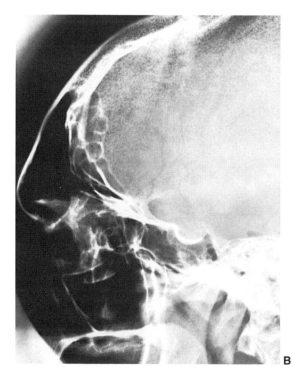

A

B

Figure 1.**1**   Large frontal sinuses in the Caldwell **A** and lateral **B** projections.

Figure 1.2 Schematic drawing of nasal cavity showing relative positions of the ostia of the sinuses. (Modified from Davies, J: Embryology and anatomy of the head, neck, face, palate, nose, and paranasal sinuses. In: Paparella, MM and Shumrick, DA, eds: Otolaryngology, Vol 1, W. B. Saunders & Co., Philadelphia, 1980, and Som, PM: The paranasal sinuses. In: Bergeron, Osborn, and Som, eds: Head and Neck Imaging. C. V. Mosby Co., St. Louis, 1984.)

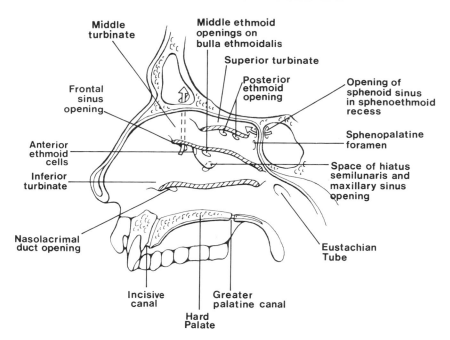

Figure 1.3 Axial CT scan, normal variant. Note the pneumatized ▶ right middle turbinate (1) as part of the right ethmoid air cells. The nasal septum (2) is deviated to the left. A right lateral recess (3) of the sphenoid sinus extends into the pterygoid bone, whereas the left pterygoid bone is solid (4). Also note the nasolacrimal duct (5) containing air on the left and soft tissue on the right, both normal.

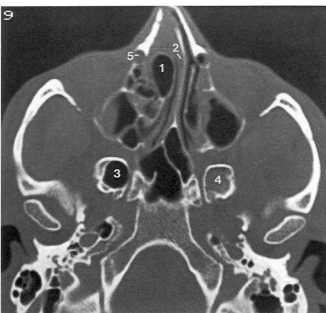

Figure 1.4 Coronal CT scan, large frontal sinuses (1) and large supraorbital cells (2). **A** is anterior to **B**.

▼

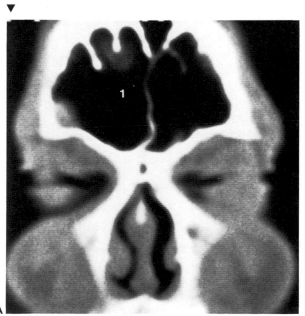

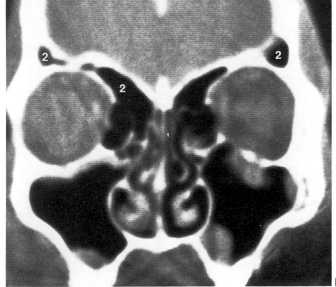

A   B

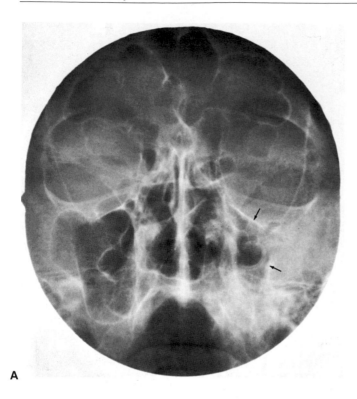

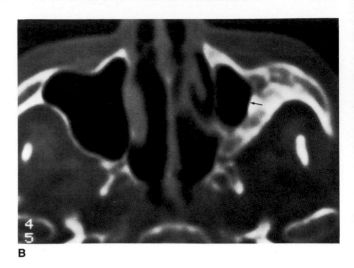

Figure 1.5   Hypoplastic left maxillary sinus. **A** Water's projection, **B** CT scan. A hypoplastic, but otherwise normal sinus (arrows) may simulate disease.

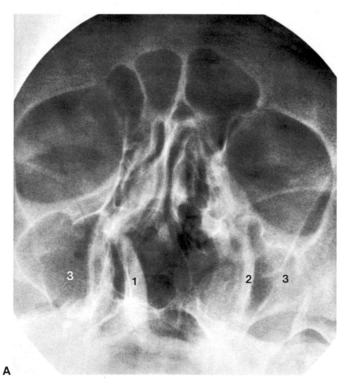

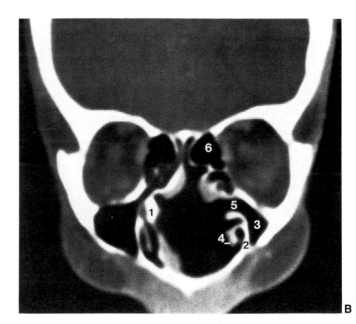

Figure 1.6   Hypoplastic maxillary sinuses and large nasal cavity. **A**) Water's projection, **B** coronal CT scan. The nasal septum (1) is deviated to the right and the medial wall of the maxillary sinus (2) is positioned laterally, resulting in very small maxillary sinuses (3), particularly on the left side. Note the hypoplastic inferior turbinate (4), the relatively large ostium of the maxillary sinus (5), and the normal appearing ethmoid sinuses (6).

Figure 1.**7** Maxillary sinus with septum, axial CT scan. The bony ▶
septum (1) extends from the infraorbital nerve canal (2) to the
medial wall of the maxillary sinus, partially separating the anterior
compartment from the main chamber of the maxillary sinus. The
nasolacrimal duct (3) is located anteriorly.

Figure 1.**8** Infected compartment, maxillary sinus. Base projection **A**, lateral tomogram **B**, showing a separate, infected compartment (arrows) in the posterior inferior portion of the left maxillary
sinus. This was opened and drained.

Figure 1.**9** Infected anterior compartment. **A** Water's projection,
B lateral tomogram. A separate anterior compartment (arrows) is
infected, making the entire right maxillary sinus appear opaque on
the plain film studies. The posterior compartment (open arrow) is
clear.

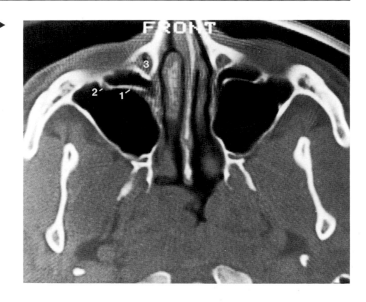

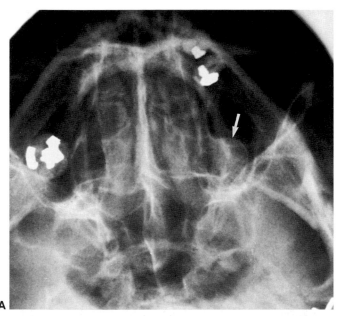
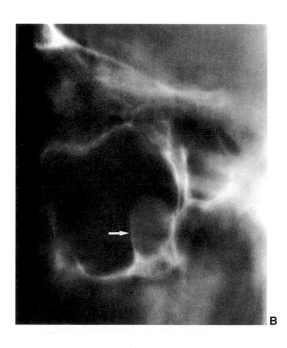

Figure 1.**8A+B**

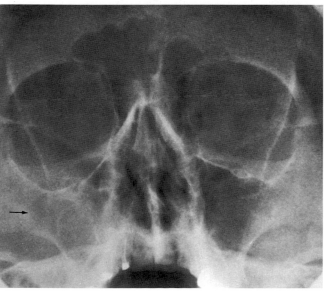
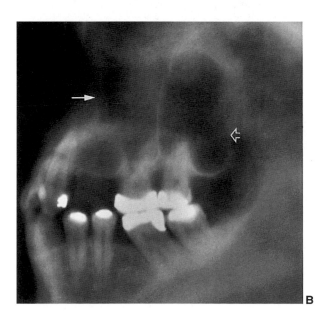

Figure 1.**9A+B**

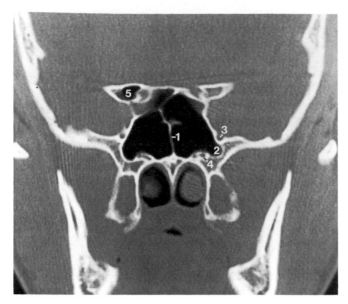

Figure 1.**10**　Normal sphenoid sinus, CT scan, coronal plane. A septum (1) separates the right and left sphenoid sinus. A small lateral recess (2) is projecting out between the foramen rotundum (3) and pterygoid (vidian) canal (4). Also note pneumatization of the right anterior clinoid (5).

extend posteriorly to the clivus and up into the dorsum sella, anterosuperiorly to the tuberculum sella and planum sphenoidalis, and out into the anterior clinoids via the tuberculum sella or optic strut. Lateral recesses of the sphenoid sinus (Fig. 1.11) extend laterally and inferiorly to the pterygoid process and greater wing of the sphenoid between the foramen ovale and rotundum and between the foramen rotundum and the pterygoid (vidian nerve) canal. Each sphenoid sinus opens to the nasal cavity behind and above the superior turbinate in the sphenoethmoidal recess (Fig. 1.2) well above the floor of the sinus.

Nasal Cavity

The nasal cavity is bounded anteriorly by two nasal bones that articulate on each side with the frontal (nasal) process of the maxilla and superiorly with the frontal bone at the nasion (see Fig. 2.6). The floor is formed by the palatine process of the maxilla and posteriorly by the palatine bone.[46] Medially, the nasal septum from front to back is made up of cartilage, the perpendicular plate of the ethmoid, and the vomer. The last articulates superiorly with the rostrum of the sphenoid bone and inferiorly with the hard palate. Laterally, the superior and middle conchae of the ethmoid bone and the inferior concha (separate bone) support the superior, middle, and inferior turbinates respectively (Figs. 2.8, 2.9). The inferior turbinate is the largest, and its turgidity may fluctuate during the day. On the plain lateral film, the inferior posterior end of the turbinate is projected over the soft palate and can simulate a polyp. It may even cause irritation to the patient and may be one of the reasons for snoring. Between the inferior turbinate and the lateral

of the maxillary sinus (floor of the orbit) is the infraorbital nerve canal (V2), which curves caudad before it exits from the anterior maxillary wall at the infraorbital foramen (see Figs. 2.1, 5.6). This canal should not be mistaken for a fracture line.

The paired **sphenoid** sinuses are separated by a septum, which is often oblique and off of the midline (Fig. 1.10). They, too, can vary considerably in size, and may be asymmetric. The sphenoid sinuses may

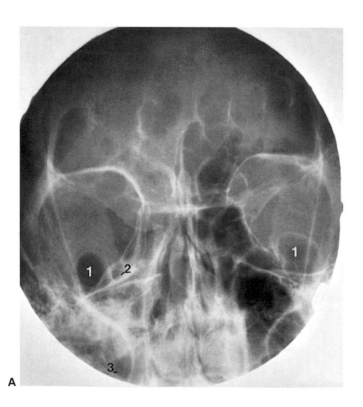

A

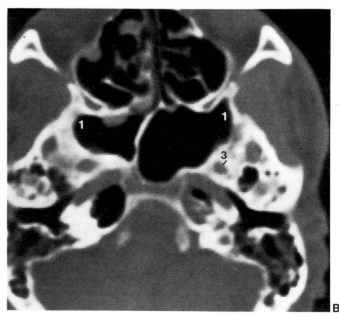

B

Figure 1.**11**　Large recess, sphenoid sinus. **A** Caldwell projection, **B** axial CT scan. Large lateral recess of the sphenoid sinus (1) projecting between the foramen rotundum (2) and foramen ovale (3) extends into the greater wing of the sphenoid bone.

nasal wall is the inferior meatus, containing the lower orifice of the nasolacrimal duct anteriorly (see Figs. 2.7, 2.9, 1.3). This duct courses through the lateral wall of the nasal cavity from the lacrimal sac located in the inferior medial corner of the orbit. The middle meatus, between the middle turbinate and lateral nasal wall, contains the maxillary sinus ostium and the hiatus semilunaris under the elevation called the bulla ethmoidalis formed by the middle ethmoidal cells (Fig. 1.2). Anterior to the hiatus semilunaris, one finds the frontonasal duct of the frontal sinus and the ostium for the anterior and middle ethmoid air cells. The superior meatus, between the small vertically oriented superior turbinate and nasal wall, contains the ostium for the posterior ethmoid cells. Behind and above the superior concha is the sphenoethmoidal recess (Fig. 1.2), the ostium for the sphenoid sinus, and the sphenopalatine foramen. The last leads from the pterygopalatine fossa to the nasal cavity.[93]

The posterior portion of the nasal cavity, the nasal choana, is bounded bilaterally by the body of the sphenoid bone, the ala of the vomer, the horizontal portion of the palatine bone, and by the medial pterygoid plate. The roof of the nasal cavity, formed by the cribriform plates, is very narrow. About 20 branches of the olfactory nerves originating from olfactory cells in the nasal mucous membrane pierce the cribriform plate to end in the glomeruli of the olfactory bulb.[47] Other foramina communicating with the nasal cavity are the incisor canal anteriorly for the greater palatine artery, and the descending and nasopalatine nerves. Posteriorly, in the floor of the nasal cavity, is the greater palatine foramen for the descending palatine vessels and the anterior palatine nerve (Fig. 1.12).

Rising vertically between the cribriform plates is the crista galli (see Fig. 2.9, 1.13), an attachment for the falx cerebri, also a part of the ethmoid bone. The

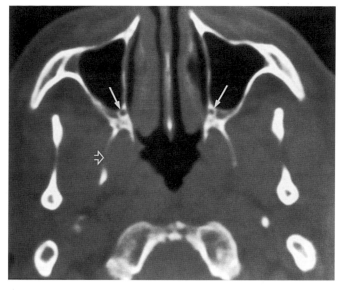

Figure 1.**12** Greater palatine foramen, axial CT scan. The descending palatine vessels and anterior palatine nerve pass through the palatine foramen (arrows). Note ossification of the pterygosphenoid ligament (open arrow) between the lateral pterygoid plate and the spinous process of the sphenoid bone.

crista galli may contain fat, but is often pneumatized and may be affected by diseases of the nasal cavity and paranasal sinuses. Similarly, the middle turbinate, also a part of the ethmoid, may be pneumatized. The middle turbinates also extend up to the cribriform plate and form an important landmark for surgery of this area. Anterior to the crista galli is the foramen cecum (Fig. 1.**14**), between the ethmoid and frontal bones. Although often impervious in the adult, it may transmit an ethmoidal vein from the nasal cavity to the superior sagittal sinus.

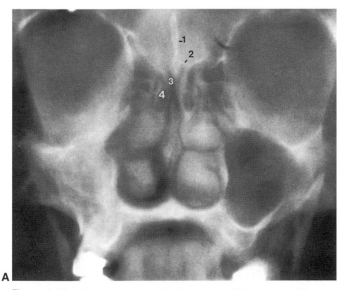

A

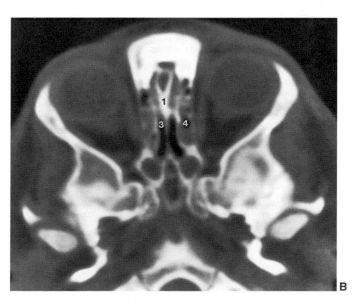

B

Figure 1.**13** Normal crista galli. **A** coronal CT scan, and **B** axial CT scan in a child showing the crista galli (1) rising vertically

between the cribriform plates (2). The roof of the nasal cavity (3) is narrow, located between the ethmoid air cells (4).

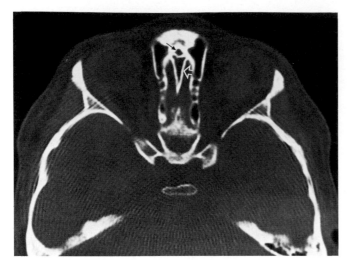

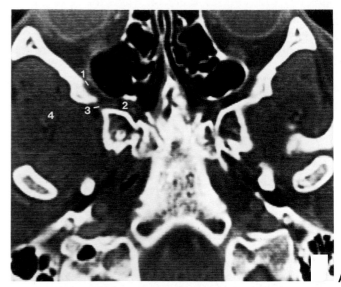

Figure 1.14 Normal foramen cecum, axial CT scan, in an infant. The foramen cecum (arrow) transmitting an ethmoidal vein from the nasal cavity is anterior to the crista galli. Note that the crista galli (open arrow) may be divergent as a variation of normal.

Figure 1.15 A–E

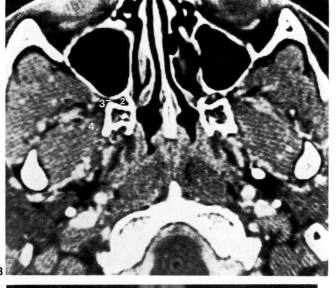

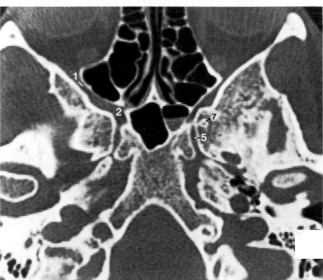

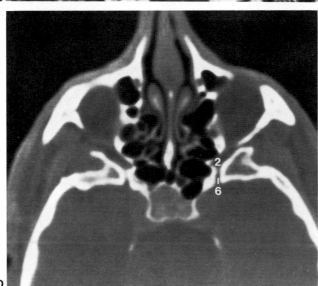

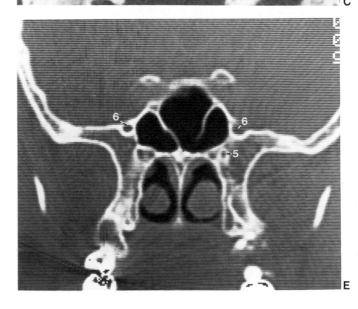

Pterygopalatine Fossa

A major crossroad between the oral cavity, nasal cavity, nasopharynx, infratemporal fossa, orbit, and middle cranial cavity is the pterygopalatine fossa.[24, 29, 92] This inverted triangular-like space is located between the posterior wall of the maxillary sinus, the pterygoid process of the sphenoid bone, and the vertical part of the palatine bone (see Fig. 2.4; 1.15).

Communications between the pterygopalatine fossa and the six adjacent spaces are as follows. The lateral edge of this space, the pterygomaxillary fissure between the lateral pterygoid plate and the maxillary sinus leads to the (1) infratemporal fossa. The sphenopalatine foramen through the vertical portion of the palatine bone transmitting the sphenopalatine vessels and the superior nasal and nasopalatine nerves – forms a communication medially between the pterygopalatine fossa and the (2) superior meatus of the nasal cavity (see Fig. 2.8 and Figs. 1.10, 1.12, 1.15). At the anterior superior aspect of the pterygopalatine fossa is the inferior orbital fissure (3), a communication with the orbit through which passes the infraorbital artery and infraorbital nerve (V2) from the foramen rotundum, a potential communication with the (4) middle cranial fossa. At the posterior superior portion of the pterygopalatine fossa is the vidian nerve, which joins the sphenopalatine ganglion within the fossa, and is accompanied by the vidian artery. Also located posterosuperiorly is the pharyngeal canal, transmitting the pharyngeal nerve and artery, a potential communication with the (5) nasopharynx. Inferiorly, at the narrow inferior portion of the pterygopalatine fossa, the pterygopalatine canal (Fig. 1.16) transmits the palatine vessels and nerves, a potential communication with the (6) oral cavity.

These various fissures and foramina provide a means of spread of infection and tumor among the nasopharynx, infratemporal fossa, orbit, nasal cavity, and middle cranial fossa.[91] These vessels and nerves found within the pterygopalatine fossa are numerous (as indicated), but the largest are the sphenopalatine ganglion (Fig. 1.16), the third portion of the internal maxillary artery, and the maxillary nerve (V2). The

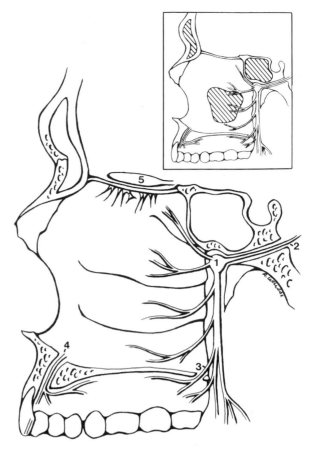

Figure 1.**16** Schematic drawing of the sphenopalatine ganglion and its branches with insert showing the sinuses. Note the sphenopalatine ganglion (1), vidian nerve within the pterygoid canal (2), the greater palatine nerve (3), nasopalatine nerve (4), and olfactory bulb (5). (Modified from Warwick & Williams: Gray's Anatomy, W.B. Saunders Co., Philadelphia, 1973.)

sphenopalatine ganglion is the largest of the parasympathetic ganglia associated with the trigeminal nerve and contains sensory roots from the palatine nerve, and a motor root from the nervous intermedius via the greater superficial petrosal nerve.[47] From the sphenopalatine ganglion, peripheral branches are distributed to the lacrimal gland, nose, palate, and oropharynx.

◀ Figure 1.**15** Pterygopalatine fossa. **A–D** axial CT scans, **E** coronal CT scan. The inferior orbital fissure (1) communicates with the pterygopalatine fossa (2) superiorly. Laterally, the pterygomaxillary fissure (3) forms a communication between the infratemporal fossa (4) and the pterygopalatine fossa (2). The pterygoid canal (5) containing the vidian nerve is seen in **C** and **E**. The foramen rotundum (6) evident in **D** and **E** forms a potential communication posteriorly and superiorly with the middle cranial fossa. The sphenoid emissary vein (7) is occasionally seen in the area as in **C**.

Chapter 2 Radiographic Findings

Radiographic evaluation of the paranasal sinuses, nasal cavity, and nasopharynx has changed considerably over the past few years. Plain film studies remain as the screening procedure of choice and are usually adequate for differentiating between normal patients and those with uncomplicated inflammatory disease.[98] Computed tomography (CT) and magnetic resonance imaging (MR) have superceded pluridirectional tomography for a more detailed assessment of the area in patients with tumors, complications of

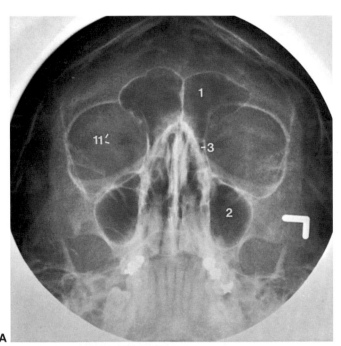

A

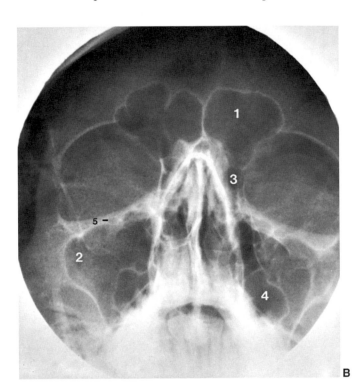

B

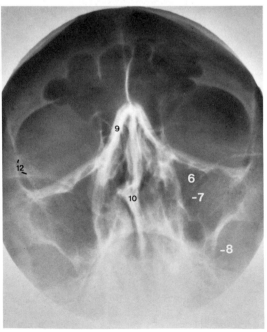

C

Figure 2.**1** Normal Water's projection, **A–C**. Three different patients to show variations in the sinuses and the normal landmarks. The frontal (1) and maxillary (2) sinuses are seen together with the anterior ethmoid air cells (3). The sinuses are fairly symmetrical. Lateral recesses of the sphenoid sinuses (4) are projected through the maxillary sinuses in **B** and **C**. The infraorbital nerve canal (5) is seen in the anterior inferior rim of the orbit. The lesser wing of the sphenoid (6), best seen in **C**, is separated medially from the greater wing by the superior orbital fissure (7). Since the latter structure is located posteriorly at the apex of the orbit, it is projected inferiorly with the elevated chin in the Water's projection. Note the foramen ovale (8), occasionally seen projected behind the floor of the maxillary sinus. The nasal bone (9) and nasal septum (10) are clearly seen. Soft tissue structures such as the palpebral fissure (11) are more subtle. The inominate line (12) of the greater wing of the sphenoid is also evident, but better evaluated on the Caldwell's projection.

infection, severe trauma, congenital anomalies and miscellaneous diseases.[22] Although CT and MR are somewhat complementary, one modality tends to be superior to the other, CT providing the better imaging of compact bone and of delicate or fine bone lattice work, whereas MR has the superior soft tissue detail.[70] Comparisons between these two modalities will be made throughout the chapter. The best understanding of the anatomical detail is obtained by correlating the plain films with the CT and MR images and with the skull itself.[81, 84]

Plain film – sinuses

The four standard projections used for the paranasal sinuses are: Water's, Caldwell, lateral, and base (submental vertex) views,[5] as shown in Figures 2.1–2.5. Supplemental studies occasionally used are the oblique (Rhese), transorbital, and the Chamberlain-Towne projections. All films are preferably obtained with the patient in an erect position using a well columnated x-ray beam parallel to the floor, permiting demonstration of air fluid levels.

Water's View

The **Water's** projection (Fig. 2.1) taken with the chin raised, is used for the evaluation of the maxillary sinuses, frontal sinuses, anterior ethmoids and the anterior rim of the orbits. With the elevated chin, the more posterior structures, such as the orbital apex, are projected inferior to the more anterior structures such as the orbital rim. The superior orbital fissure together with the anterior clinoid process and the lateral recess of the sphenoid sinus are then viewed through the maxillary sinus. The innominate line of the greater wing of the sphenoid bone is seen through the orbit. When the mouth is opened, the main body of the sphenoid sinus is visible in the midline inferior to the nasal cavity and the maxillary sinuses. With this projection, the petrous bone is projected just below the floor of the maxillary sinus. Modifications of the technique are made for individual patient problems. For instance, a questionable fluid level in the maxillary sinus is confirmed by repeating the Water's projection with the head tilted to the side (Fig. 2.2), or by having the patient placed in a decubitus position.

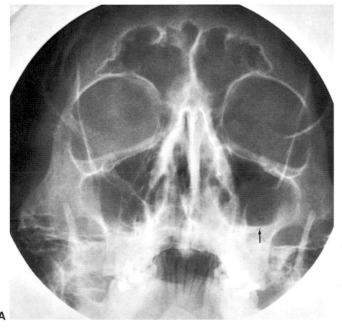
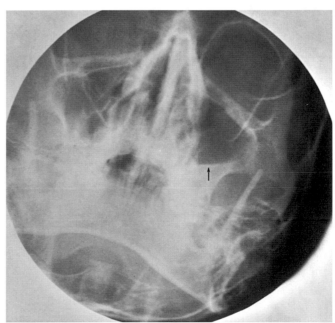

Figure 2.2 Water's projection to show fluid level. A standard Water's projection seen in **A** shows the fluid level (arrow), which shifts as shown in **B** by tilting the head to the side.

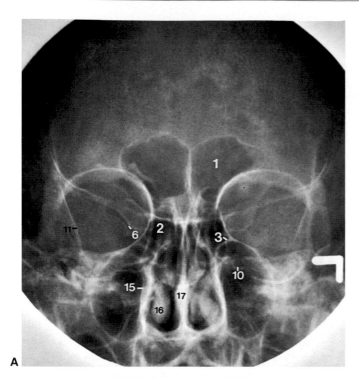

A

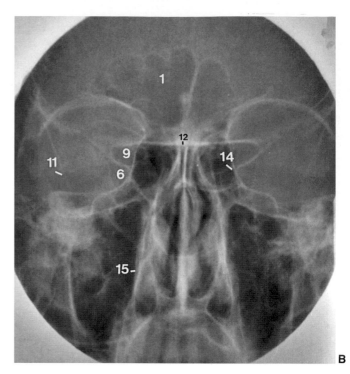

B

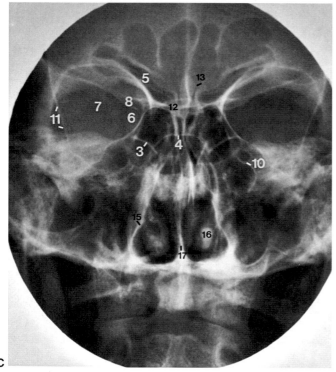

C

Figure 2.**3**   Caldwell projection, **A–C**. The frontal (1) and ethmoid (2) sinuses are seen to good advantage, but the maxillary sinuses are superimposed over the petrous portion of the temporal bone. The ethmomaxillary plate (3) and the floor of the sella (4) are best seen in **C**. Supraorbital cells (5) are an extension of the ethmoid cells over the roof of the orbit. The superior orbital fissure (6) between the greater (7) and lesser (8) wings of the sphenoid is at the apex of the orbit. The anterior clinoids (9) are pneumatized in **B** and are projected through the upper portion of the superior orbital fissure. The foramen rotundum (10) is located below the superior orbital fissure. Note the inominate line (11) of the greater wing of the sphenoid, the planum sphenoidale (12) and crista galli (13) in **C**. The lamina papyracea (14) forms the medial wall of the orbit. The medial wall of the maxillary sinus (15), inferior turbinates (16), nasal septum (17), and floor of the nasal cavity, or hard palate, are also evident.

Caldwell View

The **Caldwell** projection is modified such that the petrous bone is superimposed over the inferior orbital rim (Fig. 2.**3**). This provides the best visualization of the ethmoid air cells, the frontal sinuses, and the orbit. The medial wall of the orbit is formed by the lacrimal bone and the very delicate lamina papyracea or the paper plate of the ethmoid. The greater and lesser wings of the sphenoid bone, separated by the superior orbital fissure, are seen through the orbit.

The innominate line, a standard landmark, is formed by the greater wing of the sphenoid bone. Posterior to and superimposed behind the nasal cavity and the ethmoid sinuses are the sphenoid sinus and the sella turcica. The floor of the sella is in the midline, superimposed over the nasal cavity and ethmoid sinuses. Occasionally, an air cell may be seen extending over the orbit, a supraorbital cell arising from the ethmoid or from the frontal sinuses. With the Caldwell projection, the maxillary sinuses are difficult to evaluate because they are superimposed over the petrous bone. The cribriform plate is a small delicate bone at the base of the crista galli, forming the roof of the nasal cavity. This bone is difficult to see on plain films. However, the roof of the ethmoid sinuses, located above the level of the cribriform plate, is readily identified.

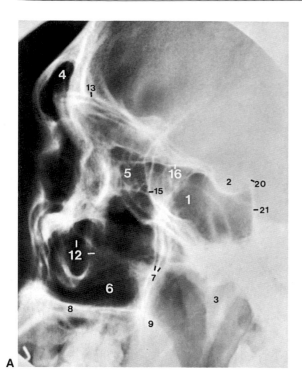

A

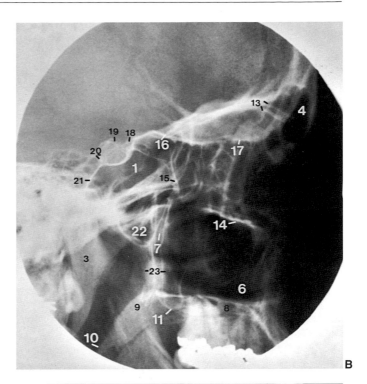

B

Figure 2.**4** Lateral projection, **A–C**. The sphenoid sinus (1), sella (2), and soft tissues of the nasopharynx (3) are seen to best advantage. The two superimposed frontal sinuses (4), ethmoid sinuses (5), and maxillary sinuses (6), are superimposed. The pterygopalatine fossa (7) between the posterior wall of the maxillary sinus and the pterygoid process is a long inverted triangle. Note the hard palate (8) and soft palate (9) with the uvula (10). The floor of the maxillary sinus (11) is located at the level of the hard palate **B** or below it **C** when the sinus is large and extending into the alveolar process. The zygoma (12) contains the lateral portion of the maxillary sinus to varying degrees. Also note the roof (13) and floor (14) of the orbit, the floor (15) of the middle cranial fossa formed by the greater wing of the sphenoid, the planum sphenoidale (16), roof of the ethmoid air cells (17), anterior (18) and posterior (19) clinoids, dorsum sella (20) and clivus (21). The lateral recess of the sphenoid sinus (22) extends inferiorly into the pterygoid behind the pterygopalatine fossa. The inferior turbinate (23) is best seen in **B**. The condylar neck (24), coronoid process (25), ramus (26), and body (27) of the mandible are best seen in **C**.

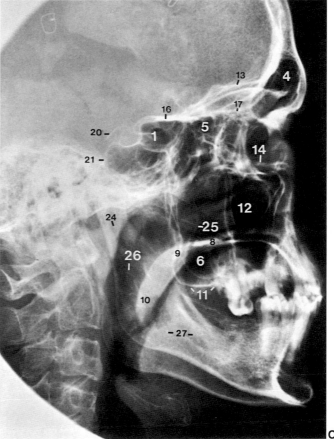

C

Lateral View

The **lateral** projection (Fig. 2.4) is needed to assess the depth of the frontal sinuses, the posterior wall of the maxillary sinuses, the pterygopalatine fossa, the sphenoid sinus, and the nasopharynx. The pterygopalatine fossa is a steeply inverted triangle located between the posterior walls of the maxillary sinus and the pterygoid plates. These areas are best visualized by a modified lateral view taken with the head rotated 5 degrees toward the film. The ethmoid and maxillary sinuses are slightly obscured by superimposed structures but can be seen, particularly when involved with a disease process. The hard palate, separating the nasal cavity from the oral cavity, may be superimposed over the floor of the maxillary sinus. However, this floor often extends inferiorly into the alveolar ridge and thus below the level of the hard palate. The

zygoma may appear as a solid triangular bone superimposed over the maxillary sinus, but again a large sinus may extend into the zygoma, making it appear as a triangular air-containing structure superimposed over the maxillary sinus. The zygomatic arch extends posteriorly from this area, superimposed over many other structures, to the temporal bone. The frontal

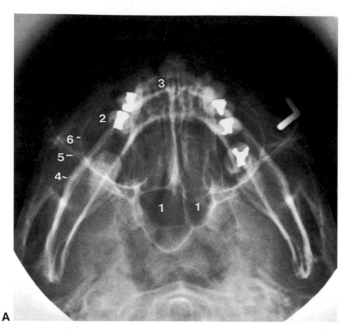

A

process of the zygoma extends superiorly to the frontozygomatic suture, forming the anterolateral wall of the orbit. Soft tissue structures seen in the nasopharynx in young people represent normal lymphoid tissue or adenoids. (This diminishes in the second and third decades.) The clivus can be seen extending from the dorsum sella down to the anterior rim of the foramen magnum. Other structures to be evaluated on the lateral film are the soft palate, the uvula with the superimposed palatine tonsils, the roof and floor of the orbit, the floor of the middle cranial fossa formed by the greater wing of the sphenoid, the mandible, tongue, valleculae, epiglottis, and larynx.

Base View

Several modifications of the **base** projection or submental vertex view are used, depending on the area of interest. The usual projection is taken with the mandible superimposed over the frontal sinus (Fig. 2.5). This shows to best advantage the entire

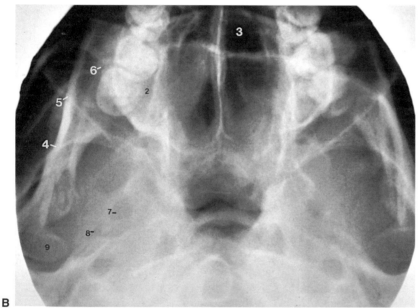

B

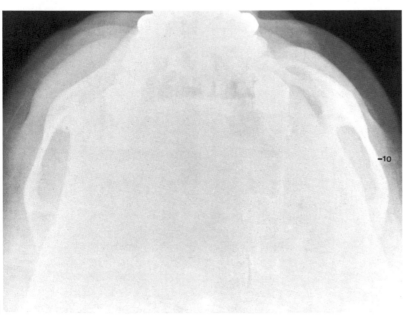

C

Figure 2.**5** Base projection, **A–C**. The sphenoid sinuses (1) are often asymmetrical as in **A** and are more difficult to see with the hyperextended projection **B**. The maxillary sinuses (2) are best seen in **A**, whereas the frontal sinuses (3) are better seen with the hyperextended base view as in **B**. Three lines forming landmarks in the base projection are the greater wing of the sphenoid (4), the straight line of the orbit (5) and more curved line of the maxillary sinus (6). The foramen ovale (7) and spinosum (8) can also be seen. The mandibular condyle (9) is located within the condylar fossa. An underexposed film **C** taken for visualization of the zygomatic arch (10) is called the "bucket handle" view.

sphenoid sinus, including the lateral recesses, the floor of the middle cranial fossa or greater wing of the sphenoid containing the foramen ovale and spinosum, the temporomandibular joint, and the petrous apices containing the petrous portion of the carotid canal. The apex of the petrous bone is separated from the sphenoid bone by the foramen lacerum. This base view is also used for evaluation of the ethmoid sinuses but the latter are often obscured by superimposition of the nasal turbinates. The **hyperextended base** projection is more useful for visualizing the anterior and posterior walls of the frontal sinuses. This hyperextended view is taken with the mandible projected anterior to the frontal bone allowing one to see the walls of each frontal sinus projected behind the symphysis of the mandible. With this modified base view, the maxillary sinus is projected slightly more anterior to the orbit but the sphenoid sinus is somewhat foreshortened. A **third modification** of the base view, taken with the mandible projected behind the frontal bone or halfway between a Water's and base view, is used primarily for evaluation of more posterior structures such as the jugular fossa. Important landmarks to be identified on the skull base are the (1) "S" shaped curve of the posterolateral wall of the maxillary sinus, (2) the gently curved to straight posterolateral wall of the orbit, and (3) the posteriorly curved wall of the greater wing of the sphenoid bone forming the floor of the middle cranial fossa.

Oblique View

Other projections used for evaluation of the paranasal sinuses include the Rhese or **oblique** view.[5] This is primarily helpful for the posterior ethmoid air cells, which are usually superimposed over the anterior ethmoid cells with the Caldwell view. The oblique projection is used more often for a study of the optic nerve canal and walls of the orbit.

Chamberlain-Towne View

The **Chamberlain-Towne** projection is useful in the evaluation of facial bones. The beam is angled caudad with the chin down and passes through the inferior orbital fissure, separating the posterior wall of the maxillary sinus from the sphenoid bone. This is occasionally used in trauma patients for assessing the posterior-superior wall of the maxillary sinus and the sphenoid bone.

Nasal Bone

The lateral projection coned down to the nasal bones and the spinous process of the maxilla depicts to best advantage the nasal bone (Fig. 2.6), the suture line between the nasal and frontal bones at the nasion, and the suture between the nasal bone and the frontal or nasal process of the maxilla. Vascular and neural grooves running parallel to the latter suture line should not be mistaken for fractures.

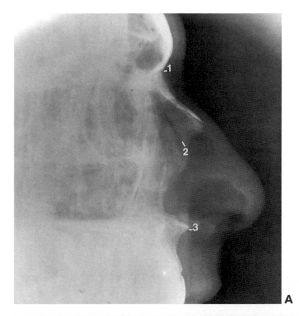
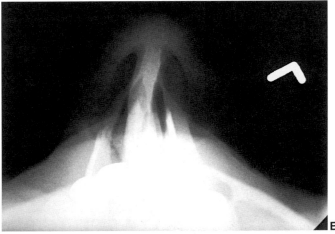

Figure 2.**6**   Nasal bones. A coned down lateral **A** and occlusal **B** film show the nasal bones. They are separated at the nasion (1) from the frontal bone. Vascular and neural grooves are parallel to the suture line (2) between the nasal bone and nasal process of the maxilla. The spinous process (3) of the maxilla is also evident. The occlusal view **B** is used for identification of any displacement of the nasal bones.

Occlusal films (Fig. 2.6) are used for the identification of medial and lateral displacement of fracture fragments of the nasal process of the maxilla and of the nasal bones. The Water's projection shows the overall appearance of the nose, nasal septum, and turbinates.

Computed Tomography

A more detailed evaluation of the paranasal sinuses, nasopharynx, skull base, and surrounding areas is achieved with CT, which has for the most part replaced pluridirectional tomography in most institutions.[12, 14, 15, 55, 111] Four or five mm slices are used in the axial and coronal plane (Figs. 2.7, 2.8). The axial plane is taken with the beam parallel to the orbito-

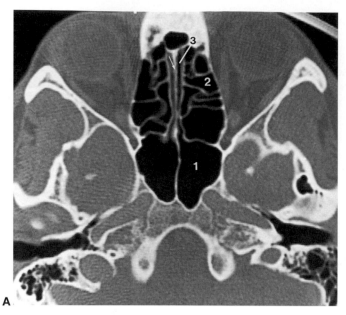

A

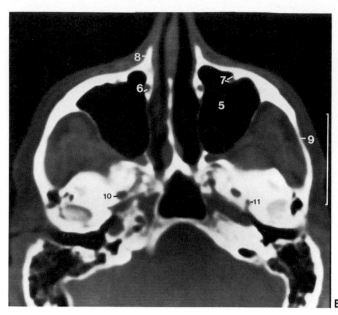

B

Figure 2.**7** CT scan, axial plane. **A** is through the sphenoid sinus (1), ethmoid sinuses (2), and top of the nasal cavity (3) with the nasal septum (arrow). **B** is through the maxillary sinus (5). Note the nasolacrimal duct (6), infraorbital nerve canal (7), nasal pro- cess of the maxilla (8), and the zygomatic arch (9). The maxillary sinus extends slightly into the zygoma on the right. Also note the foramen ovale (10) and spinosum (11).

meatal line for the skull base, and parallel to the hard palate for evaluation of the floor of the maxillary sinuses. The coronal projection is obtained by having the head hyperextended with the patient in a supine or prone position and the gantry tilted to approximate a plane 90 degrees to the orbitomeal line. By varying the tilt of the angle of the gantry during the acquisition of images, dental artifacts are minimized. The degree of angulation is determined by correlating the angle of the beam with the lateral digital radiogram acquired prior to scanning. By opening the mouth with the patient biting on a cork or sponges, improved visualization of the alveolar ridge and palate can be obtained in the coronal plane. This also separates the maxillary and mandibular teeth and again can be used to minimize dental artifacts. Thin (1.5–2 mm) sections are used for the identification of small lesions. A high resolution mode is best for obtaining bone detail. The latter is particularly important for minute detail of such fine structures as the cribriform plate with the coronal projection. Direct sagittal scans can be obtained in a cooperative patient with the head positioned parallel to the gantry, but this is difficult to do in older or in more debilitated patients.[4, 92] Reformatted images are used for visualizing the sagittal and coronal planes when hyperextended and direct lateral projections cannot be obtained. Three dimensional reconstruction has been most useful for studying facial deformity and for planning the appropriate surgical correction.[142] Intravenous contrast material is used for the identification of vessels, vascular anomalies, tumors, and abscess cavities.

Opacification is most effective with an automatic injector timed to a bolus injection of 40–60 ml of contrast, followed by a slower injection of 60–100 ml of a 60% solution. A rapid bolus injection by hand followed by a drip infusion of 300 ml of a 30% solution given through an 18 gauge needle or 20 gauge angiocath is also effective. For the more vascular lesions, a dynamic scan is achieved by obtaining rapid sequential images through the same area during and following the bolus injection.[85, 127] The rate and degree of enhancement of the area under study is measured and compared to the carotid artery and internal jugular vein. This is particularly useful in the study of enhanced lesions and in the differentiation between very vascular and less vascular masses.[126]

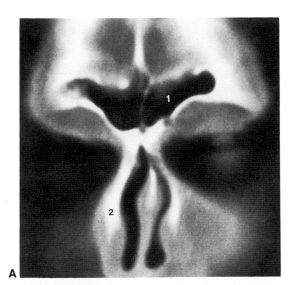

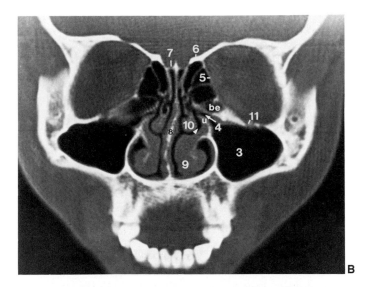

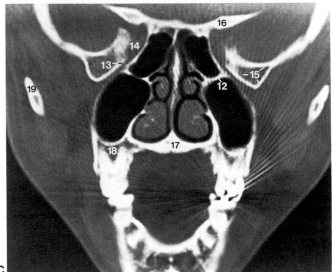

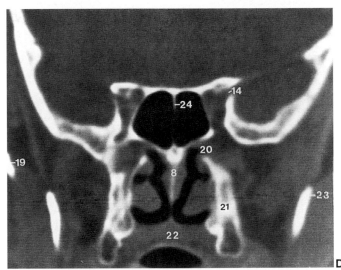

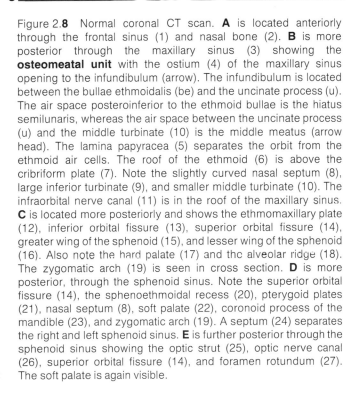

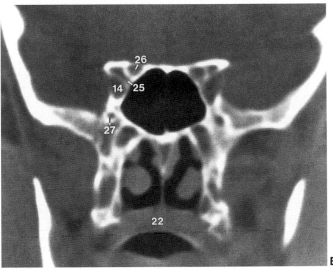

Figure 2.8 Normal coronal CT scan. **A** is located anteriorly through the frontal sinus (1) and nasal bone (2). **B** is more posterior through the maxillary sinus (3) showing the **osteomeatal unit** with the ostium (4) of the maxillary sinus opening to the infundibulum (arrow). The infundibulum is located between the bullae ethmoidalis (be) and the uncinate process (u). The air space posteroinferior to the ethmoid bullae is the hiatus semilunaris, whereas the air space between the uncinate process (u) and the middle turbinate (10) is the middle meatus (arrow head). The lamina papyracea (5) separates the orbit from the ethmoid air cells. The roof of the ethmoid (6) is above the cribriform plate (7). Note the slightly curved nasal septum (8), large inferior turbinate (9), and smaller middle turbinate (10). The infraorbital nerve canal (11) is in the roof of the maxillary sinus. **C** is located more posteriorly and shows the ethmomaxillary plate (12), inferior orbital fissure (13), superior orbital fissure (14), greater wing of the sphenoid (15), and lesser wing of the sphenoid (16). Also note the hard palate (17) and the alveolar ridge (18). The zygomatic arch (19) is seen in cross section. **D** is more posterior, through the sphenoid sinus. Note the superior orbital fissure (14), the sphenoethmoidal recess (20), pterygoid plates (21), nasal septum (8), soft palate (22), coronoid process of the mandible (23), and zygomatic arch (19). A septum (24) separates the right and left sphenoid sinus. **E** is further posterior through the sphenoid sinus showing the optic strut (25), optic nerve canal (26), superior orbital fissure (14), and foramen rotundum (27). The soft palate is again visible.

Magnetic Resonance Imaging

There are several advantages of MR over CT as listed in Table 2.1. Of particular note here is the minimal artifact caused by dental fillings and the capability of multiplanar imaging. MR, with it's superior soft tissue detail, shows to best advantage the anatomical structures, particularly with the T_1 or spin density weighted images.[3, 138] The T_2 images accentuate the differences between normal and abnormal structures. Four or five mm slices are used for the paranasal/nasopharyngeal area (Fig. 2.9), whereas thinner ($\leq$) 3 mm slices are preferable for detailed analysis of smaller areas such as the cribriform plate. Newer fast scan techniques such as FLASH and FISP may offer additional advantages, such as the capability of doing a breath holding image, evaluating flow sensitivity and having faster patient throughput. These newer techniques may also provide improved detail with thin 1 mm adjacent sections or with a 3D volume. The actual pulse sequence for T_1 and T_2 images varies with the strength of the magnet. For the Siemen's 1.0 Tesla magnet, a 256×256 data acquisition is used, spin echo technique with a TR of 0.6 seconds and a TE of 17 milliseconds for mild T_1 images. Sequential images are separated by 1 mm spacing. Four acquisitions are used for thin (3 mm) sections to improve signal to noise ratio, whereas two acquisitions are sufficient for thicker sections. For the two T_2 sequences, a TR of 3.0 seconds with a TE of 45/90 milliseconds is used with a 256×256 matrix or a 256×128 true rectangular pixel. In most instances, a head coil is used for the paranasal sinuses, nasal cavity, skull base, and nasopharynx.[153] The best detail is obtained with specially designed surface coils. Images are portrayed in the axial and coronal planes (Fig. 2.9), except in special circumstances when a sagittal plane may be preferable.

Table 2.1

Advantage MR	Advantage CT	Disadvantage MR	Disadvantage CT
No radiation	Superior bone detail	Contraindications Aneurysm clip Pacemaker Cochlear implant Pregnancy	Bone hardening artifact
Superior detail of soft tissues and brain	Availability		Dental filling
Multiple pulse sequences – T_1, T_2, etc.	Lower cost to patient		Allergy to iodinated contrast material
	Biopsy for suspect tumor	Higher cost	Radiation exposure
No bone hardening artifact	Drainage of abscess cavities	Motion artifact Respiration Vessel pulsation CSF pulsation	
Dental artifacts localized			
Multiplanar capability		Prolonged scanning time	
No intravascular iodinated contrast needed		Absence of signal from dense cortical bone and calcium	
Intrinsic sensitivity to blood flow		Critically ill patients with life support mechanisms more difficult	
		Claustrophobia more severe than with CT	

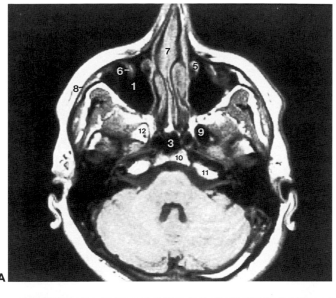
A

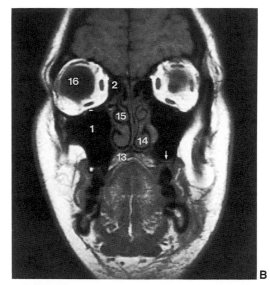
B

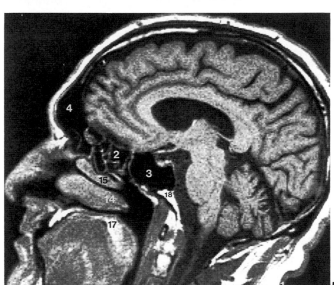
D

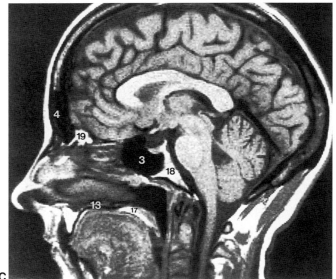
C

Figure 2.**9** MR in the axial **A**, coronal **B**, and sagittal **C** and **D** planes. The maxillary sinus (1) is clearly seen in **A** and **B**, ethmoid sinuses (2) in **B** and **D**, sphenoid sinuses (3) in **A**, **C**, and **D**, the frontal sinuses (4) in **C** and **D**. Note in **A** the nasolacrimal duct (5), infraorbital nerve canal (6), nasal septum (7), and the zygomatic arch (8). The sphenoid sinus (3) with the lateral recess (9) in the pterygoid is partially imaged **A**. High signal in the marrow of the clivus (10) **A**, petrous apices (11), and right pterygoid (12) is evident. The hard palate (13) with its underlying soft tissue is evident in the coronal plane **B**, where the floor of the

maxillary sinus (arrow) can be seen extending into the alveolar process. The inferior turbinate (14), middle turbinate (15), and ethmoid air cells are also evident. The orbit containing the globe (16), the rectus muscles, and orbital fat is also evident. **C** is a midline sagittal projection, **D** an off midline projection, both showing the sphenoid sinus (3), and the frontal sinuses (4). The inferior (14), middle (15) turbinates, and the ethmoid sinuses (2) are seen in **D**. The hard palate (13) and soft palate (17) are also evident. The clivus (18) is located above the nasopharynx. Fat in the crista galli behind the frontal sinus (19) results in a high signal.

Chapter 3   Congenital Anomalies

Congenital anomalies of the facial area (Fig. 3.1) occur as part of various craniofacial syndromes.[44, 95] Cleft lip and cleft palate are the most frequent anomalies but other less common defects are important considerations in the differential diagnosis of mass lesions of the facial area.

Anomalies may develop in the four week or younger fetus when the anterior neuropore closes in the vicinity of the optic recess.[109] At this time, mesodermal tissue is beginning to form bone, cartilage, and connective tissue. The fetal ectoderm may become entrapped with the outgrowth of the frontonasal process, a postulated explanation for ectopic gliomas, dermoids, and sinus tracts.[109] Failure to close the neuropore may result in the development of an encephalocele through the frontonasal, frontoethmoidal, or frontospenoidal complexes, producing an external, intranasal (Fig. 3.2), or nasopharyngeal encephalocele or meningocele.[115] Encephaloceles are associated with neurofibromatosis and Ehlers-Danlos syndrome.[95]

Extracranial rests of neurological tissue may result in the development of nasal gliomas, whereas defective retraction of dural elements may result in the presence of a patent dermal sinus or fistulous communication between a dermoid cyst and the intracranial cavity or falx at its attachment to the crista galli. Aproximately 15% of nasal gliomas are reported to have a fibrous connection to the subarachnoid space but no CSF connection.[95] Neuroectodermal tissue has been found extending through the foramen cecum from the falx to the nasal septum.[21] Although a nasal dermoid or nasal pit may be limited to the nose, the possibility of a sinus tract communicating with the intracranial cavity should be considered in the presence of an enlarged foramen cecum, a bifid crista galli or a broadened nasal septum. The bony defect is best identified with a CT scan. Thin section CT scans are therefore indicated in the presence of a small pit on the surface of the nose, a lipoma, or a dermoid at or near the base of the nose (Fig. 3.3), since any of these may be associated with a potential sinus tract and thus an intracranial communication directly through a defect in the nasofrontal bone or via an enlarged foramen cecum.[61] The intracranial component may lie within the falx at its attachment to the

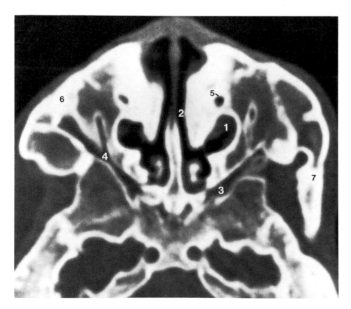

Figure 3.1   Craniometaphyseal dysplasia, axial CT scan. Severe dysplastic changes of the facial and cranial bones have resulted in hypoplasia of the maxillary sinus (1), and nasal cavity (2). Pterygopalatine fossa (3), inferior orbital fissure (4) communicating with the infra-orbital nerve canal, and the nasolacrimal duct (5) are still evident. The zygoma (6) and zygomatic arch (7) are also abnormally developed.

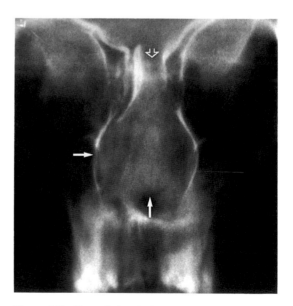

Figure 3.2   Encephalocele in nasal cavity through a defect in the cribriform plate, AP tomograms. The nasal cavity is enlarged by the mass (arrows), which projects through a defect in the left cribriform plate (open arrow).

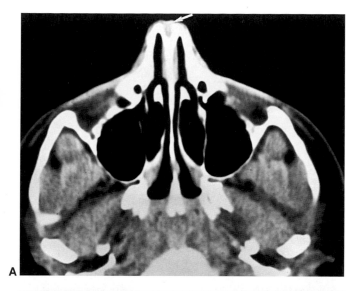

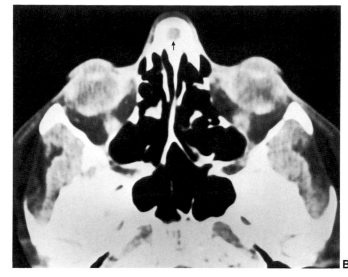

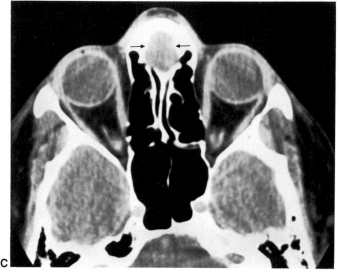

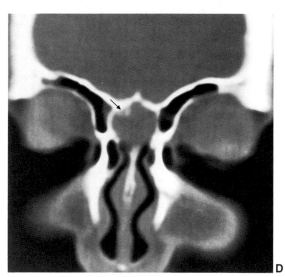

Figure 3.**3**   Nasal dermoid. Axial **A–C** and coronal **D** CT scans reveal a large dermoid (arrows) tracking from the nose cephalad in the nasal septum up to the foramen cecum. No intracranial communication was found at surgery. (Courtesy of Bertram Julian, MD and Daniel Hottenstein, MD, Harrisburg, PA.)

crista galli. Intranasal gliomas may present later in life as a tumor mass in the nares.[146]

Choanal atresia may be unilateral or bilateral (Fig. 3.**4**) as an isolated congenital anomaly, but 50% are reported to be associated with other defects.[95] The atresia occurs in one of every 5,000 to 7,000 births and is more frequent in girls than boys.[18] Although most atresias are bony, 5 to 10% are membranous.[95, 116] Some are incomplete and are then manifest as a stenosis rather than an atresia.[104] The anomaly may be associated with hypoplasia of the palatine process of the maxilla, an outgrowth of the palatal bone, a broad vomer, or an abnormality of the perpendicular plate of the palatine bone.[137] (The newborn infant is a nasal breather. Mouth breathing is a learned reflex which takes the infant from hours to days to acquire.) Choanal atresia is suspected clinically when there is respiratory distress in the neonate and is confirmed when a catheter does not pass from the nose to the oropharynx. Further confirmation of the diagnosis and delineation of the area is made by CT scan after suctioning the nasal passage and applying decongestant nose drops.

Other patients may be found with hemihypertrophy of the facial bones, mandible, and/or hemihypertrophy of the muscles on one side of the face. These may be part of various syndromes such as **Steiner's syndrome**.[23] The asymmetry may be evident at birth and become more prominent as the patients grows. It can involve the tongue as well as the other musculoskeletal structures resulting in macroglossia, either unilateral or diffuse. Conversely, hemifacial atrophy in **Romberg's syndrome** is seen sporadically, possibly as a result of trauma, and seems to be restricted to the facial structures.[23] It is apparent by one year of age with retarded development in the cartilaginous and musculoskeletal structures, causing facial distortion, unilateral enophthalmus, and hemiatrophy of the

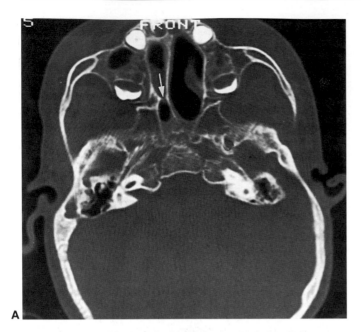

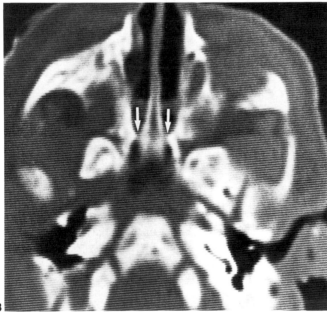

Figure 3.4   Choanal atresia, **A** unilateral, **B** bilateral, axial CT scans. Bony atresia (arrows) is evident on the right side, **A**, and bilaterally, **B**.

tongue and upper half of the lip. There are many other syndromes involving the bones and soft tissue structures of the facial area such as the **Pierre-Robin** with a cleft palate, micrognathia and glossoptosis, and the **Treacher-Collins** syndrome, a mandibulofacial dysostosis. Patients with Treacher-Collins have nonfusion of the zygomatic arches, abnormal development of the malar bones, defective orbital margins, small or absent paranasal sinuses, congenital aural atresia, and conductive deafness. Patients with **Down's syndrome** may have a high narrow palate, a bifid uvula, cleft lip and palate, and a relative macroglossia. **Crouzon's syndrome**, a craniofacial dysostosis, is secondary to premature craniosyn-

ostosis involving the lambdoid, sagittal, and coronal sutures. These patients commonly have hypoplasia of the maxilla, hypertelorism, a short upper lip, and a relative mandibular prognathism with oligodontia and macrodontia. **Apert's syndrome** has early obliteration of the cranial sutures with a high arched or cleft palate, hypertelorism, and a hypoplastic maxilla with relative prognathism of the mandible and with malocclusion. These are only a few of the multiple disorders that can be seen affecting the facial bones.

Miscellaneous

There are miscellaneous disorders affecting the paranasal sinuses, skull base, and nasopharynx to be taken into consideration. **Fibrous dysplasia** (Fig. 3.5) involving the walls of the paranasal sinuses and/or skull base may encroach on adjacent cranial nerves and cause symptoms. Monostotic fibrous dysplasia is reported to be 20–30 times more common than polyostotic.[118] These patients may present with some facial asymmetry. Whereas the growth is fairly rapid in early childhood, it tends to stabilize later in adult life. **Paget's disease** may affect the maxilla and mandible when the skull is involved. The blastic stage of Paget's disease is seen more commonly in the facial bones rather than the lytic or mixed form seen in the calvarium. The sinus and nasal cavity may be eventually obliterated. Occlusion of the ostium of the sinus can result in secondary infection. Patients with **thalassemia** (Fig. 3.6) or with a severe anemia causing hyperplasia of the bone marrow may also exhibit abnormal paranasal sinuses, obliterated by the hypertrophied marrow. Similarly, patients with **myelofibrosis** either as a primary process or as a spent phase of polycythemia rubra may present with masses in the mandible and maxilla due to extramedullary hematopoesis.[48] An expansion of the sinus or **pneumocele** is occasionally seen with encroachment on the orbital contents.[150] Measurements made in one individual would indicate that this could be related to air trapping in the sinus secondary to partial obstruction of the ostium acting as a one-way valve. If this occurs over a long period of time, the sinus may expand. Similarly, an extraction of the maxillary molar teeth in a growing child may result in an expansion of the sinus into the alveolar ridge, causing marked thinning of the bone and creating a potential for developing a fracture with minimal trauma.

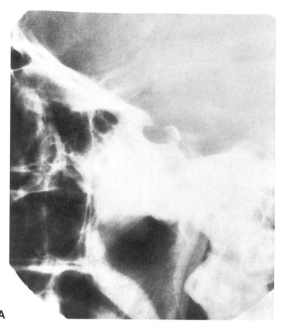

A

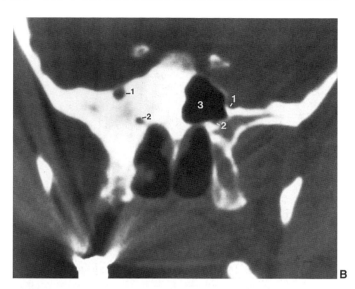

B

Figure 3.**5**   Fibrous dysplasia. **A** Lateral projection, **B** coronal CT scan, and **C** coronal MR reveal fibrous dysplasia of the sphenoid bone extending to the right, encompassing the foramen rotundum (1) and pterygoid canal (2). The right sphenoid sinus is obliterated. The left sphenoid sinus (3) and sphenoid bone including the pterygoid canal (2) and foramen rotundum (1) are normal.

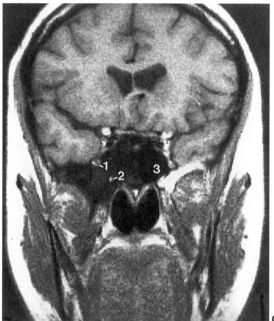

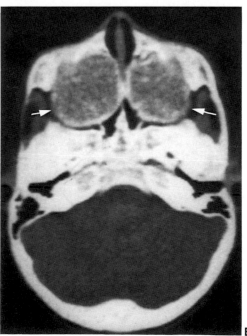

C

Figure 3.**6**   Thalassemia, **A** lateral projection, **B** axial CT scan. Hyperplasia of the maxilla (arrows) due to the thalassemia has resulted in aplasia of the maxillary sinus and in encroachment on the nasal cavity (Courtesy of Drs. C. Papavasilious, A. Gouliamos, and J. Andreou at the University Areteion Hospital of Athens, Greece).
▼

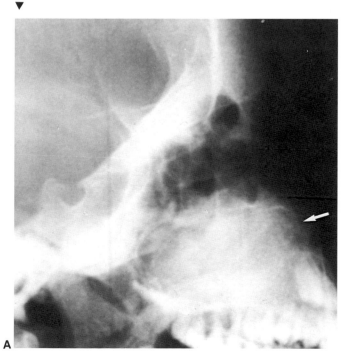

A

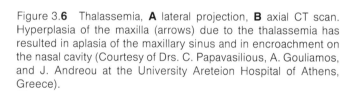

B

Chapter 4 Traumatic and Postoperative Findings

Trauma

Plain films studies are adequate (Fig. 4.1) for most patients with facial injury. Direct blows to the nose causing displaced fractures may be disfiguring and obstruct normal breathing. The degree of deformity is usually apparent on the direct lateral and occlusal film. CT scanning may be required to evaluate accompanying fractures of other bones of the face. In the nasal bone, fracture lines usually cross the vascular and neural grooves, which are parallel to the suture lines between the nasal bones and the nasal process of the maxilla (Fig. 4.1). More severe injuries are often accompanied by fractures through the spinous process of the maxilla.

Fractures with severe deformity or with complications require further study with CT. Facial fractures are often multiple, complex, and asymmetric, but they tend to fall into various categories such as the blowout fracture of the orbit, tripod injuries, and Lefort injuries. The blowout fracture (Figs. 4.2, 4.3) most commonly involves the floor of the orbit or roof of the maxillary sinus, which is depressed by the soft tissues of the orbit when displaced posteriorly by a fist, ball, or other blunt trauma to the orbit. The anterior rim of the orbit remains intact. A depressed floor fracture may be associated with inferior herniation of orbital fat or with entrapment of the inferior rectus muscle (Fig. 4.3). Either one may result in diplopia on upward gaze. Direct coronal and lateral (or reformatted lateral) 4 mm CT scans clearly demonstrate this type of injury. A medial blowout fracture involving the lamina papyracea is much less common than the inferior type (Fig. 4.4).

A **tripod** fracture (Figs. 4.5, 4.6) is the result of an oblique injury to the face with three main fracture sites: the frontozygomatic suture line, the zygomatic arch, and the maxilla (including the anterior rim of the orbit and the lateral wall of the maxillary sinus). The zygoma is often depressed with this type of injury but the direction of rotational displacement may vary depending on the direction and force of the blow (Fig. 4.6). **Lefort** fractures are a result of direct anterior facial injuries. The classification as originally

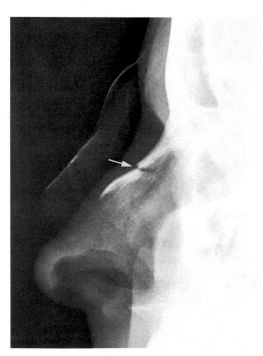

Figure 4.1 Fracture nose, lateral projection. The fracture line (arrow) crosses the nasociliary groove and shows slight displacement of the fracture fragments.

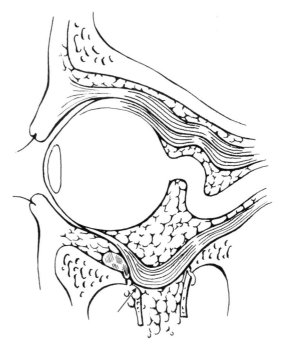

Figure 4.2 Schematic drawing of a blowout fracture. The inferior rectus muscle (arrow) is displaced inferiorly with orbital fat through the fracture defect. (Modified from Zizmor, J: Trans Amer Acad Ophthal Otolaryngol 44:733–739, 1957.)

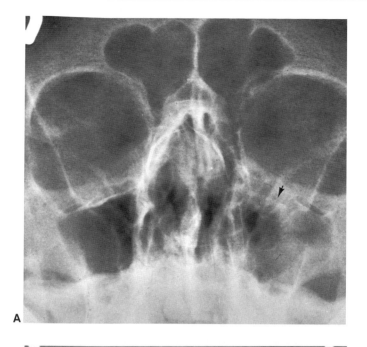

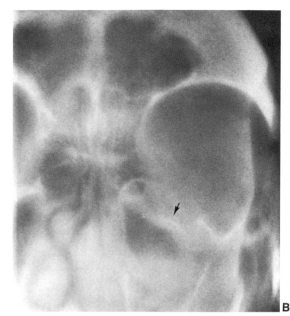

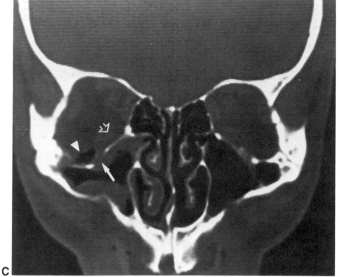

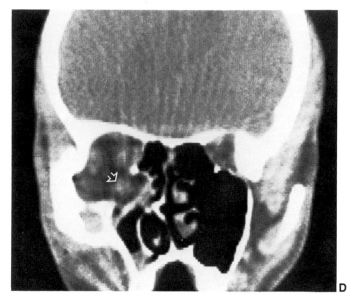

Figure 4.**3** Blowout fracture. **A** Water's projection, **B** AP tomogram, **C, D** coronal CT scans. **A** depressed fracture of the floor of the orbit (arrow) is visible on the plain film **A** but better seen by tomography **B**. Soft tissue changes in the maxillary sinus are related to submucosal bleeding from the trauma. CT shows to better advantage the position of the inferior rectus muscle (open arrow), which is normal in **C** and displaced into the fracture site in D. Orbital emphysema (arrow head) is evident in **C**.

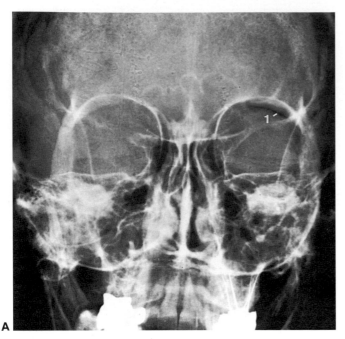

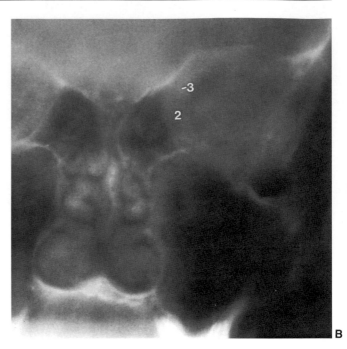

A   **B**

Figure 4.**4**   Medial blowout fracture, **A** Caldwell projection, **B** AP tomogram. Subcutaneous emphysema (1) may be the only sign of fracture as seen in **A**. Tomograms show soft tissue changes (2)

attributed to submucosal bleeding of the ethmoid sinuses due to a fracture of the lamina papyracea (3).

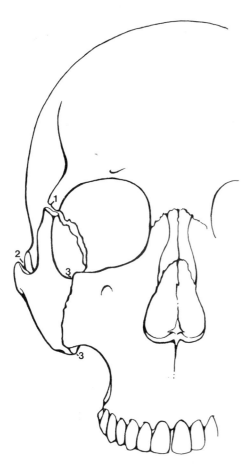

Figure 4.**5**   Schematic drawing of a tripod fracture. (Modified from Zizmor, J and Noyek, A: Orbital trauma. In Newton, TH, and Potts, DG, eds.: Radiology of the Skull and Brain. C.V. Mosby Co., St. Louis, 1971.) Fracture extends through the frontozygomatic region (1), zygomatic arch (2), anterior rim of the orbit (3), and maxilla.

described by Lefort in 1901 referred to symmetrical fractures of the facial bones extending back to and involving the pterygoid plates (Fig. 4.**7**). Since the injuries are often asymmetric, they are usually designated as Lefort-type fractures. The Lefort I injury is a horizontal fracture extending across the floor of the maxillary sinuses above the dentition line of the superior alveolar ridge, resulting in a "floating palate". Occasionally, a midpalatal split complicates this type of injury (Fig. 4.**8**). The Lefort II fracture is also called a pyramidal fracture (Fig. 4.**9**), and occurs vertically through the maxilla and across the upper nasal bone and back to the pterygoid plates. The zygoma is left intact with a "floating maxilla".[118] The most severe of this group is the Lefort III, a complete craniofacial separation (Fig. 4.**10**). The fracture line passes through the frontozygomatic sutures bilaterally, across the nose and down to the pterygoid plates resulting in a "floating face".

Complications

The cribriform plate, ethmoidal arteries, optic nerve, and internal maxillary artery are all at risk of serious injury.[57] Fractures through the orbital apex close to the optic nerve may result in blindness due to injury of the optic nerve. Trauma involving the ostium of a

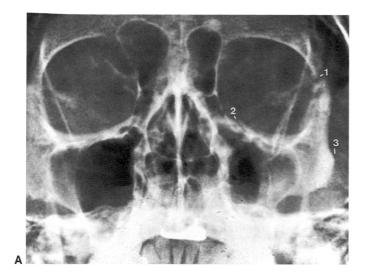

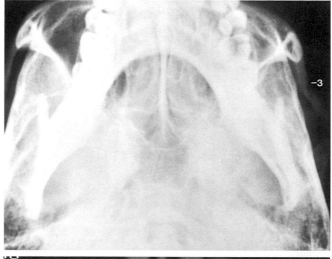

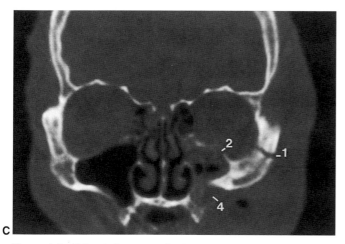

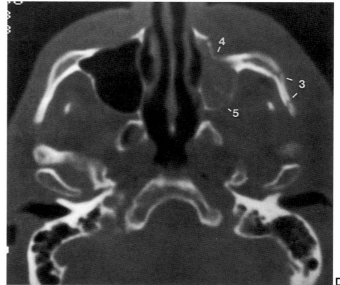

Figure 4.**6** Tripod fracture, **A** Water's projection, **B** bucket handle view, **C** coronal CT, and **D** axial CT scan. Fractures through the frontozygomatic suture (1), anterior rim (2), to floor of the orbit and the zygomatic arch (3) are clearly seen. In addition,

the fracture line through the zygomatic/maxillary area involves the wall of the maxillary sinus anteriorly (4) and posterolaterally (5). Depression of the zygoma is visible in **D** and of the zygomatic arch in **A** and **B**.

sinus may cause obstruction and the subsequent development of a mucocele. A fracture through the inner table of the skull may also be associated with tear of the dura and a cerebral spinal fluid leak. Thus, an air fluid level within the sinus might be due to blood or to cerebral spinal fluid. A tear in the dura may be associated with pneumocephalus, caused by increased pressure in the paranasal sinuses or nasopharynx. It is important to establish the presence of cerebral spinal leak because of the potential danger of meningitis. Subcutaneous emphysema in the orbit or in the soft tissue structures overlying the facial area is frequently seen by CT and again is indicative of a fracture of the adjacent paranasal sinus (Fig. 4.**4**). It should be noted that rhinorrhea may also be a manifestation of fracture of the temporal bone with an intact tympanic membrane, caused by CSF entering the nasopharynx via the eustachian tube.

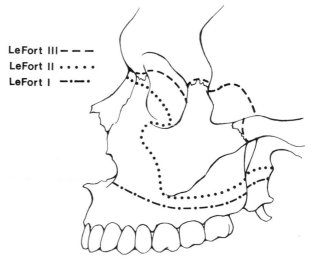

Figure 4.**7** Schematic drawing of LeFort type injuries. (After Holt, GR: Maxillofacial trauma. In Cummings et al, eds: Otolaryngology – Head and Neck Surgery. C.V. Mosby Co., St. Louis, 1986.)

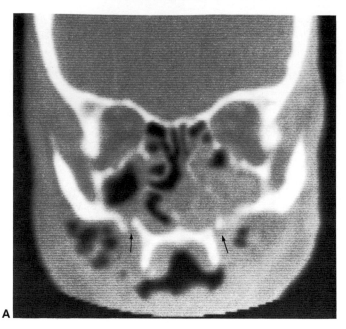
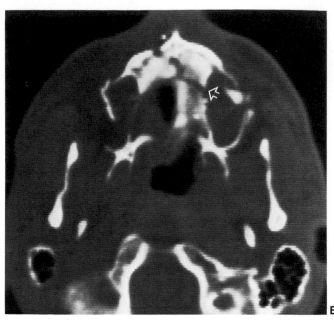

Figure 4.8   LeFort I type injury. **A** coronal CT, **B** axial CT. A "floating palate" is a result of fracture just above the superior

alveolar ridge (arrow). An associated fracture may extend through the palate (open arrow) as shown in **B**.

Postoperative Changes

Radiological changes of the paranasal sinuses are also present following any surgical procedure in the area. For instance, a lavage of the maxillary sinus is commonly followed by the presence of an air fluid level for several days following the procedure. Nasal packing used in the treatment of epistaxis and after surgical procedures can simulate the presence of a mass effect in the nose (Fig. 4.**11**) and nasopharynx.

Frontal sinuses

A simple drainage procedure through a trephine made in the superior medial margin of the orbit, used for drainage of the frontal sinus, has very little radiographic abnormality. With the **Lynch** procedure (Fig. 4.**12**), a segment of the sinus floor is removed together with an ethmoidectomy for the creation of a large drainage portal into the nose. A polyethelene tube is often used to splint the drainage pathway between the frontal sinus and middle meatus. This

operation tends to create some deformity, requires considerable postoperative care, and may be complicated by the later development of a mucocele if there is incomplete removal of the mucous membrane or stenosis of the reconstructed nasofrontal duct. Other modifications of the Lynch procedure have been developed such as the Killian operation, which has less postoperative deformity. In the Reidel approach, the anterior wall of the sinus is removed and soft tissue collapses into the sinus.[87, 107, 118] More recently, the osteoplastic flap procedure has become the operation of choice since it obliterates the sinus cavity with very minimal cosmetic deformity. The osteoplastic flap is patterned from a template of the frontal sinus traced from a Caldwell projection. The anterior sinus wall margin is traced out with a saw and the anterior wall is bent downward to expose the entire sinus cavity. The mucosa is removed and a piece of abdominal muscle or fat is used to obliterate the sinus cavity, and the anterior bony flap is then repositioned into its original place (Fig. 4.**12**).

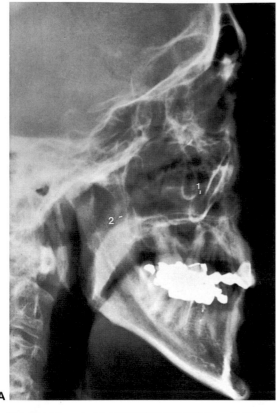

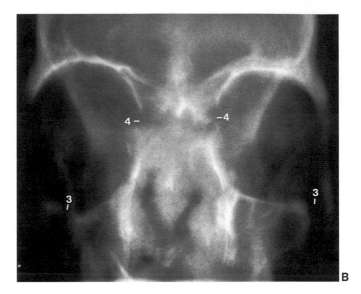

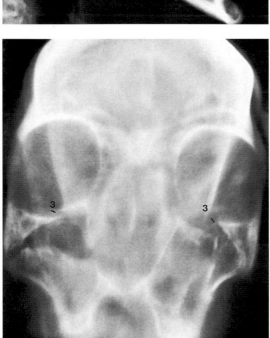

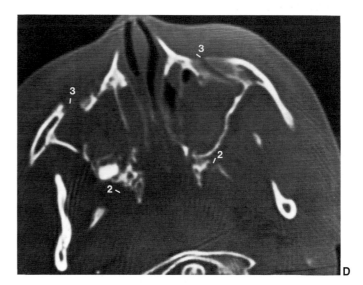

Figure 4.**9** LeFort II type fracture. Lateral projection **A**, AP tomogram **B** and **C**, axial CT scan **D**. Fracture through the midfacial area resulting in a "floating maxilla" can be seen through the zygoma (1) and pterygoid region (2) in **A**, through the junction of the maxilla with the zygoma (3) in **B** and **D**, across the nasal bone (4) in **B**. Fractures through the maxilla/zygoma area (3) and pterygoid plates (2) can also be seen in **D**.

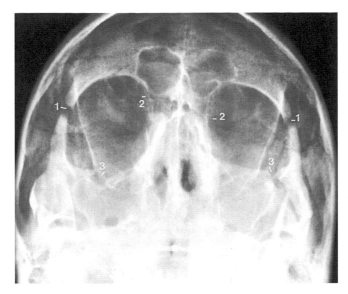

Figure 4.**10** LeFort III type fracture, a complete craniofacial separation, Water's projection. Fracture lines through the frontozygomatic area (1) and across the nasion (2) extend back to include the pterygoid plates, resulting in complete separation of the facial bones from the skull. Also note the mid-face fracture of LeFort II type injury (3).

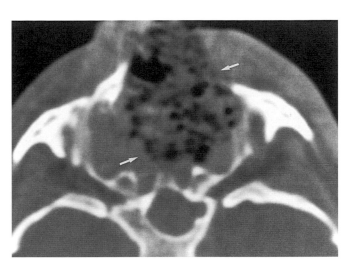

Figure 4.**11** Nasal packing (arrows) following surgery for aspergillosis of the nose and paranasal sinuses.

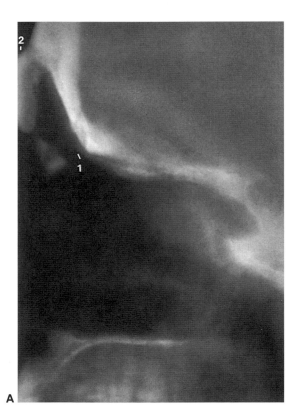

A

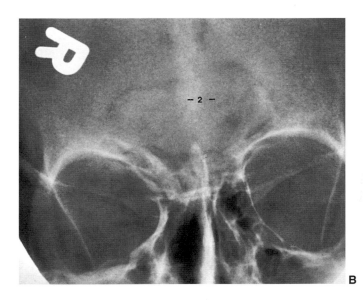

B

Figure 4.**12** Postoperative Lynch and osteoplastic procedure. **A** lateral tomogram, **B** Caldwell projection. A Lynch procedure with a large drainage shute to the nose (1) was done for recurrent frontal sinusitis. This was followed by an osteoplastic flap procedure with obliteration of the frontal sinus, replacing it with fat and muscle and then repositioning the anterior wall bony flap (2).

Maxillary Sinuses

If irrigation and antibiotics fail to clear an infection of the maxillary sinus, a nasal antrostomy or Caldwell-Luc procedure is done, assuming that a dental consultation has excluded the presence of any underlying apical dental disease. A nasal antrostomy is the creation of an opening under the inferior turbinate to provide better drainage of the maxillary sinus to the nasal cavity. If this fails, a Caldwell-Luc procedure is done in order to remove the diseased mucosa (Fig. 4.**13**). Once the infraorbital nerve has been located, an opening is made through the anterior wall of the maxillary sinus, the diseased mucosa is excised, and then a nasal antrostomy is performed along the medial inferior wall of the sinus. Postoperatively, the anterior surgical window becomes fibrotic, closing the bone defect. The antrostomy or nasoantral window is created large enough so that it will not close. Postoperatively, these sinuses may have some degree of fibrosis simulating mucosal disease. Rarely, one can see calcification or even ossification within the sinus following the surgery. Incomplete removal of the mucosa may result in the development of a secondary mucocele.

Lefort I and mandibular osteotomies performed for malocclusion are occasionally seen on scans obtained for other reasons.

A more radical operation, a total maxillectomy, is performed for removal of carcinoma of the sinus (Fig. 4.**14**). It is important to obtain baseline radiographs following radical surgery of this area in order to detect early recurrence of tumor. Progressive change following the baseline radiograph after such an operation is indicative of recurrent tumor.[131]

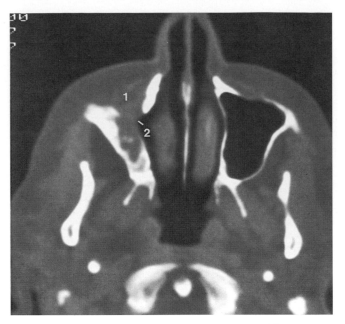

Figure 4.**13** Status post Caldwell-Luc procedure, CT scan, axial plane. An anterior surgical window (1), and nasoantral window (2) of the right maxillary sinus are evident. The wall of the maxillary sinus is thickened as a result of the chronic sinusitis and the subsequent surgical procedure.

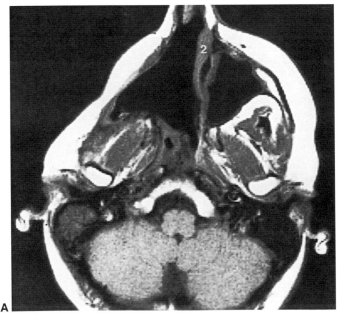

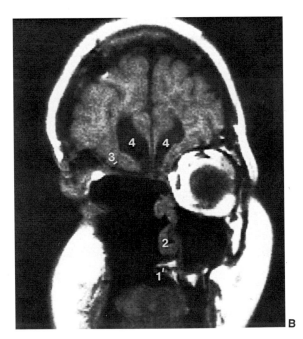

A

B

Figure 4.**14** Status post maxillectomy and resection of the orbit MR in the axial **A** and coronal **B** projections. Absence of the right zygoma, maxilla, nasal cavity, ethmoids, right side of the hard palate, and absence of the orbit are all indicative of the radical surgery for this patient with osteogenic sarcoma, maxillary sinus.

The remaining left palate (1), left turbinates (2), and the roof of the right orbit (3), are identifiable landmarks. Postoperative atrophy of the frontal lobe (4) occurred due to retraction of brain as part of the combined procedure for evaluating the roof of the ethmoid air cells and cribriform plate.

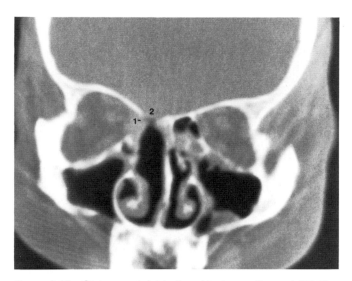

Figure 4.**15**   Status post right ethmoidectomy. Coronal CT. The walls of the ethmoid air cells and right middle turbinate have been removed, as has some of the lamina papyracea (1). The roof of the ethmoid air cells (2) has also been partially resected but the dura is left intact.

Ethmoid Sinus

Ethmoidectomy is performed for recurrent nasal obstructive polyposis, for chronic ethmoiditis, and for tumors of the ethmoid sinuses.[123, 124] The walls of the ethmoid air cells are removed, leaving the cribriform plate and roof of the ethmoid air cells intact (Fig. 4.**15**). A portion of the lamina papyracea is occasionally removed with the ethmoidectomy.

Sphenoid Sinus

The sphenoid sinus is generally approached either through an external ethmoidectomy or a transseptal route, opening the anterior wall of the sphenoid sinus. Other techniques include the transantral and transpalatal approaches. Postoperative changes are often evident in the sphenoid sinus following transsphenoidal hypophysectomy.

Chapter 5 Inflammatory Diseases

Acute Sinusitis

Diffuse thickening of the mucosa and submucosa lining the paranasal sinuses is a common finding on plain films, CT scans, and MR. Indeed, 20 to 40% of patients with an MR of the head are found to have edematous tissue of the paranasal sinuses as incidental findings. Sinusitis may accompany a viral infection but is also seen in patients with allergies (Fig. 5.1). An acutely infected sinus which is symptomatic may show thickening of the mucosa, an air fluid level, or

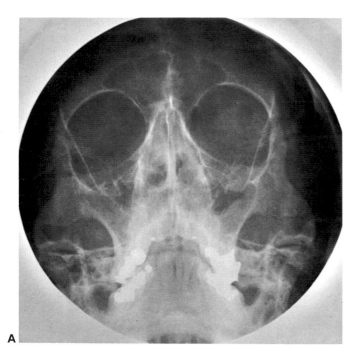

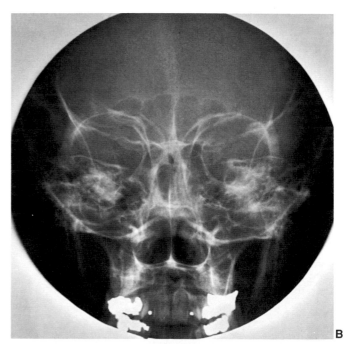

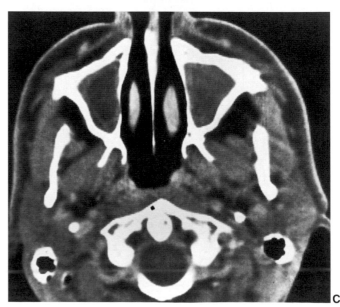

Figure 5.1 Allergic sinusitis. **A** Water's, **B** Caldwell, and **C** axial CT scan. Diffuse opacification of the paranasal sinuses is commonly seen with allergic type sinusitis.

both (Fig. 5.2). The most common cause for acute sinusitis is a viral upper respiratory tract infection.[102] A secondary bacterial infection is often caused by Streptococcus pneumoniae and Hemophilus influenza. Isolated infections of the maxillary sinus may be due to dental caries in about 20% of cases. More severe types of sinusitis occur in diabetics and in patients who are immunosuppressed by various drugs, toxins, and systemic disease. These patients are more prone to fungal infections such as mucormycosis (Fig. 5.3) and aspergillosis, which become aggressive and invade the local blood vessels, causing extensive destruction, osteomyelitis, and cerebral infarction.[37, 69, 73, 133] Treatment consists of surgical debridement and amphotericin B. Thus, the type of infection needs to be diagnosed as early as possible and treated appropriately.[143] Biopsy and special cultures may be required to establish the diagnosis of fungal infection.

Chronic Sinusitis

Chronic sinusitis is most often a complication of bacterial infection.[13, 38, 103] This may cause demineralization of the wall of the sinus and subsequent reactive sclerosis of the bone (Fig. 5.4). These changes in the wall of the sinus often indicate the presence of osteomyelitis, which requires a prolonged course of antibiotics (Figs. 5.5–5.7). Other complications of sinusitis, particularly acute sinusitis, include orbital and periorbital cellulitis, orbital abscess (Figs. 5.8, 5.9), intracranial infection (meningitis, extradural abscess, intracranial abscess), and cavernous sinus thrombosis.[71] Intracranial extension of the infection is considered to occur via the phlebitic diploic veins. Osteomyelitis of the frontal bone may be accompanied by doughy edema overlying the affected sinus and/or a subgaleal abscess causing a mass effect termed a "Pott's puffy tumor". Obstruction of the

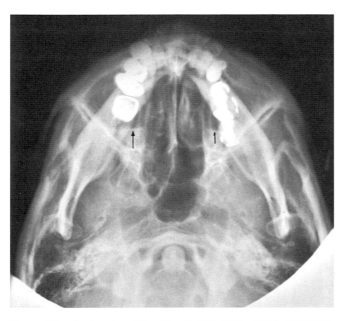

Figure 5.2   Acute sinusitis with air fluid level. Base projection shows a fluid level (arrows) in both maxillary antra.

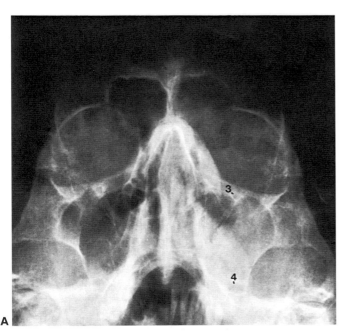

A

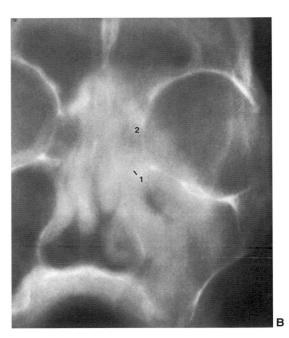

B

Figure 5.3   Mucormycosis. **A** Water's projection, **B** AP tomogram. Extensive opacification of the left maxillary, left ethmoid, and sphenoid sinuses (not shown) with minimal changes in the frontal sinuses. There is some destruction of the ethmomaxillary plate (1), walls of the ethmoid air cells (2), and floor of the sphenoid sinus (not shown). Incidentally, again note the infraorbital nerve canal (3), and the foramen ovale (4) in **A**.

ostium of a sinus, another complication of infection, may result in the development of a mucocele, which in turn may become infected and is then called a pyocele. Patients who have had an appropriate antibiotic treatment for an acute, subacute, or chronic sinusitis which does not resolve should have a biopsy to rule out the presence of any underlying tumor, particularly if the infection is limited to a single sinus and if, in the case of the maxillary sinus, an underlying dental problem has been excluded. Surgical drainage of the sinus is then indicated in order to prevent the development of more severe complications. A persistent air-fluid level following dental extraction may indicate the presence of an oral-antral fistula.

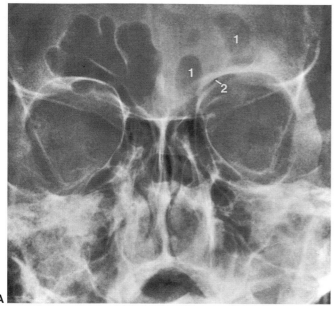

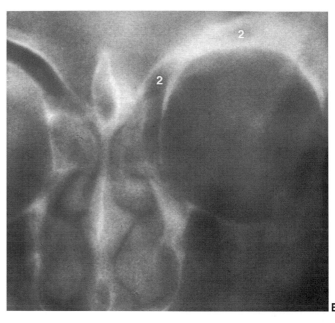

Figure 5.4   Chronic sinusitis. **A** Caldwell projection, **B** AP tomogram. The partial obliteration of the left frontal sinus (1) is due to a previous episode of sinusitis 15 years ago. Recent symptoms are due to an infection of the left supraorbital cell (2), which is also chronic, as demonstrated by some associated reactive sclerosis.

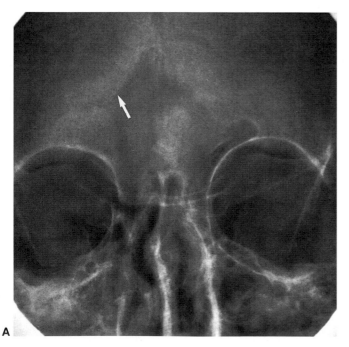

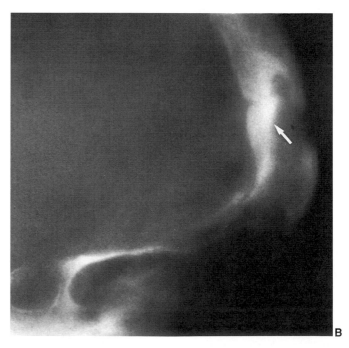

Figure 5.5   Chronic sinusitis with reactive sclerosis, frontal sinuses. **A** Caldwell projection, **B** lateral tomogram. Note sclerosis of the walls of the frontal sinuses (arrow) and loss of the sharp white cortical bone normally seen (often referred to as the mucoperiosteal membrane). This reactive sclerosis is indicative of chronic, low grade osteomyelitis of the frontal bone.

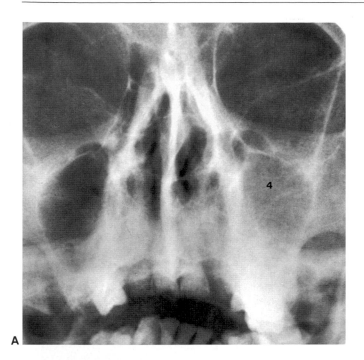

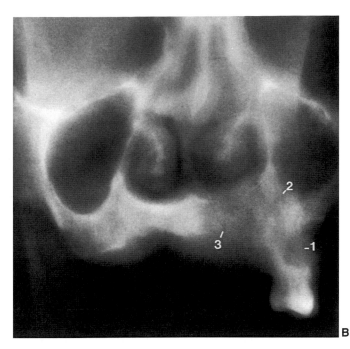

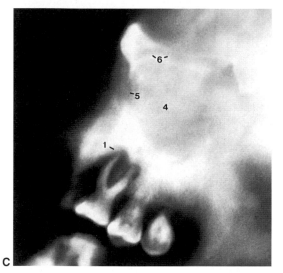

Figure 5.6 Osteomyelitis with bone destruction simulating tumor, left maxillary sinus to palate. **A** Water's projection, **B** AP tomogram, **C** lateral tomogram. A foul discharge indicated the presence of a chronic infection due to severe periapical disease with abscess around the roots of the teeth (1) as noted in **B** and **C**. The floor of the sinus (2), and left side of the hard palate (3) are partially destroyed, the sinus (4) opaque, and the anterior wall (5) partially destroyed. No tumor was found at surgery. Incidentally, note the entire course of the infraorbital nerve canal (6), roof of the maxillary sinus.

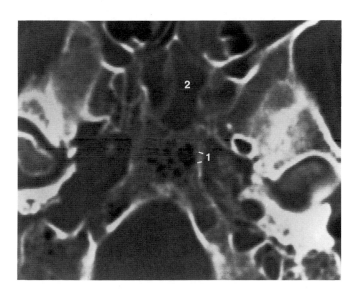

Figure 5.7 Osteomyelitis, clivus, and occipital bone secondary to sinusitis, axial CT scan. Air pockets in the clivus (1) is due to a gas producing bacteria, fusobacterium necroforum. Sinusitis of the posterior ethmoid and sphenoid sinus (2) is the cause of the osteomyelitis.

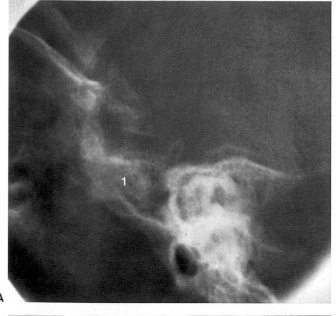

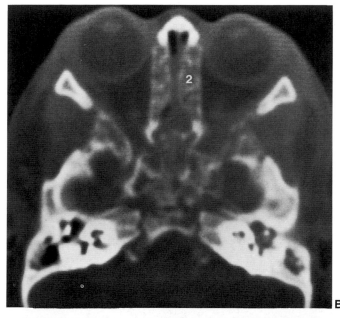

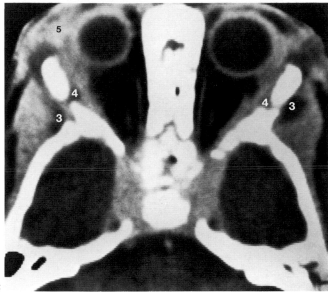

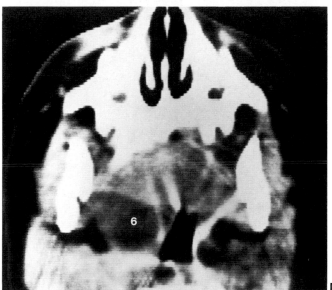

Figure 5.**8** Osteomyelitis, periorbital cellulitis, and naso-pharyngeal abscess secondary to sinusitis. **A** lateral skull, **B–D** axial CT scans. Irregularity of the sphenoid bone (1) noted on the lateral skull film **A** is due to osteomyelitis of the entire bone. The patient started with a cold, developed ethmoid sinusitis, periorbital cellulitis, followed by meningitis. Opacified ethmoid air cells (2) are evident in **B**. An abscess (3) shown in **C** is deep to the temporalis muscle and extends through the sphenozygomatic suture to the orbit (4), causing thickening of the lateral rectus muscle. The periorbital cellulitis (5) is more evident on the right side. A nasopharyngeal abscess (6) noted in **D** is due to the osteomyelitis of the sphenoid. Permission: Carter, BL, Bankoff, MS, Fisk, JD: Computed tomographic detection of sinusitis responsible for intracranial and extracranial infections. Radiology 147:739–742, 1983.)

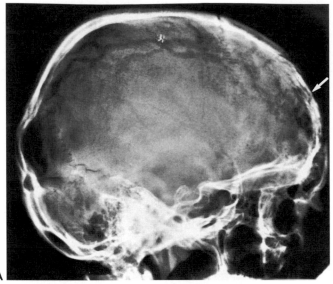

A

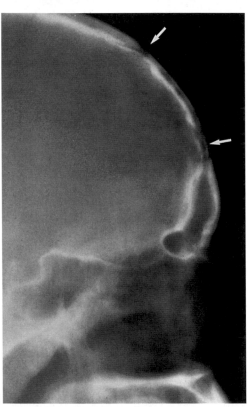

B

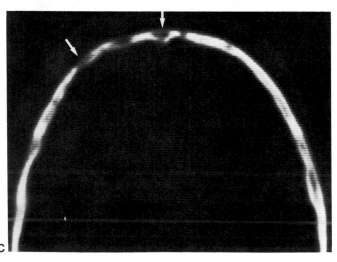

C

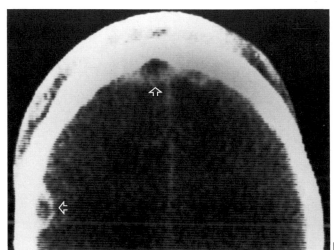

D

Figure 5.**9** Acute osteomyelitis, frontal bone with epidural abscesses secondary to sinusitis. **A** lateral projection, **B** lateral tomogram, **C** and **D** axial CT scans. Destruction of the frontal bone due to osteomyelitis (arrow) is evident on the plain films, lateral tomogram, and CT scan in **A, B**, and **C** respectively. The epidural abscess noted in **D** (open arrow) is due to the osteomyelitis. The patient had been treated for orbital cellulitis secondary to sinusitis, but the acute osteomyelitis was unsuspected. (Permission: Carter, BL, Bankoff, MS, Fisk, JD: Computed tomographic detection of sinusitis responsible for intracranial and extracranial infections. Radiology 147:739–742, 1983.)

Radiological Diagnosis

It should be noted that an air fluid level does not necessarily indicate the presence of an acute sinusitis. Knowledge of the history and physical findings are necessary to differentiate other causes of an air fluid level such as a previous antral lavage, recent trauma, recent surgical procedure, barotrauma, or hemorrhage caused by a coagulopathy defect from platelet disorders or Von Willebrand's disease.[118]

Acute sinusitis is usually evident on clinical examination, confirmed by plain film studies and followed as needed by plain studies. Complications of sinusitis are an indication for CT scan and/or MR.[13, 46, 50] CT scanning is preferable for the identification of bone destruction and osteomyelitis. MR shows to better advantage the type of soft tissue change (Fig. 5.**10**), involvement of the orbit and intracranial structures.

Figure 5.**10** Chronic sinusitis with oral-antral fistula, axial T_1 MR study. Both sinuses are opaque due to inflammatory disease. The left side is chronically infected due to an oral-antral fistula following dental extraction. Note the lower signal on the left (arrow). Some associated destruction of the posterior wall (not shown) resulted in extrusion of pus into the mouth with contraction of the pterygoid muscle in an opened mouth position.

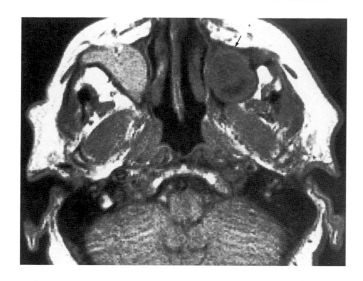

Mucocele

Obstruction of the ostium of the sinus by infection, trauma, or an underlying tumor with continued secretion of mucous results in expansion of the sinus with thinning and remodeling of the sinus wall (Figs. 5.**11**–5.**14**). This is known as a mucocele, which occurs most commonly in the frontal sinuses and less often in the ethmoid, sphenoid, and maxillary sinuses.[19, 56, 99, 129] Rarely, one can see a high attenuation within a mucocele due to increased protein content. Even more rarely seen is calcification within a mucocele. Continued expansion of the sinus encroaches on adjacent structures.[130] In the frontal sinus, this results in proptosis. In the sphenoid sinus, it may affect the cranial nerves within the cavernous sinus or the optic nerve at the orbital apex.[43] Infected mucoceles are called pyoceles.[2] Mucoceles must be differentiated from other masses in the area.[135] This is best accomplished by MR with T_1 and T_2 images or by CT scan in the axial and coronal plane.

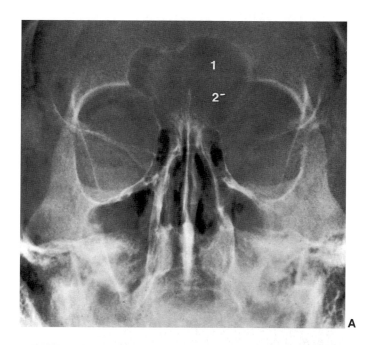

A

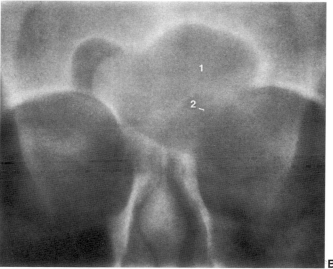

B

Figure 5.**11** Mucocele, frontal sinus. **A** Water's projection, **B** AP tomogram. An expansile mass in the left frontal sinus (1) has eroded through the superior medial wall of the orbit (2).

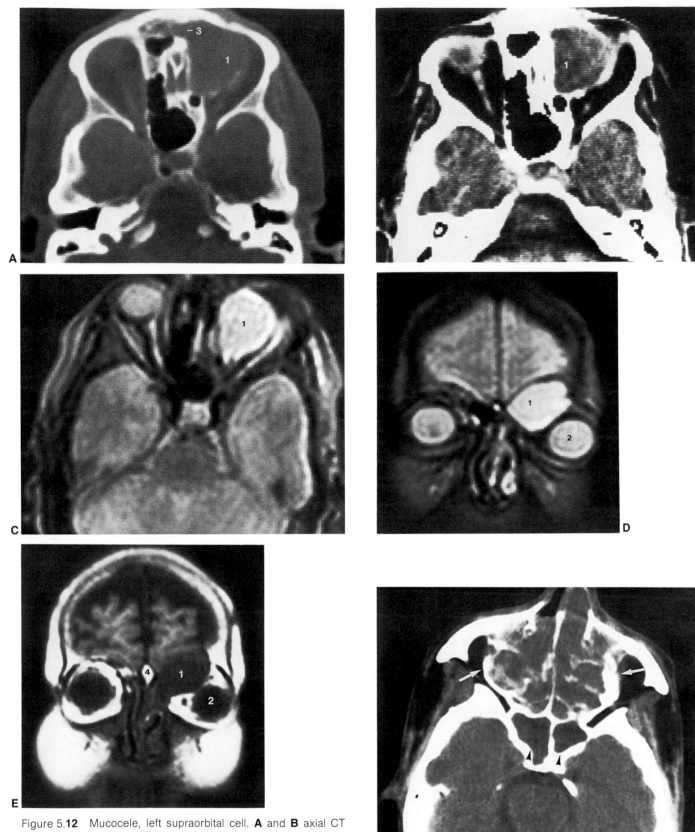

Figure 5.**12**   Mucocele, left supraorbital cell. **A** and **B** axial CT scan, **C** axial MR, **D** and **E** coronal MR. An expanded supraorbital cell (1) is encroaching on the left orbit, displacing the globe (2). The bone window **A** shows destruction of the posteriolateral wall of the frontal sinus (3) and expansion of the supraorbital cell. **B** is a soft tissue window, **C** is a T_2 MR study showing the high signal from the mucocele, **D** is a T_2 coronal image showing a high signal from the mucocele, and E is a T_1 image with a low signal due to the fluid content of the mucocele. Note the high signal from the fat content of the crista galli (4).

Figure 5.**13**   Mucocele, ethmoid air cells. Axial CT scan. The ethmoid cells are expanded bilaterally (arrows), encroaching on the orbits bilaterally. The mucocele is secondary to chronic infection. Note opacification of the sphenoid sinuses (arrow head).

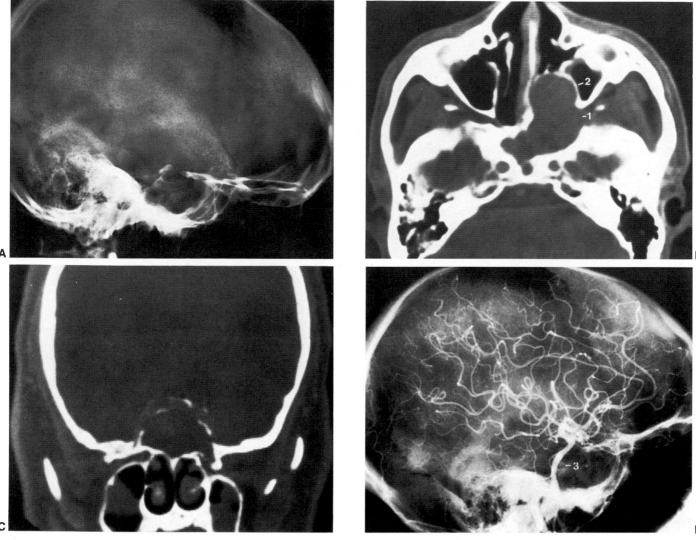

Figure 5.**14** Mucocele, sphenoid sinus. Expansion of the sphenoid sinus is barely evident on the plain lateral film **A**. Decreased vision of the left eye is due to encroachment on the optic nerve canal (not shown). **B** is an axial CT scan of a similar patient with encroachment on the pterygopalatine fossa (1) and posteromedial wall of the maxillary sinus (2). **C** is a coronal scan of another patient showing diffuse enlargement of the sphenoid sinus by a mucocele encroaching on the cavernous sinus bilaterally, causing bilateral third and sixth nerve palsy. **D** Angiogram shows posterior displacement of the carotic artery (3) due to encroachment on the cavernous sinus by the mucocele.

Retention Cyst

A secretory retention cyst due to obstruction and dilatation of a duct of a minor seromucinous gland results in a dome-shaped mass, seen most often in the maxillary sinus. A serous cyst may also be due to a loculated collection of serous, amber fluid in the submucosal connective tissue of a sinus, usually the antral floor. These are commonly seen on plain film studies, CT scans, and MR examinations (Fig. 5.15). Although most common in the maxillary sinuses, they also occur in the frontal, ethmoid, and even sphenoid sinuses. It is very rare for them to become infected but they should be differentiated from tumor masses and odontogenic cysts.[154]

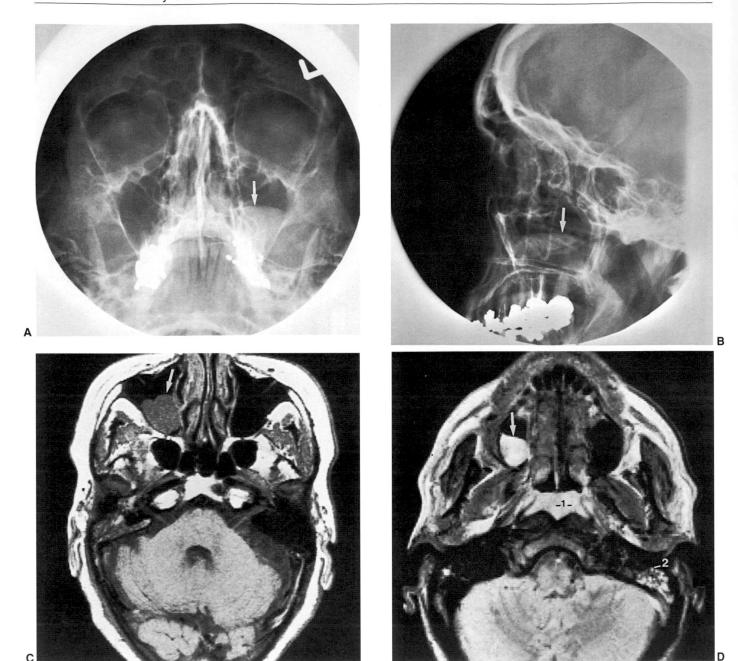

Figure 5.**15** Retention cyst. **A** Water's projection, **B** lateral projection showing a retention cyst (arrows) in the left maxillary sinus. MR studies axial plane **C** and **D** show a retention cyst in the right maxillary sinus with a T_1 image in **C** and a T_2 image in **D**. The fluid content of the cyst results in a low signal with the T_1 image **C** and a high signal with the T_2 image **D**. Note the high signal in the lymphoid tissue of the nasopharynx (1) and of the left mastoid air cells (2) in **D**, also due to inflammatory disease.

Polyps

Polyps have been divided by some authors into allergic and inflammatory types. Some are clearly associated with asthma and with idiosyncrasy to drugs, particularly aspirin. The presence of a polyp in a child should raise the question of cystic fibrosis. Histologically, polyps are characterized by edema, variable numbers of fibroblasts, and inflammatory infiltrates.

Mucous glands may be found in all. The antrochoanal polyp originates from the maxillary sinus, extends through the ostium to the nasal cavity, and through the choana into the nasopharynx (Figs. 5.**16**, 5.**17**).

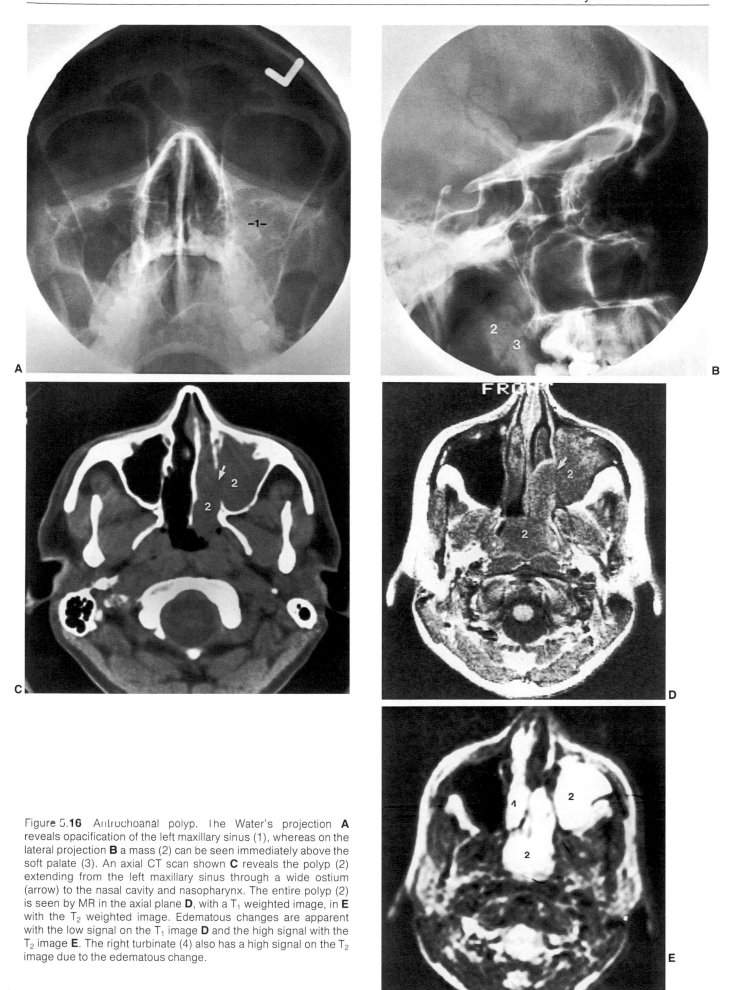

Figure 5.16 Antrochoanal polyp. The Water's projection **A** reveals opacification of the left maxillary sinus (1), whereas on the lateral projection **B** a mass (2) can be seen immediately above the soft palate (3). An axial CT scan shown **C** reveals the polyp (2) extending from the left maxillary sinus through a wide ostium (arrow) to the nasal cavity and nasopharynx. The entire polyp (2) is seen by MR in the axial plane **D**, with a T_1 weighted image, in **E** with the T_2 weighted image. Edematous changes are apparent with the low signal on the T_1 image **D** and the high signal with the T_2 image **E**. The right turbinate (4) also has a high signal on the T_2 image due to the edematous change.

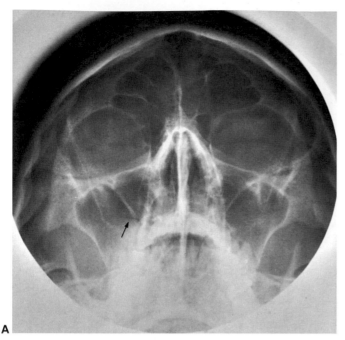

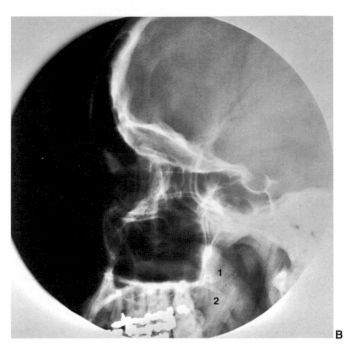

Figure 5.**17**   Antrochoanal polyp. **A** Water's, **B** lateral projection. The polyp does not have to occupy the entire sinus as evident on the Water's projection **A**, with soft tissue change with the inferior portion of the sinus (arrow), which extended through the ostium to the nasal cavity and presented in the nasopharynx (1) as shown in the lateral projection **B** overlying the soft palate (2). This was confirmed by CT scanning (not shown), MR (not shown), and by subsequent surgery.

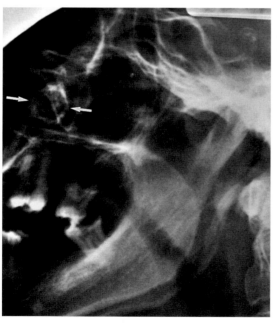

Figure 5.**18**   Rhinolith. An encrusted foreign body (arrows) is seen in the nasal cavity, lateral projection.

Allergy

Allergic reactions of the upper respiratory tract may result in characteristic changes in the nasal cavity and paranasal sinuses. These vary from mild thickening of the mucosa to complete opacification of the sinus. Hypertrophy of the nasal turbinates is common, occasionally accompanied by the presence of nasal polyps. Approximately 10% of the population has this manifestation of allergy, which is most commonly seasonal, due to a ragweed allergy, although spores from molds are also important antigens.[118] Extensive, bilateral opacification of the sinuses and diffuse polyposis are far more common in allergic disease than in bacterial sinusitis (Fig. 5.**1**).

Rhinolith

Foreign bodies within the nose and paranasal sinuses tend to become encrusted and calcified when retained for a long period of time and are thus known as rhinoliths (Figs. 5.**18**). These calcarious bodies may be endogenous as well as exogenous in origin. A nidus of purulent exudate, deposits of blood products, cellular debris, and mineral salts such as calcium phosphate and carbonate may form a rough surface. Rhinoliths may produce nasal obstruction, a malodorous nasal discharge with local pain, and epistaxis.[6] They may even project into the maxillary sinus by pressure necrosis of the nasoantral wall.[6] Foreign bodies within the nose may be self-induced, due to dental root canal fillings, to bullets, schrapnel, or buck shot.

Granulomatous Disease

There are many potential causes for granulomas of the upper respiratory tract.[96, 148] The list includes syphilis, tuberculosis, sarcoidosis, leprosy, brucellosis, rhinosclerma (due to Klebsiella), actinomycosis, blastomycosis, moniliasis, aspergillosis, and others.[79] The diagnosis is established by history and clinical testing. Granulomas due to infection should be differentiated from those due to chronic irritation from berylliosis or chromate salts, and from sarcoidosis. Other differential diagnoses include Wegener's granulomatosis (Figs. 5.**19**, 5.**20**), an autoimmune reaction to an unknown allergin which eventually

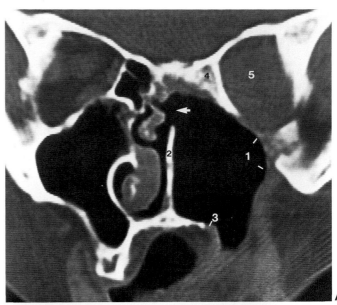

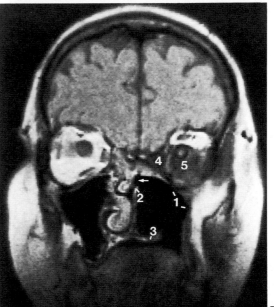

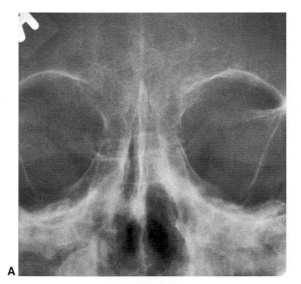

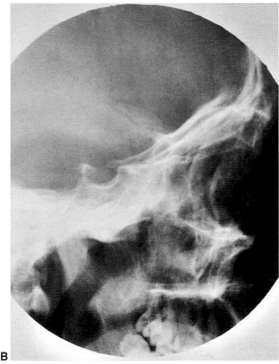

Figure 5.**19** Wegener's granulomatosis with diffuse opacification of the paranasal sinuses, obscuring detail of the walls of the sinuses as shown in the **A** Caldwell and **B** lateral projection.

Figure 5.**20** Wegener's granulomatosis with extensive bone ▶ destruction. **A** coronal CT, **B** coronal MR, **C** axial MR. The patient has had no surgery, but there is considerable destruction of the wall of the left maxillary sinus (1) as shown in **A**. In addition to destruction of the maxilla, the nasal septum (2) is partially destroyed with a perforation (arrow), the hard palate (3) partially destroyed, the turbinates missing. There is opacification of the left ethmoid cells (4) and a mass effect is present in the left orbit (5). Similar findings are evident on the MR study, T_2 **B** and T_1 **C**.

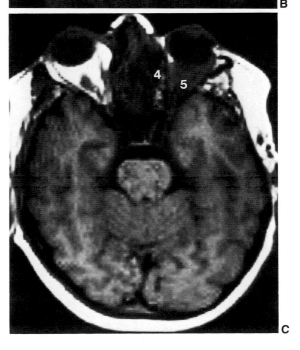

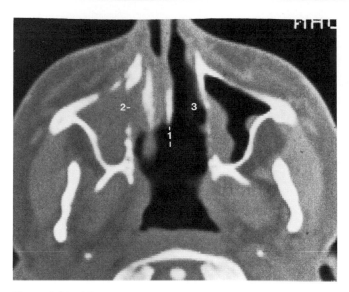

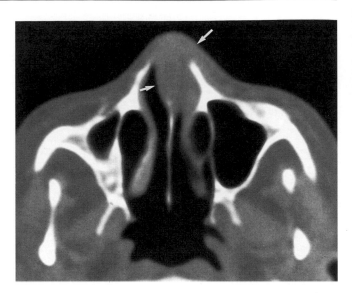

Figure 5.21 Midline granulomatosis, axial CT scan with partial destruction of the nasal septum (1), of the medial wall of the right maxillary sinus (2), and of the left inferior turbinate (3).

Figure 5.22 Chronic nasal infection due to pseudomonas. Axial CT scan. An inflammatory mass (arrow) can be seen involving the left nasal cavity and nasal septum (arrows). The patient is immunosuppressed. Also note the hypoplastic right maxillary sinus.

affects a number of organs including the lungs and kidneys, and is a granuloma with vasculitis as a distinctive feature.[67, 94] "Midline granuloma", probably a lymphomatous neoplasm rather than a true granuloma, may cause extensive local destruction but is responsive to radiotherapy (Fig. 5.21). Wegener's granulomatosis can also be very destructive locally and is usually responsive to Cyclophosphamide.[118] Nasal sarcoid may be seen in 3 to 20% of patients with systemic sarcoidosis and is manifest by multiple small granulomas of the septum and turbinates with polypoid degeneration of the mucosa. It too may be associated with bone destruction.[97, 118, 148]

Atrophic Rhinitis

An end stage of prolonged infection may result in atrophic rhinitis, an uncommon condition in the United States. Progressive chronic inflammatory changes, atrophy, and fibrosis are seen with crusting and atrophic changes of the respiratory endothelium with islands of squamous metaplasia. These patients often have foul mucous discharge, not appreciated by the patient who has lost his sense of smell.

Rhinoscleroma

Rhinoscleroma is a tumor-like expansion of the nose and upper lip, seen more commonly in Africa, Central and South America, and is caused by Klebsiella rhinoscleromatis.[7] A secondary infection in this area, now seen in immunosuppressed patients, can resemble rhinoscleroma (Fig. 5.22) and must be distinguished from other unusual disease entities such as lymphoma. Biopsy and culture is needed for establishing the diagnosis.

Chapter 6 Tumors of the Paranasal Sinuses and Nasal Cavity

Radiologic Diagnosis

If a single sinus is opaque and the underlying teeth of the maxillary sinuses are normal, the possibility of tumor should be considered, particularly if the patient has not responded to an appropriate course of antibiotics. CT scanning in the axial and coronal plane has become a standard procedure for the evaluation of a patient suspected of having a tumor.[51, 63, 120] More recently, MR has been recommended in addition to or instead of the CT scan. A good history and clinical examination are mandatory. The anatomical detail of the paranasal sinuses varies with whether or not there was previous sinus surgery and in patients with an underlying systemic disease such as Wegener's granulomatosis and other diseases (as described). The use of cocaine may cause perforation of the nasal septum. In the absence of such history, bony destruction is strongly suggestive of but not diagnostic of a malignant process. An expanded sinus is more commonly associated with a benign, slowly growing lesion but it should be remembered that benign tumors may destroy bone and malignant tumors may cause expansion of the sinus.[34, 118] The final diagnosis is made by biopsy. Benign and malignant tumors are listed in Tables 6.1 and 6.2.

Benign Tumors

Osteoma

An osteoma is seen primarily in the frontal and ethmoid sinus and can consist of very dense, compact bone, or of lamellar bone with intertrabecular fibrous tissue (Figs. 6.1, 6.2). The fibrous osteomas appear less dense on plain film studies and thus may be confused with a cyst.[118] Although usually asymptomatic, osteomas may obstruct the ostium of the sinus and result in a secondary infection, or they may grow and encroach on adjacent structures such as the orbit. They may also account for the severe sinus pain that some individuals experience during airplane flights. Multiple osteomas might indicate an underlying Gardner's syndrome. In the absence of symptoms, surgical excision is usually deferred unless serial radiographs demonstrate active growth of the lesion.

Papilloma

Papillomas are benign epithelial growths which may be polypoid or papillomatous in the nose or sinuses and are frequently multiple.[42] Squamous papilloma is one of the more common neoplasms of the upper respiratory tract, occurring most commonly in the

Table 6.1 Paranasal Sinus and Nasal Cavity Tumors-Benign

Benign

Osteoma
Papilloma
Inverting papilloma
Angiofibroma
Schwannoma
Neurofibroma
Glioma
Giant cell tumor
  Reparative granuloma
Fibrous dysplasia
Ossifying fibroma
Odontogenic
  Dentigerous cyst
  Radicular cyst
    Periodontal cyst
    Primordial cyst
    Residual cyst
  Ameloblastoma
  Odontoma

Nonodontic
  Medial or fissural cyst
  Incisive or nasopalatine cyst
  Globulomaxillary cyst
  Nasoalveolar cyst
  Aneurysmal bone cysts
Myxoma
Dermoid (Teratoma)
Polyp
  Antrochoanal polyp
Hemangioma
Pleomorphic adenoma
Meningioma
Histiocytosis
Paget's

Table 6.2 Nose and Paranasal Sinuses – Malignant-Tumors

Malignant Tumors

Squamous cell carcinoma
Lymphoma
Esthesioneuroblastoma (olfactory neuroblastoma)
Adenocarcinoma
Adenoid cystic carcinoma
Metastatic carcinoma
Lymphoepithelioma
Melanoma
Plasmacytoma
Osteogenic sarcoma
Basal cell carcinoma
Myeloma
Fibrosarcoma
Ewing's sarcoma
Chondrosarcoma
Ameloblastoma, malignant
Myxosarcoma
Hemangiopericytoma

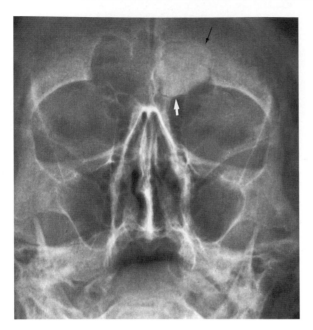

Figure 6.**1** Osteoma, left frontal sinus. Water's projection. The osteoma (arrows) is filling the frontal sinus.

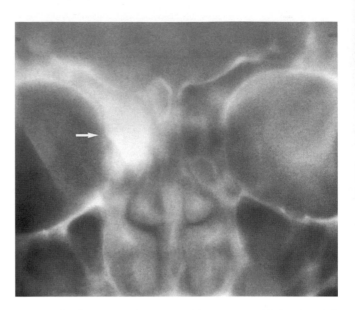

Figure 6.**2** Osteoma, right ethmoid to supraorbital cells. AP tomogram. Note the dense compact bone (arrows) adjacent to the lamina papyracea.

oropharynx, larynx, and trachea. These are treated with simple excision. An inverting papilloma (Fig. 6.3) is considered by some authors to be a variant of the epithelial papilloma and by other authors as a separate category.[77, 86] It, too, is benign microscopically but tends to be locally malignant. The term "inverting" refers to the microscopic appearance of epithelium inverting into the underlying stroma.[6] Inverting papillomas usually arise from the lateral nasal wall at the junction of the antrum and ethmoid sinus. They tend to be unilateral, causing nasal stuffiness, but they extend into the ipsilateral ethmoid and maxillary sinuses. There is a high incidence of local recurrence following inadequate removal, with occasional recurrences showing malignant degeneration or coexistent carcinoma.

Adenoma

Adenomas occur wherever there are glandular elements in the epithelium such as the nose, paranasal sinus, and nasopharynx. These may simulate a nasal polyp but are locally invasive and again show local recurrence if not completely excised. The pleomorphic adenoma arising from minor salivary glands can arise from the palate or from ectopic glands in the nares, or very rarely in a paranasal sinus. Malignant mixed tumors are much more common in the minor salivary gland than in the major glands.

Neurogenic Tumors

Tumors of neurogenic origin such as Schwannomas and neurofibromas also occur in this area but they are rare.[152] These tumors may be seen anywhere along a major nerve trunk or along a peripheral nerve branch.

Nasal gliomas are attributed to cell rests and can occur as a nodule at the base of the nose, simulating a dermoid, or as an intranasal polyp. As with other congenital anomalies in this area, a connection with the intracranial cavity should be excluded prior to any attempted removal of the tumor.

Hemangiomas

Hemangiomas must always be considered wherever blood vessels are present.[136] They may be capillary or cavernous, an isolated finding or part of a syndrome such as the Osler-Weber-Rendu syndrome. Hemangioma of the cartilaginous septum is the most aggressive, and tends to recur if not completely excised.[42, 134]

Giant cell Tumors

Giant cell tumors can also occur in this area, causing local expansion and destruction.[6, 101, 105, 125] The giant cell granuloma, called by some a "reparative" granuloma (Fig. 6.4), is considered to be a benign tumor occurring most frequently in the mandible but also in the maxilla. It is usually excised surgically. Radiation therapy is reserved for the few cases deemed inaccessible by surgery. Osteoclastoma or giant cell tumor of bone is rare, but has been reported in the sphenoid, mandible, and maxilla. Both are to be differentiated from the Brown tumor of hyperparathyroidism and from the aneurysmal bone cyst.

Others

A myxoma, arising from mesenchyme of the tooth germ tissue, is rarely found in the maxillary sinus (Fig. 6.5). It is usually benign but can grow, simulat-

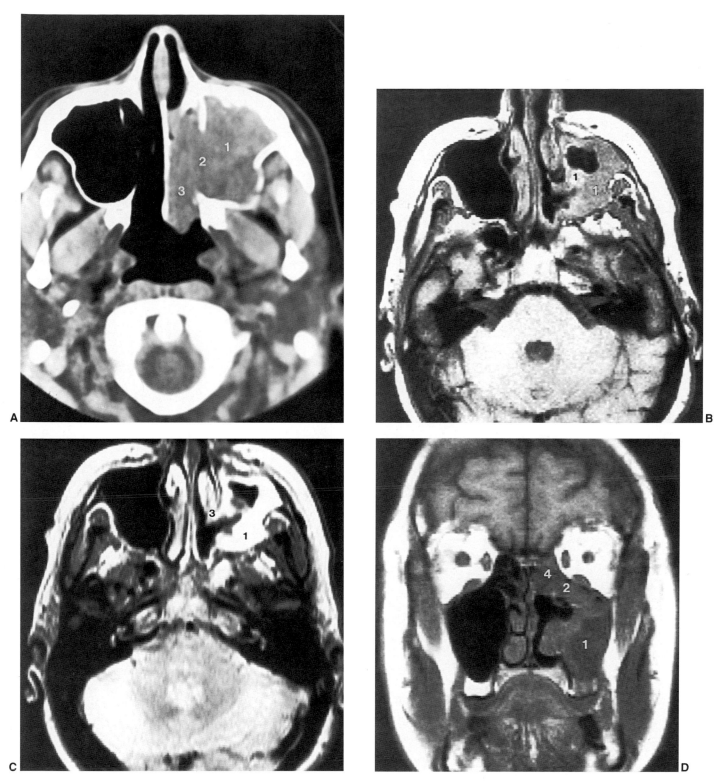

Figure 6.**3** Inverting papilloma. A large soft tissue mass occupying the left maxillary sinus (1) has extended through the medial wall (2) to the nasal cavity (3). **A** axial CT scan, **B** axial MR, T_1 image, **C** axial MR, T_2 image, and **D** coronal MR, T_1 image.

Involvement of the ethmoid air cells (4) can be seen in **D**. The soft tissue extent of the tumor is shown equally well by MR and CT but the bone detail is most readily seen by CT **A**. At surgery, an adjacent squamous cell carcinoma was also found to be present.

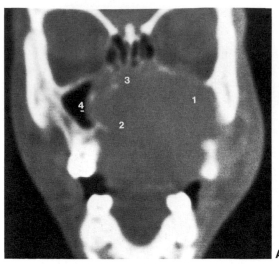

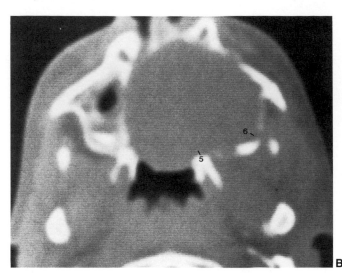

Figure 6.**4**   Giant cell granuloma. **A** coronal CT, **B** axial CT scan. A large, expansile soft tissue mass arising from the left maxilla and palate is occupying the entire left maxillary sinus (1), the palate (2), and encroaching on the nasal cavity (3), and the right maxillary sinus (4). It is also encroaching on the left pterygopalatine fossa (5). The posterolateral wall of the left maxillary sinus is expanded (6). The patient is 8 years old. The mass was resected and the patient given radiotherapy.

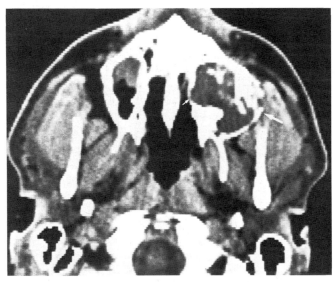

Figure 6.**5**   Myxoma, right maxillary sinus. An axial CT scan reveals an expansile lesion of the left maxillary sinus (arrows). It contained some areas of calcification.

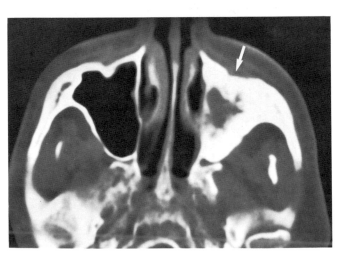

Figure 6.**6**   Fibrous dysplasia of the left maxilla. An axial CT scan shows extensive involvement of the left maxillary sinus (arrow).

ing a rapidly growing fibroma.[42, 82] The myxoma tends to recur after inadequate removal.[6] **Fibrous dysplasia** (Fig. 6.6) may occur in the bones of the head and neck as an isolated finding (monostotic) or as part of a more diffuse involvement with polyostotic fibrous dysplasia. Enlargement of the bone with fibrous dysplasia may simulate a tumor mass in the area, encroaching on the paranasal sinus and/or orbit. **Ossifying fibromas** occurring in the maxilla may have gross calcifications within the lesion. Other tumors occasionally encountered are chordoma[112] and eosinophilic granuloma (Fig. 6.7).

Many **odontogenic cysts and tumors** (Table 6.1) arise in the maxilla and mandible.[141] These include a **dentigerous cyst**, which is an epithelialized sac that develops from the enamel organ of an unerupted tooth (Fig. 6.8). Dentigerous cysts tend to be expansile, well circumscribed, and may grow at varying rates. The keratocyst arises from the enamel organ before dental hard tissues are formed and may appear as a simple or multiloculated cyst. It is aggressive and tends to recur. Multiple odontogenic cysts, especially the **keratocyst**, occur in the first and second decades as part of the nevoid basal cell carcinoma syndrome[6, 45] inherited as autosomal dominant (Fig. 6.9). These patients also have developmental anomalies of the skeleton. **Radicular cysts** of the periodontal membrane occur at the root of a carious tooth. These cysts tend to be destructive and may predispose to the development of an oral-antral fistula after tooth extraction. **Ameloblastomas** may occur in the maxilla and mandible, and are often multicystic, honeycombed-appearing tumors. They may undergo malignant degeneration and thus must be completely excised. The mesodermal type of odontic tumors arising from the mesenchyme of the tooth bud may also be seen such as the myxoma, odontogenic fibroma, and cementoblastoma. The mixed type of tumor con-

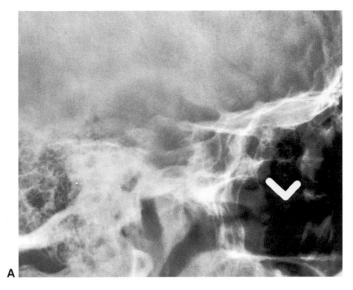

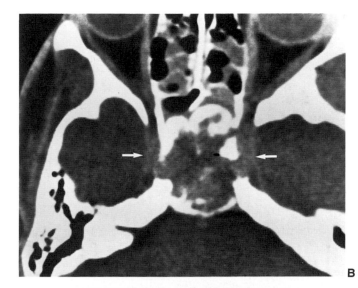

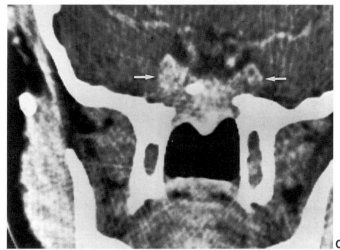

Figure 6.**7**   Eosinophilic granuloma of the sphenoid bone with extensive destruction as shown by plain film **A** and CT scan in the axial **B** and coronal **C** planes. An enhancing soft tissue mass (arrows) is replacing bone encroaching on the cavernous sinus.

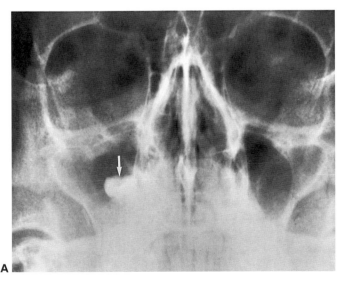

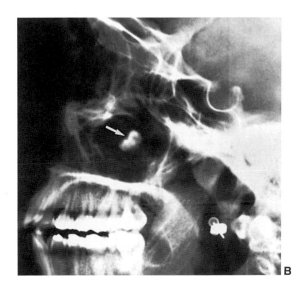

Figure 6.**8**   Dentigerous cyst, right maxillary sinus. **A** Water's projection, **B** lateral projection. A tooth (arrow) is within the dentigerous cyst.

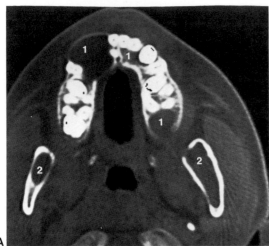

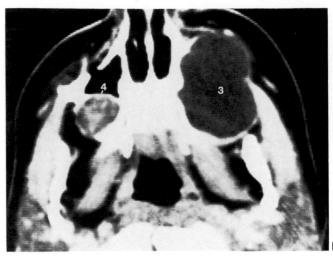

▲ Figure 6.**9** Nevoid basal cell carcinoma syndrome with multiple dentigerous cysts and kerato cysts. Axial CT scans. **A** multiple cysts, three in the maxillae (1) and one each in the ramus of the mandible (2). **B** a second patient with the same syndrome showing a large odontogenic cyst in the left maxilla (3) and a smaller odontogenic cyst (4) in the right maxilla encroaching on the sinus.

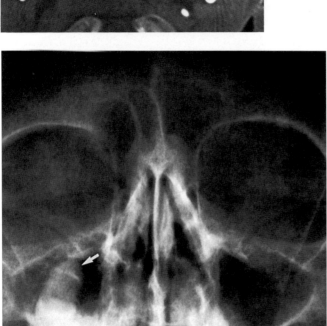

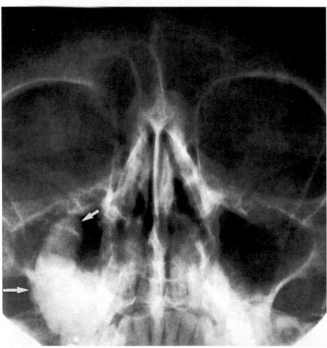

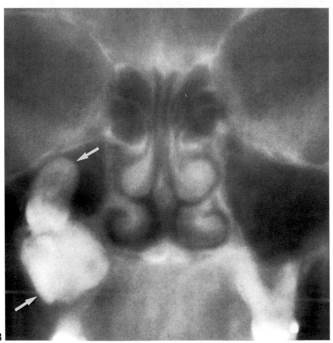

Figure 6.**10** Compound composite odontoma right. **A** Water's projection, **B** AP tomogram, **C** lateral projection. A well defined tooth and a dense mass in the alveolar process, are part of the compound, composite odontoma (arrows).

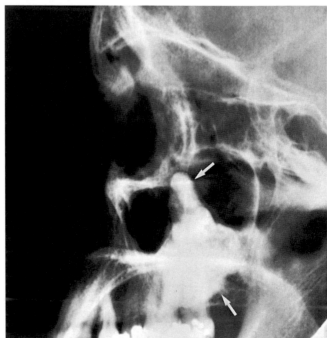

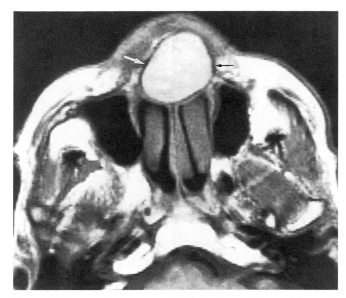

Figure 6.**11** Incisive canal cyst, MR, T₁ image. The cyst (arrows) is enlarging the incisive canal.

Figure 6.**12** Globulomaxillary cyst, left maxilla. **A** coronal CT, **B** axial CT, **C** MR, T₂. The cyst (arrows) has expanded the bone and contains proteinacious material with some calcium.

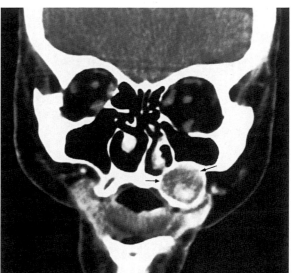

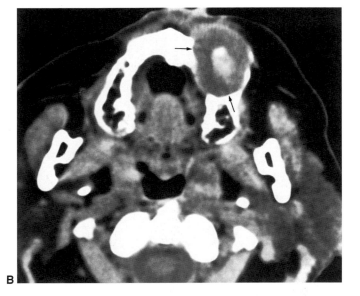

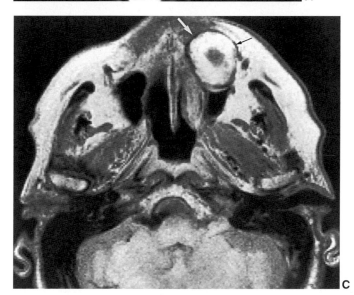

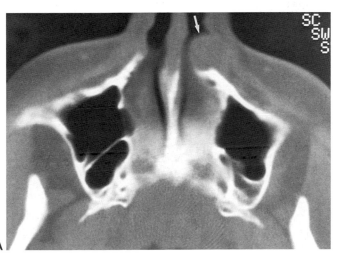

Figure 6.**13** Nasoalveolar cyst. **A** Axial CT scan, **B** MR, T₁. The cyst (arrows) is displacing the nasal process of the maxilla and has a high protein content with a strong signal on the T₁ image.

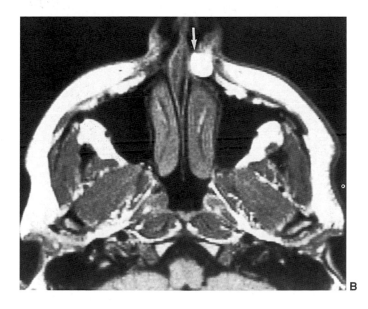

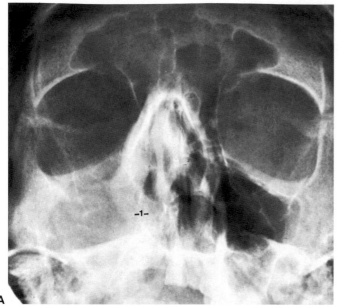

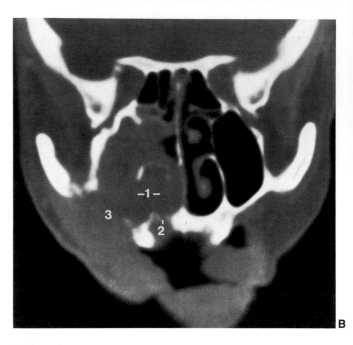

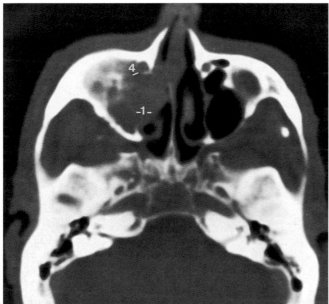

Figure 6.**14**   Carcinoma, right maxillary sinus. **A** Water's projection, **B** coronal CT, **C** axial CT scans. Destruction of the wall of the sinus is evident on plain film but better visualized by CT. Note destruction of the medial wall of the sinus (1) extending to the nasal cavity, destruction of the palate (2) and of the anterior lateral wall of the sinus (3) over to the zygoma evident in **B**. The tumor encroaches on the nasolacrimal duct (4) and extends out into the subcutaneous area (not shown).

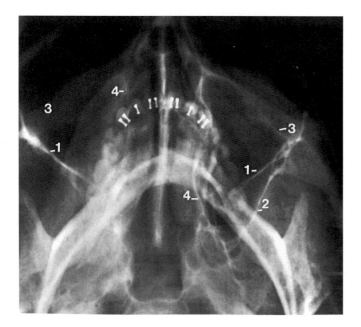

◄ Figure 6.**15**   Carcinoma, right maxillary sinus, half base projection. The posterolateral wall of the orbit (1) is intact whereas the posterolateral wall of the right maxillary sinus is destroyed [compare to normal left side (2)]. Tumor is also destroying the anterior (3) and medial wall (4) of the maxillary sinus, but these findings are somewhat subtle on the plain film study.

sisting of ectodermal and mesodermal components include the odontoma, the complex composite odontoma and the compound composite odontoma (Fig. 6.**10**).

Nonodontic cysts are named according to their location. The median or fissural cyst is frequently found in the maxilla and is usually lined by squamous epithelium. The nasopalatine cyst (Fig. 6.**11**) or cyst of the incisive canal develops from persistent epithelial debris along the nasopalatine duct.[27, 54] These cysts may become secondarily infected or activated by trauma. Other cysts in the area are the globulomaxillary cyst (Fig. 6.12), located between the lateral incisor and canine teeth, the nasoalveolar cyst (Fig. 6.13) in the lateral nasal floor, and the aneurysmal bone cyst.[68] The cysts are prone to infection, may become enlarged resulting in facial deformity and are usually excised.[8]

Malignant Tumors

Squamous cell carcinoma

Squamous cell carcinoma accounts for 80 to 90% of malignant tumors of the paranasal sinuses and nasal cavity (Table 6.2). This tumor frequently arises from the lateral wall of the nasal cavity, from the turbinates, or from the maxillary sinus (Figs. 6.14–6.19).[145] It is seen less often in the ethmoid, frontal, and sphenoid sinuses.[106]

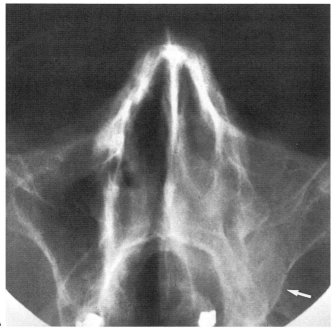

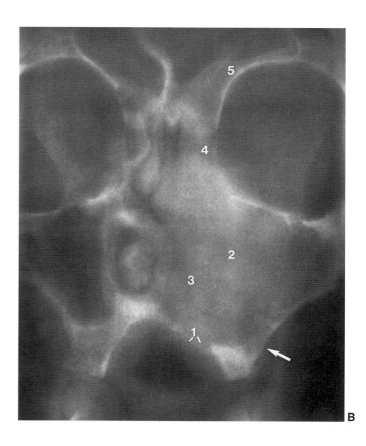

Figure 6.16 Squamous cell carcinoma, left maxillary sinus, slight expansion of sinus. **A** Water's projection, **B** AP tomogram. The left sinus is slightly larger than the right, with slight expansion of the lateral and inferior walls (arrow). There is also destruction of the palate (1), and of the medial wall (2) extending into the nasal cavity (3), ethmoid air cells (4), and left supraorbital cell (5).

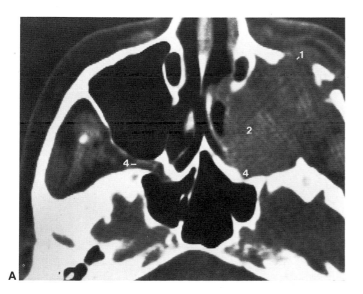

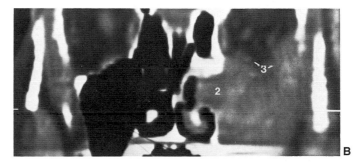

Figure 6.17 Carcinoma, left maxillary sinus. **A** axial CT scan, **B** reformatted coronal projection. A large tumor involving the sinus is causing destruction of the anterior wall (1), medial wall (2), and roof (3). Extension into the orbit resulted in diploplia, one of the presenting symptoms. Also note the posterior extension to the pterygopalatine fossa (4) on the left, whereas the comparable area on the right is normal.

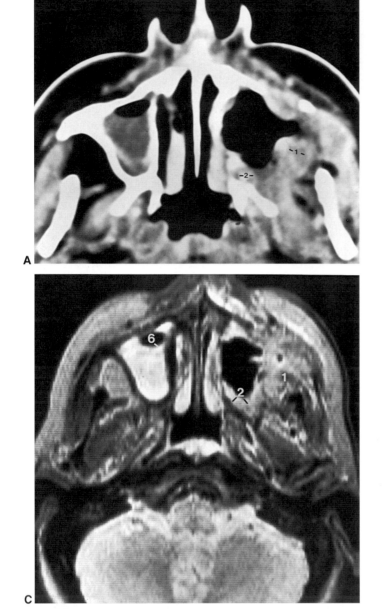

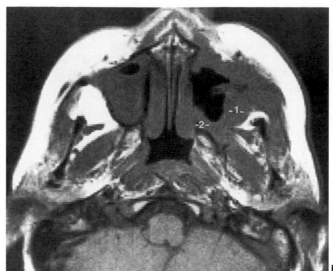

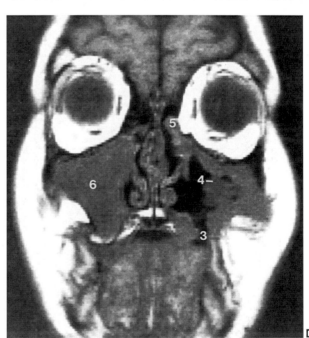

Figure 6.**18**   Carcinoma, left maxillary sinus. Axial CT scan **A**, axial MR, T₁ **B**, T₂ **C**, and coronal MR T₁ **D** all show extensive destruction including the posterolateral wall of the sinus with extension laterally to the infratemporal fossa (1) and posteriorly to the pterygopalatine fossa (2). The coronal image **D** also reveals extension inferiorly into the alveolar ridge (3) and palate. The medial wall (4) of the sinus is also destroyed and tumor is extending into the left ethmoid cells (5). Inflammatory changes in the right maxillary sinus (6) with an air fluid level **C** show a bright signal on the T₂ image; whereas tumor (1) and (2) in the left sinus has a low signal.

Soft tissue changes and local bone destruction indicate the probable presence of tumor. Superior extension to the orbit may result in proptosis as the first symptom. A malignant lesion of the maxillary sinus may also extend posteriorly to the pterygopalatine fossa, which makes surgical excision more difficult and the prognosis more guarded. Retrograde spread to the intracranial cavity may occur via an adjacent cranial nerve.

Although lymph node metastasis is relatively uncommon for squamous cell carcinoma of the maxillary sinus, 10 to 18% may show evidence of involvement of the retropharyngeal, submandibular, and jugular nodes at the time of admission.[6] Eventually 25 to 35% of these patients will show evidence of nodal metastases, whereas 10% will have more generalized metastases.[6]

Adenocarcinoma

Adenocarcinoma is much less common in the paranasal sinus, but is seen in woodworkers and cabinet makers and is attributed to the inhalation of wood dust.[66] Tumors of minor salivary gland origin and other glandular neoplasm constitute between 4 and 8% of sinonasal malignancies.[6] In order of frequency, the major types of mucous gland malignancies are as follows: adenoid cystic carcinoma, adenocarcinoma, pleomorphic adenoma, mucoepidermoid carcinoma, and undifferentiated carcinoma (Figs. 6.**20**–6.**22**).[6]

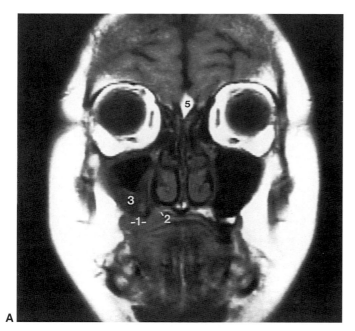

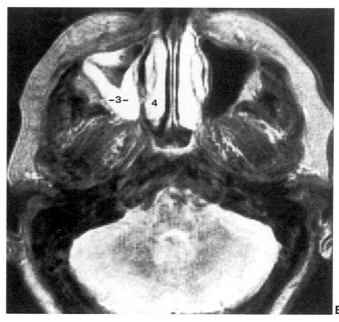

Figure 6.**19** Squamous cell carcinoma, right alveolar ridge. **A** MR coronal, T$_1$ image, and **B** MR axial, T$_2$ image. Tumor of the alveolar ridge (1) extends to the palate (2) and is associated with soft tissue changes (inflammatory) of the right maxillary sinus (3).

The high signal on the MR T$_2$ image of the inflammatory disease of the sinus and of the edematous turbinates (4) is due to infection. Tumor does not extend into the sinus. The crista galli containing fat (5) is seen in **A**.

Figure 6.**20** Adenoid cystic carcinoma of the right alveolar ridge extending into the sinus. **A** Coronal CT, **B** Coronal MR T$_1$, **C** Axial MR T$_1$. Soft tissue changes with minimal destruction of the palate (1) are evident **A**. The soft tissue change of the maxillary sinus (2) seen on all images is due to tumor. More involvement of the palate (1) with the underlying soft tissues and alveolar ridge (3) can be seen by MR **B** and **C**, which extends back to the pterygopalatine fossa (4) evident in **C**. Lateral extension to the buccinator muscle (5) is also evident by MR study.

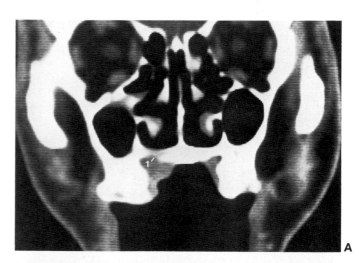

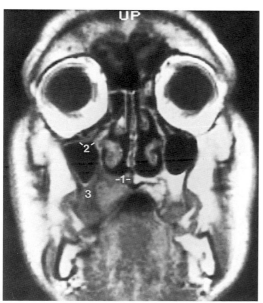

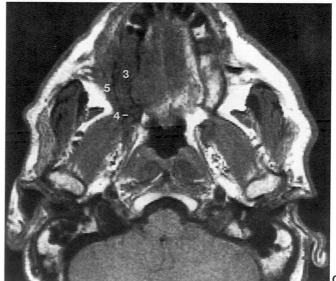

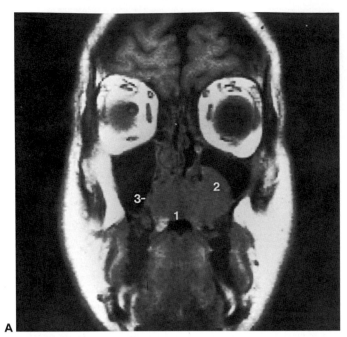

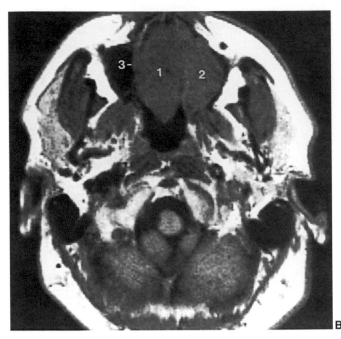

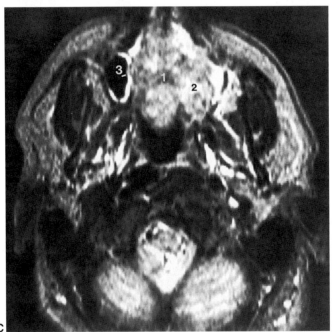

Figure 6.**21**   Adenoid cystic carcinoma of the palate. **A** Coronal MR T₁, **B** Axial MR T₁, **C** Axial MR T₂. A large tumor involving the palate (1) and left maxillary sinus (2) also barely extends to the right maxillary sinus (3). Tumor has a lower signal than the adjacent inflammatory reaction as in **C**.

Generally, minor salivary gland neoplasms are aggressive.[6, 41] Adenoid cystic carcinoma makes up about 35% of all minor salivary gland tumors.[6] They spread along perineural spaces and thus may extend back to or into the intracranial cavity, particularly along the maxillary and mandibular divisions of the trigeminal nerve.[26, 151] This is best demonstrated by CT and/or MR. Fourteen to sixteen percent of these tumors are reported to spread to regional nodes, whereas nearly 40% have more remote metastases to the lungs, bones, and brain.[6, 132]

Others

Esthesioneuroblastoma (Fig. 6.**23**) is a tumor of neural ectodermal origin, usually seen in the upper portion of the nasal cavity and ethmoid sinuses, rarely in the maxillary sinuses.[6, 122] About 11% of cases have intracranial extension.[118] Symptoms are unilateral nasal obstruction, epistaxis, nausea, headache, and rhinorrhea. Although slow growing, these tumors tend to invade and destroy adjacent bone and muscle. Meningiomas might also be seen in the nasal cavity as an extension from the intracranial cavity or very rarely as a primary tumor of the nasal cavity. Malignant melanoma also occurs as a primary tumor of the nasal cavity and maxillary sinus.[75] Rarely,

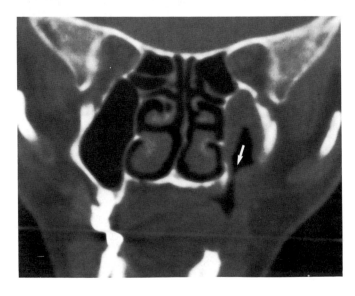

◄ Figure 6.**22**   Mucoepidermoid carcinoma, recurrent with oral antral fistula. A communication between the oral cavity and maxillary sinus (arrow) is due to destruction of bone and soft tissue by tumor which recurred after attempted surgical excision.

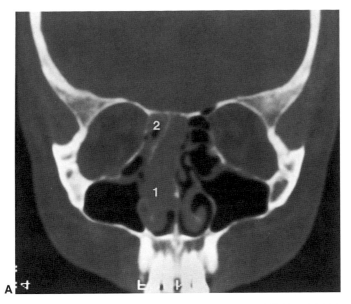

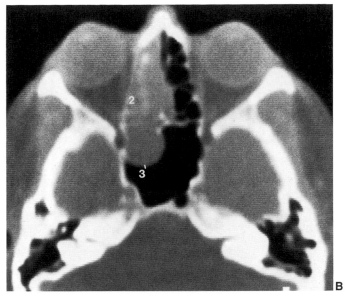

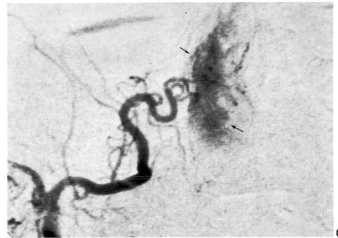

Figure 6.**23**   Esthesioneuroblastoma. **A** coronal CT, **B** axial CT, and **C** angiogram reveal a soft tissue mass in the nasal cavity (1) extending up into the right ethmoid air cells (2) and back to the sphenoid sinus (3) evident in **B**. Vascularity of the tumor (arrows) is evident with opacification of the internal maxillary artery **C**.

extramedullary plasmacytomas are seen in the para-nasal sinuses, although approximately 80% of all extramedullary plasmacytomas (Fig. 6.**24**) have been reported to be in the head and neck.[6] There seems to be a predilection for the nasopharynx, nasocavity, paranasal sinuses, and tonsils, with the more com-

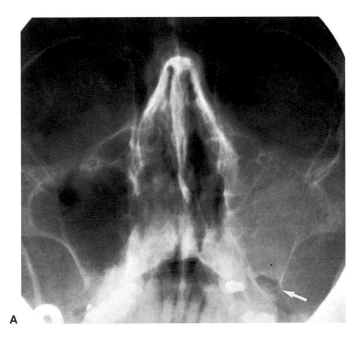

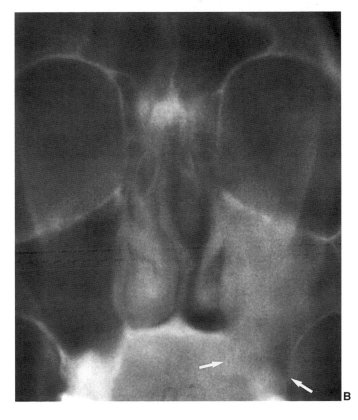

Figure 6.**24**   Plasmacytoma, left maxillary sinus. **A** Water's projection, **B** AP tomogram. Destruction of the floor of the sinus and alveolar ridge (arrows) is due to the large tumor, a proven plasmatocytoma.

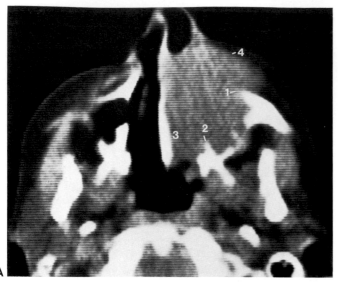

A

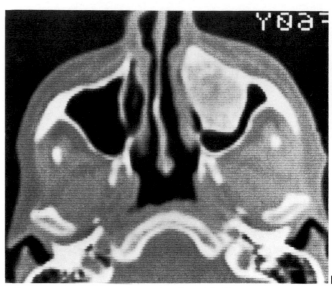

B

Figure 6.**25** Lymphoma, left maxillary sinus. Axial CT scan **A** shows a large mass with destruction of the anterior (1) and medial walls (2) of the sinus and extension into the nasal cavity (3) and

subcutaneous area anterior to the sinus (4). This was treated with radiotherapy and a scan taken several years later. **B** shows replacement of tumor by bone and fibrous tissue.

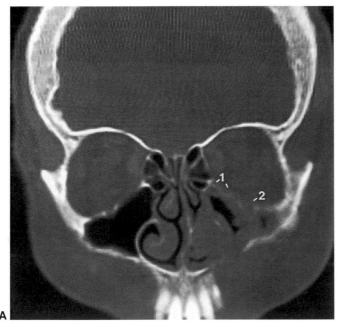

A

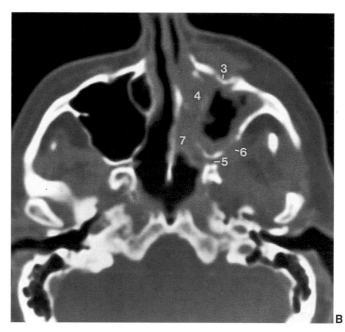

B

Figure 6.**26** Lymphoma, left maxillary sinus. **A** coronal CT, **B** axial CT. A soft tissue mass within the sinus with considerable bone destruction had at first been considered to be carcinoma but was later proven to be lymphoma. Note destruction of the floor of the orbit (1), bone destruction in the region of the infraorbital

nerve canal (2), anterior wall of the maxillary sinus (3), medial wall of the maxillary sinus (4) with extension back to the ptery-gopalatine fossa (5), and infratemporal fossa (6). Tumor mass is also extending medially to the nasal cavity (7) and anteriorly to the subcutaneous area.

mon sites being the nose and sinuses. The majority of cases are treated by surgical excision, radiation, or both.[1, 76]

Lymphomas of the nose and paranasal sinuses (Figs. 6.25, 6.26) are unusual but when present, tend to be localized to the extranodal site.[6, 117, 147] They may present with soft tissue swelling of the cheek or nose, or with nasal obstruction. The radiographic findings are non-specific showing bone destruction and a soft tissue mass. Biopsy is needed to establish the diag-

Figure 6.**28** Osteogenic sarcoma, right maxillary sinus. **A** ▶ Water's projection, **B** and **C** coronal CT, and **D** axial CT reveal a soft tissue opacification of the right maxillary sinus. This was originally diagnosed and treated as sinusitis but did not respond. Biopsy revealed osteogenic sarcoma. The tumor mass extended through the nasolacrimal duct (1) to the region of the lacrimal sac (2) and through the ethmomaxillary plate noted in **C** (3) to the ethmoid air cells (4). Absence of the turbinate and medial wall of the maxillary sinus (5) is attributed in part to the tumor and in part to the biopsy procedure. A radical maxillectomy with exenteration of the orbit was performed.

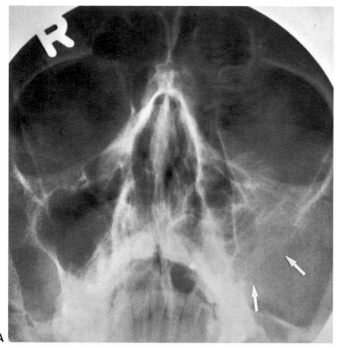

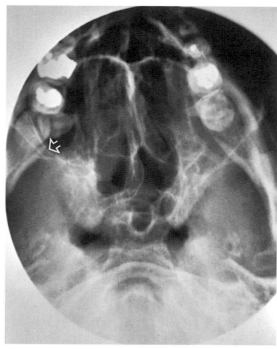

Figure 6.**27**   Rhabdomyosarcoma, left maxillary sinus and cheek. **A** Water's view, **B** Base view. Destruction of the lateral wall and floor of the maxillary sinus (arrows) is evident on the Water's projection, subsequently proven by tomography. Note absence of the "S" shaped curve of the maxillary sinus on the base projection, which is visible on the normal right side (open arrow).

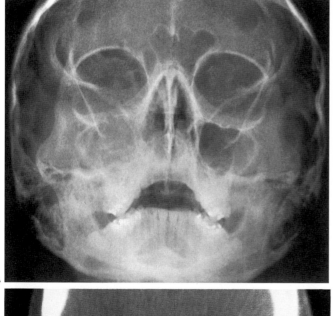

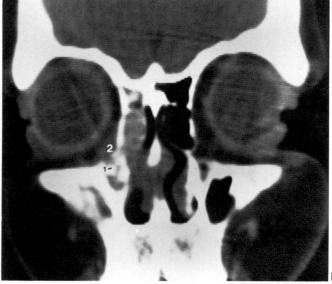

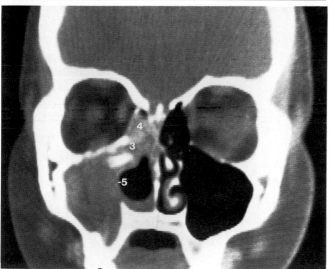

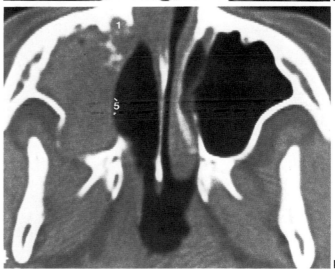

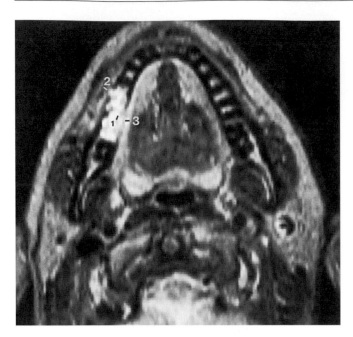

Figure 6.29 Fibrosarcoma, left mandible. Axial MR study, T_2 image reveals a high signal (1) in the region of the fibrosarcoma involving the body of the mandible on the right side. This extended slightly laterally, eroding the buccal (2) and medially eroding the lingual (3) surfaces of the mandible.

nosis.[36] When treated with radiation to the involved area, the five year survival rate ranges from 50 to 70%.[6] Concurrent generalized lymphoma is rarely seen.

In children, rhabdomyosarcoma is occasionally seen in the paranasal sinuses (Fig. 6.27), although more commonly in the orbit, infratemporal fossa, and nasopharynx.[80, 89] Various types of sarcomas such as osteogenic sarcoma (Fig. 6.28), Ewing's sarcoma, and fibrosarcoma (Fig. 6.29) are uncommon in the area but must be considered in the differential diagnosis.[90] The diagnosis is established by biopsy.[32, 110]

Metastatic Tumors

Whenever a malignant neoplasm of the paranasal sinus is encountered, the possibility of metastasis should be considered. The kidney is the most common primary site but tumors of the lung, breast, and other sites such as the prostate may also metastasize to this region.[53] Metastatic lesions can be distinguished from a primary tumor only by biopsy.

Nasopharynx and Infratemporal Fossa

Chapter 7 **Anatomy**

Nasopharynx

The nasopharynx (Fig. 7.**1**) communicates anteriorly with the nasal cavity via the choanae and inferiorly with the oropharynx beyond the soft palate.[83, 113] It is formed by the superior pharyngeal constrictor muscle with the overlying pharyngobasilar fascia extending up to the skull base. The pharyngobasilar fascia or pharyngeal aponeurosis encircles the space between the upper border of the superior constrictor muscle and the skull base. The osseous structures of the nasopharynx include the clivus, petrous apices, body of the sphenoid bone, and the upper cervical vertebrae. The longus capitis and rectus capitis muscles lie between the superior pharyngeal constrictor muscle and the skull base and upper cervical vertebra. Lymphoid tissue, the adenoids (Fig. 7.**2**), overlie these muscles and all are covered by the mucosa of the nasopharynx. Along the lateral wall is torus tubarius and the salpingopharyngeal fold, partially surrounding the pharyngotympanic or eustachian tube (Figs. 7.**1**, 7.**3**). Posterior superior to this area is the pharyngeal recess or fossa of Rosenmuller, extending as far out as the spine of the sphenoid bone. Posterolateral to the recess is the internal carotid artery, the internal jugular vein, and cranial nerves 9-12, An abscess of the retropharyngeal space or an aneurysm of the carotid artery may bulge into the lateral recess of Rosenmüller. The eustachian orifice is about 1 cm behind and slightly below the posterior portion of the inferior concha (Fig. 7.**3**). Muscles affecting tubal function and causing it to open are the tensor and levator veli palatini and the stylopharyngeus. The tensor and levator palatini muscles (Fig. 7.**3**) originate from the infralateral and inframedial wall of the cartilaginous portion of the eustachian tube respectively and from the scaphoid fossa of the pterygoid plates. They descend vertically, medial to the pterygoid muscle, to insert on the palatine aponeurosis and palatine velum. Elevation of the soft palate and contraction of the fibers of the superior constrictor muscle (Passavant's sphincter) close off the nasopharynx during deglutition.

The superior portion of the nasopharynx is concerned with respiration, and this is lined by pseudostratified ciliated columnar epithelium.[42] Inferiorly, the pharynx is more involved with eating, and the epithelium changes to a stratified squamous type. The mucosa of the nasopharynx contains a considerable number of globlet cells, minor salivary glands, and lymphoid tissue. There is an inconstant small

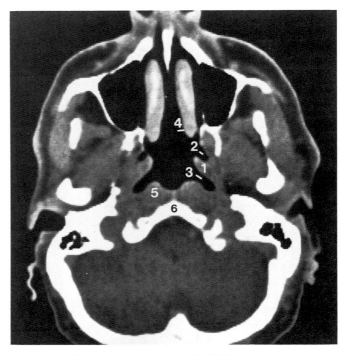

Figure 7.**1** Normal nasopharynx. Axial CT. The torus tubarius (1), eustachian tube orifice (2), and pharyngeal recess (3), are readily seen at the level of the inferior turbinate (4). The longus capitus muscles (5) form the posterior superior wall of the nasopharynx. The clivus (6) is readily seen.

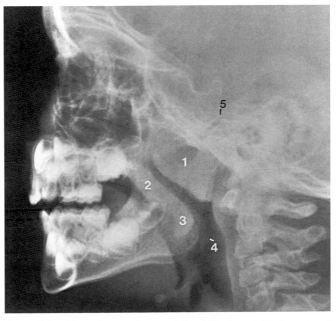

Figure 7.**2** Normal nasopharynx, lateral film in a child. Prominent adenoid tissue (1) is evident. Also note the soft palate (2), uvula (3), palatine tonsils (4), and spheno-occipital synchondrosis (5).

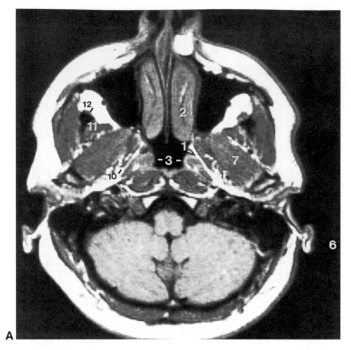

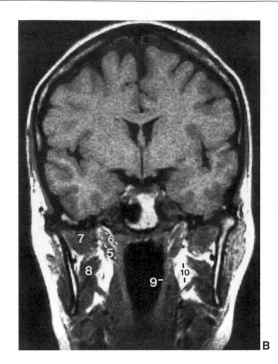

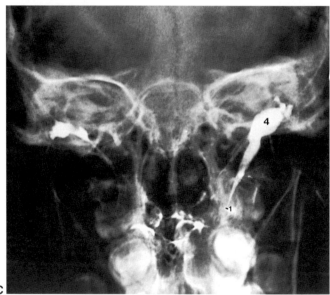

Figure 7.3 Normal nasopharynx. **A** axial and **B** coronal MR T₁ images. **C** an eustachiogram, through-orbital projection. The orifice of the eustachian tube (1) is at the level of the inferior turbinate (2). The eustachian tube is a communication between the nasopharynx (3) and the tympanic cavity (4) as seen in **C**. The tensor (5) and levator (6) palatini muscles originating from just below the eustachian tube are best seen on the coronal plane **B**. The lateral (7) pterygoid muscles, seen both on the axial **A** and coronal **B** views, and medial (8) pterygoid muscle seen on the coronal plane **B** are separated from the pharynx and the pharyngeal constrictor muscle (9) by the fat in the parapharyngeal space (10). The temporalis muscle (11) is inserting on the coronoid process (12) of the mandible in **A**.

blind pouch within or just inferior to the adenoid tissue or pharyngeal tonsil, which is known as the pharyngeal bursa (Tornwaldt's). Superior to the pharyngeal tonsil is the pharyngeal hypophysis, consisting of accessory hypophyseal tissue derived from Rathke's pouch.

Infratemporal Fossa

Lateral to the nasopharynx and pterygopalatine fossa is the infratemporal fossa (Figs. 7.3, 7.4), containing the lateral pterygoid muscle, a portion of the medial pterygoid muscle, and the inferior portion of the temporalis muscle. This fossa is found below the greater wing of the sphenoid bone, posterior to the maxillary sinus, and medial to the mandible and

zygomatic arch. It extends down to the alveolar border of the maxilla. It contains the internal maxillary vessels and the mandibular and auriculotemporal nerve. The foramen ovale (containing V3) and foramen spinosum (containing the middle meningeal artery) open to its roof. The inferior orbital fissure and pterygomaxillary fissures also open to the infratemporal fossa.

The medial and lateral pterygoid muscles together with the temporalis and masseter muscles performing the function of mastication are innervated by the mandibular nerve (V3). The pharyngeal constrictor and palatal muscles performing the function of deglutition are innervated by the vagus nerve, the pharyngeal plexus of the accessory nerve, a branch of the fifth to the tensor veli palatini, and a branch of the

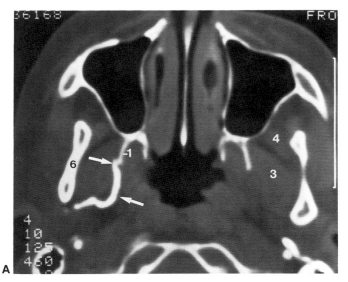 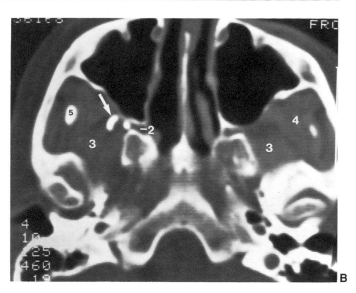

Figure 7.**4**   Normal infratemporal fossa, **A, B** axial CT scans. Previously embolized internal maxillary artery (arrows) can be seen in the infratemporal fossa, passing around the lateral ptery- goid plate (1) to the pterygopalatine fossa (2). Also note the lateral pterygoid muscle (3), temporalis muscle (4), and coronoid pro- cess (5) of the mandible (6).

ninth nerve to the stylopharyngeus muscle. Sensory nerves to the area of deglutition are conducted via the palatine and nasopalatine branches of the fifth cranial nerve and branches of the ninth or glossopharyngeal nerve. A fat plane between the muscles of deglutition and mastication is the parapharyngeal space.[119] This parapharyngeal space is an inverted pyramid extend- ing from the skull base to the submandibular space and hyoid bone as discussed in Part IV.

Chapter 8 Pathologic Findings

Congenital Anomalies

Congenital anomalies are infrequent and associated with defects in the development of the skull base. As noted earlier, failure of fusion of neural elements and of bone may result in the development of an encephalocele or meningocele through the sphenoid bone to the nasal cavity or nasopharynx. Notochord remnants, ending just caudad to the dorsal attachment of the buccopharyngeal membrane, may remain as a solid mass or as a cyst, known as Tornwaldt's cyst.[10, 140] The latter present in the second or third decade of life as persistent postnasal discharge of mucous or purulent material.[62] This is dorsal and caudad to a Rathke's pouch. The latter is the primordium of the anterior pituitary and lies anterior to the buccopharyngeal membrane.[30] Although usually obliterated, remnants of Rathke's pouch may persist as small epithelial cysts in the body of the sphenoid bone.

Mucous retention cysts (Fig. 8.1) are occasionally found in the nasopharynx and, rarely, a branchial cleft cyst derived from the second branchial arch may extend deep to the lateral pharyngeal wall as high as

C1.[140] Nasopharyngeal pseudocysts have been postulated to be the result of longus capitus perimyositis. Any of these cysts may become secondarily infected. Calcification is occasionally seen anterior to C1 secondary to peritendinitis of the longus colli tendon.[52, 144]

Inflammations

Diffuse inflammatory change of the nasopharynx or inflammatory masses (Fig. 8.2) may also occur with infection of the adenoid tissue, osteomyelitis of the clivus (see Fig. 5.7), or sphenoid bone, or with infection of the petrous apex of the temporal bone. The last may be secondary to chronic infection of the ear, to mucormycosis, to malignant external otitis secondary to a pseudomonas infection occurring in diabetics, or to granulomatous disease affecting the temporal bone such as Wegener's granulomatosis.[28] These changes may be identified with contrast enhanced CT scans or with MR. The latter has the advantage of revealing marrow changes earlier than the bone destruction seen with CT. An unusual case of hydatid cyst of the infratemporal fossa has been included to demonstrate the mass effect that may be seen with a chronic infection (see Fig. 8.12).

Benign Tumors

Angiofibroma

Benign tumors of the nasopharynx are rare, the most frequent being a juvenile angiofibroma.[9, 20, 149] They occur in teenaged boys (Figs. 8.3, 8.4), usually originating at the superior, posterolateral wall of the nasal cavity or from the nasopharynx.[31] These tumors grow into the nasopharynx and often laterally out into the pterygopalatine fossa. Local extension also occurs from there to the infratemporal fossa, superiorly to the orbit via the inferior orbital fissure and superiorly to the sphenoid sinus. It may also extend out beyond these areas to the middle cranial fossa, cavernous sinus, and sella turcica. As the tumor grows, it is accompanied by extensive local destruction of bone. The patients typically present with nose bleeds or with nasal obstruction. Although considered to be a tumor of teenaged boys, they have been reported in older patients. A few have been reported in females but the diagnosis in these instances has been questioned by some authors.

Figure 8.1 Nasopharyngeal cyst, evident on plain lateral film (arrow).

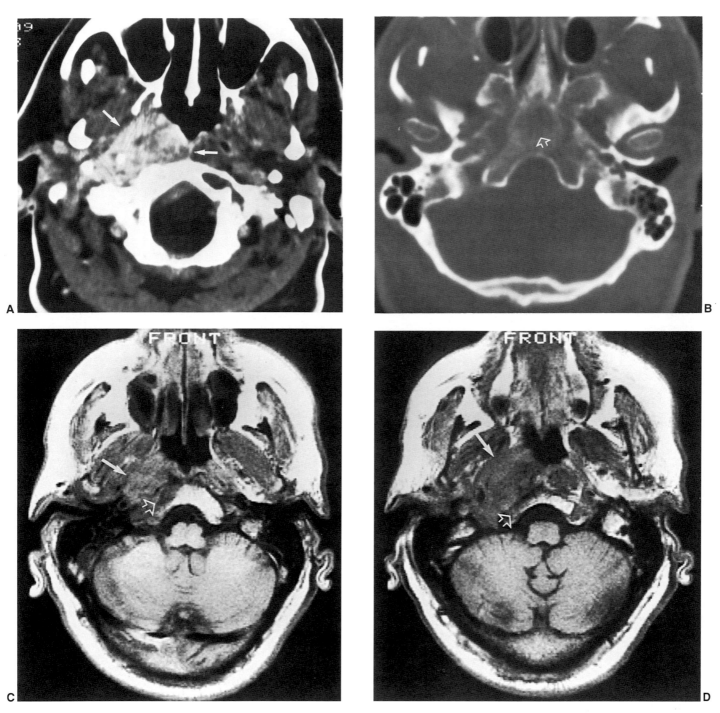

Figure 8.2 Inflammatory mass, nasopharynx secondary to malignant external otitis (pseudomonas). Axial CT scan with contrast enhancement **A** soft tissue window, **B** bone window, and MR images in the axial **C**, **D**, and coronal **E** planes. Note a mass on the right side of the nasopharynx (arrows). Bone involvement is difficult to appreciate on the CT scan **B**, but is evident (open arrow) on the MR images **C–E**. The osteomyelitis also resulted in increased uptake on the bone scan.

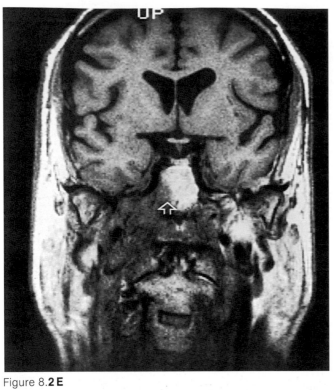

Figure 8.**2 E**

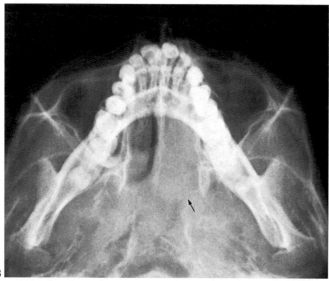

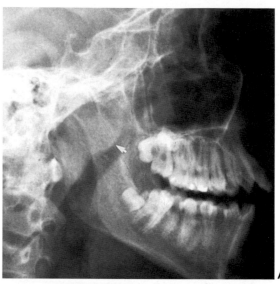

Figure 8.**3**   Angiofibroma. **A** lateral projection, **B** base projection, **C** axial CT, and **D** coronal CT after contrast injection. A soft tissue mass (arrow) in the nasopharynx **A** is extending into left nasal cavity **B**. CT scans reveal extension into the pterygopalatine fossa (1), the sphenoid sinus (2), and lateral recess of the sphenoid sinus (3).

▼

A

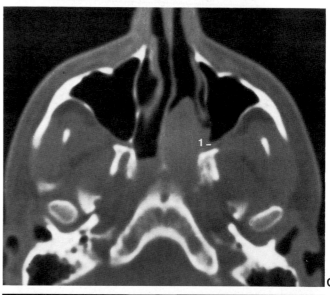

B

C

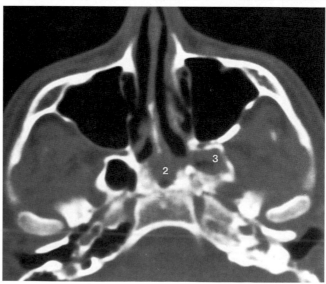

D

E

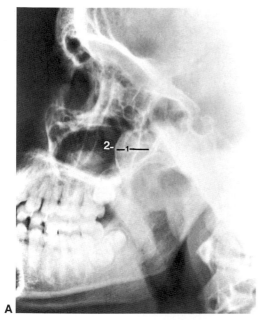

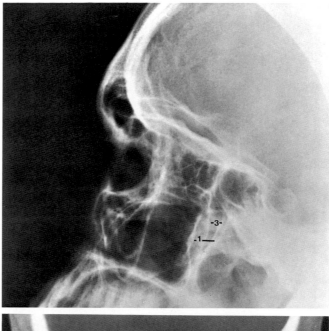

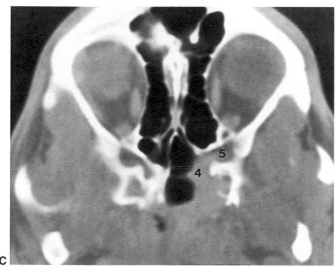

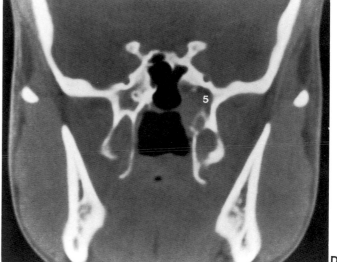

Figure 8.4 Recurrent angiofibroma. Lateral projection **A** when first seen and **B** several years later, axial **C**, and coronal **D** CT scan. The original lateral projection **A** is typical for angiofibroma extending into the pterygopalatine fossa (1) displacing the posterior wall of the maxillary sinus forward (2). These findings are

less evident several years later **B** but the left pterygopalatine fossa (1) is still larger than the right (3). CT scans **C** and **D** reveal recurrence of the angiofibroma (4) extending into the left pterygopalatine fossa (5). (Courtesy of Eric Henrickson, MD, Lawrence General Hospital, Lawrence, MA.)

Early diagnosis of an angiofibroma is now possible with CT scan using intravenous contrast enhancement or with MR. A precise determination of the extent of tumor is necessary for planning the surgical approach. Radiotherapy is sometimes used in combination with surgery for treatment of tumors which cannot be completely excised, such as those with large intracranial extension.[1, 17]

Others

Other benign growths reported in the nasopharynx are teratomas or dermoids.[58] These are seen as polypoid masses, largely fatty, but they may contain ectoderm or mesoderm.[140] They are seen most often soon after birth as a cause of nasal obstruction. CT or

MR is indicated for establishing the diagnosis and for differentiating the mass from an encephalocele or for identifying any intracranial extension of tumor. Benign adenomas from minor salivary glands usually occur at lower levels of the pharynx. Chondromas may originate from the skull base and chordomas from notochord remnant. Tumors of the sphenoid bone such as giant cell tumor, eosinophilic granuloma (see Fig. 6.7), or tumors of the sella such as chromophobe adenoma or even meningiomas may extend through to the nasal cavity or nasopharynx.[11] Other benign tumors to be considered in the area are pedunculated fibromas and vascular polyps.[72, 121] The latter are rare but can simulate an angiofibroma, although they tend to be softer in consistency and more granular in appearance.

Finally, one must consider in the differential diagnosis tumors arising from the parapharyngeal space, the carotid sheath (considered anatomically to be the posterior compartment of the parapharyngeal space) and the temporal bone. Paragangliomas arising from neural crest cells of the jugular fossa or within the perineurium of the vagus nerve at or just below the ganglion nodosum near the skull base may present in the nasopharynx.[35, 108] The intravagal tumors may be found at various sites along the course of this nerve. Although paragangliomas are usually benign, re-

gional nodal and distant metastases have been reported in greater frequency (up to 19%) with vagal paragangliomas.[6, 33] Ten percent may be multicentric in origin and up to 26% occur in patients with a familial tendency.[6]

Schwannomas and neurofibromas may arise from any of the cranial nerves found in the carotid sheath or posterior compartment of the parapharyngeal space (cranial nerves 9-12) or from the cervical nerve roots (Fig. 8.5). Schwannomas and neurofibromas may thus be seen in the nasopharynx, in the para-

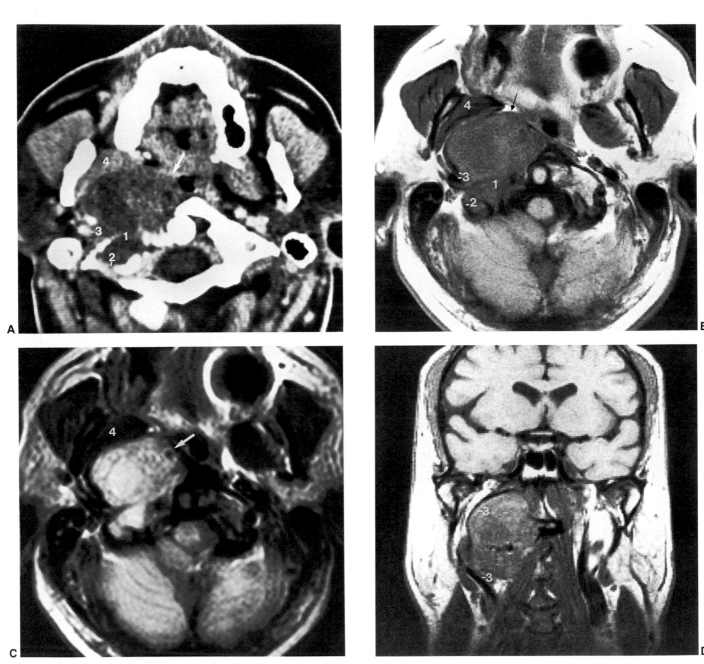

Figure 8.5   Benign Schwannoma encroaching on the right parapharyngeal space. **A** CT, **B** axial MR T_1, **C** axial MR T_2 and **D** coronal MR T_1. Recurrent right otitis media due to obstruction of the eustachian tube by a tumor mass (arrow) was noted on CT scan **A** to be causing destruction of the lateral mass of C1 (1) displacing the vertebral artery posteriorly (2), the carotid artery and jugular vein posterolaterally (3). This extended forward to encroach on the lateral pterygoid muscle (4). MR showed similar findings. The coronal image **D** also showed posterolateral displacement of the vessels by this large tumor, proven to be a Schwannoma apparently arising from C1.

pharyngeal space, or in the infratemporal fossa. Similarly, tumors of salivary gland origin such as those from the deep lobe of the parotid gland or from minor salivary glands may encroach on the parapharyngeal space and may simulate a mass lesion arising from the nasopharynx or infratemporal fossa. Meningiomas arising from the posterior fossa may also present in the nasopharynx extending directly through the skull base or through the foramen magnum. Hemangiomas and lymphangiomas can also occur in the same areas, appearing as a vascular mass in CT and in MR. An aneurysm of the carotid artery and a lipoma also have to be considered. As noted above, granulomas and inflammatory masses may simulate tumors and require biopsy for identification.

Malignant Tumors

Squamous cell carinoma (Figs. 8.6–8.9) is by far the most common type of malignant tumor of the nasopharynx.[114] It constitutes from 0.25 to 3.0% of all malignancy in Caucasions and up to 15% in susceptible Chinese.[140] This is particularly true for people from southern China. About 90% of tumors of the nasopharynx are of the epidermoid type (see Fig. 8.6), the majority being of the nonkeratinizing variety, also known as the "lymphoepithelioma". The lymphoid component of lymphoepitheliomas is said to be a passive participant in the tumor.[6] A male predominance is reported with the mean age in the late 40's.[6] Five to ten percent of the remaining tumors

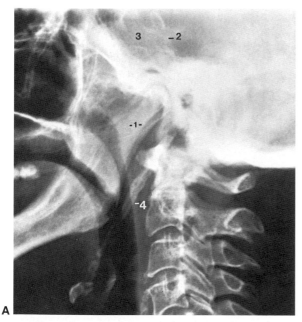

A

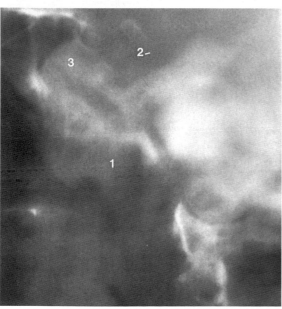

C

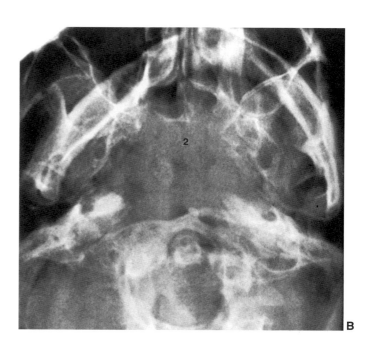

B

Figure 8.6   Carcinoma, nasopharynx. **A** lateral film, **B** base projection, **C** lateral tomogram. A soft tissue mass in the nasopharynx (1) extends through the skull base causing destruction of the clivus (2) with involvement of the sphenoid sinus (3). The extensive mass with bone destruction could be easily overlooked on plain studies. Incidentally note ossification of the stylohyoid ligament (4).

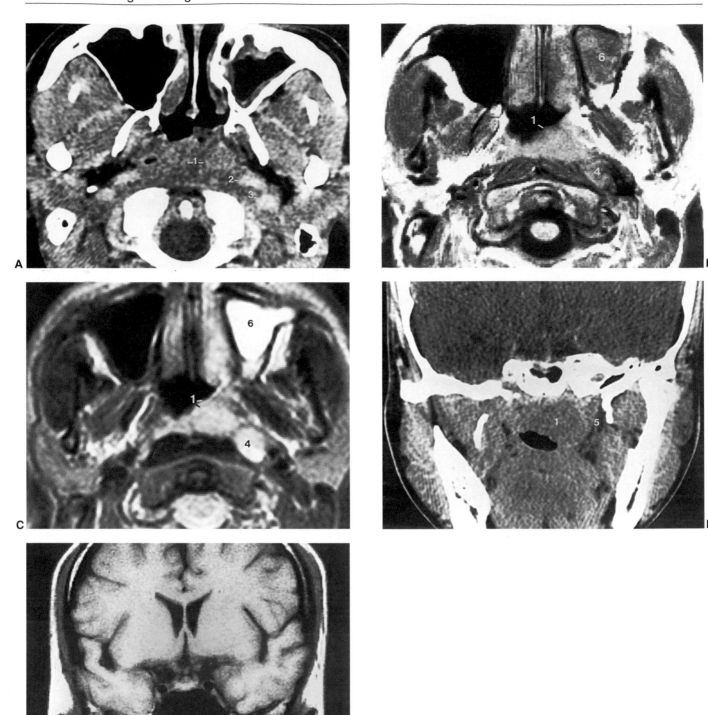

Figure 8.**7** Carcinoma, nasopharynx with nodal metastases. **A** axial CT with contrast enhancement, **B** MR T$_1$ axial, and **C** MR T$_2$ axial scans reveal a soft tissue mass (1) displacing the internal carotid artery (2) and internal jugular vein (3). A metastatic node of Rouvier (4) is easier to identify on the MR studies, **B** and **C**. The coronal CT **D** and coronal MR **E** also show the soft tissue mass (1) encroaching on the parapharyngeal space (5). The left maxillary sinus (6) is opacified due to infection.

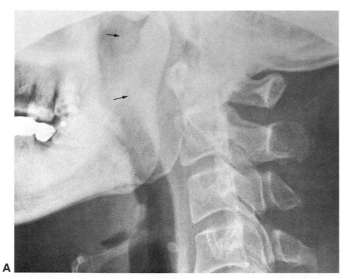

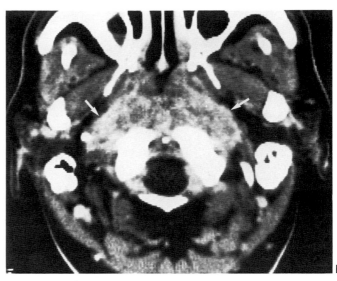

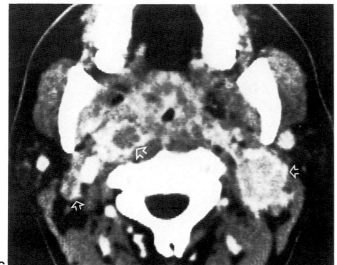

Figure 8.**8** Nasopharyngeal carcinoma with extensive nodal metastases. A soft tissue mass is evident **A** on the plain lateral projection (arrows) but is easier to identify with the contrast enhanced CT scans **B** and **C**. Extensive nodal metastases (open arrows) can be seen further caudad with the contrast enhanced axial CT scan **C**.

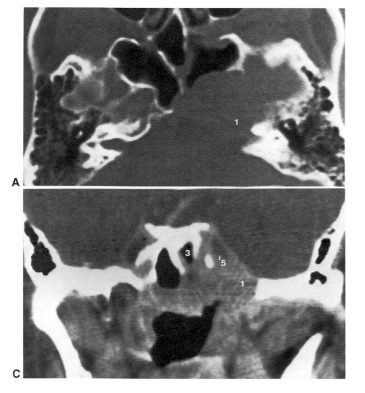

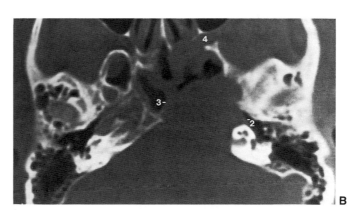

Figure 8.**9** Nasopharyngeal carcinoma with extensive bone destruction. Axial CT scans **A** and slightly more caudad **B**, enhanced coronal CT **C**. A relatively small soft tissue mass in the nasopharynx has caused extensive bone destruction. Note destruction of the petrous apex (1), extension laterally to the hypotympanum (2), forward to the sphenoid sinus (3), and to the pterygopalatine fossa (4). The tumor also encroaches on the cavernous sinus and Meckel's cave area (5) **C**.

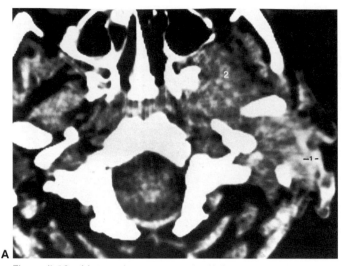

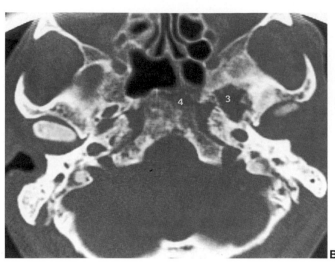

Figure 8.**10** Metastatic tumor to the infratemporal fossa and skull base from squamous cell carcinoma of the skin. Axial CT scans **A** soft tissue window caudad to **B** bone window, contrast enhanced. He presents with an apparent slight local superficial recurrence anterior to the pinna. Extensive soft tissue changes are evident by CT scan deep to the pinna (1) extending to the infratemporal fossa (2), causing destruction of the floor of the middle cranial fossa (3) and partial destruction of the clivus (4).

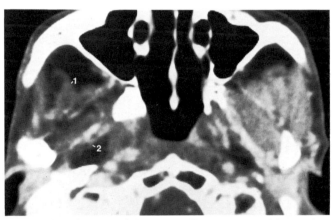

Figure 8.**11** Atrophy, right temporalis and pterygoid muscles. Atrophy of the right temporalis (1) and pterygoid muscles (2) are secondary to a previously treated carcinoma of the nasopharynx which involved the fifth cranial nerve.

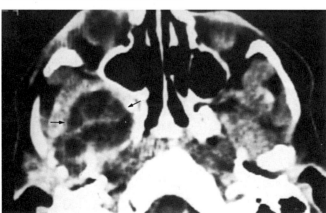

Figure 8.**12** Hydatid cyst. Infratemporal fossa. CT scan, axial plane with intravenous enhancement. Enlargement of the infratemporal fossa by a mass (arrows) with an enhancing rim has encroached on the right maxillary sinus, the pterygoid plates and pterygopalatine fossa. This was excised. (Courtesy of Springer-Verlag, Heidelberg, Radiologe, 1985, p. 236, Vol. 25. Authors: Kalovidouris A, Gouliamos A, Andreou I, Ioannovitis I, Levett J, Vlahos I, Papavasilou C.)

of the nasopharynx are reported to be malignant lymphomas.[140] Adenocarcinoma, plasmacytoma, melanoma, and other sarcomas are occasionally seen. Metastatic carcinoma, especially from the lung, kidney, and breast should also be considered in the differential diagnosis (Fig. 8.**10**).

Diagnosis

Signs and symptoms of a malignancy vary from unilateral nasal obstruction caused by the tumor mass, bloody discharge, or recurrent epistaxis, local invasion to the orbit or intracranial cavity and metastases to regional lymph nodes. Occlusion of the eustachian tube may result in a middle ear effusion and hearing loss. Patients may also have sixth nerve palsy, Horner's syndrome, or cavernous sinus syndrome with the fifth and first cranial nerves most often involved.[49] Regional nodal metastasis is present in 60 to 80% of patients, half of which may be bilateral.[140] Local spread of tumor to the parapharyngeal space is common. This includes the prestyloid compartment and the infratemporal fossa, which contains the auriculotemporal nerve and the inferior alveolar and lingual nerves. From here the tumor may extend to the tonsillar bed. Superior extension from this area would include the sphenoid bone with the foramen ovale. The tumor may also extend posteriorly to the posterior compartment of the parapharyngeal space and thus involve cranial nerves 9-12, the cervical sympathetic chain, and lymph nodes in the area.[64] Direct posterior extension to the retropharyngeal space also occurs, including the node of Rouviere and other nodes in the area. Superior extension from here may involve the sphenoid bone, the clivus, petrous apex (including the petrous portion of the carotid artery), and the intracranial cavity. When first seen, approximately 75% of the patients are apt to have metastases to cervical nodes.[74, 140] All of these patients should have CT scan with contrast enhancement in the axial and coronal plane or MR studies. The soft tissue extent of tumor is most readily identified by MR, the degree of bone destruction best evaluated by CT scan. The primary tumor may be so small as to be difficult to identify and yet it can cause extensive local destruction or have extensive nodal metastases.[39, 40, 74] In a few patients, the primary may be so small as to not be identified by either CT or MR. Such cases may require blind biopsy of the nasopharynx. CT guided biopsies are indicated for deep seated lesions which are not evident by direct visualization or palpation but which can be identified by CT. Distant metastases are said to occur in at least 20% of patients with carcinoma of the nasopharynx.[6] The treatment of choice is high dose radiotherapy.[1]

Finally, **atrophy** of the muscles in the infratemporal fossa should call to mind possible abnormalities of the skull base affecting cranial nerves 5 and 10.[49] Any abnormality involving the fifth cranial nerve may cause atrophy of the muscles of mastication (Fig. 8.11). Any abnormality involving the tenth cranial nerve may involve the muscles of deglutition, namely the pharyngeal and palatal muscles. Pseudoenlargement of the pterygoid muscles may occur after hemimandibulectomy.[24] After hemimandibulectomy, the pterygoid and masseter muscles may pull the remnant of the ramus anteriorly and superiorly, effectively shortening the lateral pterygoid muscle and making it appear to be larger than the contralateral muscle. This should not be mistaken for tumor.

References

1 Abayomi O, Bankoff MS: Planning radiotherapy for head and neck tumors. In: Carter BL, ed. Contemporary issues in computed tomography. Churchill Livingstone, London 1984

2 Atherino CCT, Atherino TC: Maxillary sinus mucopyoceles. Arch Otolaryngol 110:200–202, 1984

3 Baker SR, Latack ST: Magnetic resonance imaging of the head and neck. Otolaryng Head Neck Surg 95:82–89, 1986

4 Ball JB Jr., Towbin RB, Staton RE, Cowdrey KE: Direct sagittal computed tomography of the head. Radiology 155:822, 1985

5 Ballinger PW: Merrils atlas of radiolographic positions and radiographic procedures, fifth edition. C.V. Mosby, St. Louis 1982

6 Batsakis JG: Tumors of the head and neck. Clinical and pathological consideration, second edition. Williams and Wilkins, Baltimore 1979

7 Becker TS, Shum TK, Waller TS, et al: Radiological aspects of rhinoscleroma. Radiology 141:433–438, 1981

8 Bernstein, L: Congenital defects of the oral cavity. In: Paparella and Shumrick, eds. Otolaryngology. Saunders, Philadelphia, 1980

9 Bohman L, Mancuso A, Thompson J, Hanafee W: CT approach to benign nasopharyngeal masses. AJR 136:173–180, 1981

10 Bonneville JF, Belloir A, Mawazini H, et al: Calcified remnants of the notochord in the roof of the nasopharynx. Radiology 137:373–377, 1980

11 Carmody RF, Rickles DJ, Johnson SF: Case report. Giant cell tumor of the sphenoid bone. J Comput Assist Tomogr 7(2):370–373, 1983

12 Carter BL, Bankoff MS: Facial trauma: Computed versus conventional tomography. In: Littleton JS, Durizch ML, eds. Sectional imaging methods: A comparison. University Press, Baltimore 1983

13 Carter BL, Bankoff MS, Fisk JD: Computed tomographic detection of sinusitis responsible for intracranial and extracranial infections. Radiology 147:739–742, 1983

14 Carter BL, Karmody CS: Computed tomography of the face and neck. Semin Roentgenol 13(3):257–266, 1978

15 Carter BL, Hammerschlag SB, Wolpert SM: Computerized scanning in otorhinolaryngology. In: Pfaltz CR, ed. Advances in Otorhinolaryngology. Karger, Basel, Switzerland 1978

16 Chakeres DW: Computed tomography of the ethmoid sinuses. Otolaryngol Clin North Am 18(1):29–42, 1985

17 Chernak ES, Rodriguez-Antunez A, Jelden GL, Dhaliwal RS, Lavik PS: The use of computed tomography for radiation therapy treatment planning. Radiology 117:613–614, 1975

18 Chinwuba C, Wallman J, Strand R: Nasal airway obstruction: CT assessment. Radiology 159:503–506, 1986

19 Chui MC, Briant TDR, Gray T, Horsey WJ, Hudson AR, Tucker W: Computed tomography of sphenoid sinus mucocele. J Otolaryngol 12(4):263–269, 1983

20 Chui MC, Briant TDR, Rotenberg D, Gonsalves CC: Computed tomography and angiofibroma of the nasopharynx. J Otolaryngol 11(5):327–330, 1982

21 Clark WD, Bailey BJ, Stiernberg CM: Nasal dermoid with intracranial involvement. Otolaryngol Head Neck Surg 93(1):102–104, 1985

22 Colman MF, Hanafee WE: Diagnostic imaging of the head and neck. In: Cummings CW, Fredrickson JM, Harker LA, et al, eds. Otolaryngology Head and Neck Surgery, volume 1. C.V. Mosby Co., St. Louis 1986

23 Cotton RT, Zalzalgh: Noncleft disorders. In: Cummings CW, et al, eds. Otolaryngology Head and Neck Surgery. C.V. Mosby Co., St. Louis 1986

24 Curtin HD: Nasopharynx, infratemporal fossa and skull base. In: Carter BL, ed. Computed tomography of the head and neck. Churchill Livingstone, New York 1985

25 Curtin HD, Williams R: Computed tomographic anatomy of the pterygopalatine fossa. Radiographics 5(3):429–439, 1985

26 Curtin HD, Williams R, Johnson J: CT of perineural tumor extension: Pterygopalatine fossa. AJR 144:163–169, 1985

27 Curtin HD, Wolfe P, Gallia L, May M: Unusually large nasopalatine cyst: CT findings. J Comput Assist Tomogr 8(1):139–142, 1984

28 Curtin HD, Wolfe P, May M: Malignant external otitis: CT evaluation. Radiology 145:383–388, 1982

29 Daniels DL, Rauschning W, Lovas J, Williams AL, Haughton VM: Pterygopalatine fossa: Computed tomographic studies. Radiology 149:511–516, 1983

30 Davies J: Embryology and anatomy of the head, neck, face, palate, nose, and paranasal sinuses. In: Paparella and Shumrick, eds. Otolaryngology. Saunders, Philadelphia 1980

31 DeSanto LW: Neoplasms. In: Cummings CW, et al. Otolaryngology Head and Neck Surgery. C.V. Mosby Co., St. Louis 1986

32 Downey EF Jr, Friedman AC, Finizio J: CT of nasal chondrosarcoma. AJNR 3:80–81, 1982

33 Druck NS, Spector GJ, Ciarlsky RH, Ogura JH: Malignant glomus vagali. Report of a case and review of the literature. Arch Otolaryngol 102:534, 1976

34 Dubois PJ, Schultz JC, Perrin RL, Dastur KJ: Tomography in expansile lesions of the nasal and paranasal sinuses. Radiology 125:149–158, 1977

35 Duncan AW, Lack EE, Deck MF: Radiological evaluation of paragangliomas of the head and neck. Radiology 132:99–105, 1979

36 Duncavage JA, Campbell BH, Kun LE, et al: Diagnosis of malignant lymphomas of the nasal cavity, paranasal sinuses and nasopharynx. Laryngoscope 93:1276–1280, 1983

37 Gamba JL, Woodruff WW, Djang WT, Yeates AE: Craniofacial mucormycosis: Assessment with CT. Radiology 160:207–212, 1986

38 Gardiner LJ: Complicated frontal sinusitis: Evaluation and management. Otolaryngol Head Neck Surg 95(3):333–343, 1986

39 Gatenby RA, Mulhern CB Jr, Richter MP, Moldofsky PJ: CT-guided biopsy for the detection and staging of tumors of the head and neck. AJNR 5:287–289, 1984

40 Gatenby RA, Mulhern CB Jr, Strawitz J: CT-guided percutaneous biopsies of head and neck masses. Radiology 146:717–719, 1983

41 Goepfert H, Luna MA, Lindberg RD, White AK: Malignant salivary gland tumors of the paranasal sinuses and nasal cavity. Arch Otolaryngol 109:662–668, 1983

42 Goldstein JC, Sison GA: Tumors of the nose, paranasal sinuses, and nasopharynx. In: Paparella and Shumrick, eds. Otolaryngology. Saunders, Philadelphia 1980

43 Gore RM, Weinberg PE, Kim KS, Ramsey RG: Sphenoid sinus mucoceles presenting as intracranial masses on computed tomography. Surg Neurol 13:375–379, 1980

44 Gorlin RJ, et al. Craniofacial syndromes. In: Paparella and Shumrick, eds. Otolaryngology. Saunders, Philadelphia 1980

45 Gorlin RJ, Goltz RW: Multiple nevoid basal cell epithelium, jaw cysts and bifid rib: A syndrome. N Engl J Med 262:908, 1960

46 Granite EL: Anatomic considerations in infections of the face and neck: Review of the literature. J Oral Surg 34:34–44, 1976

47 Gray H: Gray's anatomy. Goss CM, ed. Lea & Febiger, Philadelphia 1973

48 Guy JT: Oral manifestations of systemic disease. In: Cummings, et al. Otolaryngology Head and Neck Surgery. C.V. Mosby Co., St. Louis 1986

49 Harnsberger HR, Dillon WP: Major motor atrophic patterns in the face and neck: CT evaluation. Radiology 155:665–670, 1985

50 Harrington PC: Complications of sinusitis. Ear Nose Throat J 63:58–71, 1984

51 Hasso AN: CT of tumors and tumor-like conditions of the paranasal sinuses. Radiol Clin North Am 22:119–130, 1984

52 Haun CL: Retropharyngeal tendinitis. Am J. Roentgenol 130:1137–1140, 1978

53 Henderson LT, Robbins KT, Weitzner S: Upper aerodigestive tract metastases in disseminated malignant melanoma. Arch Otolaryngol Head Neck Surg 112:659–663, 1986

54 Hertzanu Y, Cohen M, Mendelsohn DB: Nasopalatine duct cyst. Clin Radiol 36:153–158, 1985

55 Hesselink JR, New PFJ, Davis KR, Weber AL, Roberson GH, Taveras JM: Computed tomography of the paranasal sinuses and face: Part 1. Normal anatomy. J Comput Assist Tomogr 2:559–567, 1978

56 Hesselink JR, Weber AL, New PFJ, Davis KR, Roberson GH, Taveras JM: Evaluation of mucoceles of the paranasal sinuses with computed tomography. Radiology 133:397–400, 1979

57 Holt GR: Maxillofacial trauma. In: Cummings, et al, eds. Otolaryngology Head and Neck Surgery. C.V. Mosby Co., St. Louis 1986

58 Howell CG, Tassel PV, Gammal TE: High resolution computed tomography in neonatal nasopharyngeal teratoma. J Comput Assist Tomogr 8(6):1179–1181, 1984

59 Hughes GB, Sharpino G, Hunt W, Tucker HM: Management of the congenital midline nasal mass: A review. Head and Neck Surg 2:222–233, 1980

60 Inoue M, Abe H, Kobayashi T, Gillespie CA: Post traumatic internal cartoid aneurysm presenting as a nasal sinus lesion. Arch Otolaryngol Head Neck Surg 112:1093–1096, 1986

61 Jaffe, BF: Classification and management of anomalies of the nose. Otolaryngol Clin North Amer 14:989–1004, 1981

62 James AE Jr, Macmillan AS Sr, Macmillan AS Jr, Momose KJ: Thornwaldt's cysts. Br J Radiol 41:902–904, 1968

63 Jeans WD, Gilani S, Bullimore J: Effect of CT scanning on staging of tumours of the paranasal sinuses. Clin Radiol 33:173–179, 1982

64 Kalovidouris A, Mancuso AA, Dillon W: A CT-clinical approach to patients with symptoms related to the V, VII, IX–XII cranial nerves and cervical sympathetics. Radiology 151:671–676, 1984

65 Karmody CS, Carter B, Vincent ME: Developmental anomalies of the maxillary sinus. ORL 84:723–728, 1977

66 Klintenberg C, Olofsson J, Hellquist H, Sokjer H. Adenocarcinoma of the ethmoid sinuses: A review of 38 cases with special reference to wood dust exposure. Cancer 54:482–488, 1984

67 Kornblut AD, Wolff SM, deFries HO, Fauci AS: Wegener's granulomatosis. Otolaryngol Clin North Amer 15(3):673–683, 1982

68 Kuriloff DB: The nasolabial cyst-nasal hamartoma. Otolaryngol Head Neck Surg 96:268–272, 1987

69 Lazo A, Wilner III, Metes JJ: Craniofacial mucormycosis: Computed tomography and angiographic findings in two cases. Radiology 139:623–626, 1981

70 Levine PA, Paling MR, Black WC, Cantrell RW: MRI vs. high-resolution CT scanning: evaluation of the anterior skull base Otolaryngol Head Neck Surg 96:260–266, 1987

71 Lew D, Southwick FS, Montgomery WW, Weber AL, Baker AS: Sphenoid sinusitis. A review of 30 cases. N Engl J Med 309(19):1149–1154, 1983

72 Lingeman RE, Shellhamer RH: Benign neoplasms of the nasopharynx. In: Cummings, et al, eds. Otolaryngology Head and Neck Surgery. C.V. Mosby Co., St. Louis 1986

73 Liomba G, Hutt MRS: Aspergillus granuloma of the paranasal sinuses and bronchi in Malawi. Trop Geogr Med 33:169–174, 1981

74 Ljung BME, Larsson SG, Hanafee W: Computed tomography-guided aspiration cytologic examination in head and neck lesions. Arch Otolarngol 110:604–607, 1984

75 Lober PH: Histology and pathology of the nose and sinuses. In: Paparella and Shumrick, eds. Otolaryngology. Saunders, Philadelphia 1980

76 Lund VJ, Howard DJ, Lloyd GAS: CT Evaluation of paranasal sinus tumours for cranio-facial resection. Br J Radiol 56:439–446, 1983

77 Lund VJ, Lloyd GAS: Radiological changes associated with inverted papilloma of the nose and paranasal sinuses. Br J Radiol 57:455–461, 1984

78 Lusk RP, Lee PC: Magnetic resonance imaging of congenital midline nasal masses. Otolaryng Head Neck Surg 95:303–306, 1986

79 McCaffrey TV, McDonald TJ: Sarcoidosis of the nose and paranasal sinuses. Laryngoscope 93:1281–1284, 1983

80 McCauley RG, Sinks LF, Carter BL: Head and neck lesions in children. In: Carter BL, ed. Computed tomography of the head and neck. Churchill Livingstone, New York 1985

81 Mafee MF, Rasouli F, Spigos DG, et al: Magnetic resonance imaging in the diagnosis of nonsquamous tumors of the head and neck. Otolaryngol Clin North Am 19(3):523–536, 1986

82 Mallonee MS: Fibromyxoma of the pterygomaxillary fossa. Arch Otolaryngol 107:555–557, 1981

83 Mancuso AA, Bohman L, Hanafee W, Maxwell D: Computed tomography of the nasopharynx: Normal and variants of normal. Radiology 137:113–121, 1980

84 Mancuso AA, Hanafee WN: Computed Tomography and Magnetic Resonance Imaging of the Head and Neck, 2nd edition. Williams and Wilkins, Baltimore, 1985

85 Michael AS, Mafee MF, Valvassori GE, Tan WS: Dynamic computed tomography of the head and neck: Differential diagnostic value. Radiology 154:413–419, 1985

86 Momose KJ, Weber AL, Goodman M, MacMillan AS Jr, Roberson GH: Radiological aspects of inverted papilloma. Radiology 134:73–79, 1980

87 Montgomery WW, Wilson WR: Surgery of the frontal, ethmoid, and sphenoid sinuses. In: Paparella and Shumrick, eds. Otolaryngology. Saunders, Philadelphia 1980

88 Mosher HP: The applied anatomy and the intranasal surgery of the ethmoidal labyrinth. Laryngoscope 23:881–907, 1913

89 Newman AN, Rice DH: Rhabdomyosarcoma of the head and neck. Laryngoscope 94:234–239, 1984

90 Oot RF, Parizel PM, Weber AL: Computed tomography of osteogenic sarcoma of nasal cavity and paranasal sinuses. J Comput Assist Tomogr 10(3):409–414, 1986

91 Osborn AG: Pterygopalatine fossa. AJR 132:389–394, 1979

92 Osborn AG, Anderson RE: Direct sagittal computed tomographic scans of the face and paranasal sinuses. Radiology 129:81–87, 1978

93 Osborn AG, McIff EB: Computed tomography of the nose. Head Neck Surg 4:182–199, 1982

94 Paling MR, Roberts RL, Fauci AS: Paranasal sinus obliteration in Wegener granulomatosis. Radiology 144:539–543, 1982

95 Pashley N: Congenital anomalies of the nose. In: Cummings, et al, eds. Mosby, St. Louis 1986

96 Perlin E: Granulomatous and related reactions associated with malignant disease the head and neck region. Otolaryngol Clin North Am 15:699–704, 1982

97 Peterson LJ: Odontogenic infections. In: Cummings CW, Fredrickson JM, Harker LA, eds. Otolaryngology – Head and Neck Surgery, volume 2. C.V. Mosby Co., St. Louis 1986

98 Potter GD: Radiology of the paranasal sinuses and facial bones. In: Valvassori GE, Potter GD, Hanafee HN, eds. Radiology of the ear, nose, and throat. Georg Thieme Verlag, Stuttgart 1982

99 Price HI, Danziger A: Computerised tomographic findings in mucoceles of the frontal and ethmoid sinuses. Clinical Radiology 31:169–174, 1980

100 Proops DW, Mann JR: The presentation of rhabdomyosarcomas of the head and neck in children. J Laryngol Otol 98:381–390, 1984

101 Quick CA, Anderson RA, Stool S: Giant cell tumors of the maxilla in children. Laryngoscope 90:784–791, 1980

102 Rachelefsky GS: Sinusitis in children – diagnosis and management. Clin Rev Allergy 2:397–408, 1984

103 Ramsey PG, Weymuller EA: Complications of bacterial infection of the ears, paranasal sinuses, and oropharynx in adults. Emer Med Clin North Amer 3:143–160, 1985

104 Rao VM, Wechsler RJ, Carter BL, O'Hara E: Computed tomography of choanal atresia: Special considerations of the unilateral type. CT: The J Comput Tomogr 10(4):381–384, 1986

105 Rhea JT, Weber AL: Giant-cell granuloma of the sinuses. Radiology 147:135–137, 1983

106 Rice DH: Benign and malignant tumors of the ethmoid sinus. Otolaryngol Clin North Am 18:113–124, 1985

107 Ritter FN: Surgical management of paranasal sinusitis. In: Cummings, et al. Otolaryngology – Head and Neck Surgery. C.V. Mosby Co, St. Louis 1986

108 Schuller DE, Lucas JG: Nasopharyngeal paraganglioma. Arch Otolaryngol 108:667–670, 1982

109 Sessions RB: Nasal dermal sinuses – new concepts and explanations. Laryngoscope 92:1–25, 1982

110 Shapshay SM, Ossoff RH: Squamous cell carcinoma of the head and neck. Otolaryngol Clin North Amer 18:365–624, 1985

111 Shatz CT, Becker TS: Normal CT anatomy of the paranasal sinuses. Radiol Clin North Am 22:107–118, 1984

112 Shugar JMA, Som PM, Krespi YP, Arnold LM, Som ML: Primary chordoma of the maxillary sinus. Laryngoscope 90:1825–1830, 1980

113 Silver AJ, Mawad ME, Hilal SK, Sane P, Ganti SR: Computed tomography of the nasopharynx and related spaces. Part 1: Anatomy. Radiology 147:725–731, 1983

114 Silver AJ, Mawad ME, Hilal SK, Sane P, Ganti SR: Computed tomography of the nasopharynx and related spaces. Part 11: Pathology. Radiology 147:733–738, 1983

115 Simpson DA, David DJ, White J: Cephaloceles: Treatment, outcome, and antenatal diagnosis. Neurosurgery 15:14–21, 1984

116 Slovis TL, Renfro B, Watts FB, Kuhns LR, Belenky W, Spoylar J: Choanal atresia: precise CT evaluation. Radiology 155:345–348, 1985

117 Sofferman RA, Cummings CW: Malignant lymphoma of the paranasal sinuses. Arch Otolaryngol 101:287, 1975

118 Som PM: The paranasal sinuses. In: Bergeron RT, Osborn AG, Som PM, eds. Head and neck imaging excluding the brain. C.V. Mosby Co., St. Louis 1984

119 Som PM: The parapharyngeal space. In: Bergeron RT, Osborn AG, Som PM, eds. Head and neck imaging excluding the brain. C.V. Mosby Co., St. Louis 1984

120 Som, PM: The role of CT in the diagnosis of carcinoma of the paranasal sinuses and nasopharynx. J Otolaryngol 11:340–348, 1982

121 Som PM, Cohen BA, Sacher M, Choi I, Bryan NR: The angiomatous polyp and the angiofibroma: Two different lesions. Radiology 144:329–334, 1982

122 Som PM, Lawson W, Biller HF, Lanzieri CF: Ethmoid sinus disease: CT evaluation in 400 cases. Part 1. Nonsurgical patients. Radiology 159:591–597, 1986

123 Som PM, Lawson W, Biller HF, Lanzieri CF: Ethmoid sinus disease: CT evaluation in 400 cases. Part 11. Postoperative findings. Radiology 159:599–604, 1986

124 Som PM, Lawson W, Biller HF, Lanzieri CF, Sachdev VP, Rigamonti D: Ethmoid sinus disease: CT evaluation in 400 cases. Part 111. Craniofacial resection. Radiology 159:605–609, 1986

125 Som PM, Lawson W, Cohen BA: Giant-cell lesions of the facial bones. Radiology 147:129–134, 1983

126 Som PM, Lanzieri CF, Sacher M, Lawson W, Biller HF: Extracranial tumor vascularity: Determination by dynamic CT scanning. Part 1: Concepts and signature curves. Radiology 154:401–405, 1985

127 Som PM, Lanzieri CF, Sacher M, Lawson W, Biller HF: Extracranial tumor vascularity: Determination by dynamic CT scanning. Part 11: The unit approach. Radiology 154:407–412, 1985

128 Som PM, Sacher M, Lanzieri CF, Lawson W, Shugar JMA: The hidden antral compartment. Radiology 152:463–464, 1984

129 Som PM, Shugar JMA: Antral mucoceles: A new look. J Comput Assist Tomogr 4:484–488, 1980

130 Som PM, Shugar JMA: The CT classification of ethmoid mucoceles. J Comput Assist Tomogr 4:199–203, 1980

131 Som PM, Shugar JMA, Biller HF: Early detection of antral malignancy in the post maxillectomy patient. Radiology 143:509–512, 1982

132 Spiro RH, Huvas AG, Strong EW: Adenoid cystic carcinoma of salivary gland origin. A clinicopathological study of 242 cases. Am J Surg 128:513, 1974

133 Stammberger H, Jakse R, Beaufort F: Aspergillosis of the paranasal sinuses. X-ray diagnosis, histopathology, and clinical aspects. Ann Otol Rhinol Laryngol 93:251–256, 1984

134 Stassi J, Rao VM, Lowry L: Hemangioma of bone arising in the maxilla. Skeletal Radiol 12:187–191, 1984

135 Stiernberg CM, Bailey BJ, Calhoun KH, Quinn FB: Management of invasive frontoethmoidal sinus mucoceles. Arch Otolaryngol Head Neck Surg 112:1060–1063, 1986

136 Suss RA, Kumar AJ, Dorfman HD, Miller NR, Rosenbaum AE: Capillary hemangioma of the sphenoid bone. Skeletal Radiol 11:102–107, 1984

137 Tadmor R, Ravid M, Millet D, Leventon G: Computed tomographic demonstration of choanal atresia. AJNR 5:743–745, 1984

138 Teresi L, Lufkin R, Wortham D, et al: MR imaging of the intratemporal facial nerve by using surface coils. AJR 148:589–594, 1987

139 Terrier F, Weber W, Ruefenacht D, Porcellini B: Anatomy of the ethmoid: CT, endoscopic, and macroscopic. AJR 144:493–500, 1985

140 Toomey JM: Cysts and tumors of the pharynx. In: Paparella and Shumrick, eds. Otolaryngology. Saunders, Philadelphia 1980

141 Trimble LD: Odontogenesis and jaw cysts. In: Cummings, et al, eds. Otolaryngology Head and Neck Surgery. C.V. Mosby Co., St. Louis 1986

142 Vannier MW, Marsh JL, Warren JO: Three dimensional CT reconstruction images for craniofacial surgical planning and evaluation. Radiology 150:179–184, 1984

143 Wald ER, Pang D, Milmoe GJ, Schramm VL Jr: Sinusitis and its complications in the pediatric patient. Pediatr Clin North Am 28:777–796, 1981

144 Warrington G, Palmer MK: Retropharyngeal tendinitis. Br J Radiol 56:52–54, 1983

145 Weber AL, Stanton AC: Malignant tumors of the paranasal sinuses: Radiologic, clinical, and histopathologic evaluation of 200 cases. Head Neck Surg 6:761–776, 1984

146 Whitaker SR, Sprinkle PM, Chou SM: Nasal glioma. Arch Otolaryngol 107:550–554, 1981

147 Wilder WH, Harner SG, Banks PM: Lymphoma of the nose and paranasal sinuses. Arch Otolaryngol 109:310–312, 1983

148 Wilson WR: Infection and granulomas of the nasal airways and paranasal sinuses. In: Paparella and Shumrick, eds. Otolaryngology. Saunders, Philadelphia 1980

149 Witt TR, Shah JP, Sternberg SS: Juvenile nasopharyngeal angiofibroma. Am J Surg 146:521–525, 1983

150 Wolfensberger M, Herrmann P: The pathogenesis of maxillary sinus pneumoceles. Arch Otolaryngol Head Neck Surg 113:184–186, 1987

151 Woodruff WW, Yeates AE, McLendon RE: Perineural tumor extension to the cavernous sinus from superficial facial carcinoma: CT manifestations. Radiology 161:395–399, 1986

152 Zimmerman RA, Bilaniuk LT, Metzger RA, Grossman RI, Schut L, Bruce DA: Computed tomography of orbital-facial neurofibromatosis. Radiology 146:113–116, 1983

153 Zimmerman RA, Bilaniuk LT, Hackney DB, Goldberg HI, Grossman RI: Paranasal sinus hemorrhage: Evaluation with MR imaging. Radiology 162:499–503, 1987

154 Zizmor J, Noyek A: In: Paparella and Shumrick, eds. Otolaryngology. Saunders, Philadelphia, 1980

Acknowledgement: All MR studies were done under the direction of Val Runge, M.D., Chief of the MR section. His assistance, guidance, and cooperation have been of great value in the study and understanding of the images obtained. The case material was referred from Drs. Chasin, Karmody, Calcaterra, and Katz, of the Department of Otolaryngology, Dr. George Simpson, Chief of Otolaryngology, Boston University, and Dr. Papageorge, Department of Oral Surgery. Appreciation is extended to these individuals for the use of their cases. All typing and preparation of the manuscript was performed by Nancy Williams, who gave careful attention to detail, a time-consuming task. Deep appreciation is also extended to Barbara Billings for her assistance in gathering together the material, and to Collin Karmody, M.D., for carefully reviewing the manuscript.

Part III

Oral Cavity, Oropharynx, Upper Neck and Salivary Glands

Mahmood F. Mafee

Chapter 1 **Introduction**

The lips form the anterior wall of the oral cavity. The oral cavity and the pharynx unite at the palatoglossal or anterior tonsillar pillars. The anterior two-thirds of the tongue lies within the oral cavity, while its posterior one-third, the base of the tongue, projects into the oropharynx. Special features of the oral cavity include the buccal mucosa, gingiva, alveolar ridges, retromolar area (trigone) hard palate, tongue and floor of the mouth.

The oropharynx extends from the plane of the hard palate to the plane of the hyoid bone and includes palatine tonsils, soft palate, tonsillar pillars, base of the tongue, periepiglottic structures (valleculae, suprahyoid epiglottis, pharyngo-epiglottic folds and glossoepiglottic folds), pharyngeal wall, and posterior pharynx.

The neck is the junctional region between the head and the thorax. Its rostral limits are the base of the skull posteriorly, and the inferior border of the mandible anteriorly. Caudally it is bounded by the thoracic inlet and pectoral girdle, a plane which parallels the first rib. The neck contains the cervical vertebrae and muscles, larynx, pharynx, cervical esophagus, cervical trachea, thyroid and salivary glands, and vessels and nerves that supply various organs of the neck or are in transit between the head, thorax, and remainder of the body.

CT and MR have provided a major breakthrough in diagnostic medical imaging and follow-up of head and neck pathology.

CT and MR characteristics are frequently useful in differentiating benign from malignant lesions. In some instances, CT and MR studies may provide a specific diagnosis of the lesions such as dermoid cysts, hemangiomas, lipomas, and glomus tumors.

The diagnosis of malignancy in the head and neck is in the majority of cases, however, apparent from clinical examination.

Even so, mirror examination and palpation of oral and oropharyngeal tumors do not always give complete information necessary for the management of these lesions. Imaging studies are necessary to disclose the exact location of the tumor, reveal the pattern of spread and the extent of involvement of adjacent structures, and demonstrate the presence and extent of nodal disease, which are essential factors in the choice and plan of therapy. For example, in malignancies of the tongue base, the ulceration can be seen by a mirror examination, but the depth of involvement cannot be appreciated. The extent of malignancies of the body of the tongue which can be visualized by CT or MR, may aid the surgeon in his decision to perform a partial or total glossectomy. In tumors of the tonsillar area and soft palate, direct examination by palpation is sufficient for preliminary diagnosis and biopsy, but imaging studies provide essential information concerning the infiltration of deeper structures of the neck, and in the presence of metastatic nodes in the para- or retropharyngeal spaces. Lesions of the posterior oropharyngeal walls, in particular, may extend well down into the hypopharynx and cervical esophagus; in areas which may not be visible to indirect laryngoscopy. This extension can be detected by CT or MR. Clinical staging of malignant oropharyngeal lesions and determination of degree of neck node involvement are incomplete without a CT or MR evaluation of the oropharynx and nod-bearing areas of the neck.

Oral Cavity, Oropharynx and Upper Neck

Chapter 2 **Imaging**

Technique

CT imaging was performed with a high resolution scanner and MR imaging was performed with a 1.5 T (tesla) superconducting magnet with head coil. For lower neck we prefer body coil as receiver coil. The patient is placed in the supine position with the neck extended. A lateral digital radiographic (scout) image is obtained, which allows localization of the axial sections and proper angulation of the gantry in order to obtain sections parallel to the disc spaces. For CT study, we use the combination of bolus and intravenous infusion of contrast material to improve differentiation between vascular and lymph node structures (initially, an infusion of 150 ml of Hypaque-60 is given, with injection of a bolus of 30 to 40 ml of the same contrast agent through the infusion tube after at least half of the bottle is infused). In case of glomus tumors and vascular lesions, we also perform a rapid sequence, dynamic CT study of a selected cross section or multiple contiguous sections. We obtain 5-mm thick axial scans. For tonsillar, palatal, parapharyngeal, infratemporal, and salivary gland lesions, additional coronal sections will always help to better localize the lesions. For tumors of the oral cavity and pharynx, we prefer only contrast enhanced study. For lesions of the neck, including salivary glands, we obtain 10-mm thick pre-contrast axial scans, followed by contrast infusion. The non-contrast study aids detection of calcification and to appreciate the enhancement characteristics when one evaluates the post-contrast CT study. The MR examinations began with spin echo (SE) sequence of short (500–800 msec) TR (TR = repetition time) and single echo (TE = echo time of 20–25 msec), T_1-weighted (T_1w) sagittal localization, usually followed by axial and coronal SE sequence with early and late echos [TR = 2000–2500 msec TE = 20–25 msec (early echo) and TE = 70, 80 and 100 msec (late echo)]. The SE sequence of short TR and short TE provided T_1-weighted (T_1w) images. The SE sequence of long TR and short TE (early echo) provided proton density (proton-weighted = PW or spin density weighted) images and long TR and long TE (late echo) provided the T2-weighted (T_2w) images. Other technical factors included; a section thickness of 5-mm, inter-scan spacing of 1 to 1.5 mm, a 256 × 128 matrix (some with 256 × 256), two or four averages, and a field of view of 24 cm. Dynamic or fast-scan MR imaging performed using the gradient echo or "GRASS" technique. The GRASS which stands for Gradient Recalled Acquisition in the steady state; is a powerful new imaging technique. Its prime characteristic is the ability to provide T_1, T_2 and density-weighted images in a very short time. A striking feature of GRASS images is the high-intensity appearance of vascular structures, "MR angiography", specially when vessels transect the imaging slice. GRASS images are obtained with TR = 25–30 msec, TE = 12–15 msec, and a variable flip angle (10–30 degrees). The shortest TE that can be selected is 9 msec (technical minimum).

Normal Anatomy

The detailed anatomy of the oral cavity, oropharynx and neck can be found in any standard anatomy text. Because of limitation of space, the most important and practical imaging anatomy will be discussed in this chapter. For the purposes of this section of the book, it is essential to define the cross sectional anatomy visible in CT and MR images. Several CT and MR images of the normal oropharynx and upper neck are shown in Figures 2.1–2.4. The CT sections are all post-infusion images, which depict arteries and veins. The normal MR images are all spin (proton) density weighted for uniformity.

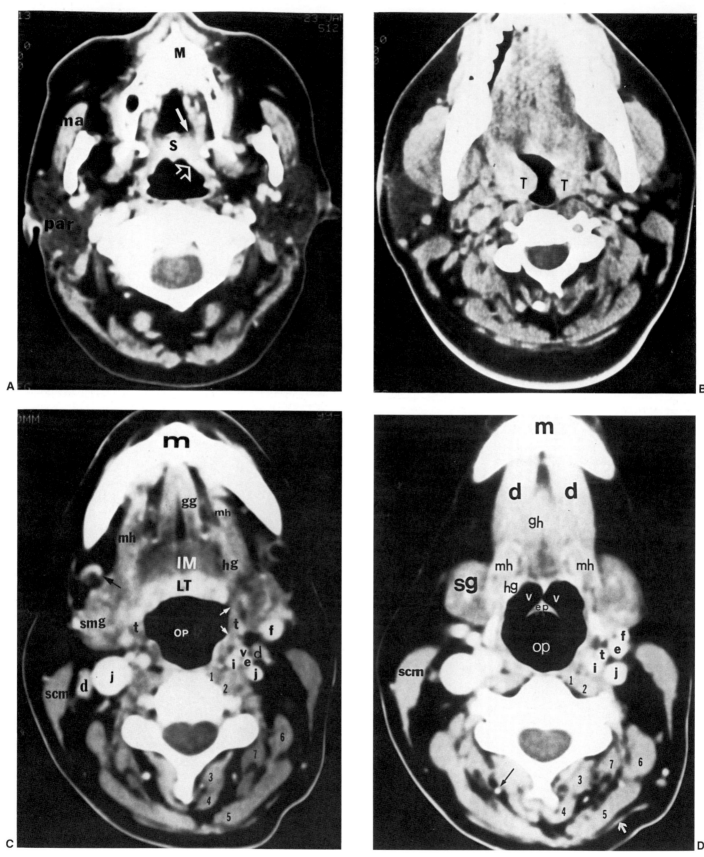

Figure 2.**1**

Figure 2.1 Normal oral cavity, oropharynx and upper neck.
A Axial post infusion CT section. This section crosses the lower maxilla = M, and the body of the axis.
par = parotid gland, s = soft palate, M = maxilla, ma = masseter muscle, white arrow = palatoglossal fold, hollow arrow = palatopharyngeal fold
B Tonsillar hypertrophy. The section crosses the body of the mandible. The image shows tonsillar hypertrophy (T), more prominent on the right. Adjacent fascial planes are normal.
C This section crosses the mid-body of the mandible where the mylohyoid muscle, mh, divides the floor of the mouth from the neck.
d = posterior belly digastric muscle, e = external carotid artery, f = posterior facial vein, gg = genioglossus muscle, hg = hyoglossus muscle, i = internal carotid artery IM = intrinsic tongue muscles, j = internal jugular vein, LT = lingual tonsil, m = mandible, mh = mylohyoid muscle, op = oropharynx, scm = sternocleidomastoid muscle, smg = submandibular gland, t = palatine tonsil, v = pharyngeal vein, black arrow = anterior facial vein, white arrows = pharyngeal contrictor muscles, 1 = longus colli muscle, 2 = longus capitis muscle, 3 = semispinalis cervicis muscle, 4 = semispinalis capitis muscle, 5 = splenius capitis muscle, 6 = levator scapulae muscle, 7 = longissimus capitis muscle.
D This section crosses the lower mandible, m, and the inferior body of the third cervical vertebra.
d = anterior belly digastric muscle, e = external carotid artery, ep = epiglottis, f = posterior facial vein, gh = geniohyoid muscle, hg = hyoglossus muscle, i = internal carotid artery, j = internal jugular vein, m = mandible, mh = mylohyoid muscle, op = oropharynx, scm = sternocleidomastoid muscle, sg = submandibular gland, t = superior thyroid artery, v = valleculae, black arrow = deep cervical vein, white arrow = trapezius muscle, 1 = longus colli muscle, 2 = longus capitis muscle, 3 = semispinalis cervicis muscle, 4 = semispinalis capitis muscle, 5 = splenius capitis muscle, 6 = levator scapulae muscle, 7 = longissimus capitis muscle.

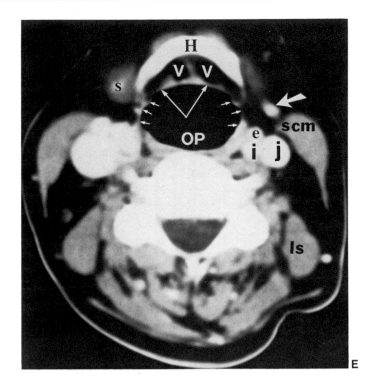

E This section passes through the body and greater horn of the hyoid bone, H, and through the body of the fourth cervical vertebra.
e = external carotid artery, H = hyoid bone, i = internal carotid artery, j = internal jugular vein, ls = levator scapuli muscle, OP = oropharynx, s = submandibular gland, scm = sternocleidomastoid muscle, v = valleculae, short white arrows = pharyngoepiglottic folds, long white arrows = epiglottis, large white arrow = posterior facial vein.

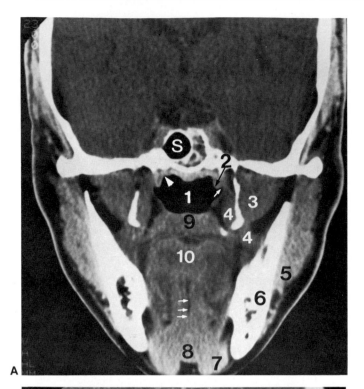

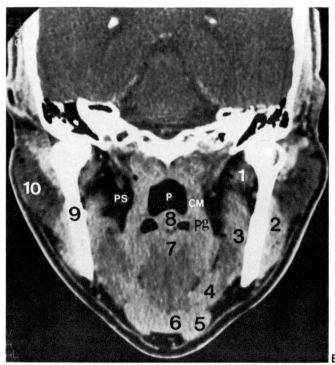

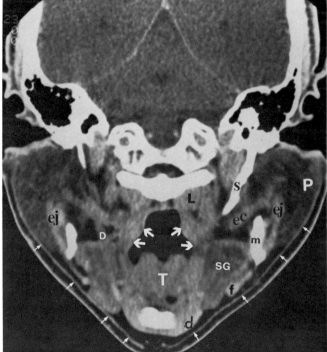

Figure 2.**2** Normal oral cavity, pharynx and upper neck. **A** This section crosses the sphenoid sinus, S, and soft palate, 9.
S = sphenoid sinus, single white arrow = eustachian tube orifice, white arrows = lingual septum, white arrowhead = Rosenmüller fossa, 1 = nasopharynx, 2 = with black arrow, torus tubarius, 3 = lateral pterygoid muscle, 4 = medial pterygoid muscle, 5 = masseter muscle, 6 = mandible, 7 = anterior belly digastric muscle, 8 = genioglossus muscle, 9 = soft palate, 10 = lingual intrinsic muscles.

B This section is 6 mm posterior to **A**.
CM = pharyngeal constrictor muscle, P = nasopharynx, pg = palatoglossal muscle, PS = parapharyngeal space, 1 = lateral pterygoid muscle, 2 = masseter muscle, 3 = medial pterygoid muscle, 4 = mylohyoid muscle, 5 = anterior belly digastric muscle, 6 = genioglossus muscle, 7 = lingual intrinsic muscles, 8 = soft palate, 9 = mandible, 10 = parotid gland.

C This section lies 6 mm posterior to **B**.
d = anterior belly digastric muscle, D = posterior belly digastric muscle, ec = external carotid artery, ej = external jugular vein, f = facial vein, L = longus colli muscle, m = mandible, P = parotid gland, S = Styloid process, SG = submandibular gland, T = tongue, small white arrows = platysma muscle, large white arrows = pharynx. Enhanced carotid sheaths are seen medial to styloid processes (S).

D This section lies 4.5 mm posterior to **C**.
D = posterior belly digastric muscle, e = epiglottis, E = external jugular vein, f = facial vein, h = hyoid bone, j = internal jugular vein, P = parotid gland, PS = pre-epiglottic space, S = submandibular gland, scm = sternocleidomastoid muscle, long white arrows = pharynx, short white arrows = platysma muscle, black arrow = digastric groove.

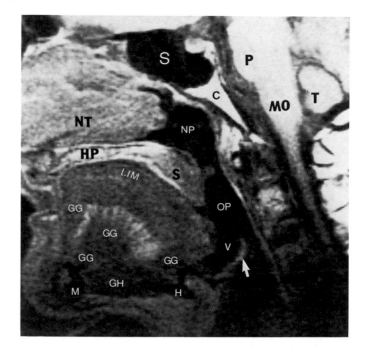

Figure 2.3 Normal oral cavity and oropharynx, MR sagittal para-median Section T₁-weighted.
C = clivus, GG = genioglossus muscle, GH = geniohyoid muscle, H = hyoid bone, HP = hard palate, LIM = lingual intrinsic muscle, M = mandible, MO = medulla oblongata, NP = nasopharynx, NT = nasal turbinate, OP = oropharynx, P = pons, black S = soft palate, white S = sphenoid sinus, T = cerebellar tonsil, V = vallecula, white arrow = epiglottis.

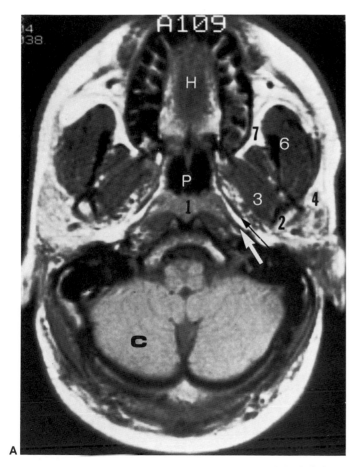

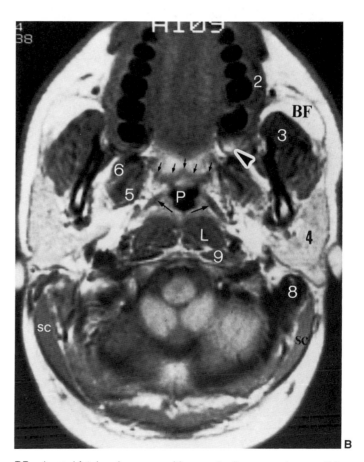

Figure 2.4 Normal oropharynx and upper neck, Axial MR Sections, Spin Density Weighted. **A** This section passes through the alveolar process of the maxilla, the nasopharynx and cerebellum.
C = cerebellum, H = hard palate, P = nasopharynx, white arrow = levator veli palatini muscle, black arrow = tensor veli palatini muscle, 1 = adenoidal pad, 2 = mandible, 3 = lateral pterygoid muscle, 4 = parotid gland, 6 = masseter muscle, 7 = buccal fat.
B This section is 6 mm inferior to **A** and crosses through the upper teeth, coronoid process and mastoid process.

BF = buccal fat, L = longus capitis muscle, P = nasopharynx, SC = splenius capitis muscle, short black arrows = pharyngopalatine muscle, long black arrow = levator palatini muscle, black white arrowhead = buccopharyngeal space, 2 = buccinator muscle, 3 = masseter muscle, 4 = parotid gland, 5 = medial pterygoid muscle, 6 = lateral pterygoid muscle, 8 = mastoid process, 9 = anterior rectus capitis.

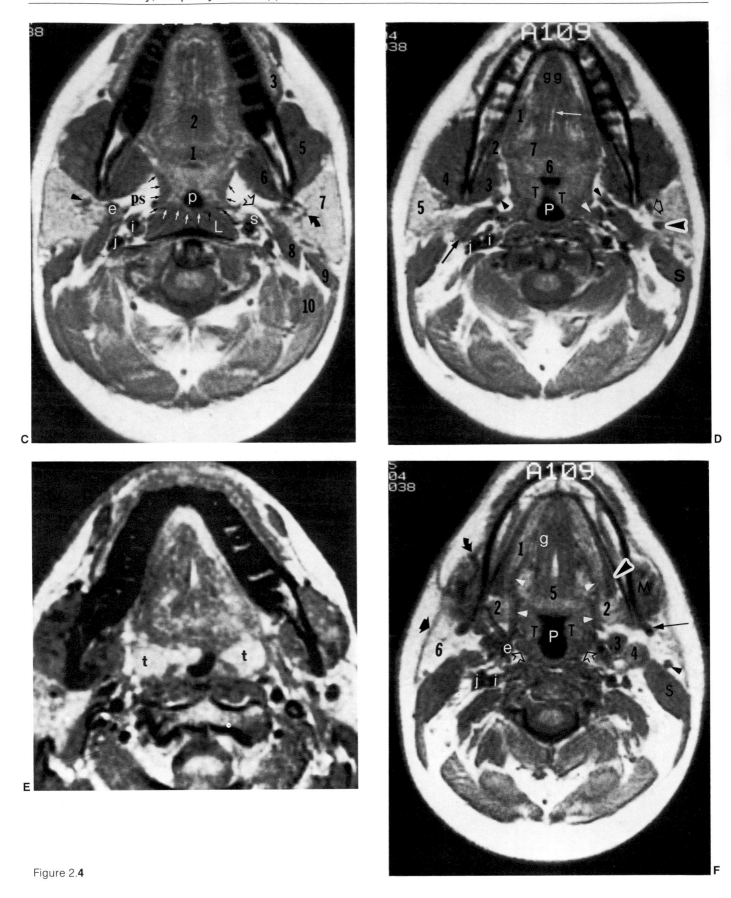

Figure 2.4

◄ **C** This section is 9 mm inferior to **B** and crosses the lower alveolar ridge.

e = external carotid artery, i = internal carotid artery, j = internal jugular vein, L = longus capitis muscle, p = oropharynx, ps = parapharyngeal fat space, s = stylopharyngeus muscle, small white and black arrows = superior pharyngeal constrictor muscle, hollow arrow = stylohyoid muscle, black curved arrow = facial nerve, black arrowhead = retromandibular vein, 1 = longitudinal intrinsic tongue muscles, 2 = transverse intrinsic tongue muscles, 3 = buccinator muscle, 5 = masseter muscle, 6 = internal pterygoid muscle, 7 = parotid gland, 8 = posterior belly digastric muscle, 9 = sternocleidomastoid muscle, 10 = splenius capitis muscle.

D This section is 6 mm inferior to **C**.

gg = genioglossus muscle, i = internal carotid artery, j = internal jugular vein, P = oropharynx, S = sternocleidomastoid muscle, T = palatine tonsils, white arrow = lingual septum, white arrowhead = stylopharyngeus muscle, black white arrowhead = external jugular vein, hollow arrow = retromandibular vein, black arrow = posterior belly digastric muscle, black arrowhead = stylohyoid muscle, 1 = hyoglossus muscle, 2 = mylohyoid muscle, 3 = internal pterygoid muscle, 4 = masseter muscle, 5 = parotid gland, 6 = longitudinal intrinsic tongue muscles, 7 = transverse intrinsic tongue muscles.

E Section at the level of the palatine tonsil and body of the mandible. The palatine tonsils, t, appear as areas of high signal intensity. The tonsils are bright because of their content of mucous glands (increased spin density) and lymphoid tissue. When the tonsils have been removed or are atrophied, the tonsillar fossae show a lower signal because of fibrous tissue and atrophy **D**.

F This section is 6 mm inferior to **D** and crosses the body of the mandible just above the mental foramina.

e = external carotid artery, g = genioglossus muscle, i = internal carotid artery, j = internal jugular vein, M = masseter muscle, P = pharynx, S = sternocleidomastoid muscle, T = palatine tonsils, white arrowheads = styloglossus muscle posterior to hyoglossus muscle, black-white arrowhead = mylohyoid muscle, black arrow = retromandibular vein, short black curved arrow = anterior facial vein, hollow arrows = pharyngeal constridor muscles, black arrowhead = external jugular vein, 1 = sublingual gland, 2 = submandibular gland, 3 = stylohyoid muscle, 4 = digastric muscle, 5 = intrinsic tongue muscles, 6 = parotid gland.

Chapter 3 Common Pathological Conditions and Inflammatory Diseases

Roentgenographic and imaging examinations of the oral cavity, oropharynx, and laryngopharynx provide valuable information that often permit rapid and accurate diagnosis and differential diagnosis of various inflammatory diseases. There are three conditions that are often associated with upper respiratory stridor of acute onset in which radiographic examination is important in diagnosis. These conditions, which occur primarily in infants and young children, are acute epiglottitis, acute laryngotracheobronchitis, and retropharyngeal abscess.

The upper airway lends itself readily to study; using conventional techniques, which show swelling and edema of soft tissues and narrowing of air passages. Frontal and lateral views of the upper airway and chest are obtained, with the patient upright, since acute respiratory obstruction may be exacerbated when the infant is recumbant. This is especially so in cases of acute epiglottitis where putting the patient in the supine position can cause more respiratory obstruction.

Every effort should be made to make the exposure during inspiration. In contrast to the adult, the airway in the child can demonstrate considerable variability. In infants and young children, crying, swallowing and expiration produce changes in the x-ray appearance of the pharyngeal soft tissues and of the trachea that can lead to diagnostic error. During expiration and particularly while crying or swallowing, and with flexion of the head, the retropharyngeal soft tissues bulge anteriorly. The trachea may deviate anteriorly and to one side (Figs. 3.1, 3.2). Views

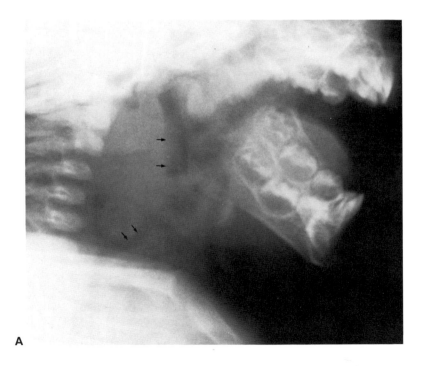

A

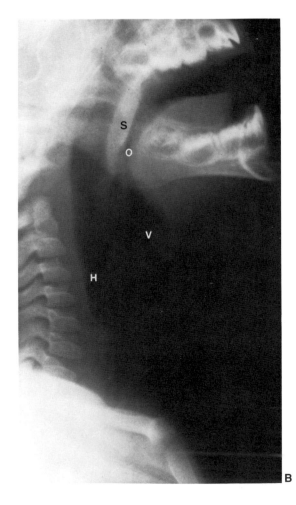

B

Figure 3.1 Lateral neck of infant, conventional film, taken with head in flexion during expiration, **A** and with head in extension (same patient) during inspiration, **B**. In **A** there is bulging of the retropharyngeal soft tissue, black arrows, mimicking a retropharyngeal abscess. In **B** the thickness of the retropharyngeal soft tissue is normal.
H = hypopharynx, O = oropharynx, S = soft palate, V = vallecule.

obtained during swallowing and phonation show elevation of the soft palate and changes in position of the epiglottis, pharynx and oropalatal airways (Fig. 3.2).

It is important to remember that in children and even in adults in acute respiratory distress, a satisfactory examination can only be made using conventional techniques, since CT and MR scanning require the patient to remain immobile for relatively long periods of time, and patients in acute respiratory distress are simply not able to maintain a constrained position for even a short period of time.

Retropharyngeal abscess is another example of the importance of appropriate conventional technique in the clinical assessment of the child with respiratory distress. In the lateral roentgenogram obtained with the infant properly positioned, the width of the prevertebral soft tissues measures from 1–1½ times the anteroposterior diameter of the adjacent cervical vertebral body. In poorly taken views, the width of the prevertebral soft tissues may increase to 2½ or 3 times the width of the vertebral body giving a false impression of pathology (Figs. 3.1, 3.2, 3.5).

In adults and children without respiratory distress, CT techniques are used to demonstrate pathology. Anatomical variations can be discovered in CT images

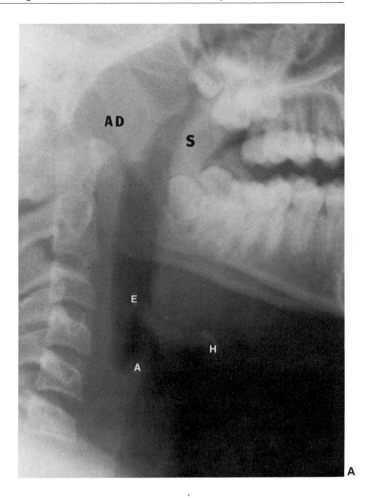

A

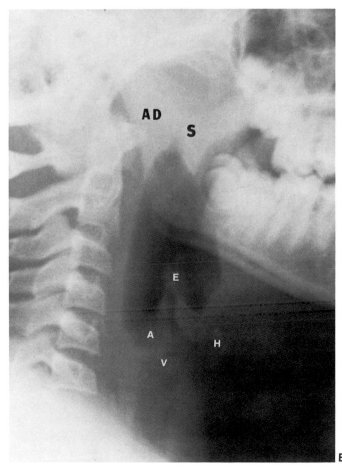

B

Figure 3.**2** Lateral conventional view of the neck of a child in ▶ quiet breathing, **A** and during expiratory phonation of "E", **B**. The change in the position of the epiglottis as well as the elevation of the soft palate which closes the nasopharynx is evident in **B**.
A = arytenoid area, AD = adenoid, E = epiglottis, H = hyoid bone, S = soft palate, V = glottis. Notice expansion of valleculae, anterior to epiglottis in B.

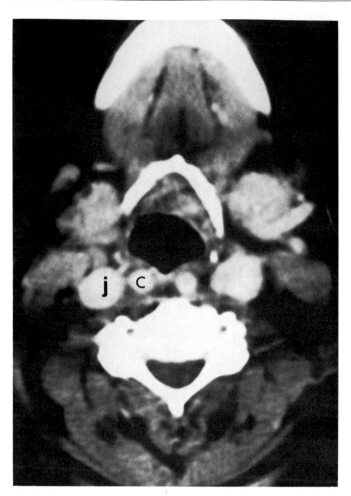

Figure 3.**3**   Abnormal course of the internal carotid arteries; Axial postcontrast CT section at the level of the hyoid bone and the mandible. The CT scan shows the internal carotid arteries, C, in the posterior pharyngeal space medial to the internal jugular veins, j.

such as in Figure 3.**3,** where the internal carotid arteries are located in the retropharyngeal space.

Infections of the Neck

Acute Epiglottitis and Angioneurotic Edema

In acute epiglottitis, which occurs most commonly in children ages three to six years, the haemophilus influenzae organism is the most common cause of infection. The disorder could be more appropriately referred to as acute supraglottitis, because the infection involves the epiglottis and the aryepiglottic folds. The diagnosis is made on a lateral conventional view of the neck, which demonstrates marked swelling of the epiglottis and aryepiglottic folds. This condition can also occur in adults, and both in children and in adults severe respiratory distress can occur. The radiologist must, of necessity, work quickly in obtaining radiographic studies.

Angioneurotic edema of the larynx is a medical emergency. The process produces a marked swelling of the base of the tongue, epiglottis, glottis, and arytenoids and post-cricoid area with obstruction of the airway (Fig. 3.**4**).

Laryngotracheobronchitis

This disorder occurs most frequently in young children between the ages of six months and three to four years. The process causes narrowing of the subglottic space. In laryngotracheobronchitis, the lateral and anteroposterior views of the airway establish that the aryepiglottic folds and prevertebral soft tissues are normal while the subglottic space is narrowed.

Retropharyngeal Abscess

In children under four years of age, retropharyngeal lymph nodes drain the regions of the nasopharynx and eustachian tubes. Infection of these nodes, which is preceded by a bacterial nasopharyngitis, may lead to retropharyngeal abscess formation. This is most common in the very young up to the age of two years, after which age it is uncommon. The disorder is an acute adenitis and cellulitis of the retropharyngeal soft tissues which, if untreated, leads to suppuration. There is marked diffuse swelling of the retropharyngeal soft tissues extending from the anterior border of Cl inferiorly to the cervical esophagus, which is best seen on the lateral conventional x-ray made during inspiration (Fig. 3.**5**).

The importance of proper radiographic technique is demonstrated in Figures 3.**1** and 3.**2,** which show how poor technique can lend to a false diagnosis of retropharyngeal abscess.

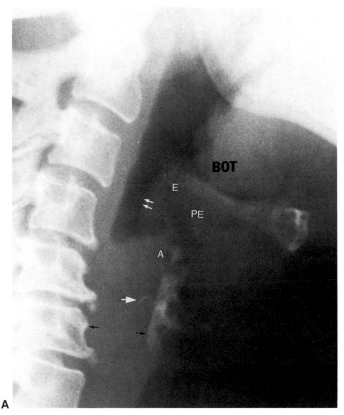

A

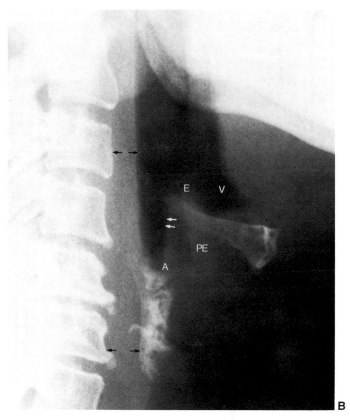

B

Figure 3.**4**   Angioneurotic edema, conventional lateral views. In **A** there is marked swelling of the base of the tongue, epiglottis, and pre-epiglottic space, arytenoid region, and post-laryngeal space. The white arrow points to the cricoid cartilage. In **B** a repeat study a few days later following treatment shows marked improvement. Notice that the base of the tongue is normal and air is seen in the vallecula. The epiglottis, aryepiglottic folds, arytenoid region, pre-epiglottic and retropharyngeal space are now normal. There is a slight persistent retropharyngeal soft tissue thickening, upper small black arrows.

A = arytenoid region, BOT = base of tongue, E = epiglottis, PE = preepiglottic space, large white arrow = cricoid cartilage, small white arrows = aryepiglottic folds, lower small black arrows = post-cricoid space, upper small black arrows = retropharyngeal soft tissue thickening.

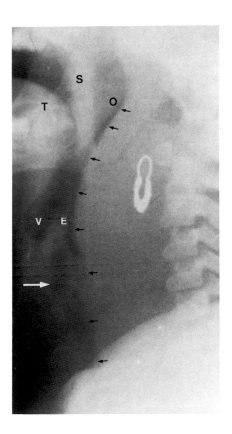

Figure 3.**5**   Retropharyngeal abscess. Lateral conventional view shows marked bulging of the retropharyngeal soft tissues indicated by the black arrows.

E = epiglottis, O = oropharynx, S = soft palate, T = tonsil, V = Vallecule, white arrow points to glottis.

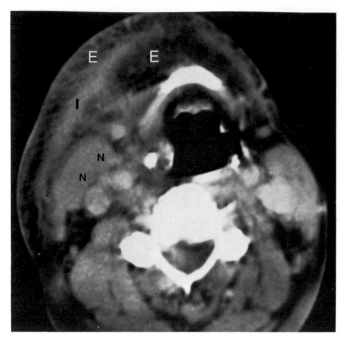

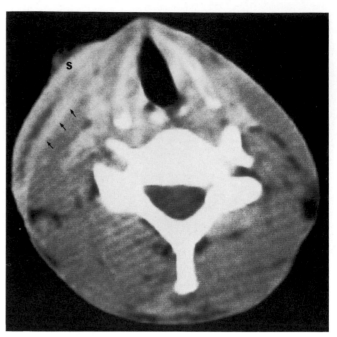

Figure 3.**6**   Cellulitis of the neck in a patient with acute lymphatic leukemia. CT scan taken at the level of the epiglottis and hyoid bone shows subcutaneous edema, E, and soft tissue induration, I. On the right side there are several enlarged lymph nodes, N.

Figure 3.**7**   Cellulitis of the neck. CT shows soft tissue thickening of the right side of the neck with marked contrast enhancement of the superficial cervical space, S, as well as the deep cervical space, blackarrows.

Deep Neck Infections

Deep neck space (DNS) infections that affect the fascial compartments of the head and neck and their contents can lead to fatal complications if not properly diagnosed and treated (Figs. 3.**6**, 3.**7**, 3.**8**, 3.**9**). Bezold's abscess, is an example of a deep neck space abscess. It is a result of a suppuration in the tip of the mastoid process which erodes the cortex of the mastoid bone medial to the attachment of the sterno-cleidomastoid muscle so that the infection spreads into the deep structures of the neck, medial to the sternocleidomastoid muscle.

The major salivary glands and congenital neck cysts are common sources of deep neck space abscesses (Fig. 3.**8**). Dental infections can also lead to suppuration of the neck spaces adjacent to the mandible. The masticator space becomes infected most often by direct extension from dental infections (Figs. 3.**9**, 3.**10**). Ludwig's angina is an infection with cellulitis and induration of the sublingual and submaxillary spaces, which also develops from dental origins.

The diagnosis of DNS infections is made by the clinician. However, with CT and MR, it is possible not only to diagnose an early abscess, but also to differentiate the abscess from a cellulitis. The CT characteristics of cellulitis include thickening of the skin and subcutaneous tissues, engorgement of the lymphatics and thickening or obliteration of the adjacent fascial planes and surrounding tissues with or without enhancement (Figs. 3.**6**, 3.**7**, 3.**9**–3.**11**).

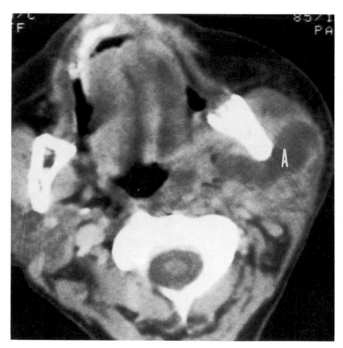

Figure 3.**8**   Parotid abscess. CT shows an abscess, A, in the retromandibular portion of the left parotid gland. The section is taken through the vertical rami of the mandible.

DNS abscesses appear as single, or multiloculated low density cystic lesions with peripheral rim enhancement and edema of the surrounding tissues (Figs. 3.**8**, 3.**10**).

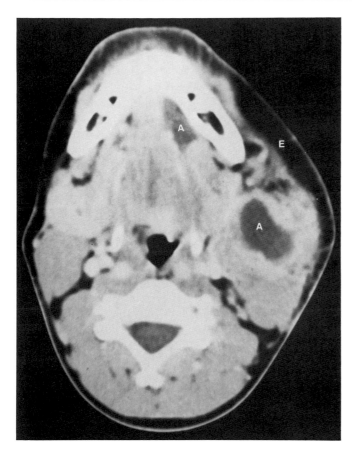

Figure 3.**9** Deep abscesses of the neck. An axial CT section through the level of the body of the mandible shows a large abscess, A, anterior to the sternocleidomastoid muscle and a smaller abscess, A, in the floor of the mouth. The lesions appear as low density areas surrounded by thick rings of enhancement. There is edema of the superficial soft tissue, E. The abscesses are in pact in the sublingual and submandibular spaces. Compare this figure with figure 2.**1C**.

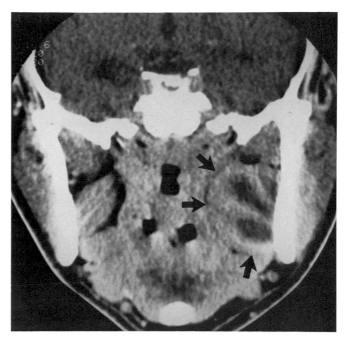

Figure 3.**10** Infection of masticatory space following tooth extraction. A coronal CT section at the level of the vertical rami of the mandible shows a multiloculated abscess indicated by the black arrows.

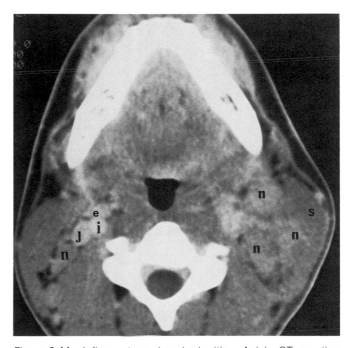

Figure 3.**11** Inflammatory lymphadenitis. Axial CT section through the body of the mandible shows enlarged, inflamed lymph nodes with infiltration of the adjacent fascial spaces. There are several enlarged lymph nodes on both sides of the neck.
e = external carotid, i = internal carotid artery, J = jugular vein, n = lymph nodes, S = sternocleidomastoid muscle. The presumptive diagnosis was mononucleosis.

Vascular complications of DNS infections include venous thrombosis and invasion of the carotid artery with hemorrhage. On CT scans, the central portion of the vessel involved is less dense than the contrast enhanced blood (see Fig. 4.**17**). A fresh thrombus may be as dense as contrast enhanced blood and for this reason may not be detectable on CT. MR, using gradient echo technique, is superior to CT scans in these cases. The thrombus in MR depending on its age appears as an area of low or high signal intensity partially or totally obstructing the vessel. The normal patent vessel appears black or as an area of no signal.

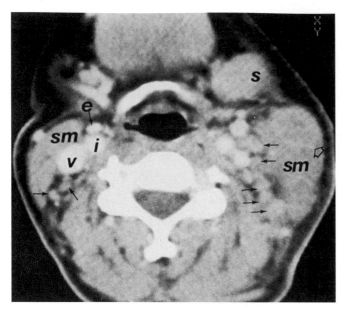

Figure 3.**12** Tuberculous lymphadenitis, post-contrast infusion axial CT scan at the level of the hyoid bone. There are several enlarged lymph nodes on the left side. The sternocleidomastoid muscle on the left is enlarged by a large lymph node adjacent to the anterior aspect of the muscle.

e = external carotid artery, i = internal carotid artery, sm = sternocleidomastoid muscle, v = internal jugular vein, black arrows = enlarged lymph nodes, hollow arrow = large node adjacent to the sternocleidomastoid.

Cervical Tuberculous Adenitis, Scrofula

Cervical tuberculous adenitis initially involves the lymph nodes of the neck with subsequent involvement of the adjacent fascial planes and musculature (Fig. 3.**12**).

On CT, there may be unilateral or bilateral masses in a lymph node-bearing area of the neck with or without significant enhancement. The fascial planes at times are not preserved and the adjacent musculature can be affected by the process. If there is central necrosis of the tuberculous lesion, the enhanced walls of the single or multichambered involved area are thicker than that which occurs in necrotic malignant metastatic neck nodes. The cold abscess of cervical tuberculous adenitis is a mass of broken down tuberculous coalescent infected lymph nodes.

Cystic Lesions of the Neck

Included here are a series of benign, congenital, or acquired cystic lesions that occur in the neck.

Ranula

A ranula is a retention cyst originating in the sublingual space and submandibular space related to obstruction of a sublingual gland or adjacent minor salivary gland. These are benign lesions and are easily recognized by examination. Ranulas can be of the simple or plunging variety. If the ranula remains within the sublingual space, it is referred to as a simple ranula. When the lesion extends from the sublingual space to involve the submandibular or parapharyngeal space, it is designated as plunging.

On CT, ranulas are seen as sharply marginated, low density, thin walled homogeneous cystic masses without septations which conform smoothly to the adjacent fascial boundries. On MR, ranulas are seen as relatively hypointense lesions on T_1-weighted images, intermediate signal intensity on spin density weighted images (Fig. 3.**13** B), and hyperintense in the T_2-weighted images (Figs. 3.**13**, 3.**14**).

Several congenital lesions that may be encountered in the oral cavity and anterior neck may be mistaken clinically or in imaging for ranulas. These lesions are anterior cystic hygromas, epidermoid cysts, dermoid cysts, teratomas, second branchial cleft cysts, and thyroglossal duct cysts.

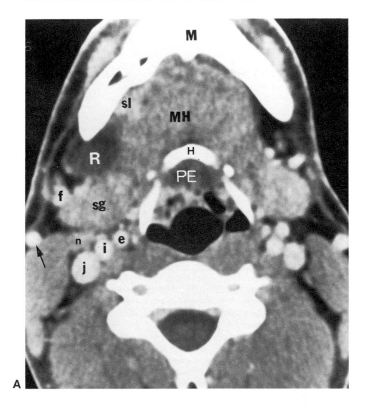

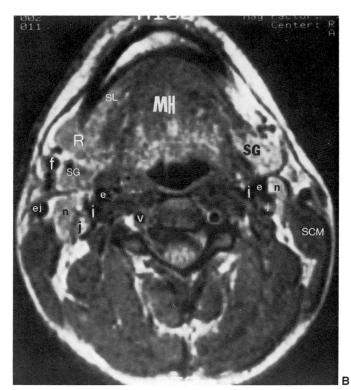

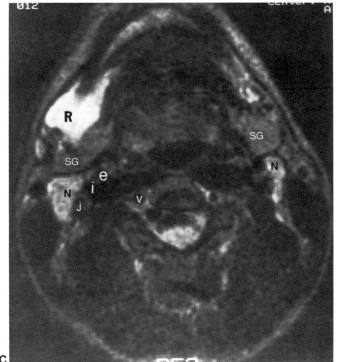

Figure 3.**13** Ranula. **A** Axial CT section with infusion at the level of the mandible shows the ranula, R, as an area of low density surrounded by a thin wall.

e = external carotid artery, f = posterior facial vein, H = hyoid bone, i = internal carotid artery, j = internal jugular vein, M = mandible, MH = mylohyoid muscle, n = lymph node, PE = pre-epiglottic space, R = ranula, sg = submandibular gland, sl = sublingual gland, black arrow = external jugular vein.

B MR, spin density weighted axial section. The ranula, R, appears as a medium signal intensity lesion.

e = external carotid artery, ej = external jugular vein, f = facial vein, i = internal carotid artery, j = internal jugular vein, MH = mylohyoid muscle, n = lymph node, R = ranula, SCM = sterno-cleidomastoid muscle, SG = submandibular gland, SL = sublingual gland, v = vertebral artery.

C MR, T$_2$-weighted axial image at the same level as **B**. The ranula, R, in this sequence has a high signal intensity.

e = external carotid artery, i = internal carotid artery, j = jugular vein, N = lymph node, R = ranula, SG = submandibular gland, v = vertebral artery.

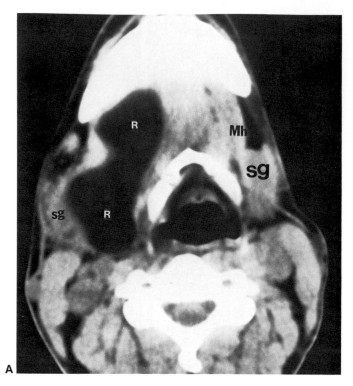

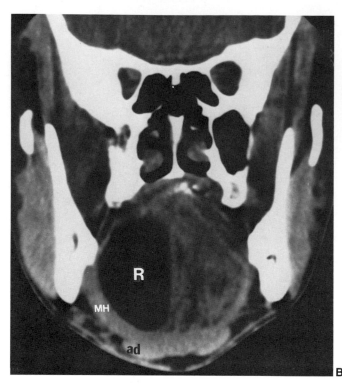

Figure 3.**14**   Ranula, plunging type. **A** Axial CT section shows a large ranula, R, in the floor of the mouth and neck displacing the right submandibular gland, sg, laterally. There is marked deformity and medial displacement of the mylohyoid muscle on the involved side, Mh.

B The coronal CT section at the level of the rami of the mandible shows the plunging ranula, R, which displaces the tongue to the left and the mylohyoid muscle, MH, inferiorly (ad is the anterior belly, of the digastric muscle).

Branchial Cleft Cysts and Fistulas

Branchial cleft cysts and fistulas arise from incomplete obliteration of the embryonic branchial apparatus.

The first branchial cleft fistulae and cysts are found entirely above the hyoid bone with an external opening in the floor of the external auditory canal. The second branchial cleft cysts and fistulae are more common and are located in the upper neck near the angle of the mandible. Third cleft fistulae and cysts have the same external openings as the second cleft, but can dip to the pyriform sinus.

A first branchial cleft cyst appears on CT as a well defined low density mass adjacent to the superficial lobe of the parotid or within the gland itself. Second branchial cleft cysts are by far the most common lesion of this type. On CT, a non-infected second branchial cleft cyst appears as a homogeneous low density, fluid filled, smoothly margined thin-walled, non-enhancing mass at the level of the mandible (Fig. 3.**15**). If the cyst has been infected, there will be varying degrees of wall thickening contrast enhancement, as well as loss of soft tissue planes around the cyst. As the protein content of the infected cyst increases, the attenuation values may approach those of muscle.

On MR, the noninfected cyst is seen as a slightly to moderately hypointense image in T_1-weighted and spin density weighted images, which become hyperintense in T_2-weighted images (Fig. 3.**15**).

When a sinus or fistula tract is present without an associated cystic component, CT and MR fail to demonstrate the lesion. In these cases, a fistulogram with injection of an iodinated contrast material will show the extent of the tract.

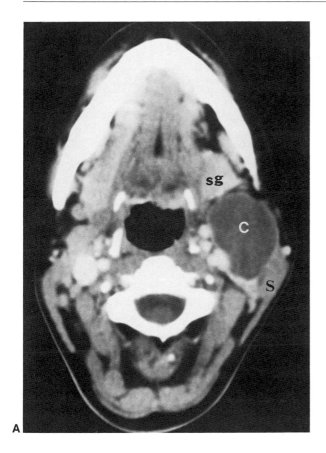

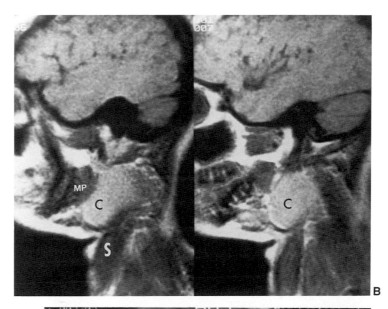

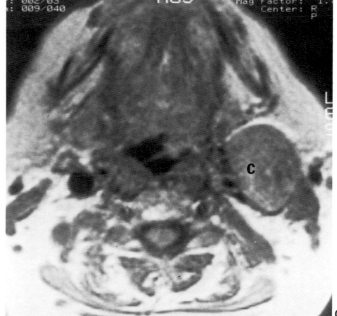

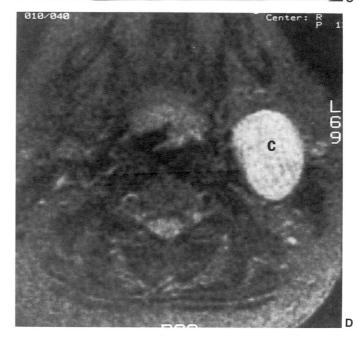

Figure 3.**15**   Second branchial cleft cyst. **A** Axial CT section through the floor of the mouth. **B** sagittal spin density weighted MR scans, **C** axial spin density weighted MR scan at a comparable level to A, **D** MR T$_2$-weighted scan at level of **A**. **A** CT scan shows a low density, smoothly marginated cystic appearing mass, **C** anterior to the sternocleidomastoid muscle, S, and posterior to the submandibular gland, sg.

B Sagittal MR spin density weighted scans show the cyst, C, of medium intensity anterior to the sternocleidomastoid muscle, S, and posterior to the medial pterygoid muscle, MP.

C Axial spin density weighted scan shows slightly hypointense mass, C, which represents the branchial cleft cyst.

D MR T$_2$-weighted scan shows a hyperintense mass, C.

Epidermoid Cysts

Epidermoid cysts in the neck are rare. They usually are located in the anterior sublingual space and anterior submandibular space (Fig. 3.16), and must be differentiated from a simple ranula. On CT, the cyst appears as a well defined, low density, non-enhancing, thin walled lesion. On MR the lesion has low signal intensity in T1 and spin density weighted images, but high intensity in T_2-weighted images.

Dermoid Cysts

Dermoid cysts are lesions similar to epidermoid cysts but contain variable skin appendages. They are usually located in the upper neck and are diagnosed before the age of three. Dermoids can be differentiated from other cysts as they contain fat. In CT, the fatty deposits appear as areas of far lower density than the fluid filling the cyst. In MR, the fluid component of the cyst is usually bright on both T1w and T2w images due to high protein fluid content. The fatty component has a high signal intensity in T1w, but low intensity in T2w images.

Thyroglossal Duct Cysts

Thyroglossal duct cysts and fistulas arise from epithelial vestiges that are retained during the descent of the anlage of the thyroid gland. The characteristic CT appearance of a thyroglossal duct cyst is that of a well circumscribed low density mass with peripheral rim enhancement (Fig. 3.17). High density lesions reflect an increased protein content within the cyst and generally correlate with a history of infection. In our study of several cases, the MR signal characteristics of these cysts are identical to ranulas and second branchial cleft cysts.

Cystic Hygroma, Lymphangioma

Cystic hygroma is a congenital, benign unilocular or multilocular endothelium-lined, fluid-containing cyst of lymphatic origin. These lesions are believed to arise from sequestrations of the primitive embryonic lymph sacs and to enlarge either because of inadequate drainage secondary to failure of communication of the lesion with the central lymphatic channels and veins or from excessive secretion of the lining cells. In most patients, the condition involves the neck. Other main sites include the axilla and, rarely, the groin. The CT appearance of cystic hygroma is that of a multiloculated, thin walled, poorly circumscribed low density mass with extension into the adjacent fascial planes. Occasionally a cystic hygroma may present as a solitary mass. On MR, the cystic masses often show a high signal intensity in all sequences due to the high protein content of the fluid. Fluid layering is occasionally seen (Fig. 3.18).

Other Neck Cysts

Other cysts that occasionally are found in the neck, but not shown in this chapter include thyroid cysts, parathyroid cysts, thymic cysts, duplication cyst of esophagus cystic schwannomas and salivary gland cysts.

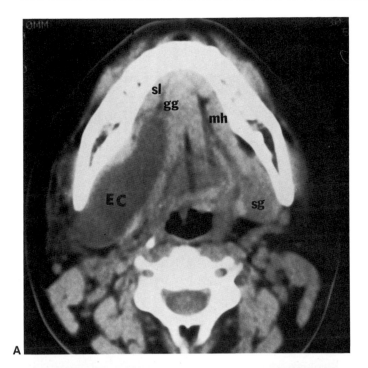

A

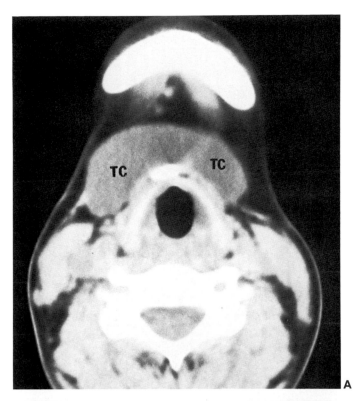

A

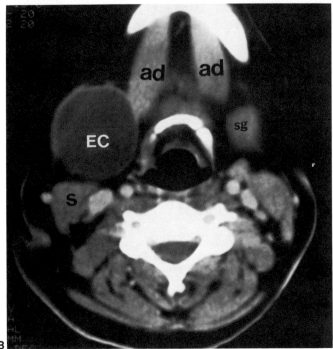

B

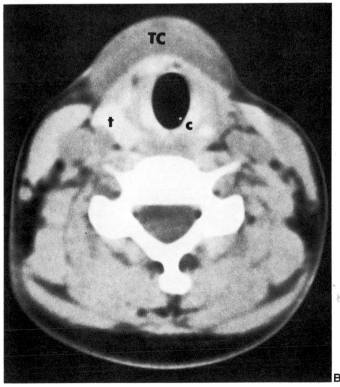

B

Figure 3.**16A** and **B**   Epidermoid cyst of the floor of the mouth, axial CT sections with infusion, at levels 1 cm apart. There is a large low density lesion, EC, in the right side of the neck surrounded by a thin capsule.

ad = anterior belly of the digastric, EC = epidermoid cyst, gg = genioglossus muscle, Mh = mylohyoid muscle, S = sternocleidomastoid muscle, sg = submaxillary gland, sl = sublingual gland.

Figure 3.**17A** and **B**   Thyroglossal duct cyst. Axial CT sections show a low density thyroglossal duct cyst, TC. C = cricoid cartilage, t = thyroid gland.

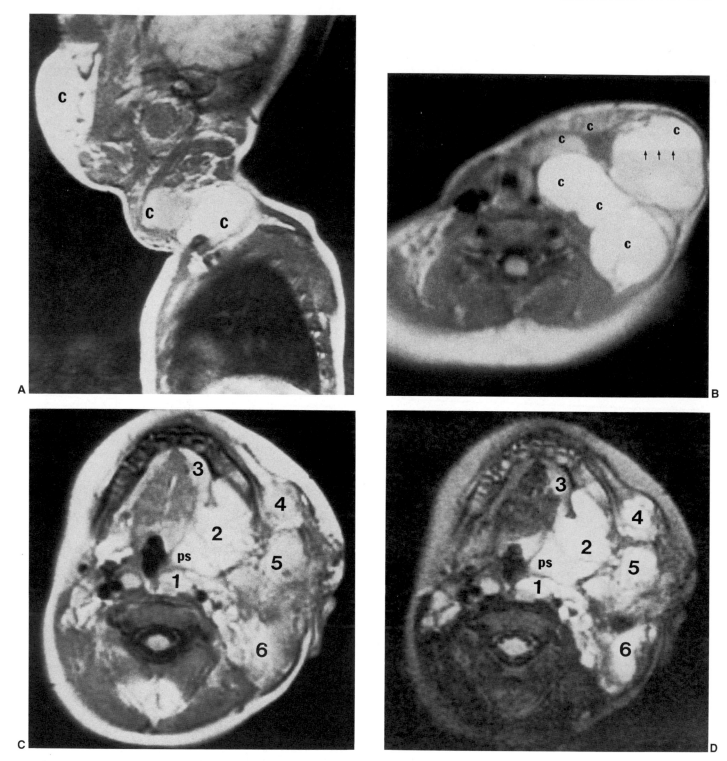

Figure 3.**18**   Cystic hygroma. **A** Sagittal T_1-weighted MR image. **B, C** Axial spin density weighted MR sections. **D** Axial T_2-weighted MR image.
There is a multiloculated thin walled mass, C, involving the entire left side of the neck. The lesion has a high signal intensity in all sequences. There is extension of the hygroma in the posterior pharynx = 1, parapharyngeal space = ps, submandibular = 2, and sublingual spaces = 3, the masticator space = 4, as well as the parotid space = 5 and the posterior triangle = 6.
The black arrows in **B** indicate layering of the fluid within the cyst.

Chapter 4   Tumors

Solid tumors are divided in this chapter into benign and malignant lesions. The solid benign tumors discussed are pleomorphic adenomas, neurofibromas, nonchromaffin paragangliomas of the carotid body and glomus vagale. The malignant lesions include carcinomas of the alveolar ridge, palate, floor of the mouth, tongue, pharynx and tonsils, metastatic neck lymph nodes and carcinoma of the major and minor salivary glands.

Solid Benign Tumors

Benign neck masses can be identified with CT and MR by their location and imaging characteristics. Salivary gland tumors are covered separately in chapter 8 of this section.

Neurogenic Tumors

Neurilemmomas or schwannomas are thought to arise from the neurolemma sheath, the Schwann cells, which are fibroblasts of the perineurium or epineurium of the pheripheral nerves. In the neck, the neurogenic tumors occur most frequently in the carotid space. The vagus nerve and sympathetic chain are the largest peripheral nerves in the neck and give rise to most neurogenic tumors. The vagus is within the carotid sheath posterolateral to the common and internal carotid arteries, while the sympathetic chain is outside the carotid sheath and medial to it.

The CT appearance of neurogenic tumors is variable (Fig. 4.1). They may be dense or lucent in noncontrast scans, and following administration of iodinated contrast material, they may show considerable, moderate or no enhancement, although nonenhanced lesions are rare. Medium to large neurofibromas can have a considerable degree of fatty infiltration and necrosis. They are either solitary or multiple masses. In patients with neurofibromatosis, diffuse overgrowth of Schwann cells and fibroblasts occurs, giving rise to plexiform neuromas. These lesions are seen as diffuse, ill defined, poorly circumscribed masses in the neck with varying degrees of contrast enhancement. The lesion may be hypo- or isodense in precontrast scans. Hypodense lesions are rare.

Neuromas of the vagus, sympathetic, trigeminal, glossopharyngeal and hypoglossal nerves, and neurofibromas arising within the parapharyngeal space, can present as masses bulging into the nasopharynx. The spectrum of MR characteristics of neurogenic tumors are presented in Figure 4.2. The neurogenic tumors are generally hypointense in T1 and hyperintense in T2 images. Unlike chemodectomas or nonchromaffin paragangliomas, neurogenic tumors usually appear relatively hypovascular on angiographic study, as well as on MR angiographic (gradient echo or fast or partial flip angle MR imaging) study.

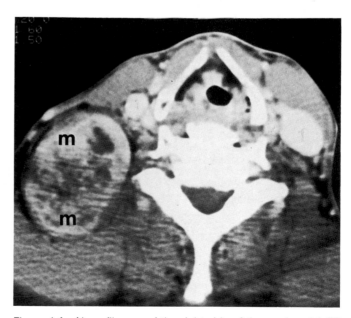

Figure 4.1   Neurofibroma of the right side of the neck, axial CT section with infusion at the level of the thyroid cartilage notch. A large, nonhomogeneous partially enhanced soft tissue mass, m, lies in the right side of the neck.

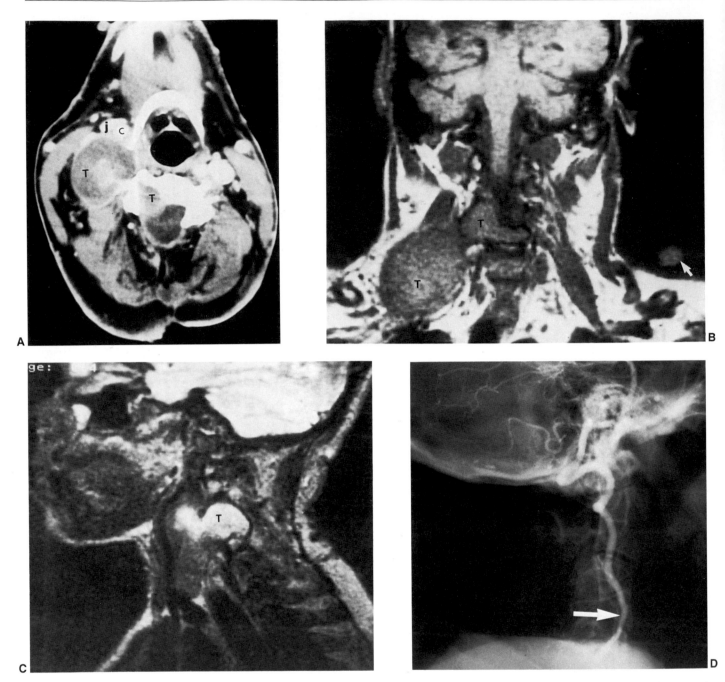

Figure 4.2   Neurofibroma, dumbbell form, spinal canal and neck.
A Axial CT section, post-contrast infusion at the level of the hyoid bone. The bilobed tumor, T, appears in the neck and spinal canal. The larger part of the tumor displaces the jugular vein, j, and internal carotid artery, c, anteriorly, The smaller lesion protrudes into the spinal canal.

B Coronal MR spin density weighted section. Both intra- and extraspinal components of the dumbbell shaped tumor, T, have a low signal intensity.
C Sagittal MR T2w image. The tumor has a high signal intensity in this sequence. The common carotid artery is displaced anteriorly.
D Vertebral angiogram, right. The vertebral artery is narrowed, arrow, due to encasement by tumor.

Carotid Body Tumors

The four main locations of glomus tissue within the head and neck are the middle ear, the site of the glomus tympanicum; the jugular fossa, which is the site of the glomus jugulare; the inferior ganglion region and cervical portion of the vagus nerve, which is the site of a glomus vagale; and finally the carotid bifurcation, which is the site of carotid body tumors. Less common locations include the larynx, orbit, nasal sinuses, and the aortic arch. Multicentricity of paraganglioma tumors of the head and neck is not uncommon.

Carotid body and other paragangliomas can often be accurately diagnosed by CT scanning (Figs. 4.3–4.5).

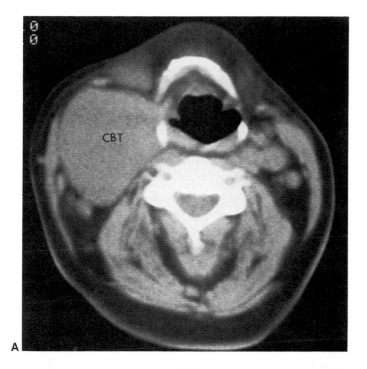

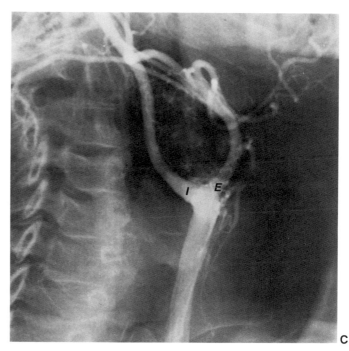

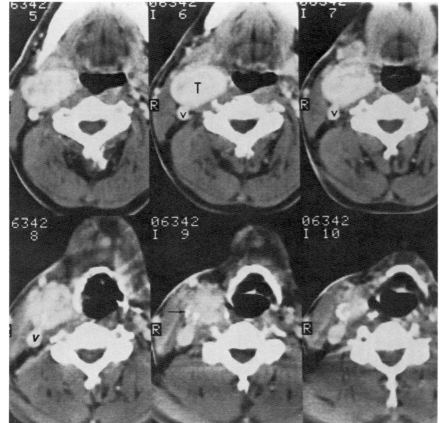

Figure 4.3   Carotid body tumor.

A Axial CT, pre-infusion section at the level of the hyoid bone. There is a large, well defined soft tissue mass, CBT, in the right side of the neck.

B Sequential dynamic CT series of carotid body tumor in another patient, similar to **A**, showing intense enhancement of the tumor mass, T. Maximum enhancement occurs in the second image. V is the jugular vein. Arrow shows the carotid artery.

C Carotid arteriogram. The tumor lies at the bifurcation of the common carotid artery. The internal carotid artery, I, is displaced posteriorly and the external carotid artery, E, is displaced anteriorly. There is a faint tumor blush between these two arteries.

They appear on non-contrast CT scans as an isodense (to muscle) homogeneous lesion. These tumors are highly vascular and thus would be expected to enhance substantially following iodinated contrast infusion. With regular drip infusion technique, bright enhancement may not be observed in all cases, because when the CT scanning is being taken through the tumor, the contrast is significantly diluted in the blood stream. Dynamic CT studies with bolus injection are of great diagnostic value for these tumors and the differentiation of these lesions from other neck masses.

The differential enhancement of glomus complex tumors and their computer generated density curves

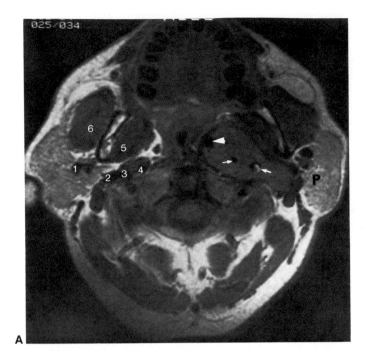

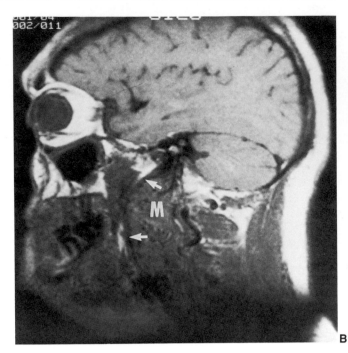

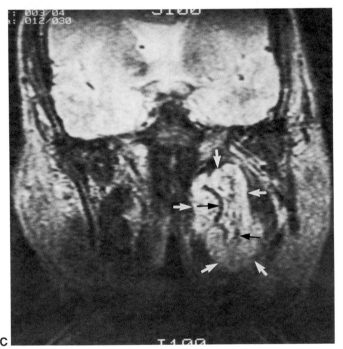

Figure 4.**4** Carotid body tumor. **A** Axial MR spin density weight-ed image. There is a large low signal intensity tumor mass on the left side of the neck medial to the parotid gland, P. The tumor displaces the left internal carotid artery medially, arrowhead. Prominent blood vessels, small arrows, lie within the tumor mass. P = parotid gland, 1 = retromandibular vein, 2 = external carotid artery, 3 = internal jugular vein, 4 = internal carotid artery, 5 = medial pterygoid muscle, 6 = masseter muscle.
B Sagittal T1w image. The low intensity mass, M, displaces the internal carotid artery anteriorly, arrows. Serpiginous areas of signal void within the tumor mass represent blood vessels.
C Coronal T2w MR section. The tumor mass has a higher signal intensity in this sequence. White arrows outline the mass and the black arrows indicate blood vessels within the tumor. All the vessels appeared as hyperintense images on gradient echo MR scans.

are characteristic, since they behave like an arterial venous malformation, and have an arterial peak (Figs. 4.**3B**, 4.**5**).

Carotid body, glomus vagale and glomus jugulare can be accurately evaluated by MR (Fig. 4.**4**). These lesions usually have an intermediate signal intensity in T1 and spin density weighted images and a moder-ately bright signal intensity in the T2 scans. When the tumor is moderate or large in size, there may be several tortuous images of no signal representing high velocity blood flow within the vessels. There may be areas of hyperintensity seen on T2 scans which probably represent sites of even-echo rephas-ing in regions of slow bloodflow or parallel bloodflow within the scan plane.

Malignant Tumors

The role of imaging studies in primary and metastatic lesions of the head and neck is to define the extent of the lesion rather than to make a specific histologic diagnosis. Tumor invasiveness, cartilage and bone destruction, and obliteration of fascial planes help differentiate malignant from benign lesions. CT and MR show the extent of the tumor and its relationship to critical adjacent structures, particularly the carotid sheath. This valuable imaging information should be used for appropriate staging of the head and neck lesions and for decision making regarding resectabil-ity, preoperative surgical mapping, radiation therapy

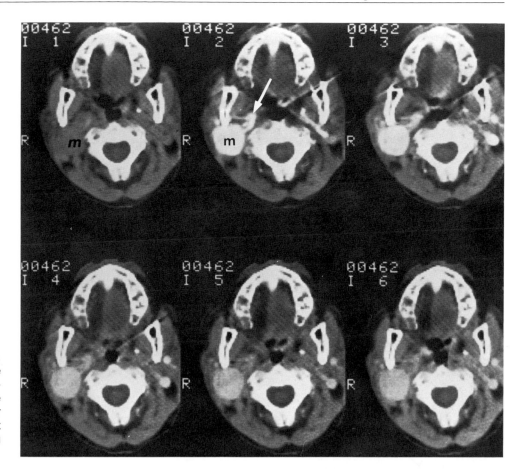

Figure 4.**5** Glomus vagale tumor, dynamic CT series obtained at the level of the tumor. All sections obtained at the same level shows the mass, m, in the right retromandibular area. The enhancement is greatest in the second image. A large feeding vessel, arrow, is visualized.

ports, and the presence of residual or recurrent tumors.

Lymphatic Spread

The principal mode of spread of squamous cell carcinoma of the head and neck is via lymphatics to the cervical nodes. The distribution of cervical node metastases to the primary echelon drainage sites of the upper aerodigestive tract is more or less predictable. Primary echelon drainage from most tumor sites in the mouth and pharynx is to the upper deep jugular chain which includes the subdigastric, jugular digastric, and jugulocarotid nodes and also the submandibular triangle. The posterior triangle is primarily involved from tumors of the base of the tongue, tonsils, and posterior pharyngeal wall (see Figs. 4.**15,** 4.**17**).

Bilateral metastases occur with midline primaries or where lymphatics are abundant and lesions invade muscle, as well as from sites where lymphatic drainage is bilateral such as the soft palate, base of the tongue, posterior pharyngeal wall and floor of the mouth (see Fig. 4.**13**).

Carcinoma of the Gingiva and Alveolar Ridges

These tumors occur primarily in the premolar and molar regions (Fig. 4.**6**). The tumors readily invade underlying bone and extend along the periodontal membrane, sulci and floor of the mouth, palate and

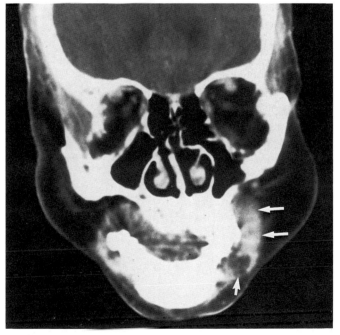

Figure 4.**6** Carcinoma of the left superior alveolar ridge, buccal mucosa, and mandible, coronal CT section with infusion. The enhanced tumor mass, arrows, involves the buccal mucosa, the upper alveolar ridge and erodes lateral aspect of the mandible.

buccal mucosa. Nodal metastases in the submandibular gland are present in one-third of the patients.

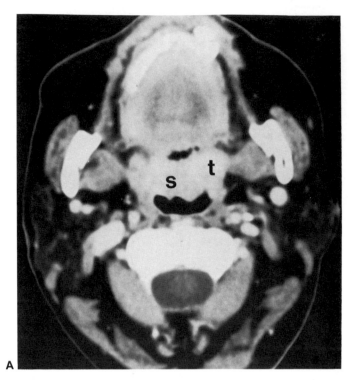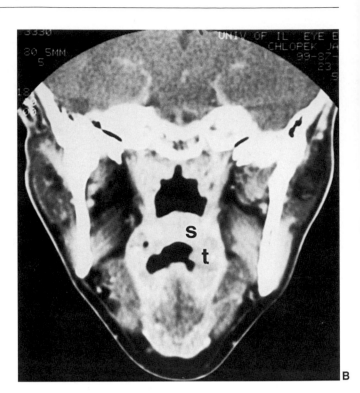

Figure 4.**7**   Carcinoma of the tonsil and soft palate; **A** axial and **B** coronal, post-contrast infusion CT sections. The soft palate, S, is thickened and the left tonsil, t, is enlarged by tumor infiltration.

Carcinoma of the Palate

The majority of malignant tumors of the soft palate are squamous cell carcinomas. Adenocarcinoma is more common in the hard palate. Other tumors that occur in this area are salivary gland lesions, lymphomas, plasmacytomas, malignant melanomas and undifferentiated tumors. Tumors of both the hard and soft palate often metastasize bilaterally or contralaterally to cervical lymph nodes. Tumors of the palate can extend into the maxillary antrum, spread to the cheek, the pterygoid muscles and contiguous structures (Figs. 4.**7**, 4.**9**, 4.**13**).

Carcinoma of the Floor of the Mouth

Malignant tumors of the floor of the mouth tend to spread rather rapidly to deep structures, because of the loose submucosal tissue in the submental and submandibular spaces (Fig. 4.**8**).

The role of CT and MR in evaluation of cancers of the floor of the mouth is to define the extent of the tumor and detect associated deep infiltration, metastatic nodal disease, involvement of the mandible and extension to adjacent structures.

Carcinoma of the Tongue

The tongue is divided by cirvumvallate papillae into the anterior two-thirds, the oral or mobile tongue, and the posterior one-third, the base of the tongue. Most oral tongue cancers are squamous cell carcinomas. Adenocarcinoma and sarcomas are rare. Extension to the adjacent structures is common and 25 to 50% of the lesions, when diagnosed, have extended beyond the oral tongue to the floor of the mouth, alveolar ridge, soft palate, pharynx or larynx. Cervical lymph node metastases are common. CT and MR are extremely helpful to define the extent of the tumor and to evaluate lymphatic metastases (Figs. 4.**10**, 4.**11**, 4.**17**).

Cancers of the posterior one-third of the tongue are relatively rare, although the area is frequently involved by extension from cancers arising from adjacent structures of the pharynx and larynx. Cancer of the base of the tongue is rarely diagnosed in its early stages. Metastases to one or both sides of the neck plus a bulky primary lesion are the usual clinical findings. When diagnosed, about three-fourths of the lesions have already spread to the oral tongue, the tonsil area, the vallecula, epiglottis, preepiglottic space, or hypopharynx.

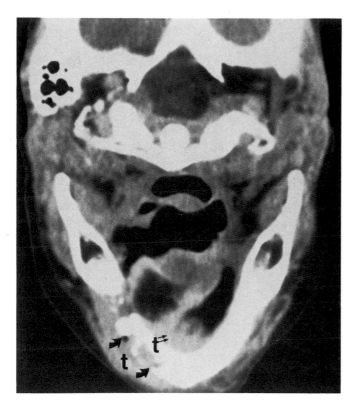

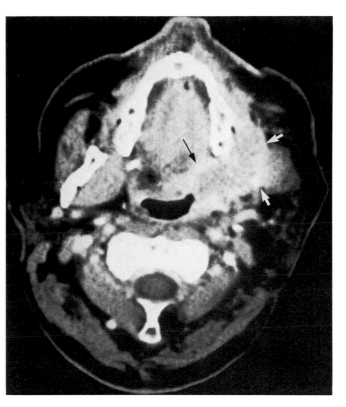

Figure 4.8 Recurrent carcinoma of the floor of the mouth, coronal CT section. The tumor, t with small arrows, extends along the floor of the mouth with erosion of the mandible, curved arrows. There is extension of the tumor, t, into the buccal mucosa. There is infiltration and necrosis of the adjacent tongue.

Figure 4.9 Recurrent carcinoma, retromolar area, axial CT sections with infusion. A large, poorly defined enhancing tumor mass involves the left retromolar area, white arrows. The tumor infiltrates the base of the tongue, black arrow. The ramus of the mandible on the left was removed at previous surgery.

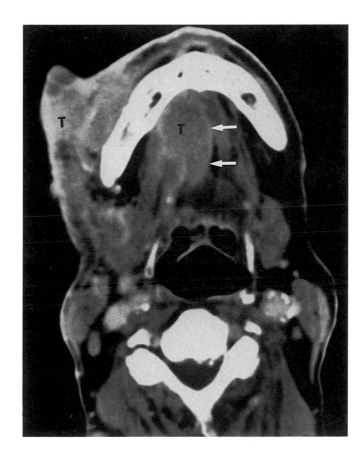

Figure 4.10 Carcinoma of the tongue and floor of mouth, axial, post-contrast infusion CT section. The extensive lesion, T, extends from beyond the midline of the tongue on the left, arrows, to the buccal mucosa on the right. The fascial planes are distorted and obliterated, and there is a subcutaneous tumor mass.

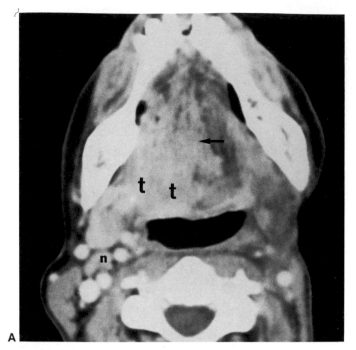

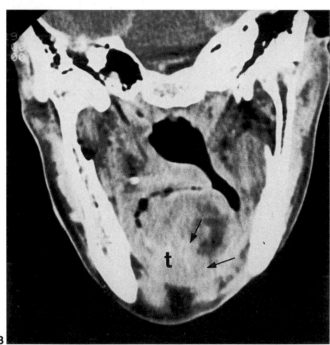

Figure 4.11   Carcinoma of the tongue; **A** axial, **B** coronal, CT post-contrast infusion sections. The enhanced tumor mass = t, involves the posterior portion of the tongue and extends across the midline = arrows. There is an enlarged lymph nodes in the axial section = n.

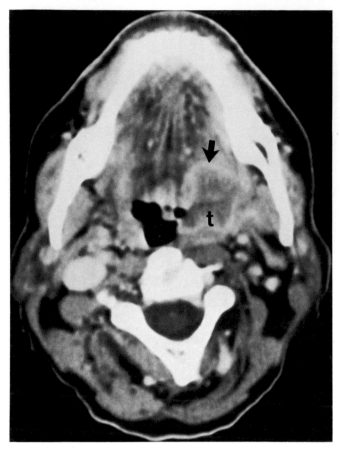

Figure 4.**12**   Carcinoma of the tonsil, axial post-contrast infusion CT section. The tumor mass = t, involves the left tonsil and extends into the base of the tongue anteriorly and into the retropharyngeal space posteriorly. The low density center of the tumor is surrounded by a thick ring of enhancement = black arrow.

Carcinoma of the Tonsil

Carcinomas of the tonsil are the most common malignancies of the oropharynx (Figs. 4.12–4.14). Most lesions are squamous cell carcinomas. Lymphoma and lymphoepithelioma are less common (Fig. 4.15). Clinically the tumors appear as ulcero-infiltrative or exophytic lesions that have extended outside the tonsil in the majority of the cases. Lymph node metastases are present in two-thirds of the cases.

Lymphoma

Lymphomas are common primary tumors of the neck. Any lymphoid structure of the body may be involved in this disorder. Cervical lymph nodes become grossly enlarged, usually without central necrosis unless the patient is receiving chemotherapy. On CT and MR, the nodes are often indistinguishable from inflammatory and non-necrotic metastatic nodes of primary carcinomas of the head or neck (Fig. 15). The diagnosis of lymphoma is often made because of involvement of other lymph-bearing structures of the neck, chest, and abdomen. Lymphomas will be discussed in chapter on lesions of the nasopharynx.

Most of the cancers of the base of the tongue have metastasized to lymph nodes when they are seen for the first time.

On CT, infiltration of the relatively low density intrinsic musculature appears as areas of higher density which enhance. Infiltration of the extrinsic muscles produce enlargement and enhancement of the involved musculature (Figs. 4.10, 4.11).

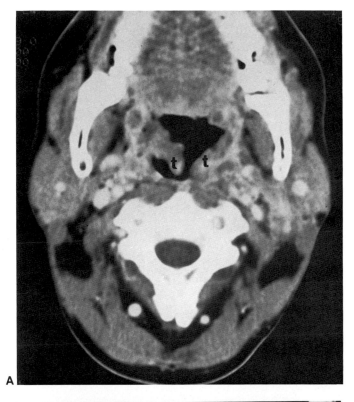

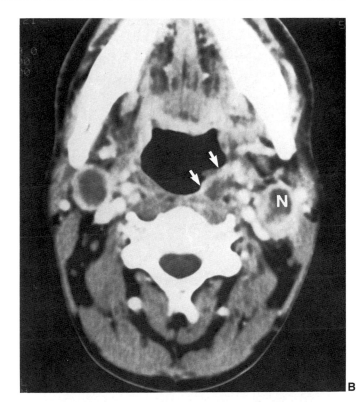

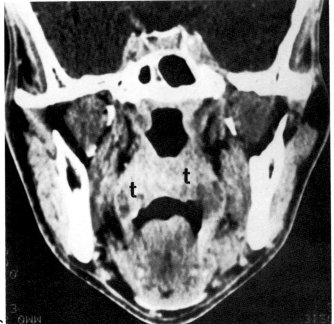

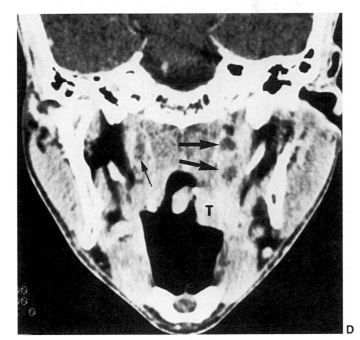

Figure 4.**13**   Carcinoma of the tonsil and soft palate; **A, B** axial CT sections with infusion.

A, B the tumor = t, involves the soft palate and left palatine tonsil, arrows. Large necrotic metastatic nodes are present bilaterally, N.

C, D coronal CT sections with contrast infusion.
C the tumor = t, infiltrates and thickens the soft palate.
D the lesion involves the left palatine tonsil = T. Several necrotic lymph nodes lie in the parapharyngeal jugular chain areas = arrows.

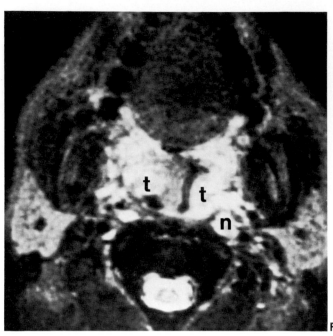

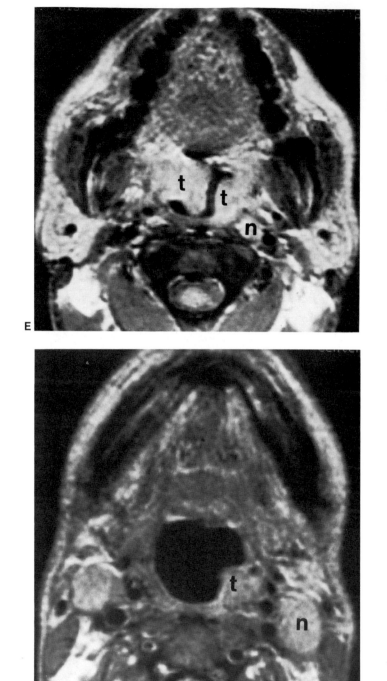

Figure 4.**13**
E axial MR spin density weighted section. The tumor of the soft palate = t, shows fairly high signal intensity in this sequence. There is an enlarged retropharyngeal metastatic lymph node on the left = n.
F axial MR T2w section at the same level as **E**. In this section the tumor, t, has a higher signal intensity.
G axial MR section, spin density weighted at a level lower than **E** and **F**. The tumor = t, is present in the left tonsil, and there are large bilateral metastatic lymph nodes = n.

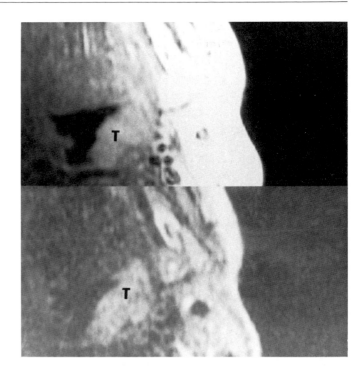

Figure 4.**14** Carcinoma of the tonsil, axial MR section, surface coil images, top, spin density weighted, and bottom, T2w images. The tumor lies in the tonsil = T, extends to the retropharyngeal mucosa and involves the base of the tongue.

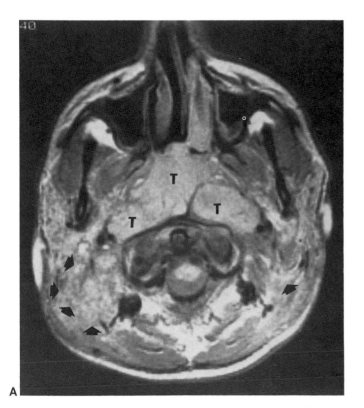

A

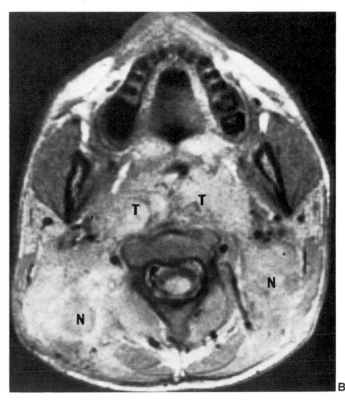

B

Figure 4.**15 A** and **B** Lymphoepitheliom of naso- and oropharynx, axial MR sections, spin density weighted. This extensive tumor − T, involves the entire oropharynx and nasopharynx.

There are extensive nodal metastases in the posterior triangle of the neck − black arrows and N. The MR features of this tumor are similar to a Hodgkin or non-Hodgkin's lymphoma.

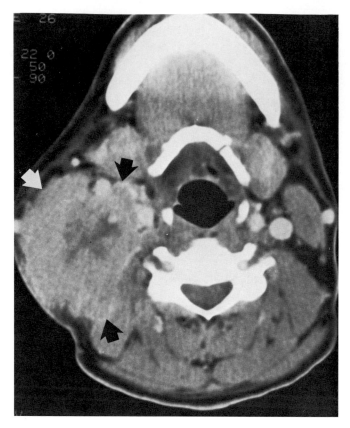

Figure 4.**16** Metastatic lymphadenopathy, axial CT sections with contrast enhancement. There is a large enhanced soft tissue mass with central necrosis in the right side of the neck indicated by the arrows.

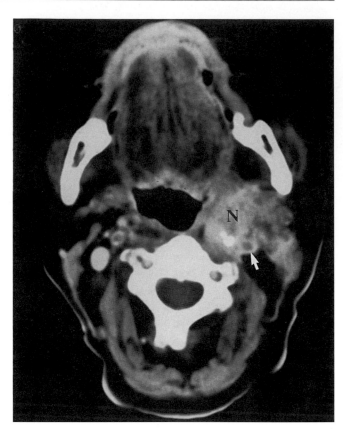

Figure 4.**17** Recurrent metastatic lymph adenopathy, post-radiation therapy for carcinoma of the tongue, axial CT post-contrast infusion section. There is a mass in the left para-pharyngeal space composed of matted metastatic lymph nodes = N. There is also a thrombus of the left internal jugular vein present indicated by the white arrow.

Metastatic Nodal Disease

The current criterion for diagnosing nodal disease on CT scan is based on size. The positive identification of single lymph nodes by CT requires bolus injection of contrast to differentiate the nodes from blood vessels, which have the same density as nodes in the pre-infusion scans (Figs. 4.**16,** 4.**17**). Any lymph node larger than 1.5 cm should be considered a positive metastatic node, though some benign hyperplastic nodes may reach 2 cm in diameter. In patients with a known primary, any enhanced or nonenhanced mass within the lymph-node bearing area with a central low density irrespective of size should be considered a nodal metastasis. Hyperplastic nodes may be as large as 1.5 cm, but have often a homogeneous density.

MR allows identification of lymph node metastases without exposing the patient to ionizing radiation or iodinated contrast infusion, since lymph nodes are clearly differentiated from blood vessels by this technique. On MR, lymph nodes have a medium signal intensity in the T1w sequence and a higher intensity in the T2w sequence (Figs. 4.**13,** 4.**15**). Lymph nodes larger than 1.5 cm are abnormal either because of neoplastic disease or inflammation.

Coalescent metastases that are caused by multiple enlarged masses of lymph nodes are relatively easily diagnosed on CT since these larger masses have a nonhomogeneous density and rarely are inflammatory in nature (Figs. 4.**16,** 4.**17**).

Currently nodal disease is staged by clinical examination only. It has been shown, however, that CT scanning can improve staging of metastatic nodal disease. Treatment of the high risk but clinically negative neck continues to be a source of some controversy and confusion. The incidence of occult metastases in advanced tumors is significant, and treatment of the clinically negative neck with radiation therapy or neck dissection has been advocated. Some clinicians, however, believe that the treatment of the neck should be delayed until the disease is evident by the presence of clinically palpable metastatic lymph nodes.

Positive CT and MR scans in patients with occult metastases should influence treatment planning and alter clinical staging. Comparisons of the accuracy of clinical examination only with combined clinical and CT or MR scans, shows that the combined approach is far superior in correctly evaluating nodal disease.

Salivary Glands

Chapter 5 Anatomy

The salivary glands consist of two groups: the three paired major glands (parotid, submandibular, and sublingual) and various minor salivary glands scattered throughout the oral cavity and pharynx. The major glands are tuboacinar in type. The minor salivary glands consist of small aggregations of glandular tissue situated beneath the oral mucosa of the mouth and to a lesser extent in the nasopharynx, nose and paranasal sinuses.

The parotid gland is the largest of the salivary glands and has a triangular shape with a convex lateral surface (Figs. 5.1–5.4). A medial, narrow portion fills the retromandibular fossa. The gland is invested with a capsule derived from the deep cervical fascia. The external carotid artery grooves the posteromedial surface before entering the gland. The carotid sheath is separated from the gland by the styloid process and muscles. The retromandibular vein formed in the upper part of the gland by the union of the maxillary and superficial temporal veins is superficial to the intraglandular part of the external carotid artery (Figs. 5.1–5.4). The facial nerve (Fig. 5.5) (also see Fig. 2.4C)

divides the parotid gland into superficial and deep lobes. The facial nerve enters the upper part of the parotid gland from the posteromedial surface and passes forward and downward behind the posterior border of the ramus of the mandible. The parotid duct, Stensen's, is approximately 5 cm long and passes forward on the external surface of the masseter muscle and through the adipose tissues of the cheek to open into the oral cavity opposite the second upper molar.

The submandibular gland is an irregularly shaped gland with a larger superficial and smaller deep lobe continuous with each other around the posterior border of the mylohyoid muscle (Figs. 5.2, 5.6) (also see figures 2.1C, D, E, figures 2.2C, D, and figure 2.4F). The superficial part of the gland extends forward as far as the posterior border of the anterior belly of the digastric muscle. From the deep part of the gland, the submandibular duct, (Wharton's duct), passes forward and opens close to the midline into the sublingual papilla on each side of the frenulum of the tongue.

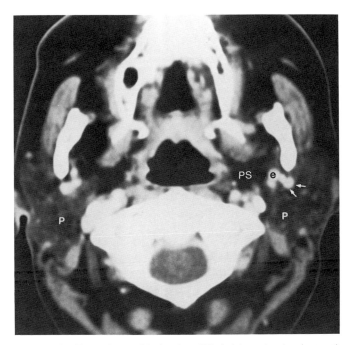

Figure 5.1 Normal parotid gland = CT. Axial contrast enhanced CT scan shows normal parotid glands = P. External carotid artery = e, retromandibular veins = arrows, and parapharyngeal space = PS.

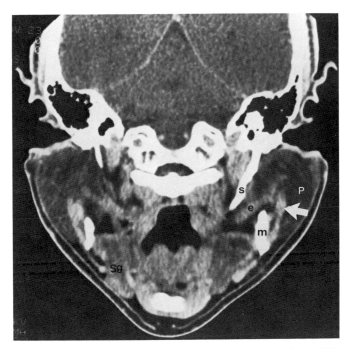

Figure 5.2 Normal parotid and submandibular glands = CT. Coronal contrast enhanced CT scan shows normal parotid gland = P, normal submandibular glands = sg, external carotid artery = e, retromandibular vein = arrow, styloid process = s, and mandible = m.

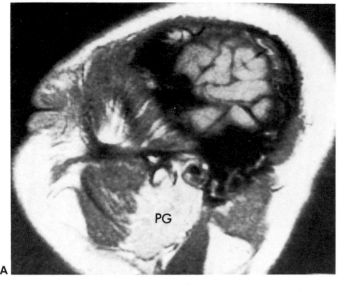

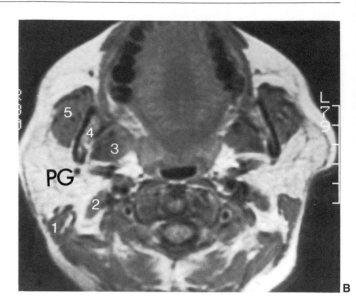

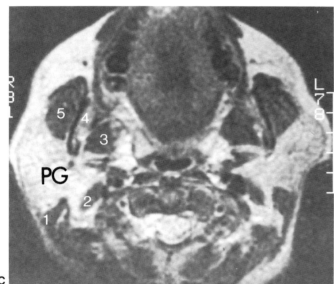

Figure 5.3 Normal parotid gland, MR. **A** sagittal T1w; **B** axial spin density; **C** axial T2w show the normal parotid gland = PG, which is hyperintense to muscles in all sequences. 1 = sterno-cleidomastoid muscle; 2 = digastric muscle; 3 = medial ptery-goid muscle; 4 = mandible; 5 = masseter muscle.

The sublingual glands, the smallest of the three main glands, are located between the mucous membrane of the floor of the mouth in contact with the mylohyoid muscle and close to the symphysis of the mandible (see Fig. 2.4F). Most of the excretory ducts, varying from 8–20, open separately in the floor of the mouth on the summit of the sublingual fold.

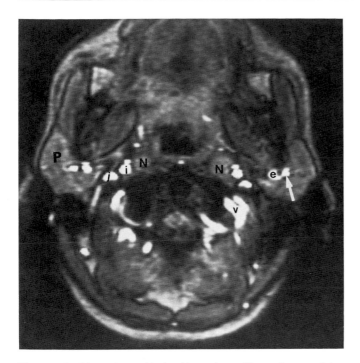

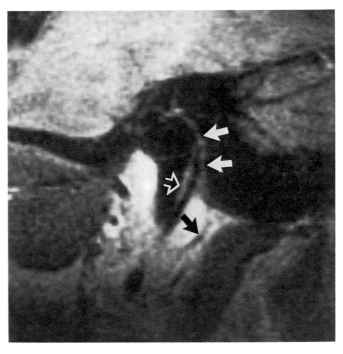

Figure 5.4 Normal parotid gland in patient with carcinoma of the nasopharynx, axial MR scan. Scan obtained with a narrow flip angle (GRASS, TR-30, TE-12 msec, θ = 30 degrees) shows parotid glands = P, with medium signal intensity similar to muscle. The normal vascular structures are hyperintense. e = external carotid artery branche, i = internal carotid artery, j = internal jugular vein, v = vertebral artery, retromandibular vein = arrow, enlarged retropharyngeal nodes, metastatic from the carcinoma = N.

Figure 5.5 Normal facial nerve, T1w sagittal MR scan. This scan shows the mastoid and parotid segments of the facial nerve = arrows, and the stapedius muscle = hollow arrow.

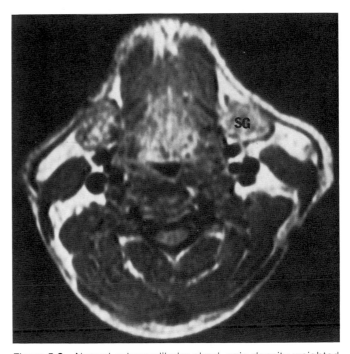

Figure 5.6 Normal submandibular gland, spin density weighted MR axial scan. The gland = SG, lies in the submandibular area.

Chapter 6 Imaging

Imaging studies of the salivary glands provide useful information that enables the physician to establish a diagnosis and select appropriate therapy. In the history and examination, it is important to establish whether the symptoms are acute or chronic, whether the disease is uniglandular or multiglandular and if there is swelling, involvement of the overlying skin, and pain. It is important to rule out the presence of systemic disease, such as sarcoidosis, lymphoreticular proliferative diseases, immunodeficiency, and metabolic or endocrine disorders.

Conventional radiography, sialography, radionucleide scan CT, CT sialography, and MR are used to:

1. determine the accurate location and map extension of the salivary gland lesions and to differentiate them from parapharyngeal masses;
2. identify neoplastic from inflammatory and other processes, and
3. differentiate, if possible, benign from malignant neoplasms.

Conventional Radiography

Calculi in the submandibular and parotid glands may be demonstrated by standard views such as oblique lateral films of the mandibular region or intraoral occlusal views or by panoramic radiography (Figs. 6.1, 6.2). Occlusal films are very useful for calculi within the anterior two-thirds of the submandibular duct. Parotid stones are best demonstrated by an antero-posterior or axial tangential view. Most (80%) salivary calculi are radio-opaque. Pre-existing calcifications which may be present in lymph nodes, tonsils, tumors and phleboliths must be differentiated from salivary calculi.

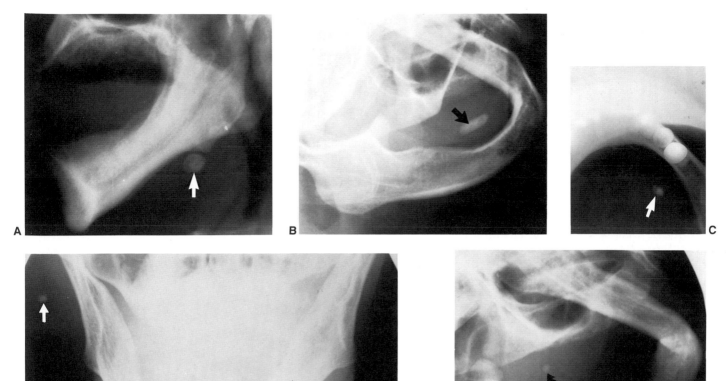

Figure 6.1   Sialolithiasis.
A Lateral conventional view of the mandibular region shows an opaque stone in the right submandibular gland, arrow.
B Lateral oblique of the mandibular region shows a stone in the Wharton's duct.

C Occlusal view shows a Wharton's duct stone = arrow.
D AP view of the parotid and cheek region shows a calculus in the Stensen's duct = arrow.
E Oblique view of the parotid and cheek area shows a calculus in the Stensen's duct.

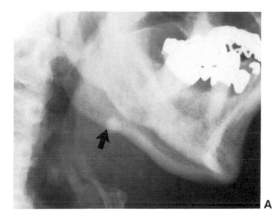

Figure 6.2   Submandibular duct calculus.
A Lateral view of the mandibular region shows a calculus = arrow.

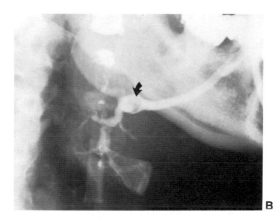

B Sialogram showing the filling defect caused by the stone in the proximal portion of the Wharton's duct. There is moderate sialectasia behind the obstruction caused by the stone, and there is irregularity of the intraglandular ductal system due to inflammatory sialadenitis.

Conventional Sialography

Sialography provides very useful information and leads to accurate diagnosis of intraductal pathology (Figs. 6.3, 7.4, 7.6, 7.10). Conventional sialography remains the study of choice for chronic inflammatory disease of the salivary glands and calculi, but this technique is no longer routinely applied in the diagnosis of salivary gland masses and tumors. CT with and without infusion, MR, and CT sialography (Fig. 6.4) demonstrate tumors far more clearly and accurately than conventional sialography (see Figs. 7.7, 8.3–8.5, 8.7–8.10, 8.14–8.17).

The three main indications for sialography are

(1) sudden acute swelling suggesting obstruction by calculus
(2) gradual progression or chronic recurrent enlargement of one or more of the salivary glands suggesting chronic infection or sialosis, and
(3) a palpable mass in the salivary gland, not identified on CT or MR.

Technique

A blunt needle should be used to avoid laceration of the papillae and perforation of the duct wall. When the papilla is too small, the orifice is dilated with graduated probes. For the injection, a slightly curved blunt needle with an olive-shaped dilatation 1 cm from the tip is preferred. The olive prevents overpenetration of the cannula, and when the olive is pressed against the orifice, backflow of the contrast media will not occur.

Cannulation may be done with the patient seated or supine. The parotid duct orifice is usually easily identified in the buccal mucosa opposite the upper second molar tooth. With careful massage of the parotid gland, a droplet of saliva can be seen at the orifice of the duct. The orifice of the submandibular duct is smaller than that of the parotid, and magnifying spectacles are often needed to identify the opening. The duct opens into the sublingual caruncle on the floor of the mouth lateral to the frenulum of the tongue.

Fat soluble contrast materials such as pantopaque and water soluble iodinated organic compounds can be used for conventional sialography (Fig. 6.3). The water soluble contrast materials do not produce images of the ductal system as clear as those made with the oily contrast media. This is because of the rapid diffusion and dilution by saliva and absorption of the contrast in the blood stream. Either water soluble or oily contrast material are satisfactory if only the ducts are to be studied.

There are three phases of sialography: duct filling, acinar filling and post-evacuation. Parenchymal opacification observed during sialography is due to normal filling of the acini with contrast material and is useful in outlining parenchymal masses. Failure of the acini to opacify is abnormal, but not specific. Any process that causes marked swelling or edema of the glands or that fills the acinar lumens or causes destruction, infiltration, or replacement of the acini may prevent acinar opacification.

Post-evacuation films taken one hour or longer after the injection are an important part of the sialographic examination. The post-evacuation film is taken to record any extravasation of contrast material and to evaluate the pattern of emptying. Delayed evacuation of contrast may be due to inflammation, obstruction, or processes associated with parenchymal destruction, such as autoimmune sialosis, chronic infection, the effects of radiation, or tumor infiltration.

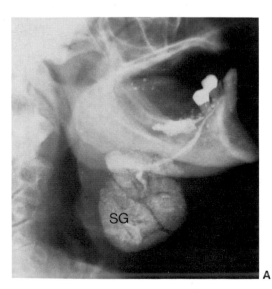

A

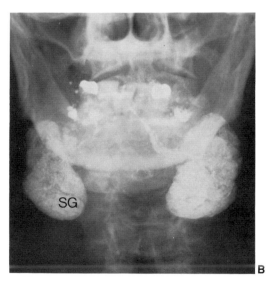

B

Figure 6.3 Normal submandibular gland, bilateral conventional sialograms, **A** lateral, **B** frontal, views, acinar opacification phase.

The submandibular glands are opacified and Wharton's ducts are seen.

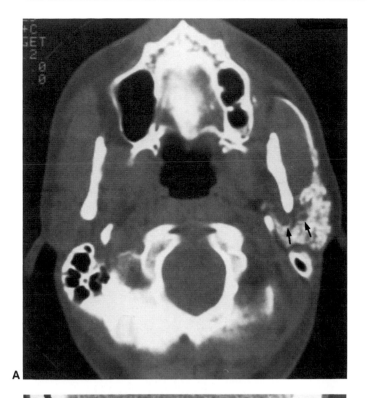

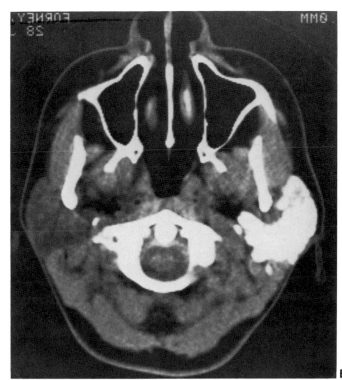

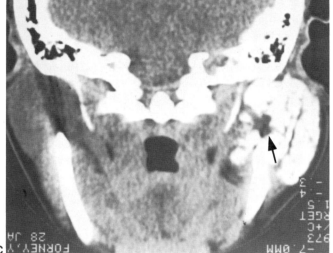

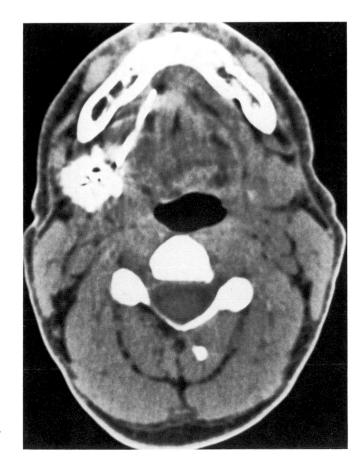

Figure 6.4   Normal parotid CT sialogram.
A The left parotid gland and Stensen's duct are opacified with pantopaque. The retromandibular vasculature is indicated by the arrows.
B The left parotid gland is densely opacified with pantopaque. The deep lobe of the parotid gland extends medial to the mandible into the pharyngeal space.
C Coronal sialogram shows good filling of the superficial and deep portions of the gland. Notice the intraparotic vasculature = arrow.

Figure 6.5   Normal submandibular gland, CT sialogram. There is ▶ opacification of the deep lobe and Wharton's duct by pantopaque.

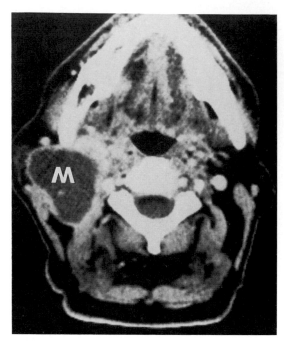

Figure 6.**6**   Branchial cleft cyst. Contrast enhanced axial CT scan. There is a well defined low density mass = M, occupying the lower portion of the right parotid gland.

Sialography is contraindicated in acute infections, since the injection of contrast material aggravates the acute symptoms. Sialography also should not be performed in iodine sensitive patients. In those patients who are planning to have thyroid function studies, sialography should be postponed until the thyroid work-up is completed.

Computerized Tomography and Magnetic Resonance Imaging

Tumors of all the salivary glands including the minor salivary glands can be demonstrated by CT and MR (see Figs. 8.3–8.5, 8.7–8.10, 8.14–8.17). However, often neither CT sections nor MR images obtained with various pulse sequences permit a specific diagnosis of salivary gland lesions. Both MR and CT can be used to determine location and extension of salivary gland masses (Figs. 6.6–6.8). MR is better for differentiating parapharyngeal space lesions from deep lobe parotid lesions and is useful in determining the relationship of parotid masses to the facial nerve. Neither CT nor MR is the method of choice for the diagnosis of chronic inflammatory salivary gland disease. CT, however, is the method of choice for the evaluation of acute inflammatory processes and abscesses and can easily detect stones in the ducts and within the glands.

CT Technique

Salivary glands are well imaged in axial sections obtained with the chin slightly elevated (see Figs. 5.**1**, 5.**2**). Whenever dental fillings are present which distort the images, the semiaxial projection with the head extended and the gantry tilted 15 to 20° should be used. The tilting angle to avoid dental fillings can be easily determined in a lateral digital scout view. The direct coronal projection is often very useful for parotid and submandibular gland lesions, and some parotid lesions are best seen in coronal images. The parotid gland is lower in density than the adjacent

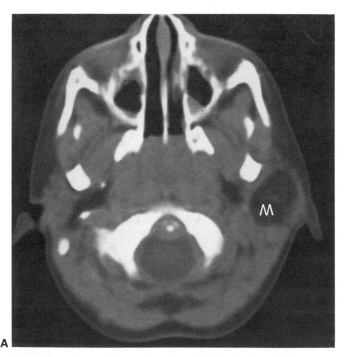

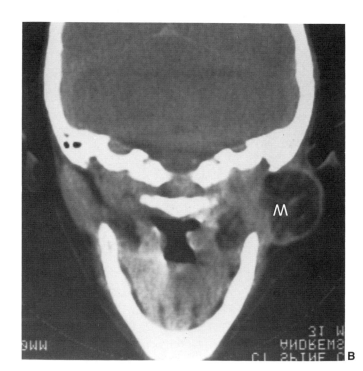

Figure 6.**7**   Dermoid cyst of the parotid gland, **A** axial, **B** coronal contrast enhanced CT scans. The left parotid gland is enlarged by an inhomogeneous low density mass = M.

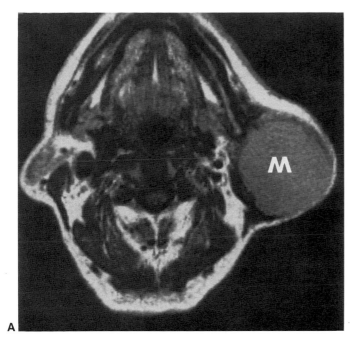

A

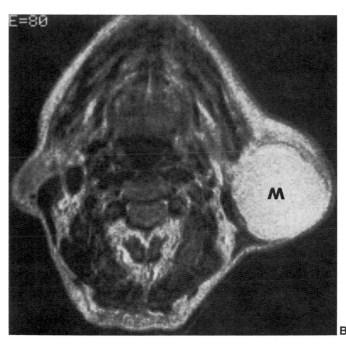

B

Figure 6.**8** Parotid cyst = MR. **A** T1w, **B** T2w, axial MR scans show a large homogeneous mass = M, enlarging the left parotid

gland. The mass has a low signal intensity in the T1w image, and high intensity in T2w image.

masseter muscle as a result of saliva and variable amounts of fat deposits within the gland. The submandibular glands are generally denser than the parotid. Most intraparotid masses are visualized by plain CT scanning, since they are denser than the normal glandular parenchyma.

Intravenous contrast enhancement results in better visualization of vascular structures (see Fig. 5.**2**) and is essential for diagnosing hemangiomas (Fig. 6.**9**). Ring enhancement may be seen in inflammatory masses (see Fig. 7.**3**). Submandibular masses are usually not recognizable in plain CT sections, since they are isodense to the gland parenchyma. At times CT sialography is required to demonstrate these lesions.

MR Technique

A 1.5 tesla superconductive magnet is used to obtain sagittal T_1-weighted (T1w) images (TR = 600 or 800 milliseconds, TE = 20 or 25 milliseconds) followed by multiple axial spin echo (2000 TR and 20 TE = spin density or proton-weighted) and (2000 TR, 80 TE = T2 weighted) sequence. In some cases, additional T_1-weighted coronal images are obtained for better evaluation of the salivary gland masses. T_1-weighted images provide the best spatial resolution and best anatomic details and T_2-weighted images provide better contrast resolution (see Figs. 5.**3**, 5.**4**, 5.**6**). On T_1-weighted images, the high signal intensity or brightness of the fat in the infratemporal area, parapharyngeal spaces, and buccal regions improve the edge definition of masticatory and parotid spaces (see Fig. 5.**3**). Tissue planes are readily identified as the parapharyngeal fat outlines the parapharyngeal and pterygoid musculature. The displacement of para-

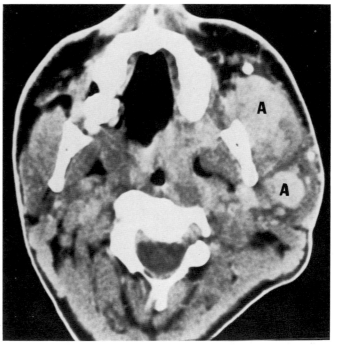

Figure 6.**9** Hemangioma of the face and parotid gland, contrast enhanced CT scan. There is an enhancing mass = A, involving the left masseter muscle and parotid gland.

pharyngeal fat raises the index of suspicion for neoplasms. Medial displacement indicates a deep lobe parotid mass and lateral displacement indicates a parapharyngeal tumor. Dense connective tissue, such as tendons and the galea aponeurotica, have a lower signal intensity than the adjacent muscle. In T1w images, the salivary glands are well outlined because their signal intensity is different from the surrounding structures, that is, lower than fat but higher than muscle and fascia.

Vascular structures such as mandibular veins and external carotid arteries are readily identified as areas of no signal within the substance of the parotid gland. However, the vascular structures are seen as hyperintense areas whenever special pulse sequences, such as fast or narrow flip-angle, dynamic or gradient echo (GRASS) techniques are used (see Fig. 5.4).

Ultrasound

Ultrasound may be useful in differentiating between intrinsic and extrinsic masses and between solid and cystic lesions.

Nuclear Medicine

Radio-isotope scanning with 99 Tc-pertechnetate is not as accurate as contrast sialography, CT, or MR in demonstrating lesions of the salivary glands. This technique is however of value in establishing the diagnosis of Warthin's tumors and oncocytomas, since these are the only tumors that regularly show an increased uptake of the isotope. It may also help in identifying subclinical involvement of the salivary gland with such systemic diseases as sarcoidosis and collagen disorders.

Chapter 7   Common Pathological Conditions

Congenital Lesions

Congenital lesions of the salivary glands are uncommon. In the first and second branchial arch syndrome, the parotid gland is sometimes absent. Congenital cysts occur in or adjacent to the salivary glands most commonly in the parotid gland (see Figs. 6.6–6.8). Congenital cystic dilatation of the major ductal system with formation of the multilocular cystic areas may be manifest in infancy or appear later. If the ducts into the cyst are patent, sialography may outline the cystic spaces.

Hemangioma

Hemangiomas may involve the salivary glands (see Fig. 6.9). Hemangiomas are classified by the type of vascular channels formed as cavernous or sclerosing. Congenital hemangioma is the most common cause of parotid swelling in the newborn.

Lymphangioma

Lymphangiomas or cystic hygromas are benign congenital lesions of lymphatic vessels. The salivary glands are involved either directly or by encroachment of a hygroma in the neck. Lymphangiomas are

seen as low density, non-enhancing images on CT (Fig. 7.1) and as hyperintense images with high signal intensity on T1w, spin density and T2w MR (see Figs. 3.18 C and D) images.

Inflammatory Diseases of the Major Salivary Glands

Inflammatory diseases may be classified as acute or chronic. Acute disorders include epidemic parotitis or mumps, and acute suppurative sialoadenitis. Imaging studies are not indicated in mumps. The chronic inflammatory diseases include chronic recurrent sialoadenitis, chronic sialectasis, sialolithiasis, chronic granulomatous disease and lymphoepithelial sialoadenopathy.

Acute Suppurative Sialadenitis with Abscess Formation

Acute suppurative sialadenitis is a bacterial infection, and the parotid gland is more frequently involved in abscess formation than the submandibular gland. CT and MR are both useful in showing the inflammation or abscess (Figs. 7.2, 7.3). There is diffuse swelling of

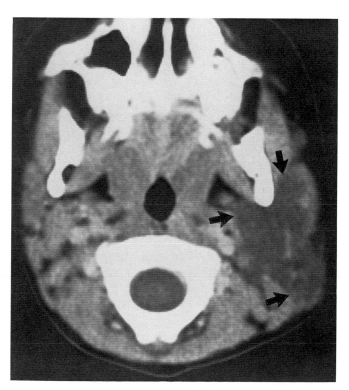

Figure 7.**1**   Cystic hygroma involving the parotid gland, contrast enhanced axial CT scan. A large low density mass involves the left parotid gland and posterior triangle of the neck = arrows.

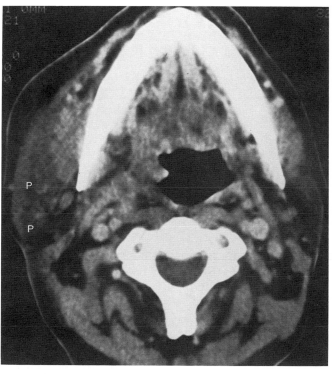

Figure 7.**2**   Acute parotitis = CT. Contrast enhanced axial CT scan shows diffuse swelling of the right parotid gland = P. There is associated subcutaneous edema.

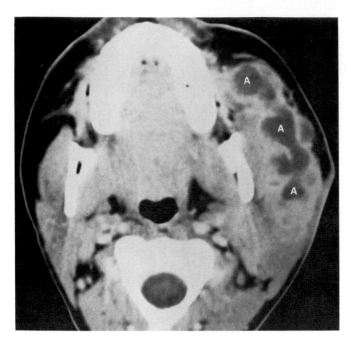

Figure 7.3 Parotid and masseter abscesses = CT. Contrast enhanced axial CT scan reveals a large mass occupying the left side of the face. The infected masseter muscle merges with the adjacent parotid gland. Multiple low density areas with ring enhancement are produced by loculated abscesses = A.

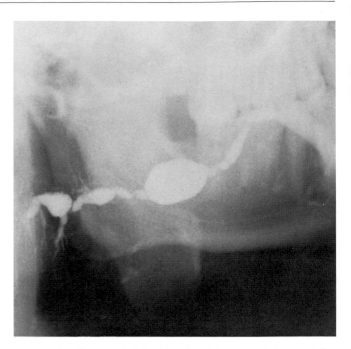

Figure 7.4 Chronic sialadenitis with sialectasis. A lateral sialogram of the left parotid gland shows dilatation of the main duct and some of the branches. There are segments of narrowing between the dilated segments.

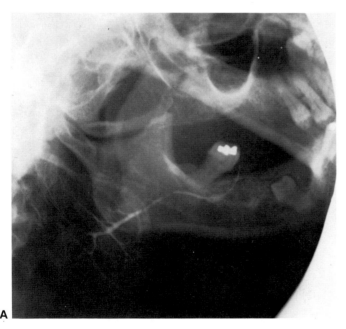

A

Figure 7.5 Chronic sialadenitis.
A Sialogram shows irregularity of the Stensen's duct and intraductal system. The intraparenchymal ducts appear narrowed and stretched.

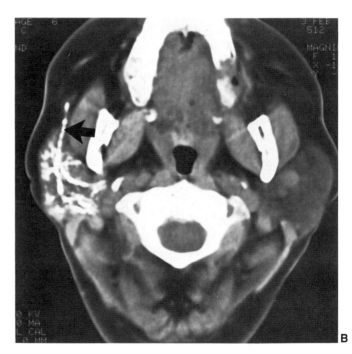

B

B CT sialogram shows irregularity and beading of the Stensen's duct = arrow and intraglandular ductal system. The filling defects are due to obstruction of some of the intraglandular ducts and parenchymal inflammatory reaction.

the gland, and the abscesses are seen as unilocular or multilocular collections of fluid. Abscesses of the submandibular gland are usually secondary to obstruction from a stone or stricture of the duct. Parotid abscesses may be complicated by inflammation of the masticatory space. Unfortunately, at times inflammatory processes may mimic neoplastic processes on CT and MR.

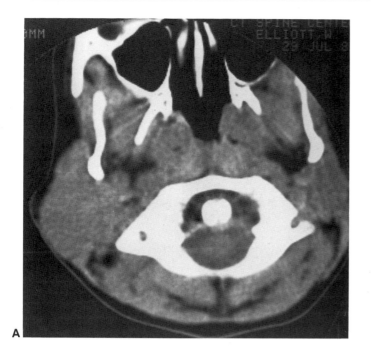

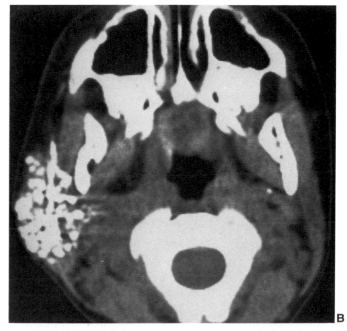

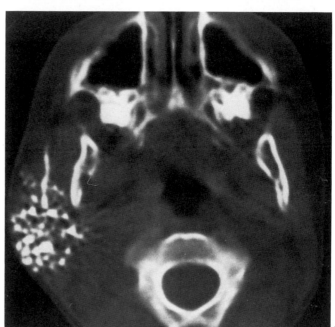

Figure 7.6   Recurrent sialadenitis in a seven-year-old male with intermittent swelling of the right parotid gland = CT.
A Plain axial CT scan shows a marked enlargement of the right parotid gland when compared with the normal, opposite gland.
B, C CT sialograms show saccular dilatation of the acini and ducts. There are several filling defects which are better appreciated in the wide window setting at **C**. These are produced by inflammatory changes and fibrosis in the stroma.

Chronic Recurrent Sialadenitis

Chronic progressive inflammatory diseases of the salivary glands are characterized by persistent swelling of the glands (Figs. 7.4–7.7). Chronic recurrent sialadenitis is characterized by a recurrent salivary gland enlargement associated with pain, tenderness and often frank pus which can be expressed from the duct. Chronic sialectasis usually is the end stage of chronic recurrent sialadenitis. Sialography in early cases may reveal a near normal ductal system with normal emptying time. In more advanced cases, sialography shows dilatation and sacculation of the intraglandular ductal system (Fig. 7.4) with marked delay in emptying time. Congenital sialectasis found in young children.

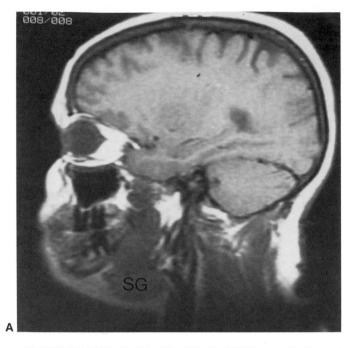

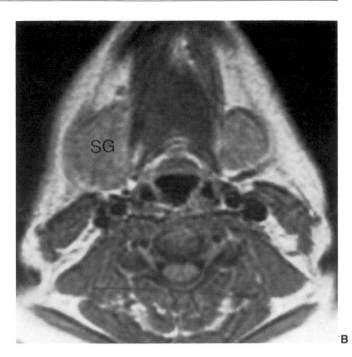

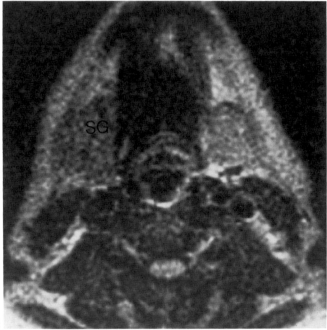

Figure 7.**7**   Chronic sialadenitis of the right submandibular gland = MR. **A** Sagittal T1w, **B** axial spin density weighted, **C** axial T2w MR images. There is enlargement of the right submaxillary gland. The lesion is hypointense in T1w, **A** and isointense in spin density, **B** images. In T2w images, the lesion is hypointense to the normal gland, indicating a chronic inflammation. At surgery chronic inflammation was confirmed. In addition a mass was found in the superior portion of the gland. The mass was isointense to remainder of the gland in all pulse sequences and therefore could not be differentiated from inflamed portion of the gland.

Chronic Progressive Disorders of the Salivary Glands

Granulomatous lesions of the salivary glands usually present as progressive, localized or diffuse painless enlargement of the gland with little inflammatory reaction. Granulomas that affect the salivary glands include sarcoidosis, tuberculosis, actinomycosis and syphilis. Salivary glands are involved in about 4% of patients with sarcoidosis (Fig. 7.**8**). Sialographic and CT findings include diffuse enlargement of the sali-vary gland, multiple small nodular densities distributed throughout the gland, or a solitary mass.

Post-Irradiation Sialadenitis

This condition is characterized by acute swelling, tenderness and pain, which subside within a few days. The irradiated gland usually remains more dense on plain CT and will show increased enhancement following contrast infusion (Fig. 7.**9**).

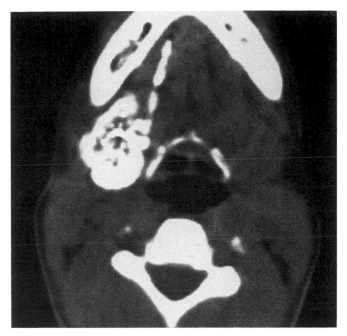

Figure 7.**8** Sarcoid of the right submandibular gland = CT. An axial CT sialogram shows enlargement of the right submandibular gland. Several filling defects are due to sarcoid granulomas.

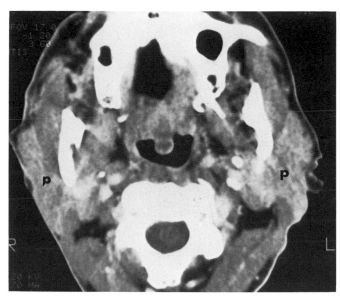

Figure 7.**9** Post-irradiation sialadenitis = CT. Contrast enhanced axial CT shows diffuse increased enhancement of the enlarged parotid glands = p, due to mucositis and vasculitis.

Figure 7.**10** Sjögren's Syndrome, conventional sialogram. ▶
A Lateral sialogram immediately after injection.
B Delayed sialogram, lateral view. There are multiple, small globular collections of contrast material within the parotid gland in **A**, and delayed emptying of the acini in **B**.

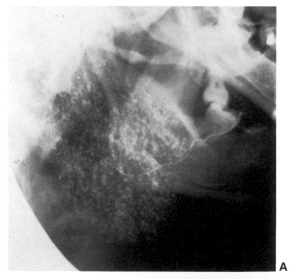

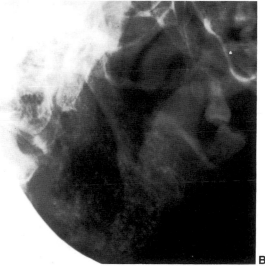

Benign Lymphoepithelial Sialadenopathy

This specific lesion affecting the salivary glands can be distinguished by clinical, radiological and pathological criteria. The etiology of this disease is most likely an autoimmune process. The disease is usually seen in women beginning at the age of 40 to 50. Clinically there is recurrent diffuse swelling of the salivary glands associated with mild pain and tenderness. The disease is usually multiglandular, although often only the parotid gland is affected. Typically, there are no systemic signs, but there may be superimposed acute bacterial infections secondary to stasis of secretion. The disease process is also known as autoimmune sialosis, benign lymphosialadenopathy, chronic lymphoepithelial sialadenopathy, non-obstructive sialectasis, and punctate parotitis.

In Sjögren's Syndrome, an autoimmune disease, the involvement of the salivary glands is associated with keratoconjunctivitis sicca, xerostomia, and rheumatoid arthritis (Figs. 7.**10**, 7.**11**). The term Mikulicz Disease has been used clinically for instances in

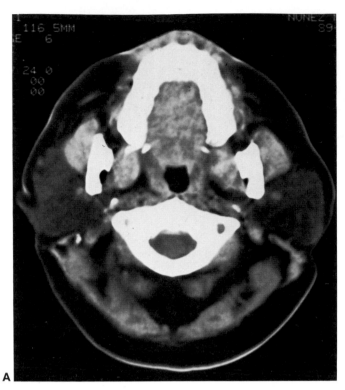

A

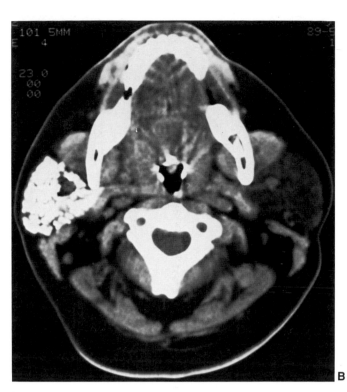

B

Figure 7.11   Sjögren's Syndrome = CT.
A Axial CT, plain scan, same patient as in Fig. 7.**10** shows enlargement of parotid glands.

B A CT sialogram shows globular filling of the parotid gland on the right side.

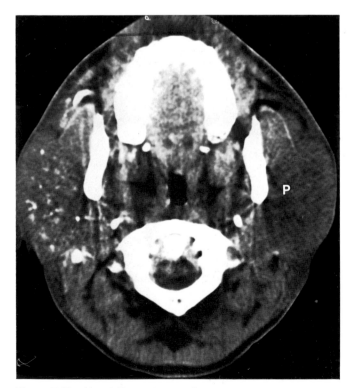

Figure 7.**12**   Non-inflammatory salivary gland enlargement of diabetes = CT. Axial CT shows enlargement of both parotid glands = P. The CT sialography on the right shows multiple irregular collections of contrast.

which parotid and lacrimal gland enlargement, keratoconjunctivitis sicca, and xerostomia are present without systemic symptoms. Other collagen disorders may be associated with benign lymphoepithelial sialadenopathy as well including systemic lupus erythematosus, scleroderma, polyarteritis, and polymyositis.

Metabolic and Endocrine Related Salivary Gland Disorders

Noninflammatory salivary gland enlargement has been associated with a variety of metabolic and endocrine disorders such as diabetes (Fig. 7.**12**), gout, vitamin deficiency, malnutrition, and in children with cystic fibrosis.

Chronic Sialolithiasis

About 85 to 90% of salivary gland calculi occur in the submandibular gland, while 10% occur in the parotid (see Figs. 6.**1**, 6.**2**). Stones in the sublingual glands are rare. In the submandibular gland, the calculi usually form at the hilum of the gland or are found in the ductal system. Symptoms of a salivary gland stone may include intermittent swelling and colicky pain with eating. The diagnosis is made by manual palpation, probing of the duct, and x-ray studies. Most (75 to 80%) of the salivary gland calculi are radio-opaque and can be demonstrated in plain roentgenographic studies or nonenhanced CT. If no calculus is demonstrated on plain film or CT, conventional sialography will reveal radiolucent stones. There is dilatation of the duct proximal to the obstruction and delayed emptying of contrast material. If there is complete obstruction, the ductal system beyond the calculus, of course, will not fill.

Stricture of the Salivary Gland Ducts

Stricture of the parotid or submandibular gland duct can be congenital or caused by calculus, trauma, infection or neoplasm (see Figs. 7.4, 7.5). The symptoms are similar to those of salivary gland calculi, with intermittent swelling, pain with eating, and superimposed infection secondary to stasis. Diagnosis is made by conventional or CT sialography.

Chapter 8 Tumors

Tumors of the salivary glands usually arise from the gland epithelium. The most common benign neoplasms are mixed tumors of pleomorphic adenomas, and Warthin's tumors or papillary cystadenoma lymphomatosum, other adenomatous lesions, hemangiomas, lipomas and other benign mesenchymal lesions (Figs. 8.1–8.9). The most frequently occurring malignant lesions arising from the epithelial structures include malignant mixed tumors, squamous cell carcinomas, mucoepidermoid carcinomas, and adenocarcinomas of various types (Figs. 8.10–8.17).

More rare lesions arise from contiguous or intraglandular structures such as seventh nerve neuromas (Fig. 8.9), lymphomas, sarcomas, and malignancies of adjacent structures. When there is an associated seventh nerve paralysis, the prognosis for successful treatment of the malignant tumors is very poor.

Tumors of the salivary glands constitute less than 3% of all head and neck neoplasms. About 70 to 80% of all salivary gland tumors arise in the parotid gland. Approximately 80% of parotid tumors are benign, while 50% of submandibular and minor salivary gland tumors are malignant.

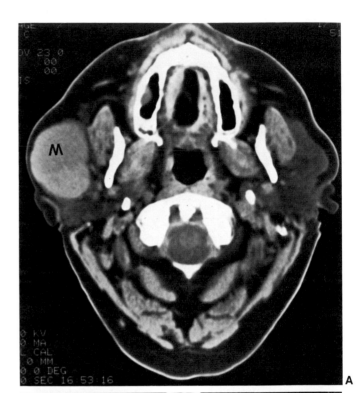

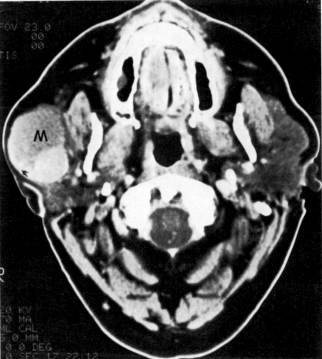

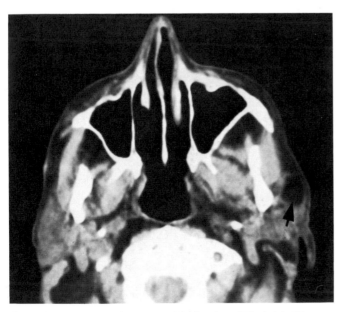

Figure 8.1 Lipoma of the parotid gland = CT. Axial CT scan shows the lipoma involving the superficial portion of the left parotid gland = arrow.

Figure 8.2 Pleomorphic adenoma = CT. Parotid gland, **A** plain, and **B** enhanced CT scans. In **A** the right parotid gland is enlarged by a large inhomogenous mass = M. Following infusion, **B** the irregular enhancement of the tumor is apparent. The presumptive diagnosis in this patient was pleomorphic adenoma.

Figure 8.**3** Pleomorphic adenoma, parotid gland = CT. Axial CT ▶
sialogram shows a well circumscribed mass = M, in the deep
lobe of the left parotid gland.

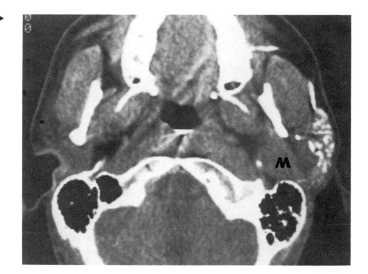

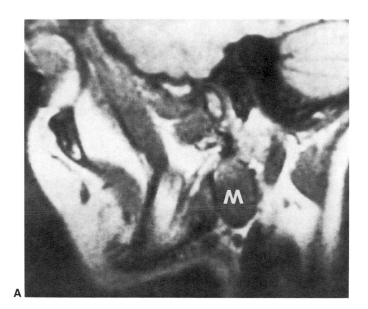

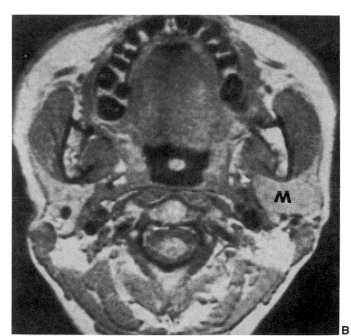

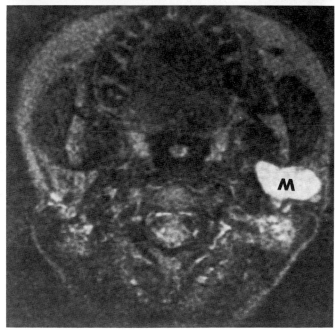

Figure 8.**4** Pleomorphic adenoma = MR. **A** sagittal T1w; **B** axial
spin density weighted; **C** axial T2w MR scans. A well defined
mass = M, lies in the left parotid gland. The tumor is of low signal
intensity in T1w, **A**; intermediate in spin density, **B**; and high
intensity in T2w, **C** images. The facial nerve and retromandibular
vasculature are displaced posteriorly.

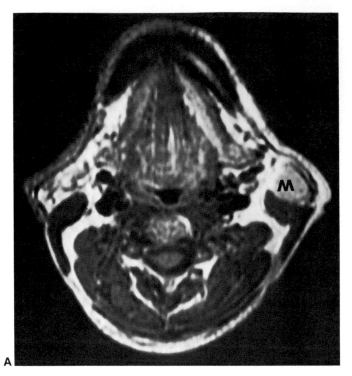

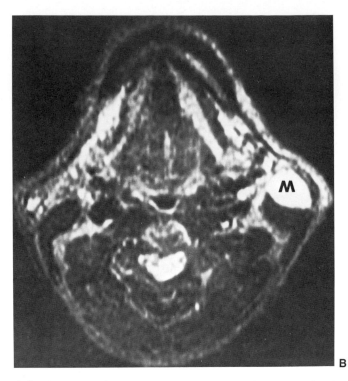

Figure 8.5 Pleomorphic adenoma = MR. **A** Axial spin density weighted and **B** axial T$_2$-weighted MR scan showing a well defined mass = M, in the tail of the left parotid. The tumor signal is intermediate in **A** and hyperintense in **B**.

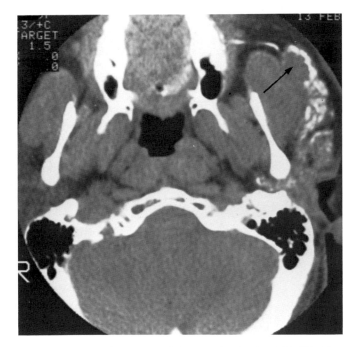

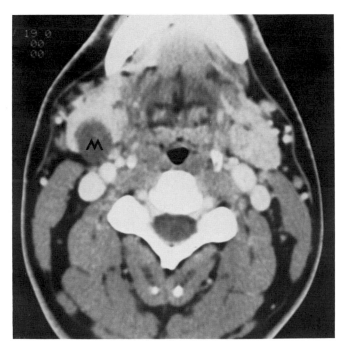

Figure 8.6 Warthin's tumor of the parotid gland = CT. CT sialogram shows a tumor mass, arrow, within the superficial portion of the left parotid gland displacing stensen's duct laterally.

Figure 8.7 Submandibular pleomorphic adenoma = CT. Enhanced axial CT scan shows a well defined non-enhancing mass = M, replacing the posterior portion of the right submandibular gland. Notice marked enhancement of the normal submandibular glands.

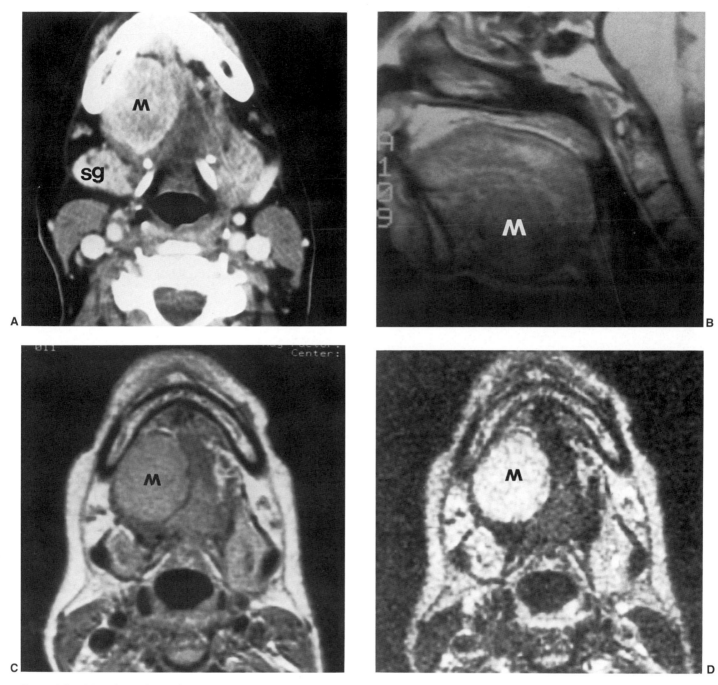

Figure 8.8   Adenoid cystic carcinoma of the minor salivary gland of the floor of the mouth, **A** CT, **B, C, D** MR.
A contrast enhanced axial CT scan shows a large enhancing mass = M, anterior to the submandibular gland = sg. **B** sagittal

T1w, **C** axial spin density weighted and **D** axial T2w MR scans show a large mass = M, on the floor of the mouth. The mass is hypointense to muscle in T1w, **B**; isointense to muscle in spin density weighted, **C**; and hyperintensive in T2w, **D** scans.

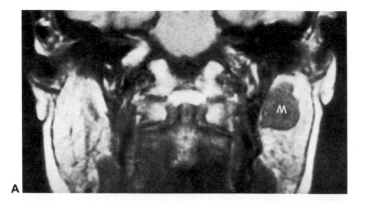

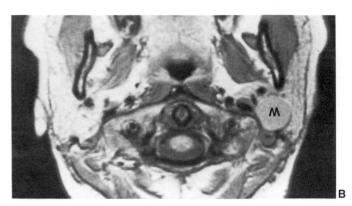

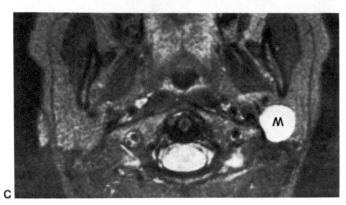

Figure 8.**9**   Facial nerve neuroma = MR. **A** coronal T1w, **B** axial spin density weighted and **C** T2w MR scans which show a well defined mass = M, within the left parotid gland. The intensity of the mass is low in T1w, **A**; medium in spin density weighted, **B**; and high in T2w, **C** images.

CT Appearance of Salivary Gland Tumors

Differentiation of benign and malignant tumors by CT is not the primary goal of this examination. CT becomes important in demonstrating the total extent of the disease, local lymphadenopathy, and distant metastases. The CT appearance of cysts is similar to that of cysts in other organs of the body. Generally cysts have thin walls, are well circumscribed, and contain water density material. If the fluid is proteinacious, the cyst may appear dense.

Benign mixed tumors are typically sharply circumscribed and lie in an otherwise normal gland (Figs. 8.**3**, 8.**5**, 8.**10**, 8.**11**). In the parotid, on plain CT the mass is seen because tumors have a higher density than the normal gland parenchyma. Submandibular tumors are often not detected because of the higher density of the normal submandibular gland, and CT with contrast infusion or CT sialography is indicated when a tumor is suspected.

The CT appearance of Warthin's tumor, the second most common benign tumor of the parotid gland, is non-specific (Fig. 8.**6**). The lesion usually appears as a well circumscribed mass within or on the surface of the parotid gland.

Although histologically these tumors often have cystic components and some mucoid fluid within them, the CT characteristics are not specific since the cystic spaces are very small. Some Warthin's tumors have a multiple lobular appearance that has been compared to a bunch of grapes.

Malignant tumors may be sharply circumscribed or have indistinct margins due to extension beyond the glandular tissue into the adjacent fat space and fascial planes (Figs. 8.**10**–8.**17**). Large tumors invade adjacent anatomic structures and extend into the facial canal, external auditory canal, middle ear, base of the skull, lateral pharyngeal spaces, and infratemporal fossae.

Enhancement with contrast material is sometimes useful for better visualization of the lesions and differentiation of benign from malignant tumors. Benign mixed tumors often show nonhomogeneous enhancement of the well defined tumor mass (Fig. 8.**2**). In Warthin's tumors, the enhancement may be inhomogenous due to the presence of cystic components in the lesion. Malignant tumors show a nonspecific and a non-uniform enhancement of the mass which often merges with the enhanced densities of the surrounding muscles.

MR Appearance of Salivary Gland Tumors

MR, similar to CT, is useful in the evaluation of salivary gland masses (Figs. 8.**5**, 8.**9**, 8.**10**, 8.**11**). MR, like CT helps to differentiate extrinsic lesions such as cervical nodes and parapharyngeal masses from parotid masses. MR may give some indication of the relationship of the parotid mass to the facial nerve. Although MR cannot give a histologic diagnosis, it does give an indication of the general morphology of the tumor. Rounded, sharply marginated, well encapsulated tumors tend to be benign, while irregu-

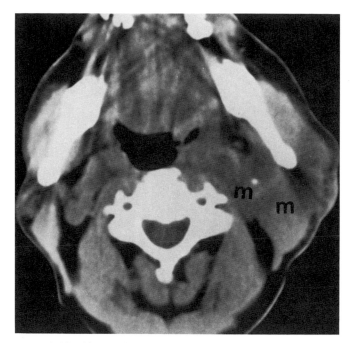

Figure 8.**10** Mucoepidermoid carcinoma = CT. A plain axial CT scan shows a large inhomogeneous mass = m, involving the superfical and deep lobes of the parotid gland. The tumor extends into the parapharyngeal space, distorting and displacing the lateral wall of the pharynx, medially.

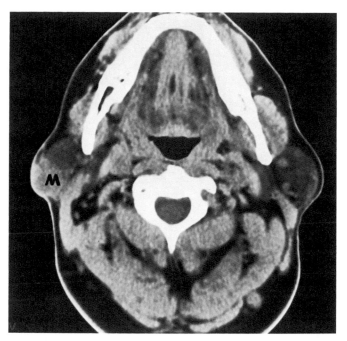

Figure 8.**11** Mucoepidermoid carcinoma, highly malignant = CT. Plain axial CT scan shows a high density mass = M, involving the posterior portion of the right parotid gland. There is involvement of the subcutaneous tissue evident by comparison with the normal subcutaneous tissue on the opposite side. Except for the subcutaneous invasion which is strongly suggestive of aggressive lesion, the CM appearance of the lesion is identical to a benign parotid mass.

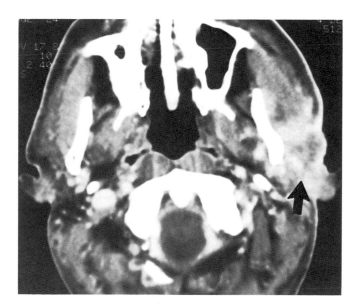

Figure 8.**12** Recurrent mucoepidermoid carcinoma = CT. Contrast enhanced axial CT scan shows inhomogeneous enhancement of the enlarged left parotid gland = arrow, with infiltration of the adjacent masseter muscle.

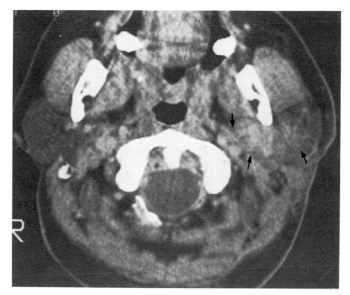

Figure 8.**13** Adenocystic carcinoma of the parotid gland with facial paralysis = CT. Axial CT with infusion shows infiltration and enlargement of the left parotid gland, including the deep lobe, by a nonhomogeneous mass = arrows. This lesion was not palpable clinically.

lar and diffuse tumors are usually malignant. Lipomas, cysts, lymphangiomas, and hemangiomas may be specifically differentiated from other salivary tumors. In cystic lesions, the signal intensity depends upon the characteristics of the fluid, whether serous or mucous. Most salivary gland tumors are seen by MR as intermediate or low intensity masses on T1w and spin density weighted images, and as high signal intensity lesions on T2w images (Figs. 8.**4**, 8.**5**, 8.**8**). The tumors, when they are small, have a homogeneous appearance. Mixed signal intensities may be present, particularly in large lesions due to areas of frank cystic degeneration. Similar areas of mixed signal intensities also are seen in inflammatory lesions.

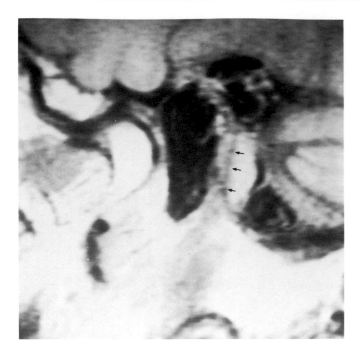

Figure 8.14   Adenocarcinoma of the parotid gland with extension into the temporal bone = MR. A sagittal T1w MR image obtained with surface coil. The facial nerve (arrows) is grossly enlarged. Perineural growth of the tumor had extended to the internal auditory canal.

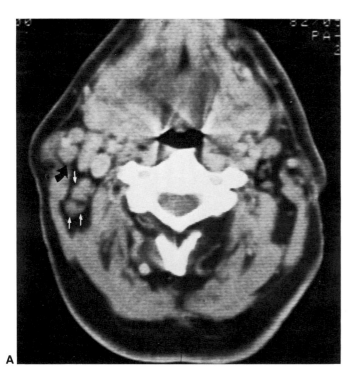

A

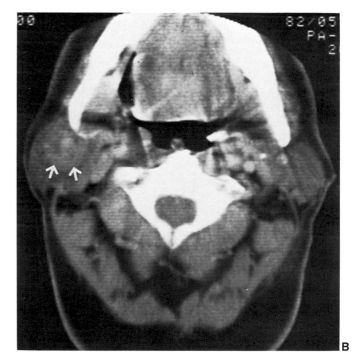

B

Figure 8.15   Lymphoma, parotid gland = CT.
A Axial CT scan shows lymph nodes in the right side of the neck under and anterior to the sternocleidomastoid muscle = arrows.

B Axial CT scan cephalad to A, shows enlargement of the right parotid gland by a nonhomogeneous infiltrate = arrows.

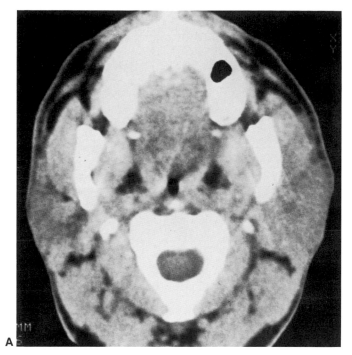

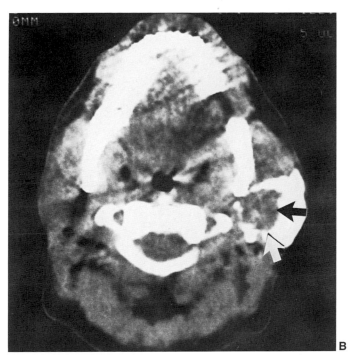

Figure 8.**16** Sarcoma of the left parotid gland = CT.
A Contrast enhanced axial CT scan shows a non-specific enlargement of the left parotid gland. The tumor is isodense with the remainder of the gland and, therefore, could easily be over-

looked. There is effacement of the posterior aspect of the masseter muscle.
B CT sialogram outlines an irregular sarcomatous mass = arrows.

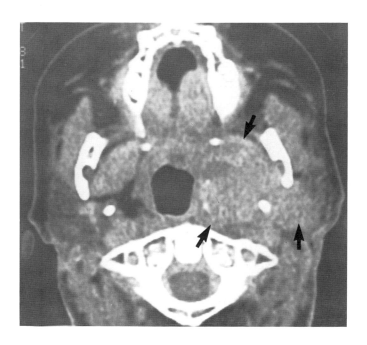

Figure 8.**17** Carcinoma of the left tonsil = CT. A contrast enhanced axial CT scan shows a left parapharyngeal mass = arrows, infiltrating the parotid gland.

Part IV

Hypopharynx and Larynx

William N. Hanafee

Chapter 1 **Introduction**

The vast majority of requests for imaging of the larynx and hypopharynx are related to malignant tumors. Occasionally patients present with post-traumatic deformities or benign masses that simulate malignant tumors. When the presenting symptom is a lymph node mass, the radiologic study of the larynx and hypopharynx may be in the search for a primary tumor.

Dysphagia, chronic aspiration, and airway problems are handled effectively clinical examination or barium studies. The more chronic type of airway obstruction may benefit from body sectional imaging, but most of the acute patients should receive treatment first to be followed by a more detailed study of etiology.

Indication for Study

The role of radiology in all of the tumor masses about the larynx is to delineate deep infiltrations and deep extensions rather than mucosal disease. Clinical examination either by direct or indirect laryngoscopy remains the examination of choice for visualizing mucosal detail (Fig. 1.1). In the past, contrast laryngography could prove useful in correlative studies of laryngeal function and mucosal changes, but the information concerning deep infiltrations was always indirect or implied. With the advent of CT and now MR, the role of imaging in demonstrating deep extensions of a tumor is becoming much more clear. Either CT or MR can be used to demonstrate the deep infiltrations of malignant laryngeal and hypo-

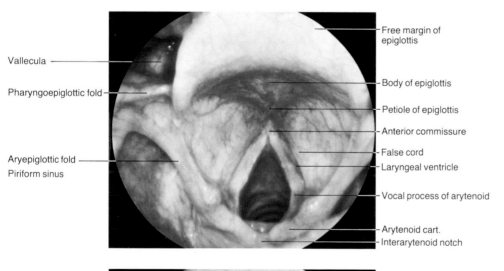

Vallecula

Pharyngoepiglottic fold

Aryepiglottic fold
Piriform sinus

Free margin of epiglottis

Body of epiglottis

Petiole of epiglottis

Anterior commissure

False cord

Laryngeal ventricle

Vocal process of arytenoid

Arytenoid cart.

Interarytenoid notch

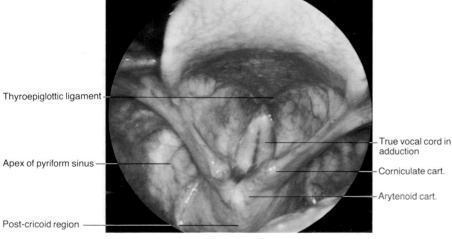

Thyroepiglottic ligament

Apex of pyriform sinus

Post-cricoid region

True vocal cord in adduction

Corniculate cart.

Arytenoid cart.

Figure 1.**1** Endoscopic view of the normal larynx.

A View of the larynx during quiet respiration. The vocal cords are fully abducted and the entire laryngeal vestibule and subglottic region can be visualized.

B View of the larynx during phonation. The arytenoid cartilages rotate medially and also glide medially to bring the two true vocal cords together. The movement of the arytenoid cartilages brings the aryepiglottic folds medially and widens the laterally placed piriform sinuses. The inferior most extent of the piriform sinuses is known as the apex. It lies at or slightly below the level of the true vocal cords.

pharyngeal tumors. Both modalities have their advantages and disadvantages. The indications for either study are changing as technical improvements occur in both MR and CT. Opinions expressed in printed form are frequently outmoded quickly because of the rapid changes taking place in technical developments. For the time being it would seem that the advantage of laryngeal imaging ist with MR. This would be related to the availability of axial, sagittal as well as coronal sectioning. The multiple projections permit more accurate measurement of superior – inferior extension of tumor masses. The contrast available with MR is superior to that of CT in differentiating tumor masses from musculature. The larynx and piriform sinus regions have an abundance of loose areolar tissue, which gives an extremely bright signal that contrasts with the lower signal of malignant tumors. This fact makes demonstration of tumors quite simple, since the long T1 of tumors

causes a loss of signal on T1 weighted pulsing sequences when there ist deep infiltration of the larynx by tumors.

Knowledge of the TNM classifications (38) of tumors is quite helpful in determining the need of an imaging modality (see Table 1.1).

Tumors of the larynx can be divided into supraglottic cancers, true cord tumors, and subglottic lesions. Most of the supraglottic and subglottic lesions require imaging to show extent of tumor and to assist in management by precision radiation therapy (2, 26) or voice conservation surgery (21, 28).

Both modalities are based on an exacting knowledge of the extent of tumor masses. The indications for study of true cord tumors may be listed as follows:

1. T1 Tumors. Early tumors are frequently limited to the junction of anterior and middle thirds of the true vocal cord with no impairment of mobility, and no imaging is necessary. These patients

Table 1.1 Definitions: TNM Classification

Primary Tumor (T)

TX Minimum requirements to assess the primary tumor cannot be met

TO No evidence of primary tumor

Supraglottis

Tis Carcinoma in situ

T_1 Tumor confined to site of origin with normal mobility

T_2 Tumor involves adjacent supraglottic site(s) or glottis without fixation

T_3 Tumor limited to larynx with fixation or extension to involve postcricoid area, medial wall of piriform sinus or preepiglottic space

T_4 Massive tumor extending beyond the larynx to involve oropharynx, soft tissues, of neck, or destruction of thyroid cartilage

Glottis

Tis Carcinoma *in situ*

T_1 Tumor confined to vocal cord(s) with normal mobility (including involvement of anterior or posterior commissures)

T_2 Supraglottic or subglottic extension of tumor with normal or impaired cord mobility

T_2 Tumor confined to the larynx with cord fixation

T_4 Massive tumor with thyroid cartilage destruction or extension beyond the confines of the larynx, or both

Subglottis

Tis Carcinoma *in situ*

T_1 Tumor confined to the subglottic region

T_2 Tumor extension to vocal cords with normal or impaired cord mobility

T_3 Tumor confined to larynx with cord fixation

T_4 Massive tumor with cartilage destruction or extension beyond the confines of the larynx, or both

Nodal involvement (N)

NX Minimum requirements to assess the regional nodes cannot be met

NO No clinically positive nodes

N_1 Single clinically positive homolateral node 3 cm or less in diameter

N_2 Single clinically positive homolateral node more than 3 but not more than 6 cm in diameter or multiple clinically positive homolateral nodes, none more than 6 cm in diameter

N_{2a} Single clinically positive homolateral node more than 3 cm but not more than 6 cm in diameter

N_{2b} Multiple clinically positive homolateral nodes, none more than 6 cm in diameter

N_3 Massive homolateral node(s), bilateral nodes, or contralateral node(s)

N_{3a} Clinically positive homolateral node(s), one more than 6 cm in diameter

N_{3b} Bilateral clinically positive nodes (in this situation, each side of the neck should be staged separately; i.e. N_{3b}: right N_{2a}; left, N_1)

N_{3c} Contralateral clinically positive node(s) only

Distant Metastasis (M)

MX Minimum requirements to assess the presence of distant metastasis cannot be met

MO No (known) distant metastasis

M_1 Distant metastasis present

Location of Tumor

Supraglottis

Ventricular band
Arytenoid
Suprahyoid epiglottis
Infrahyoid epiglottis
Arytenoepiglottic fold

Glottis

Vocal cords (including commissures)

Subglottis

(From: Beahrs OH, Myers MH: Manual for Staging of Cancer. Second edition. Philadelphia: JB Lippincott Company 1983: 37–42.)

require biopsy for proof of diagnosis and should be treated with either voice conservation surgery or radiation therapy.

2. T2 Tumors. The tumor is confined to the true vocal cords. It can involve the false cord or adjacent subglottis space but does not involve the vocal process of the arytenoid or other cartilage. The cord ist mobile. These patients need imaging to confirm that there is no deep infiltration prior to biopsy.

3. T3 Tumors. These are vocal cord tumors that have some degree of vocal cord fixation. They involve adjacent areas of the larynx but have not extended beyond the confines of the larynx. These individuals also need imaging because the limits of voice conservation surgery have been extended and many of the patients can be cared for conservatively with a reasonably good voice resulting. They also need delineation of their infiltrations for precision radiation therapy.

4. T4 lesions. These are massive tumors with cartilage destruction or extension beyond the confines of the larynx or both. They require radical surgery as a life saving procedure, and imaging is only occasionally needed to confirm the widespread extensions of the tumor beyond the confines of the larynx.

Technique

Regardless of whether MR or CT is used as the imaging modality, patient cooperation and positioning are extremely important for orientation within the larynx. Axial sections should always be made in the plane of the true vocal cords. With CT this may require angling of the gantry or altering the patients position with multiple cushions in order to get the lumen of the larynx perpendicular to the plane of scan. In a similar manner, MR sections in the axial plane should be parallel to the plane of the true vocal cord, while coronal sections should be made with the patient's head looking directly to the ceiling so that symmetry of the two sides can be compared. On the sagittal projections, some type of system using cursor lines or similar techniques should be employed to ensure that the midline section is truly in the midline plane of the larynx. This is important for visualization of the status of the anterior commissure.

Many patients will have difficulty managing secretions during a CT or MR study. Five to ten second CT sections can be performed during breath holding. Similary, if gradient echoes are available with MR, the MR scan time can be reduced to 3 to 8 seconds for rapid imaging. In the absence of either of these techniques, one must resort to imaging during quiet respiration. A few minutes to watch the patient breathe while he is in the recumbent position can be very valuable. With a little practice the patient can be instructed not to make large excursions that will cause vertical shifts in the position of the larynx. Also, tongue motion or jaw motions will move the entire pharyngeal musculature and hence the position of the larynx.

CT Factors

Since most of the patients presenting for imaging of the larynx have moderately advanced tumors, visualization of lymph node chains becomes a matter of concern. Intravenous contrast is necessary to determine which densities are due to blood vessels and which are due to lymph nodes. A convenient technique for CT of the larynx is as follows.

1. An intravenous infusion of 150 ccs of 60% contrast material is started. For supraglottic tumors, the initial scans are begun low to allow time for a concentration of contrast material to build up and opacify blood vessels. True cord tumors are begun at the level of the hyoid bone and the sectioning progressing in a caudal direction. This is related to the direction of spread for lymph node metastases, with supraglottic tumors spreading cephalad while true cord tumors metastasize posterolaterally or inferiorly.

2. Sections are taken at 5 mm intervals from the angle of the mandible to 1 cm below the inferior thyroid notch. If nodes are visible in the scan, the sections are continued higher or lower until all disease has been covered.

3. The level of the true vocal cords is marked, and 5 sections each 1.5 mm thick are taken at 1 mm intervals. The multiple thin sections give a better appraisal of spread to the vital structures in the immediate vicinity of the true vocal cords.

MR Pulsing Sequences

If available, surface coils should be used for all examinations to improve signal to noise ratios. (Fig. 1.**2**). The entire examination is performed with T1 weighted pulsing sequences because of the abundance of bright signal coming from the larynx and paralaryngeal spaces. T2 pulsing sequences make the tumor become a bright signal that does not yield contrast with adjacent areas regardless of whether one is looking at the primary tumor within the larynx or metastatic tumor within lymph nodes. A convenient technique is as follows.

1. Axial T1 weighted pulsing sequences (TR500, TE28, 5 mm thick sections at 7 mm intervals) from the hyoid bone to the upper trachea lying 1 cm below the thyroid notch. In order to cover this wide area in axial sectioning, it may be necessary to increase the TR to 800 or 900 milliseconds.

2. Five sections in the coronal plane and 5 sections in the sagittal plane are usually sufficient to cover the entire larynx plus the nodal bearing regions adjacent to the jugular vein.

Three-dimensional data acquisition and gradient echoing imaging will probably change these factors dramatically.

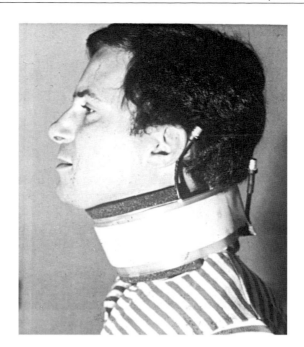

Figure 1.**2**   Solenoid surface coil.
The surface coil for larynx examination consists of approximately two turns of antennae material. This same coil can be used on larger or smaller patients because the exact number of turns is not crucial to producing high signal. The number of turns can vary from 1¾ to 2½ turns.

Chapter 2 Anatomy

The larynx and hypopharynx can be thought of as two organs. The true vocal cords and regions below the true vocal cords functionally behave much more like trachea, whereas the supraglottic larynx and piriform sinuses behave more like gastrointestinal tract.

Embryologically, the true vocal cords are part of the tracheobronchial bud, while the supraglottic larynx is part of the buccopharyngeal anlage[3]. The piriform sinuses resemble oral cavity even more precisely with the expansivity of their muscular walls and rich lymphatics.

The "two organs" must coordinate functions in a precise fashion to play the main role of the larynx, which is a sphincter. The sphincter functions to separate respiration from deglutition, and it performs the act of vocalization. The cartilages that form the skeleton of the larynx are unique forms of hyaline and fibroelastic cartilage. They support both intrinsic and extrinsic muscles and ligaments (Fig. 2.1).

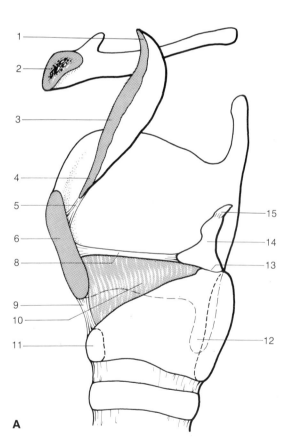

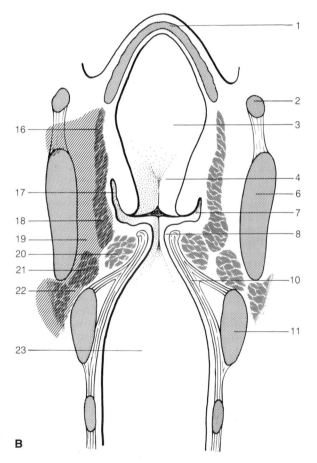

Figure 2.1 Diagrammatic representation of laryngeal cartilages and paralaryngeal space.
A View of the right half of the larynx on midsagittal cut.
B Midcoronal view of the larynx looking from behind. 1. Suprahyoid epiglottis, 2. hyoid bone, 3. body of epiglottis, 4. petiolus of epiglottis, 5. thyroepiglottic ligament, 6. thyroid cartilage, 7. laryngeal ventricle, 8. vocal ligament, 9. cricothyroid membrane, 10. conus elasticus, 11. cricoid cartilage, 12. inferior cornu of thyroid cartilage, 13. cricoarytenoid joint, 14. arytenoid cartilage, 15. corniculate cartilage, 16. aryepiglottic muscle, 17. appendix of the laryngeal ventricle, 18. the lateral thyroarytenoid muscle, 19. paralaryngeal space (shaded area), 20. vocal muscle, 21. lateral cricoarytenoid muscle, 22. inferior extension of the paralaryngeal space, 23. trachea.

Laryngeal Skeleton

The MR appearance of the laryngeal skeleton at various age groups is very disconcerting. At times, the cartilages may give a bright signal, while at other times they are visible by a signal void due to calcification. Often, the combination of the two signal levels average out to make the cartilages blend with the surrounding tissues.

Cricoid Cartilage

The cricoid cartilage is a signet ring in configuration and forms the very basis of the larynx. It supports the vocal ligament and the principal muscles of the spincter. The cricoid cartilage is a complete ring with a broad lamina posteriorly and a narrow arch anteriorly. The cricoid cartilage supports two arytenoid cartilages that lie on the broader posterior rim near the posterolateral margin of the lamina or signa portion of the cartilage. The paired thyroid cartilages articulate with the lateral borders of the posterior portion of the cricoid cartilage.

With aging, calcifications begin to take place in the surfaces of the lamina of the cricoid cartilage. Usually there is hyaline cartilage preserved in the midline of the cricoid lamina. Calcifications in adults are usually present in the superolateral surfaces of the cricoid lamina that service the articulation with the arytenoid cartilages[14, 35].

The medullary cavity of the cricoid lamina, with calcifications of the lateral shoulders, serves as an important landmark at both MR and CT. This usually will denote the level of the true vocal cords. At CT the medullary cavity will be low density surrounded by adjacent calcified cartilage. An MR bright signal will come from the medullary cavity, with a low signal coming from the calcified areas and some of the cartilaginous areas (Fig. 2.2). A low signal from calcifications in parts of the arytenoid cartilages, plus a bright signal from the medullary cavity of the cricoid lamina and arytenoid cartilages, give the exact location of the true vocal cords.

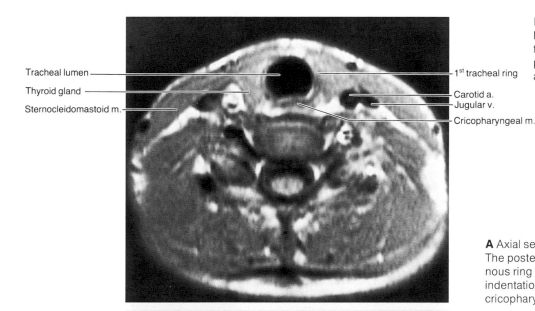

Tracheal lumen

Thyroid gland

Sternocleidomastoid m.

1st tracheal ring

Carotid a.
Jugular v.

Cricopharyngeal m.

Anterior ring of cricoid cart.

Laterale cricoarytenoid m.

Inferior cornu of thyroid cart.
Cricoid lamina

Strap m.

Inferior margin
thyroid ala

Posterior
cricoarytenoid m.

Figure 2.2   MR of the normal larynx – axial view. Sections were taken at 3 mm intervals using a T1 pulsing sequence (TE28, TR500, 2 averages 256×256 matrix.)

A Axial section through the first tracheal ring. The posterior circumference of the cartilaginous ring is incomplete, which produces an indentation in the lumen caused by the cricopharyngeal muscle (arrowheads).

B Scan through the entire ring of the cricoid cartilage. The anterior ring of the cricoid cartilage is partially calcified, giving low signal regions. Note that there are no appreciable soft tissues lying to the lumen side of the cricoid cartilage.

Figure 2.**2**

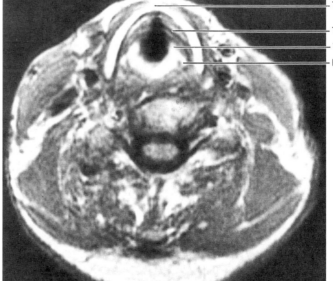

Anterior jugular v.
Thyroid cart.
Inferior surface
true vocal cord
Cricoid lamina

Sternocleidomastoid m.
Carotid a.
Internal jugular v.
Pharyngeal constrictor m.

C Section through the undersurface of the true vocal cord. The plane of section is slightly angulated so that thyroid cartilage is well visualized along with the cricoid lamina. The inferior surface of the true vocal cords are producing some soft tissues lying medial to the thyroid cartilage.

Thyroid symphysis

True vocal cord
Vocal process of arytenoid
Muscular process of aryteno

D True vocal cord level. The true vocal cord level can be recognized when arytenoid cartilages and cricoid lamina are in the plane of section. One can be absolutely certain of the level if the vocal process of the arytenoid cartilages are in the plane of section.

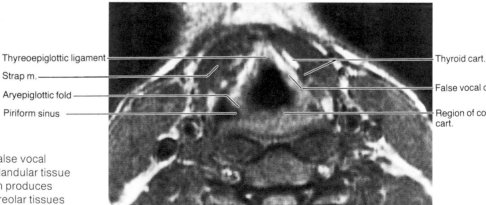

Thyreoepiglottic ligament
Strap m.
Aryepiglottic fold
Piriform sinus

Thyroid cart.

False vocal cord

Region of corniculate cart.

E False vocal cord level. The false vocal cords have an abundance of glandular tissue and loose areolar tissue, which produces very bright signal. The loose areolar tissues create a broad space that continues on the undersurface of the thyroid cartilage as the paralaryngeal space.

Figure 2.**2**

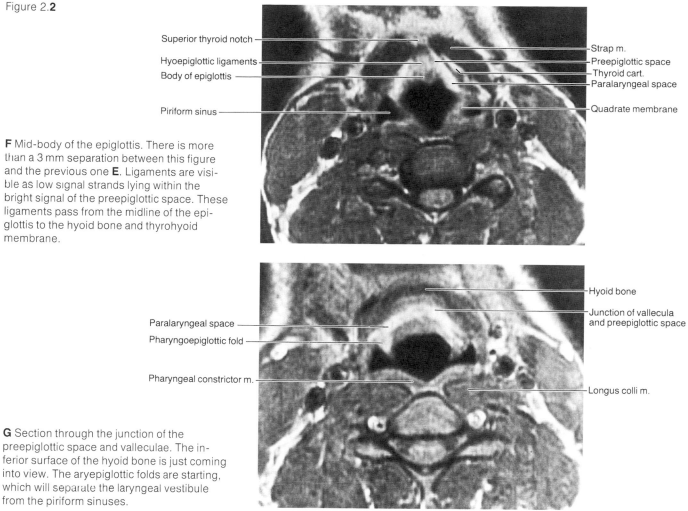

Superior thyroid notch
Hyoepiglottic ligaments
Body of epiglottis

Piriform sinus

Strap m.
Preepiglottic space
Thyroid cart.
Paralaryngeal space

Quadrate membrane

F Mid-body of the epiglottis. There is more than a 3 mm separation between this figure and the previous one **E**. Ligaments are visible as low signal strands lying within the bright signal of the preepiglottic space. These ligaments pass from the midline of the epiglottis to the hyoid bone and thyrohyoid membrane.

Paralaryngeal space
Pharyngoepiglottic fold

Pharyngeal constrictor m.

Hyoid bone
Junction of vallecula and preepiglottic space

Longus colli m.

G Section through the junction of the preepiglottic space and valleculae. The inferior surface of the hyoid bone is just coming into view. The aryepiglottic folds are starting, which will separate the laryngeal vestibule from the piriform sinuses.

Arytenoid, Corniculate and Cuneiform Cartilages

The combination of the three paired cartilages gives the posterior support to the true vocal cords and aryepiglottic folds. The primary support is supplied by the arytenoid cartilages, which rest on the posterolateral shoulder of the cricoid lamina. From the anterior inferior margin of the arytenoid cartilage, a vocal process extends forward that gives support to the vocal ligament. The arytenoid cartilages are capable or a rotary action as well as an anteroposterior and lateral gliding action. This is accomplished through multiple muscular attachments to the arytenoid cartilages that fan out much like ropes supporting a tent post.

The arytenoid cartilages calcify quite early so that on CT they appear as dense calcifications. (Fig. 2.3). On MR one would expect them to be low in signal but actually they have a bright signal. This is presumably related to the medullary cavity and interspersed cartilage. The arytenoid cartilages and the paired corniculate cartilages, which lie at their superior pole, support the aryepiglottic folds, which can be rotated medial to lateral along with the true vocal cords during breathing and return toward the midline dur-

ing valsalva or swallowing to close the airway. The very small cuneiform cartilages lie in the aryepiglottic folds along the superior margin. The arytenoid cartilages are viewed without superimposed cricoid lamina when the scan is at the level of the false vocal cords. At the level of the true vocal cords some arytenoid cartilage, vocal process, and cricoid lamina should be in the plane of section on axial projections.

Thyroid Cartilages

The thyroid cartilage is actually a single shield-shaped cartilage that protects and supports the anterior portion of the larynx. It has a prominent notch superior and inferiorly which gives the thyroid cartilage the appearance of having a midline symphysis. The true vocal cords attach slightly below the midpoint anteriorly. Finger-like processes project from the posterosuperior and inferior margins of the thyroid alae and are called the superior and inferior cornua respectively. The inferior cornu articulates with the cricoid lamina while the superior cornu extends cephalad to the region of the hyoid bone.

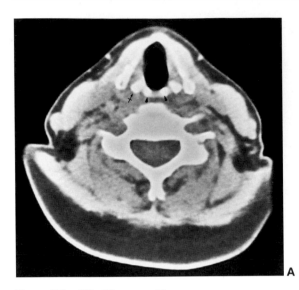

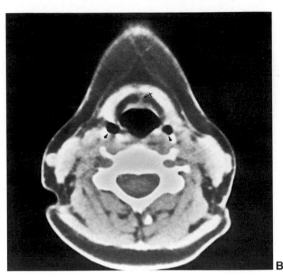

Figure 2.**3** CT of the normal larynx.
A Section through the level of the true vocal cords shows the arytenoid cartilages (single cross-hatched arrow) resting on the cricoid lamina. (arrowheads). The arytenoid cartilages support the true vocal cord. The thyroid cartilages in this patient are incompletely calcified.

B Axial scan through the body of the epiglottis. This section corresponds to the superior margins of the arytenoid cartilages. The piriform sinuses are seen lateral to the aryepiglottic folds (arrowheads). The midline ligaments that extend from the hyoid bone to the body of the epiglottis are visible in the preepiglottic space. (cross-hatched arrow).

Hyoid Bone

The hyoid bone marks the junction of oral pharynx with hypopharynx. It provides attachment for the strap muscles and the diaphragm of the floor of the mouth. It also gives origin to the lateral border of the tongue. The hyoid bone ist tripartite secondary to its embryologic origin. It has a central body and two lateral wings.

The anterior and posterior digastric tendons attach to the superolateral margin of the hyoid. This is an important CT and MR landmark for the jugular digastric lymph node, which lies at the crotch of the two tendons.

A dense membrane extends from the thyroid cartilage to the hyoid bone; the thyrohyoid membrane. This membrane gives origin to important ligament structures that fan out in the midline posteriorly to support the epiglottis.

Epiglottis

The epiglottis ist leaf-shaped and composed of elastic cartilage that is extensively perforated. It does not calcify and must remain extremely flexible to perform its function of inverting as a trap door over the larynx during the act of swallowing. The superior margin of the epiglottis has epithelium both anterior and posterior, and is spoken of as the free margin. Anterior to the free margin of the epiglottis, the valleculae lies between the epiglottis and base of the tongue. The space is rich in lymphatics and may be filled by the lingual tonsils. Posterior to the epiglottis marks the entrance to the laryngeal vestibule.

Inferiorly the body of the epiglottis becomes quite pointed (the petiole) and terminates as a 4 mm long thryoepiglottic ligament that attaches the petiole to the posterior surface of the thyroid cartilage immediately above the level of the true vocal cords. From the posterolateral margins of the body of the epiglottis are the aryepiglottic folds. They are made up of the quadrangular membrane and muscular bundles from the arytenoid. The aryepiglottic folds separate the piriform sinuses from the laryngeal vestibule. From the lateral borders of the epiglottis, a second pair of ligaments courses directly laterally to the pharyngeal wall; these are the pharyngoepiglottic folds (see Fig. 1.**1**).

Laryngeal Soft Tissues

The mucous membrane that lines the laryngeal vestibule and piriform sinuses rests on a generous bed of loose areolae tissue containing numerous mucous and serous glands. A space is created lying medial to the thyroid cartilage and cricoid cartilages which is called the paralaryngeal space. This is a continuum that contains the intrinsic muscles of the larynx. The space communicates freely with the preepiglottic space. Despite this anatomical freedom of space, the larynx is divided into distinct compartments related to embryology and lymphatic drainage[32, 31].

Preepiglottic Compartment

The major portion of the epiglottis lies above the level of the thyroid cartilage. Nevertheless a space is created between the epiglottis and the thyrohyoid membrane. Midline ligaments divide the anterior compartment into two lateral compartments, which then are continuous posterolaterally with the space lying medial to the thyroid cartilage and lateral to the aryepiglottic folds. Lymphatic drainage from the preepiglottic space is almost exclusively unilateral and drains superiorly and posterolaterally[16]. The primary nodes of drainage are in the lympathic channels above and below the level of the hyoid bone surrounding the anterior border of the jugular vein.

Lateral Paralaryngeal Spaces

The parapharyngeal spaces form a continuum medial and posterior to the thyroid ala but are limited medially below the true cords by the conus elasticus[11, 10]. The paired spaces continue anteriorly as the preepiglottic space. The parapharyngeal spaces are composed of an abundance of loose areolar and elastic tissue whose function is to supply the capability of muscular motion, allow a rocking action of the thyroid on the cricoid cartilage, and permit expansion of the piriform sinuses when they must balloon to allow passage of a bolus of food. The concept of a continuum is an extremely important relationship because only the lymphatic drainage respects a separation of supraglottic larynx from true vocal cords and subglottic region. Part of the posterior free access to the space is closed off by the pharyngeal constrictures, which sweep around the posterior margin of the thyroid alae to insert into the lateral surface of the ala of the thyroid cartilages. This closure by the pharyngeal constrictures means that lymphatic drainage must extend posterosuperiorly through the thyrohyoid membrane or posteroinferiorly adjacent to the cricoid lamina.

The lymphatic drainage of the aryepiglottis folds, which form the medial wall of this space, drain inferiorly and posterolaterally between the cricoid lamina and inferior border of the thyroid cartilage (Fig. 2.4).

Part of the parlaryngeal space is made up of the musculature of the true vocal cords, which are the vocalis muscle and the thyroarytenoid muscles. From within the true vocal cord and extending lateral to the thryoid cartilage, lymphatic drainage is distinctly separate from the supraglottic larynx. The drainage may be anterior or posterolateral. Anteriorly at the junction of the true vocal cords lies a special area known as the anterior commissure. At this level the mucosa lies directly on perichondrium of the thyroid cartilage. Below this level lies the crico-thyroid membrane, which is penetrated by lymphatics that drain anterior to small lymph nodes known as dolphine nodes in the anterior neck.

Subglottic space lies beneath the level of the true vocal cords and represents the transition from larynx to tracheal lymphatics. As one descends to the first tracheal rings, the lymphatic drainage is more circumferential rather than lateralized so there are rich

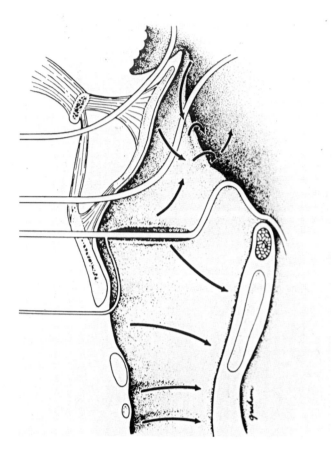

Figure 2.**4** Lymphatic drainage of the larynx. The supraglottic larynx drains superiorly and posteriorly to high jugular nodes and jugular digastric nodes. The true vocal cords and subglottic region drain to the mid-jugular and lower jugular nodes together with some anterior drainage to dolphine nodes lying anterior to the trachea. These two compartments are quite sharply separated at the laryngeal ventricle. The separation is probably related to the embryologic origin of the supraglottic larynx from the primitive buccopharyngeal anlage, while the true cords lower from the tracheobronchial buds.
(Courtesy of Batsakis: Tumors of the Head and Neck, 2nd Edition. Baltimore, Williams and Wilkins, 1979).

anastomoses between the two sides. This rich complex of lymphatics communicates inferiorly with the tracheal mucosal lymphatics.

Aryepiglottic Folds

The aryepiglottic folds (as the name implies) pass from the arytenoid cartilages to the lateral margins of the epiglottis. They separate the laryngeal vestibule from the piriform sinuses. During the resting state they tend to rotate laterally, obliterating the major portion of the lumina of the piriform sinuses or they may be at approximately a 45 degree angle with the midsagittal plane. During a Valsalva maneuver they fold medially and anteroposteriorly upon themselves to obliterate the airway of the laryngeal vestibule.

The aryepiglottic folds are intermediate signal strength on MR and intermediate density on CT. The

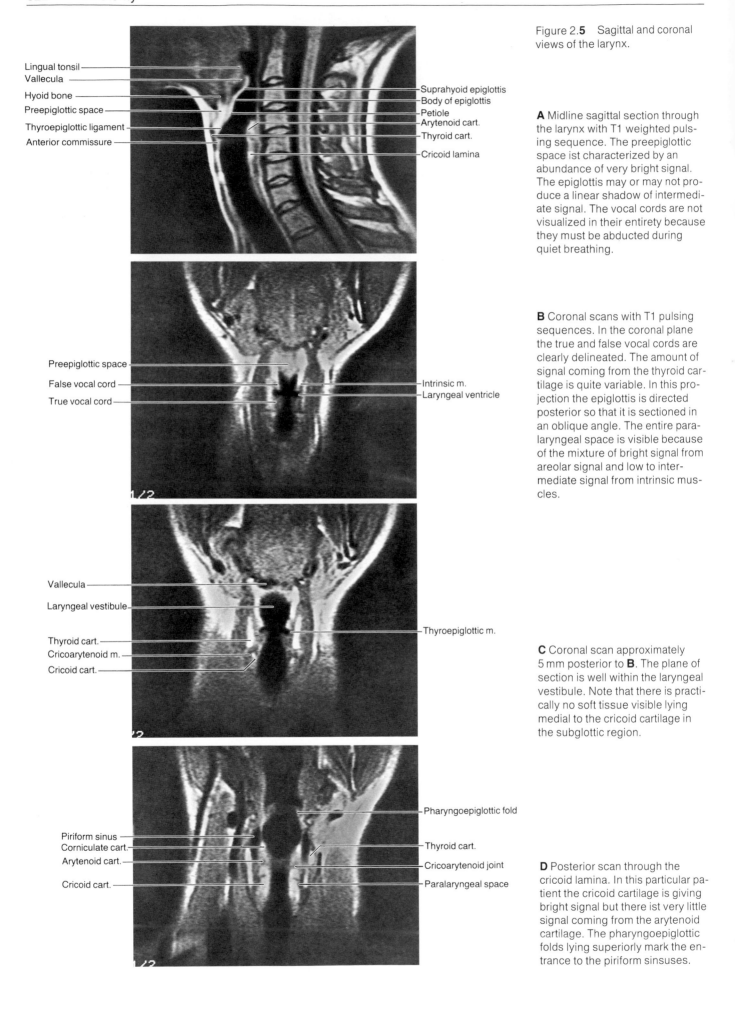

Figure 2.5 Sagittal and coronal views of the larynx.

Lingual tonsil
Vallecula
Hyoid bone
Preepiglottic space
Thyroepiglottic ligament
Anterior commissure

Suprahyoid epiglottis
Body of epiglottis
Petiole
Arytenoid cart.
Thyroid cart.
Cricoid lamina

A Midline sagittal section through the larynx with T1 weighted pulsing sequence. The preepiglottic space ist characterized by an abundance of very bright signal. The epiglottis may or may not produce a linear shadow of intermediate signal. The vocal cords are not visualized in their entirety because they must be abducted during quiet breathing.

Preepiglottic space
False vocal cord
True vocal cord

Intrinsic m.
Laryngeal ventricle

B Coronal scans with T1 pulsing sequences. In the coronal plane the true and false vocal cords are clearly delineated. The amount of signal coming from the thyroid cartilage is quite variable. In this projection the epiglottis is directed posterior so that it is sectioned in an oblique angle. The entire paralaryngeal space is visible because of the mixture of bright signal from areolar signal and low to intermediate signal from intrinsic muscles.

Vallecula
Laryngeal vestibule
Thyroid cart.
Cricoarytenoid m.
Cricoid cart.

Thyroepiglottic m.

C Coronal scan approximately 5 mm posterior to B. The plane of section is well within the laryngeal vestibule. Note that there is practically no soft tissue visible lying medial to the cricoid cartilage in the subglottic region.

Piriform sinus
Corniculate cart.
Arytenoid cart.
Cricoid cart.

Pharyngoepiglottic fold
Thyroid cart.
Cricoarytenoid joint
Paralaryngeal space

D Posterior scan through the cricoid lamina. In this particular patient the cricoid cartilage is giving bright signal but there ist very little signal coming from the arytenoid cartilage. The pharyngoepiglottic folds lying superiorly mark the entrance to the piriform sinsuses.

corniculate cartilages and the cuneiform cartilages that lie in these folds are usually not visible on CT or MR.

Piriform Sinuses

The paired piriform sinuses are intimately related to the larynx but are actually part of the gastrointestinal tract. They serve as a conduit for food from the oral pharynx to the cervical esophagus. The degree of distention of the lumen of the piriform sinus is related to physiologic maneuvers or swallowing of a bolus of food. The anterior inferior margins of the piriform sinuses are known as the apices, and usually lie at a level of or slightly below the true vocal cords. This relationship ist extremely important to surgical management of cancers, and should constantly be born in mind.

The loose areolar tissue forming the bed of the mucosa of the piriform sinus gives a very bright signal and is easily detected. Posteriorly the pharyngeal constrictures form a boundary to the lumina of the piriform sinuses, and the musculature can be seen as a low signal band encircling the posterior pharyngeal wall. Anterosuperiorly, a fold separates the piriform sinuses from the vallecula. This is the pharyngoepiglottic fold, which lies on a plane perpendicular to the aryepiglottic fold.

True and False Vocal Cords

The true vocal cords extend from the vocal processes of the arytenoids to the posterior inner surface of the thyroid cartilage. They are composed of a vocal ligament, which is covered along the free margin by mucosa, and intrinsic muscles. They unite anteriorly at the anterior commissure, and posteriorly a broad space separates the two cords, which is the space between the two arytenoid cartilages and their vocal processes. The bulk of the true vocal cords is made up of two muscles – the vocalis muscle, which originates from the arytenoid cartilages and inserts into the vocal ligament anteriorly, and the thyroarytenoid muscle, which is another of the intrinsic muscles of

the larynx. As the name implies, the latter passes from the arytenoid posteriorly to the thyroid cartilage (Fig. 2.5).

From the free margin of the true vocal cords and attaching to the vocal ligaments are membranes that fan out inferiorly to envelop the cricoid ring. These are rather tough membranous folds that lie just beneath the mucosa and are called the conus elasticus. They form an important barrier to the spread of tumors, and they direct lymphatics from the depths of the vocal cords posterolaterally and inferiorly.

The false cords are cephalad to the true vocal cords and are separated from them by a space called the laryngeal ventricle. The false cords are composed primarily of areolar tissue and glandular tissue plus some of the thyroepiglottic musculature. In the middle of the anterior third of the false vocal cord, an extension of mucosa extends superiorly from the laryngeal ventricle into the paralaryngeal space. This is known as the appendix of the laryngeal ventricle or saccule. It continues superiorly and posteriorly in the paralaryngeal space for a varying distance (usually –12 mm). Dilatation beyond 22–25 mm constitutes a pathologic condition called laryngocele or mucocele. The function of the appendix of the laryngeal ventricle is to secrete a thin mucous to lubricate the true vocal cords.

Intrinsic Musculature

The remainder of the intrinsic muscles that lie in the lateral wall of the larynx course from the arytenoid cartilages to the cricoid cartilages. These are the medial and lateral cricoarytenoid musculature. They serve to rock the cricoid cartilage on the thyroid cartilage.

Posteriorly, muscle bundles pass directly between the two arytenoid cartilages and between the posterior surface of the cricoid lamina and the arytenoid cartilages. These muscle bundles appear as low signal regions on MR and can be identified in the vast majority of MR examinations.

Chapter 3   Pathologic Conditions of the Larynx and Hypopharynx

Since MR or CT is primarily used for treatment planning rather than as a purely diagnostic procedure, there is an even greater need for close correlation with clinical examination. The clinician will inspect the larynx and piriform sinuses either with direct and indirect methods assessing mucosal changes and physiology. Depending on patient cooperation, pattern of tumor growth, and other factors, specific areas may represent pertinent gaps of information needed for making a pre-surgical or pre-radiation therapy decision. The surgeon may say, "I can get that information at the time of surgery", which is correct. On the other hand, the patient deserves to be informed as fully as possible concerning the sacrifices he must make regarding voice, swallowing, and quality of life. Also with adequate preoperative information, a more orderly surgical approach can be conducted. The most common problem areas during the clinical examinations are the deep infiltrations beneath the mucosa[21]. If the infiltrations involve the cricoarytenoid joint, mobility of the true cord is limited or even fixed, which can be easily detected by the examining clinician. Unfortunately other tumor manifestations can also produce cord fixation, such as a bulky tumor in the ventricle that restricts mobility of the true cord, nerve involvement, or preexisting trauma that has resulted in cartilage deformities[23].

Tumors that have extended below the level of the cords can be extremely difficult to visualize in the uncooperative patient. Even at direct laryngoscopy, tumors that have extended posteriorly beneath the posterior commissure can escape detection. Extensions anteriorly through the cricothyroid membrane or superiorly into the base of the tongue means a far advanced tumor. Such information is not easily obtainable on indirect inspection.

Last, the problem of lymph node metastases can be so difficult that even the most astute clinician needs whatever diagnostic aids are available[21]. Nodes lying high under the sternocleidomastoid muscle are extremely difficult to palpate. Nodes that have extended extracapsulary and involve the carotid artery are difficult to judge preoperatively.

Pathology

The vast majority of laryngeal cancers are squamous cell carcinomas. Rarely, tumors begin from the supporting structures or cell rests in the mucosa. The total of non-squamous cell carcinomas of the larynx probably does not exceed 2%[3,5].

The degree of differentiation of squamous cell carcinoma bears an important relationship to therapeutic management. Well differentiated keratinizing tumors most commonly originate from the true vocal cords. Less well differentiated tumors that infiltrate more widely are mostly from the supraglottic larynx[16]. In general, all laryngeal tumors tend to be more well differentiated tumors, which is part of the reason why voice conservation procedures can be used so effectively. Some surgeons operating on small tumors that do not have deep infiltration feel quite comfortable with 2 to 3mm of surgical margin around the tumor mass. The growth patterns of even more aggressive undifferentiated tumors of the supraglottic larynx are confined to compartments, so that voice conservation surgery or precision radiation therapy is still entirely feasible. As one passes laterally to the piriform sinuses, a different "breed" of tumor is frequently encountered. These lesions are of the gastrointestinal tract and tend to be less well differentiated, more widely infiltrating, and more difficult to manage with close surgical margins or narrow field radiation therapy ports[25].

Regardless of the growth pattern, one must constantly remember that histologic diagnosis is not possible by any known radiologic means, and the spread of disease tissue is the only information possible by body sectional imaging. Nevertheless this appraisal of deep infiltration ist precisely the type of information required for tumor management.

True Cord Tumors

T1 Lesions

T1 tumors are carcinomas confined to the true cords with normal mobility. T1A lesions involve one cord while T1B lesions involve both. Lymph node metastases are rare, and generally no imaging techniques are requested with early tumors unless the patient is uncooperative or the lesion involves the anterior commissure. Under these circumstances the clinician may be worried about subglottic extension (Fig. 3.1). Thyroid cartilage invasion is rarely caused by T1A cord tumors. Only when there is subglottic extension does one see involvement of the anterior inferior surface of the thyroid cartilage[30,29]. Early tumors frequently arise from the mid-portion of the true cord, while origins near the vocal process are quite

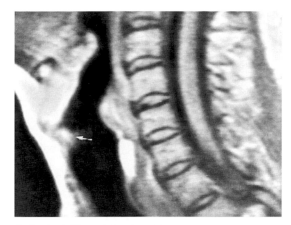

A Sagittal T1 weighted pulsing sequence through the midline shows the tumor mass at the anterior commissure (arrow). The mass does not extend superiorly into the preepiglottic space or inferiorly into the subglottic space.

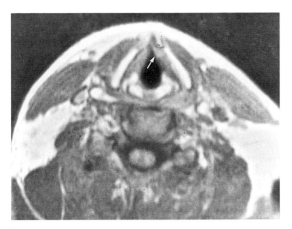

B Axial section through the true vocal cord. On this section the tumor is seen to involve the anterior third of the left vocal cord (arrow). The tumor extends to the anterior commissure but does not involve the right vocal cord. The posterior half of the vocal cord including the vocal process of the arytenoid are entirely normal.

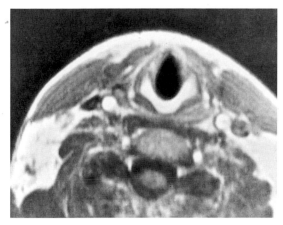

D Coronal scan through the anterior third of the true vocal cords shows the tumor mass on the left (arrow). In this instance the signal is mixed within the tumor. Note that the intrinsic muscles lying lateral to the tumor are relatively normal in appearance and there is no evidence of extension of the tumor deep to the level of the muscles.

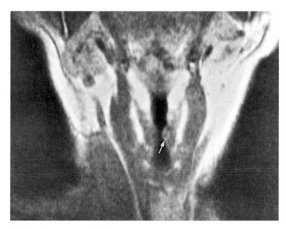

C Section through the subglottic region at the level of the cricoid lamina. There is a normal amount of "fullness" of the under-surface of the true vocal cords. The cricoid lamina shows normal mineralization. The strap muscles lying anterior to the thyroid cartilage are normal. One could not be certain about the status of the thyroid cartilages on this section since the entire left of the thyroid cartilage does not give signal. This ist not an unusual finding.

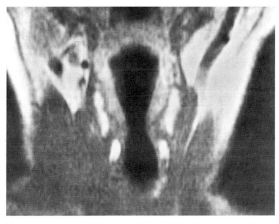

E Section through the middle third of the vocal cords shows the airway is perfectly normal. The intrinsic muscles show normal pattern and there is no evidence of any subglottic extension.

Figure 3.**1**   T1 true vocal cord tumor.

unusual. The tumor may originate in a region of leukoplakia, but this diagnosis and the differential diagnosis of invasive carcinoma is beyond the scope of any radiologic imaging modality. Only when there is a significant degree of deep infiltration can one suggest invasive carcinoma.

Early lesions require meticulous positioning of the patient and slice selection to be certain that the vertical extent of a tumor can be clearly delineated. Axial sections that are taken in an oblique plane may spuriously suggest anterior commissure involvement, when actually the plane of the section may pass from true cord to the thyroepiglottic ligament or even into the petiole and inferior extremity of the preepiglottic space. On axial sectioning with both CT and MR, there should be no significant soft tissue lying posterior to the inner surface of the thyroid cartilage when the patient is scanned in quiet respiration. With the cords adducted during phonation, one cannot be certain about the status of the anterior commissure.

The thickness of the vocal cords at the level of the anterior commissure ist normally in the range of 3 to 4 mm. Any thickening beyond 5 mm raises the question of subglottic extension. This type of thickening is best evaluated by sagittal MR. On CT one must usually rely on the visualization of the anterior ring of the cricoid cartilage and determine if the tumor ist approaching this cartilage to make a definitive diagnosis of subglottic extension.

Anterior to the cricothyroid membrane, the strap muscles should be carefully scrutinized. Any significant asymmetry is an indication of advanced disease that has escaped the confines of the larynx.

Since the lymphatic drainage and compartmentalization of the larynx is such that tumors from the anterior commissure spread inferiorly, it is rare to see extension of an early lesion into the preepiglottic space prior to extensive involvement of the subglottic region and laryngeal ventricle.

Coronal MR scanning will show mucosa with bright signal on T1 weighted studies. Slightly further laterally, the low density of the vocalis muscle and thyroarytenoid muscle is visualized in the normal vocal cord. There should be a high signal region lying just

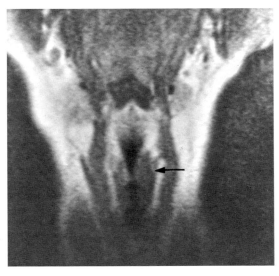

A Coronal section shows loss of normal bright signal on the left (arrow) which involves both the true and false vocal cord.

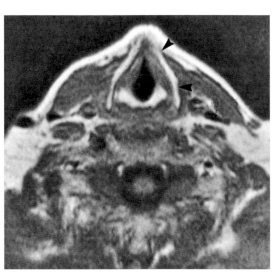

B Section through the inferior surface of the vocal cords shows fullness of the left vocal cord (arrowhead) but the thyroid cartilage is intact.

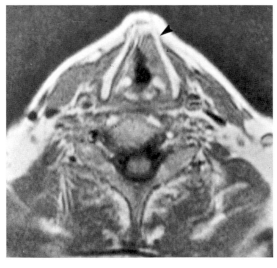

C Section through the true vocal cord shows tumor extending from the anterior commissure (arrowhead) to the posterior third of the vocal cord. The arytenoid cartilages are intact.

Figure 3.**2**   T2 transglottic tumor with limited cord mobility.

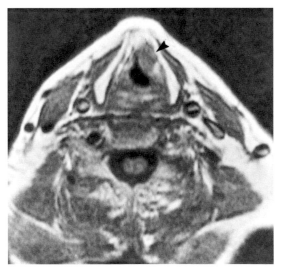

D Section through the false vocal cords shows the loss of bright signal in the paralaryngeal space with a sharply circumscribed region of tumor (arrowhead). The tumor does not extend posteriorly to the aryepiglottic fold region.

beneath the thyroid cartilage and deep to the intrinsic muscles. At times, the thyroid cartilage cannot be seen, especially in young individuals. Fortunately, in the more advanced age groups where carcinoma of the larynx is more likely to occur, the thyroid cartilage has a medullary cavity which can be clearly delineated as bright signal surrounded by low signal from calcified cartilage.

T2 True Vocal Cord Tumors

T2 Tumors are true cord tumors that have spread to involve the adjacent false cord, subglottic region, or preepiglottic space without vocal cord fixation. The tumor almost invariably crosses the anterior commissure (Fig. 3.2). The degree of vocal cord mobility is an extremely important aspect to tumor staging. Unfortunately the lack of mobility may be related to invasion of the cricoarytenoid joint (being the most ominous prognostic sign). Other causes of limited mobility include bulky tumor masses, replacement of the thyroid arytenoid and vocalis muscles or direct nerve invasion[10]. Invasion of the thyroid alae ist unusual and microscopic in nature. Only a rather marked subglottic extension results in involvement of the thyroid cartilage symphysis.

The degree of involvement of mucosa along the superior surface of the true cord is of considerable interest to the clinician. He wishes to know if the mucosa involvement extends to the extreme lateral portion of the laryngeal ventricle. If there is infiltration in the lateral portion of the paralaryngeal space, spreads can accompany the lymphatics of the supraglottic larynx. With the deep infiltration of the musculature of the true vocal cord, the direction of spread can be related to the conus elasticus. This tought membrane will direct laterally placed tumors to the space between the cricoid and thyroid cartilages.

If the tumor mass is predominantly superficial and spreads inferior to the margin of the vocal ligament, the tumor will tend to stay in the mucosa, being confined by the conus elasticus. Under these circumstances involvement of the posterior commissure is more likely to occur, and information regarding the mucosa overlying the cricoid lamina and extending into the tracheal lumen is extremely important (Fig. 3.3).

CT and MR are not designed to give physiologic information, but motion artifacts, although annoying, can indicate mobile vocal cords. Unfortunately when motion artifacts degrade the image, it is frequently impossible to see how far laterally the tumor has spread. In axial CT scanning there should be a low density plane lying immediately adjacent to the inner surface of the thyroid cartilage. Disruption of this low signal plane can be an early indication of extensive lateral spread. Again, meticulous technique of patient positioning is essential for orientation as to cephalocaudad extent of tumor. The vocal process of the arytenoid is usually visualized on the thin sections, and any extensions posteriorly and medial to the

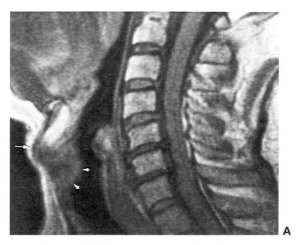

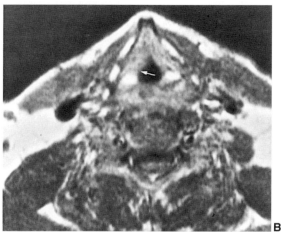

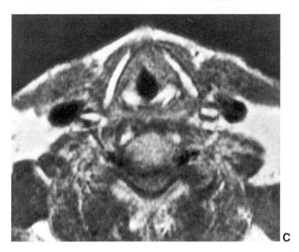

Figure 3.**3**   Advanced T2 true vocal cord tumor.

A Sagittal section shows the mass involving the anterior commissure and subglottic region (arrowheads). There is loss of the normal bright signal from the inferior portion of the preepiglottic space (arrow).

B Section through the true vocal cord shows the tumor extends almost to the level of the arytenoid cartilages and may involve the vocal process of the arytenoid on the right (arrow). The thyroid cartilage is grossly intact and the strap muscles lying anterior to the thyroid cartilage show no evidence of distortion.

C Section through the under surface of the true vocal cords shows bilateral thickening but more on the left. Tumor involves the anterior commissure. Note that the strap muscles lying external to the thyroid cartilages are well preserved. Although the tumor is rather far advanced, the vocal cords were both mobile on clinical examination.

vocal process indicate the tumor has involved the mucosa lying on the anterior surface of the cricoid lamina. This has ominous prognostic significance for voice conservation either by radiation or surgery. Care should be taken to visualize this posterior commissure region when the patient is in quiet respiration. During Valsalva maneuver or breath-holding, the mucosa of the subglottic region may lapse into folds that appear like soft tissue masses on the cricoid cartilage.

On MR the vocalis muscle and thyroarytenoid muscles have approximately the same density as most infiltrating tumors. One should carefully note the symmetry of these muscle bundles with the normal side and also identify symmetry of other intrinsic muscle bundles that lie between the cricoid cartilage and the inferior border of the thyroid cartilage. These intrinsic muscles are the medial and lateral cricothyroid muscles and become infiltrated when a tumor has infiltrated inferiorly in the paralaryngeal space.

The strap muscles lying anterior to the cricothyroid membrane should be symmetrical. Any elevation or distortion of these muscle bundles indicate an advanced disease process.

A nodal spread is directly related to the size of the tumor mass and to some extent its degree of differentiation. When the tumors have involved regions beyond a true vocal cord, the incidence of metastases increases to the range of 25 to 50%. If the spread is predominantly subglottic, the lymph nodes should be searched thoroughly in the mid and lower neck. If the spread has occurred to the supraglottic region, sectioning should extend to above the level of the hyoid bone.

T3 True Cord Tumors

These lesions involve regions adjacent to the true cord with fixation of the true cord. Imaging is extremely important in these patients because the limits of voice conservation surgery have been extended to include removal of portions of the cricoid lamina and subglottic larynx.

If one mobile arytenoid can be left with half of a vocal cord, the patient may still be able to produce a functioning voice although a permanent tracheostomy is necessary for respiration. This type of surgical decision is usually weighed with the possibility of performing total laryngectomy and using some of the newer artificial speech mechanisms that involve prosthetic materials communicating the upper trachea with the esophagus. Many are now in clinical use such as the "duck bill", the Panje button, Modified Panje button, and so on.

The most important imaging information to be obtained concerns the status of the cricoid cartilage. Since this is a foundation of the larynx, the cricoid cartilage cannot be removed without destabilizing the entire larynx. Fixation implies tumor extending into the cricoarytenoid joint. On CT or MR the superior margin of the cricoid is usually destroyed and is

manifest by a lack of calcification in one side. This is usually accompanied by destruction of all or part of the arytenoid cartilage.

At times the joint is not destroyed but the tumor has insinuated itself between the posterior margin of the thyroid cartilage and the cricoid cartilage. This bulky mass then widens the space and mechanically interferes with arytenoid cartilage mobility. Axial scans should show symmetry in the space between the cricoid lamina and the thyroid cartilage in a normal patient.

As the tumor extends laterally in the laryngeal ventricle, it may extend into the appendix of the laryngeal ventricle or occlude the appendix. The obstructed appendix will dilate and obscure or distort the true vocal cords. The dilated appendix in itself will not cause fixation of the cord but may contribute to limited mobility. On imaging, the appendix is usually filled with a mucoid homogenous material. There may be small amounts of air present in the lumen. Non-homogeneity of the signal from within the appendix or contrast enhancement on CT within the lumen of the appendix implies that tumor hasn't actually invaded into the appendix.

The combination of axial and coronal scanning can be quite helpful using MR to tell the amount of tumor that has spread onto cricoid cartilage. The anterior ring of the cricoid cartilage can be evaluated on axial scanning. However, if the tumor has extended slightly below the anterior commissure but not reached the cartilaginous ring, it is difficult to give an exact measurement of tumor extent without sagittal imaging provided by MR. Posteriorly if the tumor has spread toward the lumen side of the cricoid signet, a reasonably accurate estimate of the degree of involvement can be made. When the tumor has spread laterally, outside the confines of the conus elasticus, contrast on CT is not quite as sharp, and precise measurements are more difficult. Coronal, sagittal, and axial MR will help to find these limits because partial excision of the cricoid lamina is still a very viable alternative to total laryngectomy in selected cases.

Last, imaging in the T3 true cord tumor may show extensions beyond the confines of the larynx with involvement of the piriform sinuses or other neck structures. Lymph node involvement in this group is much more common and at times can preclude curative surgery.

T4 True Cord Tumors

By its definition, T4 lesions have spread beyond the confines of the larynx (Fig. 3.4). Usually treatment has been chosen on the basis of clinical examination, and the only surgical decision to be made concerns the possibility of life-saving total laryngectomy. As a general rule, imaging does little to influence what happens to the larynx, and the information derived from radiologic studies is primarily related to lymph nodes and other vital structures in the neck. Coronal

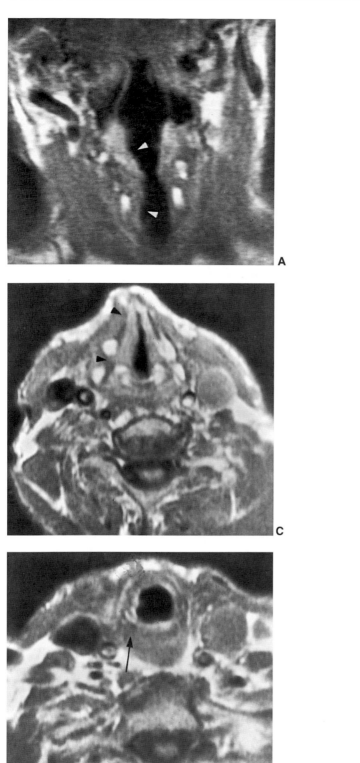

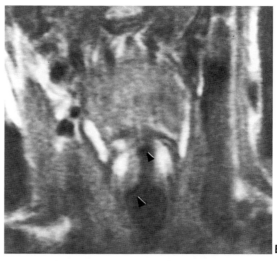

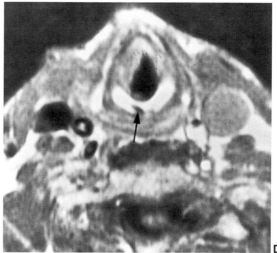

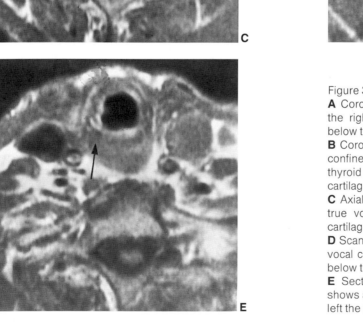

Figure 3.**4** T4 true cord tumor with spread to the upper trachea.
A Coronal scan shows the transglottic tumor predominately on the right, spreading superiorly in the false cord and inferiorly below the cricoid cartilage (arrowheads).
B Coronal scan through the posterior airway shows the masses confined to the mucosa (arrowheads). The space between the thyroid cartilage and cricoid cartilage is normal and the arytenoid cartilages are not destroyed.
C Axial scan through the true vocal cord shows the entire right true vocal cord has been invaded by tumor but the thyroid cartilage is intact (arrowheads).
D Scan through the cricoid lamina shows tumor beneath the true vocal cords and a nodal tumor is seen in the midline posteriorly below the posterior commissure (arrow).
E Section through junction of cricoid with the upper trachea shows a nodular tumor on the right, confirming that the tumor has left the larynx and is in the upper trachea.

and axial sectioning is usually geared toward gathering information regarding the carotid artery and degree of extension to lymph nodes in the lower neck.

Since the tumors have spread widely they are usually in the supraglottic and subglottic larynx. Cartilaginous involvement is much more common. The involvement is frequently of the anterior inferior margin of the thyroid cartilage or the posterior inferior margin of the thyroid alae. Cricoid and arytenoid cartilage are usually involved as described in T3 lesions. If there is any doubt, this radiologic demonstration of cartilage involvement will confirm that radiation therapy is little more than palliative in these advanced cases. When looking for a thyroid cartilage involvement, a general rule is to concentrate on areas where ossification has taken place. These regions seem much more prone to tumor invasion.

Supraglottic Larynx Tumors

The TNM classification has been developed for supraglottic larynx cancer and is based on spread from the site of origin. T1 lesions are confined to the site of origin, with advancing stages related to spread beyond the compartment of origin. The site of origin of a supraglottic larynx cancer is of equal prognostic significance to the local spread of a tumor. They might be classified as follows:

1. Free margin of the epiglottis (suprahyoid epiglottis).
2. Infrahyoid epiglottis
3. False vocal cord
4. Aryepiglottic fold (marginal supraglottic).

The general spread of supraglottic larynx cancers is divided in the midline into two lateral compartments and divided at the laryngeal ventricle for superior/inferior extent of tumor[13]. Lesions will usually remain unilateral if the mucosal disease is unilateral. Part of the explanation is because the epiglottis is perforated, and tumors from the mucosa may infiltrate deeply once they have crossed the midline on the mucosa. The preepiglottic space is separated by the hyoepiglottic ligaments, which course in the midline.

In general, supraglottic larynx cancers spread to lymph nodes at a much earlier stage than true cord tumors[16]. The overall instance of metastases is approximately 55% regardless of staging. Despite the high incidence of nodal disease, cartilage invasion is surprisingly low. The tumor may be adjacent to the perichondrium, but deep invasion into the medullary cavity of the thyroid cartilage is indeed rare and then only occurs in far advanced disease[9].

Suprahyoid Epiglottic Carcinomas

Supraglottic laryngeal cancer or cancer of the free margin of the epiglottis is usually an exophytic type of growth that eventually spreads to the lateral pharyngeal wall and anteriorly into the valleculae. Because of the ease of examination of this region, they are usually diagnosed at an earlier stage, but neglected tumors can invade into the tongue base.

In CT or MR the free margin of the epiglottis will be thickened to two or three times its normal dimensions. The bright signal that is normally visible in the submucosa as seen by MR is obliterated. The extensions of tumor into the lateral pharyngeal wall through the pharyngoepiglottic fold are manifest by lack of bright signal of the areolar tissue and thickening of the regions (Fig. 3.5). The tumors are usually accompanied by a moderate amount of reactive edema so that the exact differentiation of tumor from edema may be difficult.

The extensions into valleculae also present diagnostic difficulties whether examined by CT or MR. The lingual tonsils may closely simulate the signal of tumor as seen by MR, and the bulk of these lesions will appear as exophytic tumor masses. Asymmetery is so common that other criteria must be utilized for lingual tonsil invasion. For superficial spread into the lingual tonsils, clinical examination and biopsy are the gold standard. Once deep invasion into the tongue base has occurred, MR can give valuable information because the superior longitudinal intrinsic muscle bundles of the tongue form a distinct line in the tongue base that is easily visible on axial projections. If the signal from the tumor has invaded through this muscle bundle, one can be relatively certain that the disease has advanced to an extralaryngeal location.

Tumors of the free margin of the epiglottis may invade into the preepiglottic space for varying distances. They will usually not extend to the petiole region until later because the lymphatic drainage from the upper epiglottis is superiorly and laterally. If the tumor originates on the lateral free margin of the epiglottis, the tumor will respect the midline for a considerable period of time.

Infrahyoid Epiglottic Tumors

Probably one of the most valuable contributions of laryngeal imaging is related to voice conservation surgery for lesions of the body of the epiglottis[4, 27, 28]. These tumors respect their compartments of origin for a considerable period of time. Because of the distinct separation between supraglottic larynx and true vocal cords at the level of the ventricle, surgical margins can be quite close with considerable confidence. The tumors are late to invade into the tongue base or into the anterior commissure and subglottic region via the thyroepiglottic ligament (Fig. 3.6). As the tumors spread onto the lateral margin of the epiglottis, they gain access to the paralaryngeal space and involve the medial walls of the piriform sinus.

CT imaging will show loss of the low density of the fat in the preepiglottic space while MR will show a loss of the bright signal of this same region due to the infiltration of tumor. Because of the abundance of bright signal of MR in the paralaryngeal space, the superior and inferior extent of these tumors is readily documented.

False Vocal Cord Tumors

The false vocal cords are relatively silent areas, so usually tumors have spread beyond this region by the time the patient seeks medical assistance. The tumor spreads superiorly and laterally to involve the paralaryngeal space and the aryepiglottic folds. On CT or MR they can be identified quite readily by the wiping out of bright signal from the paralaryngeal space and distortions of the aryepiglottic folds. The vocal cord may become fixed if the lesion has spread posteriorly in the aryepiglottic fold to involve the cricoarytenoid

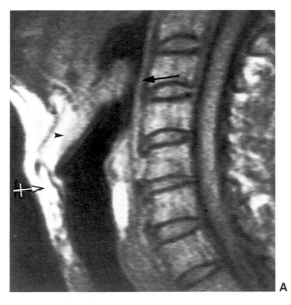

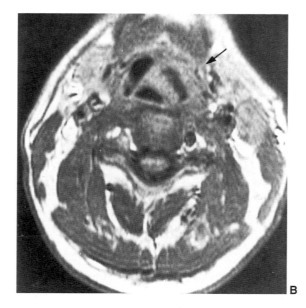

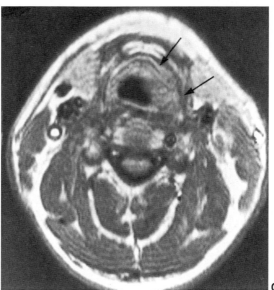

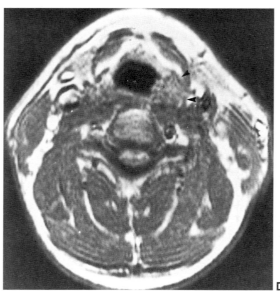

Figure 3.5 Supraglottic carcinoma of the free margin of the epiglottis.

A Midline sagittal section shows bulbous enlargement of the free margin of the epiglottis (arrow). Part of the bright signal of the preepiglottic space has been replaced by the tumor (arrowhead). The extreme inferior portion of the preepiglottic space is entirely normal, as is the anterior commissure (cross-hatched arrow).

B Axial section through the free margin of the epiglottis shows the thickening of the epiglottis extending predominantly to the left of midline. The tumor has extended into the valleculae to the junction of valleculae with tongue base on the left (arrow).

C Axial section through the lower margin of the hyoid bone shows the tumor is extending down on the body of the epiglottis and on the lateral pharyngeal wall (arrows). Between the two arrows, the tumor is bulging against the strap muscles adjacent to the hyoid bone.

D Scan through the lower body of the epiglottis and thyroid cartilage show the tumor is no longer visible in the preepiglottic space. There is some tumor still present along the lateral pharyngeal wall (arrowheads).

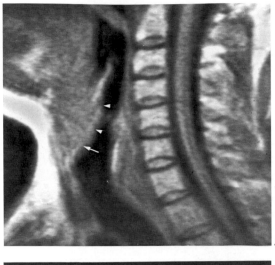

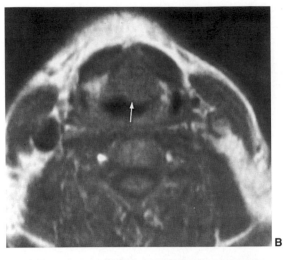

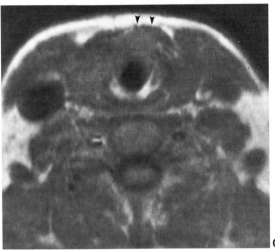

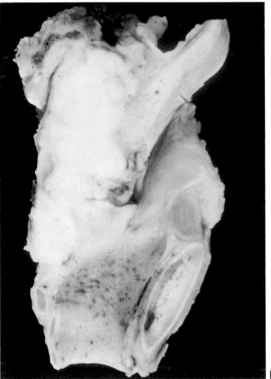

Figure 3.**6**   Supraglottic carcinoma with subglottic extension.
A Sagittal section through the midline demonstrates total replacement of the bright signal that normally comes from the preepiglottic space. The bulky tumor mass bulges into the airway (arrowheads). Although the vocal cords appear to be perfectly normal on both indirect and direct laryngoscopy, tumor can be seen to extend down below the level of the anterior commissure. (arrow).
B Axial section through the mid-epiglottis shows the bright signal has been totally replaced in the preepiglottic space (arrow). The tumor is bilateral in the preepiglottic space.
C Axial section through the mid-cricoid lamina shows the tumor has a circumferential growth pattern in the mucosa almost totally surrounding the lumen. Anteriorly, the tumor has broken through the cricothyroid membrane and causes anterior bulging of the strap muscles on the left (arrowheads).

D Midline sagittal section of the operative specimen. The tumor arising on the petiole of the epiglottis has invaded extensively throughout the preepiglottic space and followed the thyroepiglottic ligament inferiorly to the subglottic region. Note that all of the inferior extension of tumor is beneath the mucosa. This is why the vocal cords appeared perfectly normal at inspection.

joint. Nodal disease ist occasionally the presenting symptom. The tumor spread to the mid and high jugular nodes can be demonstrated quite nicely on axial or coronal scans (Fig. 3.7).

Marginal Tumors (Aryepiglottic Folds)

The differentiation of aryepiglottic fold tumors from piriform sinus cancers is usually made on clinical examination rather than by any of the imaging mo-

dalities. These tumors have almost invariably spread to involve major portions of the piriform sinus by the time they are discovered. They spread much like the false vocal cord tumors with early lymph node metastases. They do respect the superior-inferior compartmentalization at the level of the laryngeal ventricle, but the posterior limits of the tumor are much more likely to involve the arytenoid cartilage. Most of the discussion on piriform sinus cancers can be applied to the marginal tumors (Fig. 3.8).

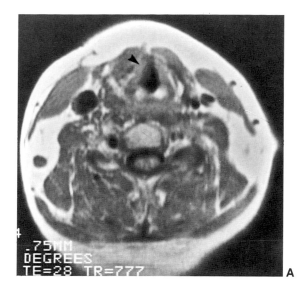

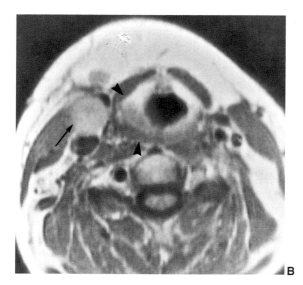

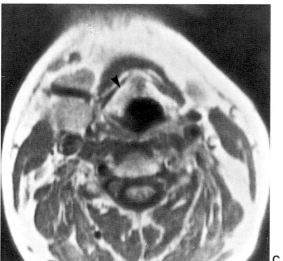

Figure 3.**7**   False vocal cord tumor.
A Section through the false vocal cords shows the bulky tumor mass bulging into the airway (arrowhead). When the tumor is extremely bulky like this, it is difficult to tell whether the tumor has extended onto the true cord or merely pushes the true cord down.
B Lower epiglottis. The tumor has extended posterolaterally to involve the aryepiglottic fold (arrowheads). The preepiglottic space and anterior portions of the paralaryngeal space are free of tumor. Tumor is also visible in a node lying anterior to the jugular vein (arrow). A smaller node is visible anterior to the external jugular vein. Some small reactive nodes are visible lying posterolateral to the jugular vein on the right.
C Axial section through the mid-epiglottis shows the tumor has extended beneath the mucosa in the paralaryngeal space and replaced the bright signal of the paralaryngeal space (arrowhead). The midline ligaments have kept the tumor confined unilaterally.

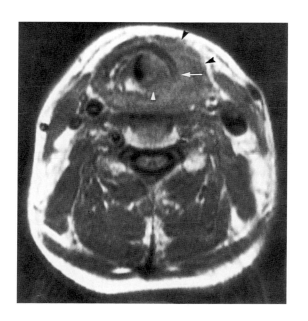

Figure 3.**8**   Piriform sinus cancer with cartilage destruction. Axial section through the lower margin of the vocal cord shows that this massive tumor has extended posterolaterally in the paralaryngeal space to destroy the left half of the cricoid cartilage (white arrowhead). The tumor has then extended laterally around the external surface of the thyroid cartilage lifting off the strap muscles (arrowheads). The tumor destroys the posterolateral margin of the thyroid cartilage, and there is a typical greater destruction of the outer table than the inner table of the thyroid cartilage (arrow).

Piriform Sinus Cancers

Strictly speaking, piriform sinus cancers are part of the hypopharynx and gastrointestinal tract rather than the larynx and respiratory tract. The tumors tend to infiltrate much more widely and are much more anaplastic in their histology[18, 1, 33].

The presenting symptoms of patients with piriform sinus cancers are usually dysphagia and voice change but not hoarseness. Patients may have vague sensations of discomfort in the throat or frequently describe a referred pain to the ear. Voices of patients with a bulky piriform sinus cancer or supraglottic larynx cancer have frequently been referred to as "potato voices". This ist quite different than hoarseness and may be compared with a person talking with a mouthful of "marbles".

Because of the richness of lymphatics in the piriform sinus mucosa, these tumors tend to spread in a circumferential pattern and involve the lateral and posterior pharyngeal wall rather early. They are slow to invade into the preepiglottic space because of the lymphatic drainage. Contralateral spread in the preepiglottic space is unusual unless the tumor is far advanced[13]. Piriform sinus cancers insinuate themselves between the cricoid lamina and the posterior and inferior margin of the thyroid cartilage. They may invade the cricoarytenoid joint or the posterior border of the thyroid cartilage. Cartilage invasion is much more frequent with piriform sinus cancers than with supraglottic larynx cancers (see Fig. 3.**8**).

The pharyngeal constrictors tend to confine the direct spread of this tumor and prevent it from escaping into the vascular spaces of the neck. Since the pharyngeal constrictors insert on the middle third of the outer surface of the thyroid cartilage, the tumor will infiltrate along the outer surface of the thyroid cartilage. It then gains access to the medullary cavity of the thyroid cartilage by following the blood vessels that penetrate the outer surface of the thyroid cartilage. This is the reason one frequently sees more erosion of the outer surface of the thyroid cartilage than the inner surface.

Another route of spread of the piriform sinus cancers is the paralaryngeal space superiorly and over the top of the thyroid cartilage through the thyrohyoid membrane. This dumbbell type of growth is much less frequent than the posteroinferolateral extension between the thyroid cartilage and cricoid cartilages.

Pharyngeal Wall Tumors

Carcinomas arising from the lateral and posterior pharyngeal walls are not common, but they are not rare. Although they extend for considerable distances, they tend to be confined by the prevertebral fascia. Although this fascia is quite tough, the tumor masses will eventually erode through the prevertebral fascia and invade the longus colli muscle bundles. Demonstration of muscle invasion is much easier by MR because of the improved contrast between muscle and tumor than by CT scanning with contrast. Muscle invasion is usually considered a sign of inoperability, so that MR becomes the examination of choice in these patients. T1 weighting pulsing sequences are usually adequate. If surface coils are not available and additional information is needed, T2 weighted pulsing sequences will show the tumor as very bright signal within low signal coming from muscles supporting the head and neck.

Post-Cricoid Cartilage Tumors

Post-cricoid tumors are usually secondary to cervical cancers that have extended superiorly or piriform sinus cancers that have extended postero-medially. A primary tumor arising from the post-cricoid region can be extremely difficult to diagnose clinically because of the poor visibility of this region on direct and indirect laryngoscopy.

CT or MR can show the edematous changes in the arytenoid regions and tumor masses in the post-cricoid region. If the tumor is flat, infiltrative diagnosis can be extremely difficult.

Post-Radiation Larynx

Following radiation therapy, diffuse edema is usually present within the larynx for a period of 3 to 4 months. Persistence of edema beyond this period is an ominous sign of either early chondronecrosis or persistent tumor. The diagnosis of persistent or recurrent tumor in the edematous larynx is difficult if not impossible by most imaging and many clinical means[37, 8]. The edematous changes within the larynx produce a signal that closely simulates that of recurrent tumor. Only when there ist a discrete mass or ulceration can one suggest the diagnosis of persistent or recurrent tumor. Ward and colleagues[37] performed laryngectomies on a group of patients who had persistent edema and **negative** biopsies. The laryngectomies were necessary because of incapacitating symptoms. Sixty percent of these larynxes showed microscopic tumor at the time of pathologic examination. Given the high likelihood of tumor in a setting of persistent edema, one should view any localized expansion as tumor until proven otherwise.

Benign Conditions

The vast majority of benign processes are handled by clinical inspection and biopsy. Only a few noteworthy examples are discussed here because they present a confusing clinical picture and are frequently mistaken for hidden tumors. Others are extremely rare and are usually not the subject of a radiologic investigation.

Laryngoceles

Laryngoceles are dilatations of the appendix of the laryngeal ventricle (saccule) that may be caused by voice abuse or obstruction of the natural opening of this gland-like structure. Laryngoceles will expand in the paralaryngeal space and may eventually extend superiorly over the top of the thyroid cartilage to penetrate the thyrohyoid membrane. If the laryngocele ist confined to the laryngeal vestibule and bulges into the airway, it is spoken of as an internal laryngocele. Those that have passed through the thyrohyoid membrane are referred to as external laryngoceles.

Laryngoceles may be filled with either air, retained secretions, or a combination of secretions and tumor. Tumors arising in the saccule have been reported, but more likely tumors within the laryngoceles are secondary to true cord tumors that have extended into the laryngeal ventricle and saccule.

Laryngoceles are important because they may be mistaken for extensions of malignant tumors or they may produce respiratory obstruction if acutely infected. On CT studies they are of homogenous low density unless they are air containing or contain variable amounts of tumor[6, 34].

In MR, laryngoceles are usually of low signal, which may be due to fluid or air or both. If T2 weighted pulsing sequences are used, the laryngoceles become homogenously bright because of the water and protein content. The homogenous nature of the signal from a benign laryngocele should be the first clue to the diagnosis. The diagnosis is easily made because laryngoceles begin in the false cord, so that scans made inferiorly at the level of the true cord will be entirely within normal limits.

Amyloid

The larynx may be effected by deposits of primary or secondary amyloid[15, 12]. These appear as low signal regions usually found in the paralaryngeal spaces. The masses of amyloid will interfere with the voice or function of the laryngeal sphincter. The local effects of amyloid can be identified nicely by CT or MR, and there is no specific signal to differentiate them from malignant tumor infiltrations.

Benign Tumors

A variety of benign lesions may effect the larynx. The most common is papilloma, which may be singular or multiple. They may occur in the pediatric age group and effect the tracheobronchial tree as well as the larynx.

Chondromas of the larynx are also quite rare and are more likely to arise from the cricoid ring. As yet the MR appearance of chondroma has not been described but one can suspect that it would be of intermediate signal since information is readily available concerning the CT appearance of chondromas[38]. On CT they show areas of cartilage matrix and a mass usually in association with the cricoid signet.

Trauma

Based on clinical presentation of the patient, imaging of the larynx for trauma can be classified as either acute or chronic. The acute forms can be further subdivided into blunt trauma, penetrating injuries and iatrogenic trauma. The vast majority of acute injuries are handled with life-saving procedures to establish an airway and repair soft tissue lacerations. Until the availability of CT and now MR, little attention was paid to the underlying cartilaginous injuries.

Iatrogenic Trauma

Traumatic intubation during general anesthesia is the most common cause of injury. The injuries are usually limited to surface abrasions of the laryngeal mucosa and occasionally penetrating injuries of the pharyngeal wall. True perforations within the larynx are rare.

One of the more frequent types of injuries is dislocation of an arytenoid during passage of an endotracheal tube. Invariably the displaced arytenoid is dislocated anteriorly so that the cord will appear paretic. This type of an injury can cause consternation if there has been thyroid surgery or other maneuvers near the recurrent laryngeal nerve.

At CT or MR, the arytenoid will be displaced anteriorly and the aryepiglottic fold will fold medially, causing a widening of the piriform sinus[20]. Replacement usually results in complete recovery provided the trauma is recognized within a reasonable period of time.

Acute Blunt Trauma

An anteriorly directed blow to the larynx will compress the cartilages against the cervical spine. The cricoid ring may fracture much like the pelvis (Fig. 3.9). One type of injury is a vertical fracture through the cricoid signet and bilateral fractures through the anterior ring of the cricoid cartilage. If there is not too much posterior displacement of the anterior ring and so significant hematoma, the airway may stay reasonably well preserved[20, 17].

Another mechanism of trauma is for a blow to be directed anteriolaterally to the larynx which results in a shattering or longitudinal fractures through the thyroid cartilage. One ala of the thyroid cartilage may be folded inward to cause laryngeal airway compromise. If there is little in the way of significant hematoma formation, the patient may not even seek medical attention and attribute to the injury a little "soreness" together with some hoarseness which subsides in two to three weeks.

More severe trauma with a great deal of shearing forces can result in the entire trachea being severed from the larynx or a complete evulsion of the epiglot-

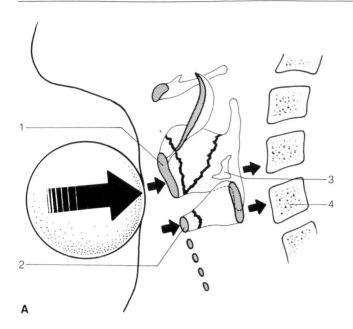

A

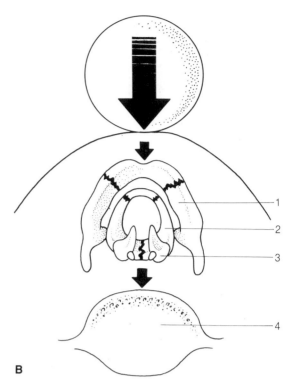

B

Figure 3.9 Distribution of force to the larynx. **A** Diagrammatic lateral projection of a ball striking the anterior surface of the larynx and **B** the view from above. The larynx is trapped between the force of the ball and the vertebral bodies posteriorly. The thyroid cartilages may shatter with an oblique fracture, vertical fracture, or combination of both to allow posterior displacement of the symphysis. The cricoid fracture must occur in two places since the cricoid is a ring. A bilateral anterior fracture may displace a segment of the ring posteriorly. The major impact may be with the signet of the cricoid against the spine. One or two fractures through the signet are accompanied by an anterior ring fracture allowing both halves to be displaced laterally. 1. Thyroid cartilage, 2. cricoid cartilage, 3. arytenoid cartilage, 4. cervical vertebral body.

tis. The more massive type of injuries produce severe respiratory obstruction and are treated by emergency surgery. If possible, cartilage imaging should be performed so that appropriate repairs can be conducted prior to the patient leaving the hospital.

Old Trauma

Consequences of old trauma to the larynx can produce a well definable clinical syndrome. Patients present with five diagnostic symptoms:

1. Soreness in the side of the "throat", especially at the end of the day after they have done a lot of talking.
2. Sensation of food sticking in the throat.
3. Failure to remember the traumatic incident.
4. A bulging mass at the level of the false cord, with intact mucosa, will be detected upon clinical exam.
5. Distortion of the thyroid cartilage with "embuckling" at the site of old injury will be demonstrated by CT or MR.

Old injuries of the cricoid cartilage are diagnosable by distortions of the normal circular pattern of the cricoid lumen (Fig. 3.10). Frequently the lateral portions of the cricoid ring are rotated laterally and there may be a "twisting" deformity whereby one lateral portion of the ring is directed inferiorly and the other is directed superiorly. This will also cause asymmetry of the position of the arytenoid cartilages even though they still rest on the cricoid signet.

Summary

Imaging of the larynx is primarily related to malignant disease and defining the extensions of tumor that lie below the mucosa. The vast majority of tumors are diagnosed by clinical inspection and history but occasionally a piriform sinus cancer or vallecular cancer may escape detection and be discovered by imaging.

Benign lesions are so rare that clinicians frequently request assistance in confirming the presence of a tumor and differentiating some of the more specific lesions such as laryngoceles, chondromas, and other solid tumors.

MR examinations have replaced CT to a large extent because of the availability of coronal, sagittal and axial sections. Gradient echo imaging and improvements in resolution will greatly expand and modify the imaging possibilities in the larynx as seen by MR.

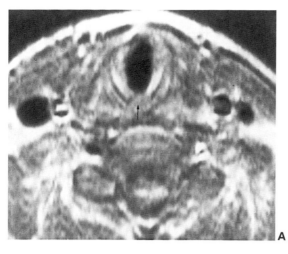

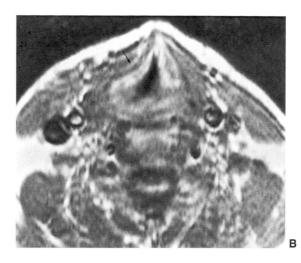

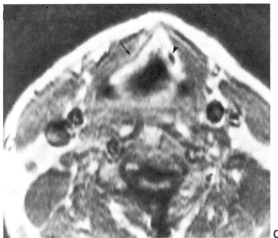

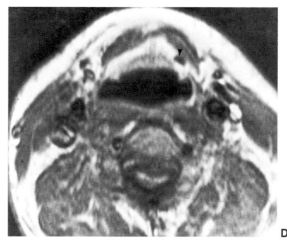

Figure 3.**10**   Old laryngeal fracture with incidental laryngocele.
A Axial section through the cricoid lamina shows the cricoid ring has been destroyed and now is more oval in shape due to a midline fracture through the cricoid lamina (arrow).
B Section through the false vocal cord. There ist "inbuckling" of the thyroid cartilage (arrow). This is the typical location of cartilage deformity, creating the false impression of a paralaryngeal space mass.

C Axial section through the lower epiglottis. The thyroid cartilage deformity is not quite as severe in the superior portion of the laryngeal vestibule. In the opposite paralaryngeal space, one notices a region of signal void corresponding to superior extension of the appendix of the laryngeal ventricle (arrowhead).
D Axial section through the upper body of the epiglottis. The laryngeal deformity has almost disappeared but one can still trace the dilated appendix of the laryngeal ventricle (arrowhead). This laryngocele did not escape through the thyrohyoid membrane and therefore ist classified as a small internal laryngocele.

References

1   Archer CR, Yeager VL: Evaluation of laryngeal cartilages by computed tomography. J. Comput. Assist. Tomogr. 1979, 3:604–611.

2   Baclesse F: Carcinoma of the larynx: Radiotherapy of laryngeal cancer, clinical radiological and therapeutic study: Follow-up of 341 cases treated at the Foundation Curie from 1919 to 1940. Br. J. Radiol. 1949; 3:5–62.

3   Batsakis JG: Tumors of the Head and Neck: Clinical Pathological Consideration, ed 2. Baltimore, Williams & Wilkins, 1979. P. 223.

4   Bocca E, Pignataro O, Oldini C. Supraglottic laryngectomy: 30 years of experience. Ann. Otol. Rhinol. Laryngol. 1983; 92:14–18.

5   Fox JC: Supporting tissue neoplasms of the larynx. Surgery Gynecology and Obstetrics. Volume 131. Page 99. 1970.

6   Glazer HS, Mauro MA, Aronberg DJ, et al: Computed tomography of laryngoceles. AJR 140: 549–552, 1983.

7   Hanson DG, Mancuso AA, Hanafee WN: Pseudo mass lesions due to occult trauma of the larynx. Laryngoscope 92: 1249–1253, 1982.

8   Harnsberger HR, Mancuso AA, Muraki AS, Parkin JL: The upper aerodigestive tract and neck: CT evaluation of recurrent tumors. Radiology 1983; 149: 503–509.

9   Kirchner JA: One hundred laryngeal cancers studies by serial section. Ann. Otol. Rhinol. Laryngol. 78: 689, 1969.

10   Kirchner JA, Owen JE: Five hundred cancers of the larynx and pyriform sinus: Results of treatment by radiation and surgery. Laryngoscope 1977; 87: 1288–1303.

11   Kirchner JA, Som ML: Clinical and histologic observations on supraglottic cancer. Ann. Otol. 1971: 80: 638–644.

12 Kyle RA, Bayrd ED: Amyloidosis: review of 236 cases. Medicine 54: 271, 1975.

13 Larsson S, Mancuso AA, Hoover L, et al: Differentiation of pyriform sinus cancer from supraglottic laryngeal cancer by computed tomography. Radiology 141: 427–432, 1981.

14 Lufkin RB, Larsson SG, Hanafee W: NMR anatomy of the larynx and tongue base. Radiology 148: 173–175, 1983.

15 McAlpine JC, Fuller AP: Localized laryngeal amyloidosis: a report of a case with a review of the literature. J. Laryngol. 78: 296, 1964.

16 McGavran MH, Bauer WC, Ogura JH: The incidence of cervical lymph node metastases from epidermoid carcinoma of the larynx and their relationship to certain characteristics of the primary tumor. Cancer 14: 55–66, 1961.

17 Maceri D, Mancuso AA, Bahna M, et al: Value of computerized axial tomography in severe laryngeal injury. Arch. Otolaryngol. 108: 449–551, 1982.

18 Mafee MF, Schild JA, Valvassori GE, et al: Computed tomography of the larynx: Correlation with anatomic and pathologic studies in cases of laryngeal carcinoma. Radiology 1983; 147: 123–128.

19 Mancuso AA, Calcaterra TC, Hanafee WN: Computed tomography of the larynx. Radiol. Clin. North. Am. 1978; 16: 195–208.

20 Mancuso A, Hanafee W. Computed tomography of the injured larynx. Radiology 1979; 133: 139–44.

21 Mancuso AA, Hanafee WN: Elusive head and neck cancers beneath intact mucosa. Laryngoscope 93: 133–139, 1983.

22 Mancuso AA, Maceri D, Rice D, Hanafee WN: CT of cervical lymph node cancer. AJR 136: 381–385, 1981.

23 Mancuso AA, Tamakawa Y, Hanafee WN: CT of the fixed vocal cord. AJR 135: 429–434, 1980.

24 Millian RR, Cassisi NJ: Larynx. Management of Head and Neck Cancer: A Multidisciplinary Approach. Philadelphia, Lippincott, 1984, chap 19.

25 Millian RR, Cassisi NJ: Hypopharynx: Pharyngeal Walls, Pyriform Sinus and Postcricoid Pharynx. Management of Head and Neck Cancer: A Multidisciplinary Approach. Philadelphia, Lippincott, (in press), chap 21.

26 Ogura JH, Henneman H: Conservation surgery of the larynx and hypopharynx – selection of patients and results. Can. J. Otolaryngo 2: 11–16, 1973.

27 Ogura JH, Marks JE, Freeman RB: Results of conservative surgery for cancers of the supraglottis and pyriform sinus. Laryngoscope 1980; 96: 591–600.

28 Ogura JH: Supraglottic subtotal laryngectomy and radical neck dissection for carcinoma of the epiglottis. Laryngoscope 1958; 68: 982–1003.

29 Oloffsson J: Specific features of laryngeal carcinoma involving the anterior commissure and subglottic region. Can. J. Otolaryngol 4: 618–630, 1975.

30 Oloffsson J, van Nostrand AWP: Growth and spread of laryngeal and hypopharyngeal carcinoma with reflections on the effect of preoperative irradiation. 139 cases studied by whole organ serial sectioning. Acta. Otolaryngol. (Suppl. 308): 1–84, 1973.

31 Pressman JJ, Simon M, Morell C: Anatomic studies related to the dissemination of cancer of the larynx. Am. Acad. Ophth. Otolaryngol. Trans. 64: 628–638, 1960.

32 Pressman JJ: Submucosal compartmentation of the larynx. Anal. Oto. Rhinol. Laryngo. 77: 165–172, 1956.

33 Silverman PM, Bossen EH, Fisher SR, et al: Carcinoma of the larynx and hypopharynx: Computed tomographic-histopathologic correlations. Radiology 1984; 151: 697–702.

34 Silverman PM, Korobkin M: Computed tomographic evaluation of laryngoceles. Radiology 145: 104, 1982.

35 Stark DD, Moss AA, Gamsu G, et al: Magnetic resonance imaging of the neck. Part. I Normal anatomy. Radiology. 1983; 150: 455–61.

36 TNM Classification: American Joint Committee on Cancer: Staging of Cancer of the Head and Neck Sites and of Melanoma 1980. Article No. 31.

37 Ward PH, Calcaterra TC, Kagan AR: The enigma of post radiation edema and recurrent or residual carcinoma of the larynx. Laryngoscope 1975; 85: 522–529.

38 Weber AL, Shortsleeve M, Goodman M: Cartilaginous tumors of the larynx and trachea. Radiol. Clin. of North America 16 (2), 261–271, 1978.

Index